Other related titles:

You may also like

- PBPC091Z | Komaitis | Digital Climate Change: The slow death of the open Internet (In Focus) | 2026
- PBPC088 | Botterman | Technology and Policy Synergy for Internet Governance: Frameworks, strategies and case studies | 2025
- PBTE118 | Soman | Advances in Quantum Communications and Machine Learning for the Quantum Internet: Theory and practice | 2025
- PBPC070 | Raj | Engineering the Metaverse: Enabling technologies, platforms and use cases | 2025

We also publish a wide range of books on the following topics:
Agricultural Engineering and Technology
Applied Physics
Built Environment
Computing and Networks
Control, Robotics and Sensors
Electrical Regulations
Electromagnetics and Radar
Energy Engineering
Healthcare Technologies
History and Management of Technology
IET Codes and Guidance
Materials, Circuits and Devices
Model Forms
Nanomaterials and Nanotechnologies
Production, Design and Manufacturing
Security
Telecommunications
Transportation

All books are available in print via https://shop.theiet.org or as eBooks via our Digital Library https://digital-library.theiet.org.

IET COMPUTING SERIES 086

Web X.O

Enabling secure, intelligent, and inclusive digital futures

Edited by
Muhammad Tariq and Houbing Herbert Song

The Institution of Engineering and Technology

About the IET

This book is published by the Institution of Engineering and Technology (The IET).

We inspire, inform and influence the global engineering community to engineer a better world. As a diverse home across engineering and technology, we share knowledge that helps make better sense of the world, to accelerate innovation and solve the global challenges that matter.

The IET is a not-for-profit organisation. The surplus we make from our books is used to support activities and products for the engineering community and promote the positive role of science, engineering and technology in the world. This includes education resources and outreach, scholarships and awards, events and courses, publications, professional development and mentoring, and advocacy to governments.

To discover more about the IET, please visit https://www.theiet.org/.

About IET books

The IET publishes books across many engineering and technology disciplines. Our authors and editors offer fresh perspectives from universities and industry. Within our subject areas, we have several book series steered by editorial boards made up of leading subject experts.

We peer review each book at the proposal stage to ensure the quality and relevance of our publications.

Get involved

If you are interested in becoming an author, editor, series advisor, or peer reviewer, please visit https://www.theiet.org/publishing/publishing-with-iet-books/ or contact author_support@theiet.org.

Discovering our electronic content

All of our books are available online via the IET's Digital Library. Our Digital Library is the home of technical documents, eBooks, conference publications, real-life case studies and journal articles. To find out more, please visit https://digital-library.theiet.org.

In collaboration with the United Nations and the International Publishers Association, the IET is a Signatory member of the SDG Publishers Compact. The Compact aims to accelerate progress to achieve the Sustainable Development Goals (SDGs) by 2030. Signatories aspire to develop sustainable practices and act as champions of the SDGs during the Decade of Action (2020–30), publishing books and journals that will help inform, develop, and inspire action in that direction.

In line with our sustainable goals, our UK printing partner has FSC accreditation, which is reducing our environmental impact on the planet. We use a print-on-demand model to further reduce our carbon footprint.

Published by The Institution of Engineering and Technology, London, United Kingdom

The Institution of Engineering and Technology (the "**Publisher**") is registered as a Charity in England & Wales (no. 211014) and Scotland (no. SC038698).

Copyright © The Institution of Engineering and Technology and its licensors 2026

First published: 2026

All intellectual property rights (including copyright) in and to this publication are owned by the Publisher and/or its licensors. All such rights are hereby reserved by their owners and are protected under the Copyright, Designs and Patents Act 1988 ("**CDPA**"), the Berne Convention and the Universal Copyright Convention.

With the exception of:

(i) any use of the publication solely to the extent as permitted under:

a. the CDPA (including fair dealing for the purposes of research, private study, criticism or review); or
b. the terms of a licence granted by the Copyright Licensing Agency ("**CLA**") (only applicable where the publication is represented by the CLA); and/or

(ii) any use of those parts of the publication which are identified within this publication as being reproduced by the Publisher under a Creative Commons licence, Open Government Licence or other open source licence (if any) in accordance with the terms of such licence, no part of this publication, including any article, illustration, trade mark or other content whatsoever, may be used, reproduced, stored in a retrieval system, distributed or transmitted in any form or by any means (including electronically) without the prior permission in writing of the Publisher and/or its licensors (as applicable).

The commission of any unauthorised activity may give rise to civil or criminal liability. Please visit https://digital-library.theiet.org/copyrights-and-permissions for information regarding seeking permission to reuse material from this and/or other publications published by the Publisher. Enquiries relating to the use, including any distribution, of this publication (or any part thereof) should be sent to the Publisher at the address below:

The Institution of Engineering and Technology
Futures Place,
Kings Way, Stevenage,
Herts, SG1 2UA,
United Kingdom

www.theiet.org

Whilst the Publisher and/or its licensors believe that the information and guidance given in this publication is correct, an individual must rely upon their own skill and judgement when performing any action or omitting to perform any action as a result of any statement, opinion or view expressed in the publication and neither the Publisher nor its licensors assume and hereby expressly disclaim any and all liability to anyone for any loss or damage caused by any action or omission of an action made in reliance on the publication and/or any error or omission in the publication, whether or not such an error or omission is the result of negligence or any other cause. Without limiting or otherwise affecting the generality of this statement and the disclaimer, whilst all URLs cited in the publication are correct at the time of press, the Publisher has no responsibility for the persistence or accuracy of URLs for external or third-party Internet websites and does not guarantee that any content on such websites is, or will remain, accurate or appropriate.

Whilst every reasonable effort has been undertaken by the Publisher and its licensors to acknowledge copyright on material reproduced, if there has been an oversight, please contact the Publisher and we will endeavour to correct this upon a reprint.

Trade mark notice: Product or corporate names referred to within this publication may be trade marks or registered trade marks and are used only for identification and explanation without intent to infringe.

Where an author and/or contributor is identified in this publication by name, such author and/or contributor asserts their moral right under the CDPA to be identified as the author and/or contributor of this work.

British Library Cataloguing in Publication Data
A catalogue record for this product is available from the British Library

ISBN 978-1-83724-534-5 (hardback)
ISBN 978-1-83724-535-2 (PDF)
ISBN 978-1-83724-536-9 (EPUB 3)

Typeset in India by MPS Limited

Cover image credit: Busakorn Pongparnit | Moment via Getty Images

Contents

Preface

The Internet has never been a static invention; it lives, breathes, and evolves with us, and with each evolution, it rewrites the terms of how humanity connects, creates, and governs itself. From the static pages of Web 1.0 to the social ecosystems of Web 2.0, and now to the trustless, decentralized protocols of Web 3.0, this journey across web generations has fundamentally altered how people, organizations, and governments conduct their affairs. Now we stand at a more consequential threshold. Web X.0 is not a single technology, nor a single transition; it is a journey, one that carries artificial intelligence, blockchain, quantum computing, the metaverse, and brain–computer interfaces forward together, fusing into one intelligent, autonomous digital ecosystem that deepens with every step. This new web will anticipate our needs before we articulate them, protect our identities without demanding our constant vigilance, and dissolve the boundary between physical and virtual in ways no prior generation has encountered. Yet every leap forward casts new shadows: cyberattacks grow more sophisticated, privacy erodes under hyper-personalization, governance struggles to keep pace with autonomous systems, and the digital divide threatens to separate not merely the connected from the unconnected, but the empowered from the permanently left behind.

This book was conceived with a clear mission, to treat Web X.0 as what it actually is: a sum, not a collection of parts. Grounded in real-world deployments across healthcare, governance, finance, and urban infrastructure, and anchored in scenario-based analysis, it moves beyond documenting what exists to modelling what is coming, and what choices made today will determine whether that future is equitable or exclusionary. Throughout, we demonstrate how Web X.0 directly advances the United Nations Sustainable Development Goals, because technology deployed with intention and governed with wisdom is never neutral.

Web X.0 is not a distant prophecy. It is already present in the algorithms shaping public discourse, the digital twins modelling our cities, and the decentralized platforms redefining finance, education, and governance across continents. The question is not whether this future will arrive; it is what kind of future it will be, and who will have shaped it. This book is written for researchers seeking technical rigor, for professionals navigating rapid technological change, for policymakers balancing innovation against accountability, and for anyone who wishes to understand the digital world being built around them. We invite you to read, reflect, and join us in that work.

AF904502

Web X.0

List of abbreviations

Acronym	Definition
ACO	Ant Colony Optimization
AE	Auto Encoder
AEA	Autonomous Economic Agent
AER	Audio Emotion Recognition
AGI	Artificial General Intelligence
AI	Artificial Intelligence
AIS	Artificial Immune System
AJAX	Asynchronous JavaScript and XML
AML	Anti-Money Laundering
AoI	Age of Information
AoI-FLC	AoI-aware Federated Learning-based Communication
API	Application Programming Interface
AR	Augmented Reality
ARPANET	Advanced Research Projects Agency Network
ASR	Automatic Speech Recognition
BBS+	Boneh–Boyen–Shacham Signature Scheme
BCI	Brain–Computer Interface
BERT	Bidirectional Encoder Representations from Transformers
BFT	Byzantine Fault Tolerance
BS	Base Station
CBDC	Central Bank Digital Currency
CBM	Condition-Based Maintenance
CCC	Concordance Correlation Coefficient
CCDF	Complementary Cumulative Distribution Function
CCIP	Cross-Chain Interoperability Protocol
CDN	Content Distribution Network
CERN	Conseil Européen pour la Recherche Nucléaire (European Organization for Nuclear Research)
CIA	Confidentiality, Integrity, and Availability
CNN	Convolutional Neural Network
CPS	Cyber-Physical Systems
CPU	Central Processing Unit
CT	Cipher Text
CUDA	Compute Unified Device Architecture
CV	Computer Vision
DAG	Directed Acyclic Graph
DAO	Decentralized Autonomous Organization
DAOs	Decentralized Autonomous Organizations
Dapp	Decentralized Application
DDPG	Deep Deterministic Policy Gradient

(Continues)

(*Continued*)

Acronym	Definition
DeFi	Decentralized Finance
DeSci	Decentralized Science
DID	Decentralized Identifier
DIDs	Decentralized Identifiers
DIF	Decentralized Identity Foundation
DLT	Distributed Ledger Technology
DoS	Denial of Service
DP	Differential Privacy
DPoS	Delegated Proof of Stake
DQN	Deep Q-Network
DRL	Distributed Reinforcement Learning
DT	Digital Twin
E2EE	End-to-End Encryption
ECC	Elliptic Curve Cryptography
ECG	Electrocardiogram
EEG	Electroencephalography
her	Electronic Health Record
eMBB	Enhanced Mobile Broadband
EMI	Electromagnetic Interference
ERT	Emotion Recognition Technology
EU	European Union
EVM	Ethereum Virtual Machine
FHIR	Fast Healthcare Interoperability Resources
FIDO	Fast IDentity Online
FL	Federated Learning
G20	Group of Twenty
GAN	Generative Adversarial Network
GCN	Graph Convolutional Network
GDP	Gross Domestic Product
GDPR	General Data Protection Regulation
glTF	Graphics Language Transmission Format
GMM	Gaussian Mixture Model
GNN	Graph Neural Network
GPD	Generalized Pareto Distribution
GPT	Generative Pre-trained Transformer
GPU	Graphics Processing Unit
GSR	Galvanic Skin Response
HCC	Human-Centric Computing
HCI	Human–Computer Interaction
HE	Homomorphic Encryption
HICSS	Hawaii International Conference on System Sciences
HMC	Human–Machine Collaboration
HMD	Head-Mounted Display
HMI	Human–Machine Interaction
HMM	Hidden Markov Model
HRI	Human–Robot Interaction
HTML	HyperText Markup Language
HTTP	Hypertext Transfer Protocol

(Continues)

(*Continued*)

Acronym	Definition
IBC	Inter-Blockchain Communication
IDA	Intelligent Digital Assistant
IDPS	Intrusion Detection and Prevention System
IDS	Intrusion Detection System
IEEE	Institute of Electrical and Electronics Engineers
IETF	Internet Engineering Task Force
IIoT	Industrial Internet of Things
IoT	Internet of Things
IP	Intellectual Property
IPFS	InterPlanetary File System
ISO	International Organization for Standardization
ISP	Internet Service Provider
IT	Information Technology
ITU	International Telecommunication Union
JSON	JavaScript Object Notation
JSON-LD	JavaScript Object Notation for Linked Data
KG	Knowledge Graph
KYC	Know Your Customer
LIME	Local Interpretable Model-agnostic Explanations
LLM	Large Language Model
LSTM	Long Short-Term Memory
MDP	Markov Decision Process
MDRL	Multi-Agent Deep Reinforcement Learning
Meta	(Formerly Facebook, Inc.)
MEV	Maximal Extractable Value
MFA	Multi-Factor Authentication
MiCA	Markets in Crypto-Assets Regulation
ML	Machine Learning
MLOps	Machine Learning Operations
mMTC	Massive Machine-Type Communication
Mosaic	NCSA Mosaic (early web browser)
MPEG	Moving Picture Experts Group
MQTT	Message Queuing Telemetry Transport
MR	Mixed Reality
MSE	Mean Squared Error
NaaS	Neuromorphic-as-a-Service
NeRF	Neural Radiance Field
NFT	Non-Fungible Token
NIST	National Institute of Standards and Technology
NLG	Natural Language Generation
NLP	Natural Language Processing
NLU	Natural Language Understanding
NPC	Non-Player Character
NREL	National Renewable Energy Laboratory
NSAI	Neurosymbolic Artificial Intelligence
OECD	Organization for Economic Co-operation and Development
OEF	Open Economic Framework
OID4VCI	OpenID for Verifiable Credential Issuance

(Continues)

(*Continued*)

Acronym	Definition
OID4VP	OpenID for Verifiable Presentations
ONNX	Open Neural Network Exchange
OPA	Open Policy Agent
OpenXR	Open Extended Reality Standard
OWL	Web Ontology Language
PbD	Privacy by Design
PBFT	Practical Byzantine Fault Tolerance
PER	Packet Error Rate
PET	Privacy-Enhancing Technology
PIoT	Power Internet of Things
PLC	Power Line Communication
PoA	Proof of Authority
PoET	Proof of Elapsed Time
PoS	Proof-of-Stake
PoW	Proof-of-Work
PQC	Post-Quantum Cryptography
PROV-O	Provenance Ontology
PSO	Particle Swarm Optimization
PT	Plain Text
PTSD	Post-Traumatic Stress Disorder
PV	Photovoltaic
QC	Quantum Computing
QKD	Quantum Key Distribution
QML	Quantum Machine Learning
QPU	Quantum Processing Unit
R&D	Research and Development
RAG	Retrieval-Augmented Generation
RATS	Remote Attestation Procedures
RDF	Resource Description Framework
ReRAM	Resistive Random-Access Memory
RF	Random Forest
RFC	Random Forest Classifier
RL	Reinforcement Learning
RNN	Recurrent Neural Network
RSA	Rivest–Shamir–Adleman (cryptographic algorithm)
RWA	Real-World Asset
SDG	Sustainable Development Goal
SER	Speech Emotion Recognition
SHACL	Shapes Constraint Language
SHAP	SHapley Additive exPlanations
SKOS	Simple Knowledge Organization System
SLAM	Simultaneous Localization and Mapping
SME	Small and Medium-sized Enterprise
SMPC	Secure Multi-Party Computation
SNN	Spiking Neural Network
SPARQL	SPARQL Protocol and RDF Query Language
SSI	Self-Sovereign Identity
SSL	Secure Sockets Layer

(Continues)

(*Continued*)

Acronym	Definition
STDP	Spike-Timing-Dependent Plasticity
SVM	Support Vector Machine
TCP/IP	Transmission Control Protocol/Internet Protocol
TD	Thing Description
TLS	Transport Layer Security
TOU	Time-of-Use
TPS	Transactions Per Second
TPU	Tensor Processing Unit
TTS	Text-to-Speech
TVL	Total Value Locked
UAV	Unmanned Aerial Vehicle
ULAoI	Ultra-Low Age of Information
ULAoI-DT	Ultra-Low Age of Information Guaranteed Digital Twin
UN	United Nations
UN SDGs	United Nations Sustainable Development Goals
UNDP	United Nations Development Program
UNESCO	United Nations Educational, Scientific and Cultural Organization
URI	Uniform Resource Identifier
URLLC	Ultra-Reliable Low Latency Communication
USD	Universal Scene Description
UX	User Experience
VC	Verifiable Credential
ViT	Vision Transformer
VQ	Virtual Queue
VR	Virtual Reality
W3C	World Wide Web Consortium
WAC	Web Access Control
WASI	WebAssembly System Interface
WASM	WebAssembly
WCAG	Web Content Accessibility Guidelines
WebRTC	Web Real-Time Communication
WoT	Web of Things
XAI	Explainable Artificial Intelligence
XCMP	Cross-Chain Message Passing
XML	eXtensible Markup Language
XR	Extended Reality
ZK	Zero-Knowledge
ZKP	Zero-Knowledge Proof
ZTA	Zero-Trust Architecture
5G	Fifth Generation Mobile Network
6DoF	Six Degrees of Freedom
6G	Sixth Generation Mobile Network

About the editors

Muhammad Tariq is a professor and head of the School of Engineering, and director of the Smart Technologies and Applied Intelligence Research (STAIR) Lab, at FAST National University of Computer and Emerging Sciences (NUCES), Islamabad, Pakistan. He serves as a NATO Science for Peace and Security (SPS) director and has been consistently listed among Stanford University's Top 2% Scientists worldwide for three consecutive years. His research expertise spans cybersecurity, blockchain, Internet of Things, artificial intelligence, digital twins, smart grids, and intelligent transportation systems. He has published 85+ papers in high-impact journals and co-authored a seminal book on smart grids with renowned researchers. He has served as a national high-end foreign expert for China in 2017, 2019, and 2023, contributing to state-funded research initiatives, and has secured and led national and international R&D projects partnering with industry leaders. At the government policy level, he serves as a member of the Government of Pakistan's National AI Task Force, playing an active role in shaping the national technology strategy. As a senior IEEE member, he has held leadership roles including chairman of the IEEE Peshawar Subsection (2019–23) and chairman of conference activities for the IEEE Islamabad Section (2023 to date). He is also the founding chairperson of the Pukhtunkhwa Open Source Foundation (POSF). He holds a PhD from Waseda University, Tokyo, Japan, as an MEXT scholar, and a postdoc from Princeton University, NJ, USA, as a Fulbright scholar, under the supervision of Prof. H. Vincent Poor.

Houbing Herbert Song is a professor, founding director of the NSF Center for Aviation Big Data Analytics (Planning), associate director for leadership of the DOT Transportation Cybersecurity Center for Advanced Research and Education (Tier 1 Center), and director of the Security and Optimization for Networked Globe Laboratory, University of Maryland, Baltimore County, MD, USA. He is also a distinguished visiting fellow of the Scottish Informatics and Computer Science Alliance (SICSA) in the UK. His research interests include AI and machine learning, big data analytics, cyber-physical systems, Internet of Things, and cybersecurity and privacy. He is the editor of 10+ books, the author of more than 100 articles, and the inventor of two patents. He is an IEEE fellow, an Asia-Pacific Artificial Intelligence Association (AAIA) fellow, an ACM distinguished member, and a full member of Sigma Xi. He received his PhD degree in electrical engineering from the University of Virginia, Charlottesville, VA, USA.

Chapter 1

The evolution of the web: from Web 1.0 to Web X.0

Muhammad Tariq[1], Irum Saba[2] and Sana Saleh[1]

Abstract

The chapter lays the conceptual and historical groundwork for the development of the web from its beginnings to the convergent Web X.0 paradigm. Following the path of Advanced Research Projects Agency Network (ARPANET) and the pioneering work of Tim Berners-Lee at European Organization for Nuclear Research (CERN), through the read-only documentation infrastructure of Web 1.0, the participatory platforms of Web 2.0, and the decentralized protocols of Web 3.0, the chapter argues that web generations are best thought of as overlapping, i.e., layered structures rather than replacements. A three-part model on technological enablers, user behavior changes, and economic paradigms describes the rising level of generational change and the self-reinforcing nature of innovation. Analysis eliminates terminological confusion of numerated futures (Web 4.0–Web 6.0) by locating them as functional dimensions: intelligent, sensory, and autonomous systems whose combination forms Web X.0. Cross-generational patterns, as control paradigms, the development of trust, and data economies, data architectures, and security, also display some recurring trends as they situate new problems. The chapter, based on empirical data on adoption measures, market concentration, energy use, and regulatory changes, provides the fundamental basis for further analysis of certain technologies and their effects on society.

1.1 Introduction: the accelerating digital epoch

The trajectory of the Internet represents one of the most profound and rapid accelerations of technological capability in human history. To fully comprehend

[1]Department of Computer Engineering, School of Engineering, Smart Technologies and Applied Intelligence Research (STAIR) Lab, National University of Computer and Emerging Sciences (NUCES), Pakistan
[2]Department of Electrical Engineering, School of Engineering, Smart Technologies and Applied Intelligence Research (STAIR) Lab, National University of Computer and Emerging Sciences (NUCES), Pakistan

the Web X.0 paradigm, which promises intelligent, autonomous, and immersive digital experiences, we must trace the path that leads to this point. This journey involves more than sophisticated code or faster processors. It includes fundamental paradigm shifts that reorganize the network's design, the user's agency, and the online world's economics. The web versions are continuously evolving, i.e., Web 1.0 had read-only, static addresses; Web 2.0 featured dynamic, interactive websites; and Web 3.0 pointed to a decentralized, trustless future. Each of these stages resulted from the convergence of new economics, rising user needs, and technological brilliance. This chapter begins our exploration of this major transformation. It lays the conceptual and historical groundwork for the rest of the book, which explores the safe, intelligent, and inclusive potential of Web X.0.

The early Internet design, developed from research projects like ARPANET in the late 1960s, was both resilient and interoperable. It utilized packet-switching technologies, such as Transmission Control Protocol/Internet Protocol (TCP/IP), to construct a network architecture without a central authority [1]. This backbone served as an efficient but covert means of file transfer and communication for government employees, researchers, and academic cliques in the decades that followed. The turning point occurred in 1989, when CERN scientist Tim Berners-Lee proposed a mechanism to control the lab's information flow, which was causing the management to have restless nights. His vision of the "World Wide Web" was a universal, interconnected information framework founded on three fundamental yet revolutionary pillars: HyperText Markup Language (HTML), the document construction language; the Uniform Resource Identifier (URI), the method for disparate identification; and the Hypertext Transfer Protocol (HTTP), the access protocol utilized across the network [2]. This was the conceptual leap from a network of computers to a web of information.

The actual spark for popular adoption emerged with the invention of the graphical web browser. Early text-based browsers like Lynx predate this period, but the NCSA Mosaic's 1993 release marked a turning point. For the first time, text and images could be rendered simultaneously in an intuitive graphical interface, transforming the web from a tool for command-line experts into an accessible "information superhighway" for the general public. This led to a period of rapid expansion and business interest that was briefly known as the Web 1.0 era. However, this was merely the start of a series of events. A self-reinforcing loop caused the subsequent generations of the web to emerge more rapidly. New user behaviors brought about by technological advancements create new business prospects that support further technical research and development. This accelerating feedback loop explains why it took about ten years for the static Web 1.0 to evolve into the social Web 2.0, while the concepts of Web 3.0 first gained substantial traction a few years after Web 2.0's peak popularity, with the convergence into Web X.0 well underway (Figure 1.1).

This book explores the case that the development of the web can be better understood as a process of accumulation and complex convergence rather than as a sequence of neat, discrete replacements. The paradigms overlap; Web 1.0's static websites still coexist with Web 2.0's social websites, which are further challenged and enhanced by Web 3.0's decentralized protocols. The nomenclature "Web X.0" is thus

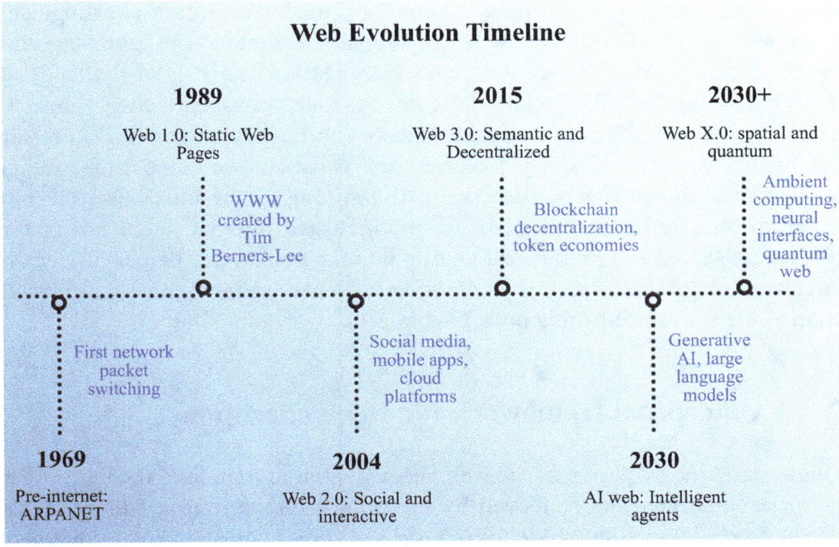

Figure 1.1 Evolution of the Web from ARPANET to Web X.0

intentionally selected. The "X" denotes a fluid, open-ended future, a realization that the next chapter is not defined by a single monolithic technology such as blockchain, but by the mutually enhancing interplay of many frontier technologies. Web X.0 denotes the moment when artificial intelligence (AI), decentralized architectures, immersive extended reality (XR), the Internet of Things (IoT), and next-generation connectivity, such as 5G and 6G, combine, producing a more intelligent, reactive, and embedded-in-the-physical-world digital ecosystem than the world has hitherto seen.

This history is not an imaginary academic game for practitioners and researchers in computing, telecom, cybersecurity, and public policy. Instead, it is a necessary prism for interpreting the present and foreseeing future directions. The security issues that plague us nowadays, such as central-platform data breaches and decentralized-network smart-contract attacks, are the logical result of the architecture decisions made by earlier generations. By 2024, the Internet is expected to have an estimated 4.95 billion users worldwide. Web 2.0 sites are taking the overwhelming share of user interaction, with active blockchain wallets estimated at 80–100 million, or roughly 2% of the total number of Internet users, and growing at an average rate of 30% per year [3]. The arguments over data sovereignty, Internet privacy, and platform control are so heated because of the economic regimes established during the Web 2.0 period, when the five leading technology firms had valuations totaling tens of trillions of dollars. Similarly, the need for future network infrastructure, the ethics of AI, and the governance of virtual worlds become clearer through lessons from the predecessors of previous disruptions.

Our chapter's main goal is to provide a strong conceptual framework for understanding these generations of the web. We will unpack the technological catalysts, user interaction shifts, and economic model evolutions, distinguishing among Web 1.0, Web 2.0, and Web 3.0. We shall examine how each stage overcame the deficiencies of the one before it while creating a new set of challenges and opportunities. We shall finally pull these threads together as a prelude to presenting the concept of Web X.0 as not a future fantasy but the natural, convergent result of these historical trajectories. By looking back at where we came from, we give ourselves the critical vantage necessary to confront the promises as well as the dangers of the intelligent, autonomous, and inclusive Internet future taking form. This context serves as a prelude for getting into the book's detailed excursions into particular technologies, security consequences, and societal repercussions that comprise the substance of this book (Table 1.1).

1.2 A conceptual framework for web generations

To understand the evolution of the web, it is essential to transcend the naive idea of successive improvements conveyed by the quantitative suffixes "1.0," "2.0," and "3.0." A more compelling model of thought is layered development, convergence, and symbiotic progression. Imagine the digital world as a vast, ancient metropolis, populated and rebuilt over countless millennia, rather than a single piece of code. In this city, Gothic churches represent the monolithic platforms of Web 2.0. Encircling them, glass-and-steel skyscrapers stand for the decentralized protocols of Web 3.0. Beneath the streets, ancient Roman aqueducts illustrate the foundational protocols of Web 1.0. These layers are not isolated: the new Web X.0 district emerges as the intelligent, networked urban tissue that unites these disparate architectural styles. This unity enables new forms of interaction and value creation that were previously impossible. By viewing the digital world in this way, it becomes clear why elements of every generation persist today. Change, therefore, is often a continuation rather than an abrupt break.

Thus, the word "Web X.0" is a well-considered and practical decision. The "X" serves as a stand-in for an open, diverse future that is not limited to a single defining technology. While Web X.0 is the site of synergistic convergence where many technical frontiers meet and support each other, Web 3.0 is thought to be essentially identical to decentralization and blockchain. It is here that lies truly transformative power. AI is given trust and auditability through decentralized data sources and verifiable computation. Blockchain networks become more intelligent and scalable through AI-based optimizations and off-chain computations. Immersive metaverses become economically relevant and persistent with the blending of decentralized asset ownership and AI-based non-player characters. This is the fundamental argument of Web X.0: its defining feature is not a given technology, but rather emergent properties derived from their profound integration (Figure 1.2) [4].

These generational shifts are not random; rather, they result from a strong feedback loop among three key factors: changes in economic models, user

Table 1.1 A comparative framework of web generations

Web generation	Core paradigm	User's primary role	Key enabling technologies	Dominant economic model	Primary unit of value	Approximate scale (2024)
Web 1.0	Read-only	Consumer	HTML, HTTP, and early browsers	Banner advertising, direct sales	Content/page views	~500M users (peak)
Web 2.0	Read–write	Creator and product	AJAX, APIs, cloud, and mobile	Targeted advertising and platform fees	User data a attention	~5B users; top 5 platforms revenue >$1.5T annually
Web 3.0	Read–write–trust	Owner and stakeholder	Blockchain, smart contracts, and DApps	Tokenomics, DeFi, and NFTs	Digital assets and tokens	~80–100M wallet users; $80B DeFi TVL
Web X.0	Read–write–trust–intuit	Participant in an intelligent ecosystem	AI, IoT, advanced cryptography, and XR	AI-driven services and tokenized economies	Predictive insight and experience	Emerging; projected >$10T economic impact by 2030 [5]

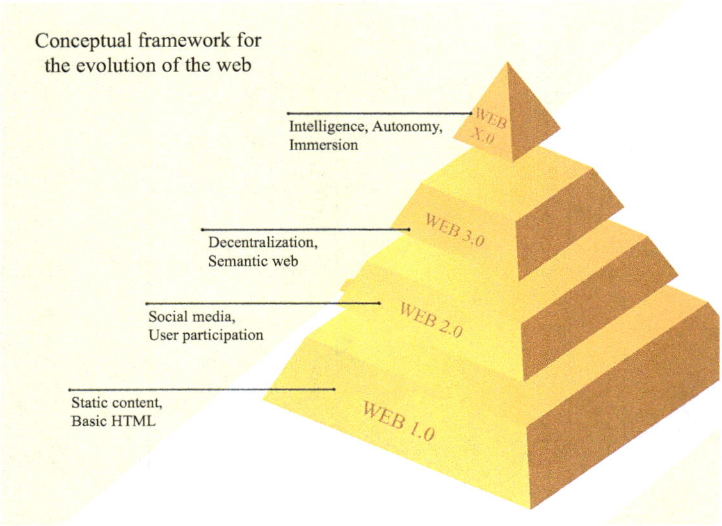

Figure 1.2 Conceptual pyramid illustrating the evolution of the web from Web 1.0 to Web X.0, showing technological, economic, and regulatory drivers

behavior, and technical enablers. This three-way engine provides a forecasting prism to comprehend past disruptions and anticipate future ones.

1. Technological enablers: These are the fundamental innovations that make new things possible. A necessary step toward the rich media of Web 2.0 was the switch from dial-up modems to broadband (a telecom breakthrough). In a similar vein, Web 3.0's trustless transactions were made possible by the cryptography invention of blockchain, a computing/science advance. Neuromorphic computing advancements, quantum-resistant cryptography, and the low-latency possibilities of 6G networks are some of the enablers for Web X.0.
2. Shifts in user behavior: Although technology offers opportunities, its direction is determined by user adoption. Text-based Web 1.0 was unable to satisfy users' desire for more interactive and engaging online experiences as broadband Internet proliferated. The desire for greater user autonomy has increased recently amid growing user disenchantment with Web 2.0 features such as data surveillance, content filtering, and platform monopolies. This has directly fueled interest in Web 3.0 alternatives. User behaviors for Web X.0 are changing to include a readiness to delegate work to self-governing agents and to engage with more customized, relevant, and interesting digital experiences.

This model requires a major clarification of terminology. It must be well articulated between the numbered futures (Web 4.0, 5.0, and 6.0) and the relationship between Web X.0 and the numbered futures (Web 4.0, 5.0, and 6.0). These numerated labels characterize different layers of convergent Web X.0 instead of being sequential. The term Web 4.0 refers to the intelligence layer that incorporates AI and machine learning into the network. The human ability to perceive and respond to emotions and physical surroundings is the sensory and affective layer, which is Web 5.0. Web 6.0 includes the network layer of autonomy—networks with the ability to act and coordinate independently. Web X.0 is not the seventh generation but a synthesis of these dimensions to a convergent whole that is interoperable. Such conceptualization fixes the seeming explosion of the generational into a rational structure of overlapping and mutually supporting technological changes [6].

3. Economic model: This system of incentives that propels and maintains every generation. The concept of targeted advertising was made possible by the technological capacity for dynamic content (Web 2.0) and the user behavior of creating and disseminating information. This, in turn, generated the capital that capitalized on the enormous scale of the platform economy. New economic models, including token-based incentivization, decentralized finance (DeFi), and creator economies based on non-fungible tokens (NFTs), have been enabled by blockchain technology and by user demand for sovereignty. Although the Web X.0 economic model is still in the early stages of development, it is likely to involve complex value exchanges between AI and humans, micro-transactions for AI services, and novel ways to value data and attention in immersive environments.

It also showcases the ultimate development process of the concept of digital trust. In Web 1.0, the only trust lay with the content publisher (e.g., a university or a reputable company). Web 2.0 transfers this trust to the sites themselves. We entrusted Facebook with our social data, Google with our searches, and Amazon with our payments. This was an institutional trust. Web 3.0 foresees a disruptive break from algorithmic and cryptographic trust, where one does not trust an arbitrary node but rather the open, auditable, immutable code within the blockchain protocol. Web X.0 will predominantly require a contextual trust hybrid framework, in which AI will testify on behalf of reputation and identity, cryptographic assertions will assure transactional integrity, and decentralized governance mechanisms will provide for accountability, all operating interactively as per the specific interaction [7].

Those who oppose the decentralization paradigm raise significant questions that should be addressed. Some have also proposed that systems built on blockchain tend to replace, rather than eliminate, trust relationships, with institutions giving way to developers, miners, or protocol governance procedures that are less transparent to regular users [8]. Some have argued that the energy use of Proof-of-Work consensus systems—even Bitcoin, which uses about 150 terawatt-hours each year, is an equal power user to the national electrical requirements of Argentina—invalidates claims of sustainability, yet moves to Proof-of-Stake (which scales down to about 99.9% power usage) mitigate this issue [9]. These critiques do not discount the potential of Web 3.0, but they highlight that decentralization is a trade-off design space and not a clear answer.

In addition, it is necessary to differentiate between the Semantic Web, an original vision for Web 3.0 espoused by Tim Berners-Lee, and the Decentralized Web that has largely defined the term among the public. The Semantic Web was designed to make data machine-readable so that intelligent agents could automatically interpret and interlink information. Although advancements have been made (e.g., through schema.org), its complete vision has yet to be realized. The Decentralized Web, based on blockchain, aims to disintermediate trust and return control of data and assets to users. It is argued that Web X.0 might be the ideal combination of these two visions: a web where data is not only machine-readable (Semantic) but also user-owned and verifiably authentic (Decentralized), creating an environment that is conducive to truly intelligent and autonomous agents acting on our behalf [10]. With its emphasis on convergence, feedback loops, and changing trust models, this conceptual framework offers the essential lens through which to examine the subsequent detailed history and evaluate the prospects of the intelligent digital future.

1.3 Web 1.0: the read-only web (the information foundation)

The period, spanning somewhere between 1991, when the general public first learned of the World Wide Web, and the early years of the first decade of the 2000s, is now classified under the term Web 1.0. The first phase is the one most suitable for describing the so-called "Read-Only Web" or the "Static Web." This was an altogether non-interactive computer environment by today's standards, with the one-way principle of information delivery. One must come to it not as the primeval precursor but as the groundbreaking innovations that created the very notion of broadly available, inter-associated information.

The design of Web 1.0 was beautifully simplistic, based on the straightforward client–server architecture. The user machine had the client program—the web browser, for example, the NCSA Mosaic, Netscape Navigator, or subsequently, Microsoft Internet Explorer. The browser would issue the request, utilizing the HTTP, for a file from a distant server that hosted the HTML pages. The server's activity remained straightforward: it would find the specified file and send the entire static page back to the client by rendering the page on the user's monitor. The interaction remained straightforward and linear, practically entirely mapped to the clicking activity of moving from one document to the next via hyperlinks, an activity characterized by the father of the Web itself, Tim Berners-Lee [11], as "browsing" [11].

This technological parsimony shaped the Internet's social and economic architecture. Content creation was a technological undertaking limited to a tiny group of webmasters, developers, and institutions with the necessary technology, software, and connectivity. For the vast majority, the function was merely passive. The websites served as web equivalents to traditional media, such as digital catalogs for enterprises, web magazines for publishers, or catalogs for early e-commerce ventures. The concept of "user-generated content" did not exist on a large scale. In contrast, individual homepages did exist, often hosted by services such as GeoCities; they primarily catered to people interested in learning basic HTML and thus amounted to isolated cases of individualization in a vast sea of professionally produced content. This dynamic formed a clear divide between information publishers and users, similar to the patterns of TV and print broadcasting, but characterized by a single factor: unparalleled accessibility and scope.

As a result, these economic models accurately represented the fixed broadcast period. Display advertisements, particularly banner ads, were the most common means of revenue creation. The introduction of the first clickable banner ad, sponsored by HotWired (the online subsidiary of *Wired* magazine) on behalf of AT&T in 1994, was a watershed moment in digital commerce [12]. Although e-commerce was in its infancy and generally looked with suspicion due to security concerns, it began to gain respectability. Amazon, which was founded as an online bookstore in 1994, and eBay, which was originally known as AuctionWeb in 1995, pioneered the adoption of the online selling model, emphasizing the importance of customer trust through the implementation of secure transaction protocols such as Secure Sockets Layer and customer-centric policies. The economic value was generated from the material itself, which included product descriptions, news articles, and software downloads, as well as the potential audience for advertisers. Aside from rudimentary server logs that tracked page visits, user information was not yet recognized as the valuable commodity it would later become.

To dismiss Web 1.0 as a technologically unsophisticated era would be a profound misjudgment of its historical impact. Its revolutionary achievement was the democratization of information access on a global scale. For the first time in history, an individual with a dial-up modem and a phone line could, from their home, access a vast and growing repository of human knowledge. University libraries, government documents, scientific papers, and news from across the globe became instantly available, collapsing geographical and institutional barriers that had previously restricted the flow of information. This had a leveling effect, empowering students, researchers, and curious minds in ways that were previously unimaginable. It planted the seeds for a more informed and interconnected global citizenry. The web's fundamental principle of hyperlinking created a non-linear, associative structure of knowledge, allowing users to follow their curiosity from one topic to another in a way that a static encyclopedia or library shelf never could.

From the standpoint of cybersecurity and infrastructure, the anxieties of the Web 1.0 era seem almost nostalgic by today's measures, but set the stage for the basic challenges of the digital era. The outright threats were directed at the infrastructure itself. The vulnerability of servers became a prime target, as hackers attempted to deface websites, a sort of cyber-equivalent of graffiti aimed more at notoriety than financial motives. Denial-of-Service attacks, meant for the purposes of swamping servers and taking websites down, became a disruptor. Network-based attacks, such as the sniffing of unencrypted packets, presented a risk to sensitive information, although the level of critical transactional data remained limited compared to today. The security paradigm remained a matter of the perimeter: the aim remained protection for the server, the central strongpoint containing the valuable information. The client, or the user, remained a benign endpoint. This naiveté would be radically reversed when platforms become more dynamic and user-driven.

The basic constraints of Web 1.0 were preprogrammed into its design. Its immobility made it unsuitable for use in settings that require contact, cooperation, or real-time customization. Upgrading to a website required hand-editing and uploading HTML files, which did not suit the dynamic, talkative nature of modern social networks or mobile devices. Rather than functioning as a platform or app, it was primarily a document-oriented web. However, this limitation served as a catalyst for innovation. Users' expectations grew as they became accustomed to the vast amount of information available on the Internet. They wanted to create, not simply read; they wanted to generate rather than receive. With the growing need for interactivity and user participation, and the inevitable advancement of technological capabilities, a dramatic shift occurred that would define the next ten years: the creation of the participatory Web 2.0. The read-only, static web had mostly created the infrastructure foundation; the next iteration would be to build a dynamic, engaged, and complicated civil society on top of it.

1.4 Web 2.0: the social and participatory web

This transition to Web 2.0, which occurred in the early to mid-2000s, is widely regarded as one of the most profound paradigm shifts in the field of digital technology. While Web 1.0 can be compared to a library, Web 2.0 represents a worldwide collaborative workshop, a dynamic town square, and a personalized broadcasting media that are all merged together. This era, known as the "Social Web" or "Participatory Web," saw a significant shift from a static, read-only medium to a dynamic, read–write media, with the user transitioning from passive consumer to active contributor and collaborator. Its ideology shifted from broadcasting material to end users to rendering services that enabled end users to create, share, and remix content collaboratively. It was not the result of a single invention, but rather a series of technological advancements, a shift in Internet connectivity, and a revolutionary shift in user behavior that collectively redefined the primary role and economic growth of the Internet.

The technical foundations of Web 2.0 included a series of advances that enabled a highly interactive and agile user experience. The breakthrough of AJAX (Asynchronous JavaScript and XML) in 2005 was a watershed moment. Before AJAX, when a user interacted with a webpage, such as by filling out a form, the entire page had to be reloaded from the server. AJAX enables web browsers to communicate with servers in the background, allowing them to fetch small amounts of data and dynamically change page components. This innovation encouraged the development of complex, dynamic web applications that behaved smoothly like desktop programs, paving the way for products such as Google Maps (which allowed users to drag and drop maps without reloading) and Gmail (which allowed for the smooth opening and arrangement of messages) [13]. In addition, the deliberate use of Application Programming Interfaces (APIs) became an important unifying feature of the web. APIs enabled websites to provide crucial capabilities, allowing programmers to "mash up" data from various sources to develop entirely new apps. For example, a real estate portal may superimpose rental information over a Google Map, delivering a more valuable service than each component separately.

The advent of cloud computing enabled the development of this technology stack. During the Web 1.0 era, each organization had its own hardware servers, which were costly and difficult to scale. Cloud computing firms, such as Amazon Web Services (founded in 2006), provided scalable, on-demand storage and computing services via the Internet. This invention made world-class infrastructure readily available, allowing a few people to quickly expand their reach into a global market base without incurring significant upfront capital expenses. The combination of ubiquitous broadband connectivity, which replaced dial-up, solid cloud infrastructure, and AJAX-based user interfaces, facilitated the development of the platform economy. Platforms such as Facebook, YouTube, Wikipedia, and Twitter primarily facilitated the creation of interactive spaces in which users created value for themselves rather than providing content. The material created, social networks, and data acquired from user interactions became the foundation of these websites.

This resulted in a fundamental shift in the dominant economic paradigm. Banner advertising that exemplified Web 1.0 simplicity evolved into sophisticated, data-driven targeted ads. User engagements on a site, such as liking, viewing videos, and searching for products, resulted in an unprecedented amount of personal data. The data was then analyzed to create extraordinarily sophisticated psychological and behavioral profiles, allowing advertisers to send highly personalized messages. "Surveillance capitalism," as coined by Shoshana Zuboff, characterizes this paradigm, which has launched certain "Big Tech" to new levels of scale, wealth, and influence [14]. In some ways, the user was transformed into a commodity, with their data and attention serving as raw material for advertisers to trade.

Web 2.0 had cultural and political ramifications that were paradoxical and extended. It was a positive catalyst for new grounds of international cooperation and content democratization. Wikipedia used collective intelligence to produce the largest encyclopedia in the world, currently available in more than 300 languages and containing more than 60 million articles. Social platforms enabled marginalized voices and contributed to the emergence of recorded roles in political mobilizations, from the Arab Spring to climate activism. YouTube enabled the development of creative economies that currently help millions of content creators around the world, and Etsy and similar sites enabled artists to reach global markets.

Nonetheless, the concentration of information and power produced deep evils that need a long-term critical evaluation. According to the hypothesis of Shoshana Zuboff, surveillance capitalism, the paradigm that transformed the human experience into data of behavior to be extracted, processed, and sold by the platform, has little transparency or consent [14]. The processes behind this change are structural:

platforms fight over who will attract users, developing an incentive system based on algorithms that reward emotionally resonant, frequently false information. Whistleblower testimony has revealed internal Facebook studies showing that algorithmic amplification of divisive content boosted engagement but worsened social polarization [15]. The monopoly of market power: Google has a market share of about 90% in search advertising, and Meta and Google together account for about 50% of all worldwide digital advertising revenue, resulting in unchecked private regulation of public discourse [16]. It is not just bad corporate behavior that is a systemic critique of the system; rather, it is these structural dynamics that have led to calls for decentralized alternatives. It is important to understand this criticism in all its richness to realize why Web 3.0 and Web X.0 are proposing architectural solutions rather than just behavioral ones.

1.5 Web 3.0: the decentralized and semantic web

Web 3.0 is a literal response to the perceived shortcomings of the centralized Web 2.0 paradigm, pushing for a complete architectural and philosophical rethinking of the Internet. Unlike Web 2.0, which consolidated power and data into a few corporate silos, Web 3.0 envisions a decentralized Internet built on open standards, peer-to-peer topologies, and cryptographic identification. Its philosophical shift shifts trust away from centralized intermediaries like social media companies and financial institutions and toward decentralized, transparent, and auditable codebases. Its ideology, typically expressed as "don't trust, verify," seeks to redistribute authority and ownership to end-user persons. The key to understanding this matter is recognizing that Web 3.0 actually covers two mutually exclusive but possibly complementary visions: the years-dreamed-of Semantic Web, aimed at making data machine-readable and intelligence-connected, and the more recently emerging Decentralized Web, aimed at disintermediating trust. The unification of the two visions holds the potential for a genuinely intelligent and user-oriented Internet future.

The underlying technology of the Decentralized Web is blockchain, a decentralized, immutable ledger that stores transactions in a verifiable and permanent manner. Initially deployed as the backbone of Bitcoin, blockchain technology enables the development of trustless systems in which parties can interoperate without a trusted third party. Leveraging this, platforms such as Ethereum went one step further and introduced the concept of smart contracts, self-executing contracts, whereby the terms of the agreement are written into code. Programmable contracts execute actions automatically when predetermined terms and conditions are met, allowing the development of sophisticated, decentralized applications (DApps) that run on a peer-to-peer network rather than a central server. This tech stack uses native cryptocurrencies or tokens that serve as both an incentive mechanism for network participants (e.g., miners or validators) and a medium of exchange in these new digital economies.

These technologies have spawned completely new economic models, challenging the traditional corporate form. Tokenization makes any physical or digital asset to be represented as a one-of-one, tradable token on a blockchain. This forms the basis for DeFi, a marketplace of financial services (lending, borrowing, and trading) based on blockchain without the involvement of banks or brokers. Likewise, NFTs use tokenization to enable deterministically verifiable digital scarcity and ownership for unique items such as digital art, collectibles, and in-game possessions. The most extreme innovation may well be the Decentralized Autonomous Organization (DAO), an organization represented by a set of agreed-upon rules encoded as a transparent computer program, controlled by its members (via governance tokens) and not by a central government. DAOs outline a new form of human collaboration and organizational rulemaking, which exists internationally and operates independently according to community accord.

An empirical evaluation of Web 3.0 adoption reveals both positive achievements and existing constraints. By Q1 2024, valuations of all protocols in DeFi had topped $80 billion, compared to about $180 billion at its highest point in 2021, illustrating continued user demand for disintermediated financial services [17]. Etherion handles 1–1.5 million transactions per day, but during peak demand, gas prices often exceed 20–50 per transaction, making most applications cost-prohibitive for the average user. Transaction volumes, some 10-fold smaller than Ethereum mainnet and at fees of less than $0.10, are now supported through layer-2 scaling subsystems (Arbitrum, Optimism, and zkSync), indicating that scalability trends are technically feasible. Still, user experience remains disjointed [18].

There are serious points of friction in user adoption. According to Blockchain.com statistics, the number of users of decentralized applications is about 5–10 million, which is a significant difference compared to the number of verified wallet users (around 85 million globally), indicating that retention is a problem. In usability studies, the barriers consistently include the cognitive burden of using the seed phrase, unfamiliar to traditional Internet users; the lack of instantaneity in the transaction confirmation process; and the practical difficulty of achieving cross-application identity portability, whilst conceptually appealing [19]. These measures put the successes of Web 3.0 into perspective and benchmark the level of adoption within the mainstream.

The key promises of Web 3.0 are profound. It offers user sovereignty and data ownership, where individuals control their own identity and data through tools like self-sovereign identity (SSI) rather than surrendering it to platforms. Censorship resistance is a fundamental advantage of decentralized networks, which lack a centralized authority capable of blocking material or banning users from the site. Furthermore, networks enable greater financial inclusion by offering open-access monetary services to people with Internet connections, bypassing traditional intermediaries. However, these advantages are balanced by major hurdles encountered in earlier stages of expansion. Scalability remains a serious concern, as large blockchain networks like Ethereum often experience high transaction fees and sluggish processing times during surges in demand. User Experience (UX) is typically clumsy, requiring users to manage cryptographic keys and engage with sophisticated interfaces, posing a substantial obstacle to widespread adoption. Furthermore, the industry faces significant regulatory uncertainty, as governments around the world struggle to apply appropriate classification and regulation to cryptocurrencies, DAOs, and DeFi protocols without suffocating innovation. Finally, the energy consumption required for some consensus techniques, particularly Proof-of-Work, has sparked legitimate concerns about environmental sustainability.

Concurrently, Tim Berners-Lee's initial notion for the Semantic Web remains a cornerstone of the future Web 3.0 vision. It makes web content more meaningful to some extent by employing standards such as RDF (Resource Description Framework) and OWL (Web Ontology Language), making data intelligible to machines. This would enable software agents with intelligence to automatically comprehend, reason with, and interconnect information from disparate sources, achieving the dream of a genuinely "intelligent" web. Though development has come more slowly than originally expected, the ideals of the Semantic Web come into sharper focus against the backdrop of the big data era and the advent of AI. The intermixture of decentralized data ownership (from the Decentralized Web) and machine-readable data structures (Semantic Web) would unlock robust new use cases. One would involve a user authorizing an AI software agent to access their securely stored, semantically enhanced medical records from a variety of providers, deriving customized health insights without providing their data to a central platform. As a result, Web 3.0 is more than just decentralization; it is a convergence of root levels to produce a wiser, more egalitarian, and user-governed Internet—a necessary prerequisite for the future integrated Web X.0.

The decentralization thesis is to be subjected to critical examination. Despite arguments for total disintermediation, empirical studies show that, in so-called decentralized systems, concentration persists. The production of Ethereum blocks is also not open in practice. However, Proof-of-Stake theory is concentrated in select large staking providers, with Lido controlling about 30% of staked Ether (ETH) and centralized exchanges holding large additional shares [20]. Governance participation in large DAOs is less than 10% of total token owners, which creates a factual control by active minorities. Depending on the code, additional code dependencies add a layer of trust: most DeFi protocols are forked from audited codebases of more dominant projects such as Uniswap or Compound, which pose systemic risk due to shared vulnerabilities. These observations do not disprove the value of Web 3.0 but indicate that decentralization is more of a spectrum and not a binary property, and that governance, economic concentration, and technical dependencies need to be given as much focus as consensus mechanisms.

1.6 Web X.0: the convergent future—intelligence, autonomy, and immersion

Web X.0 is the hypothetical, convergent synthesis in which the existing technological trends are headed, not a fourth wave as such, but rather the unified ecosystem that will arise during the concomitant maturation of AI, blockchain, IoT, XR, and next-generation connectivity. This difference eliminates terminological wars introduced in parts of the literature on futures: Web 4.0 (intelligent), Web 5.0

(emotional/sensory), and Web 6.0 (autonomous systems) are different functional dimensions that Web X.0 brings together into a single entity [21]. The connection is structural rather than chronological. These dimensions will co-evolve in parallel, just as Web 2.0 did not supersede Web 1.0 but added interactivity to solid foundations; these dimensions will evolve based on interoperability standards, developed infrastructure, and evolving user practices. The X represents this multidimensional integration, the place where, in the past, separate technological frontiers were discontinuities, but which has now become a reinforcement of one another rather than a coexistence.

The transition from user-led tools to agent-controlled environments is the key feature that distinguishes Web X.0. Individuals will engage with the virtual environment via extremely advanced AI agents that work for them. Such agents will go beyond chatbots' fundamental capabilities, evolving into long-lived, semi-automated creatures capable of handling complex operations across a variety of platforms. For example, a person's agent may be able to sign contracts with a DAO for a freelancer project, manage their portfolio of investments in DeFi protocols based on real-time market data, and consult their smart home IoT device to improve energy efficiency while also absorbing the user's preferences and making proactive recommendations. This intelligent web will be powered by Ambient Intelligence, which embeds computations in the environment in an elegant and simple manner, resulting in a hybrid digital–physical workplace that is always active, context-aware, and responsive.

This intelligent agency will be made up of a convergent stack of technologies. The verifiable and decentralized qualities of blockchain and smart contracts will serve as a trust layer, making AI decision-making auditable and transparent, and digital real estate really owned. The intelligence layer will be made up of AI and machine learning, with a focus on improvements in large language models (LLMs) and neuro-symbolic AI. The physical data layer will be comprised of the IoT and sensor networks, which will connect the digital and physical worlds by perceiving a continuous stream of real-world data. The interface and experience layer will be made up of immersive technologies such as Virtual Reality (VR), Augmented Reality (AR), and the Metaverse, which will expand interaction beyond displays and into spatially oriented, 3D environments. Finally, the ultra-reliable, low-latency communication of 5G and forthcoming 6G networks will serve as the underlying core connectivity layer, connecting all of these components in real time.

The economic and social architectures of Web X.0 are likely to undergo substantial reengineering. The economy will be a combination of human and machine interactions, combining AI-driven service economies with advanced tokenized asset markets. Value creation will be centered on generating predictive information, providing individualized experiences, and enabling autonomous task fulfillment. Socio-interactions will become increasingly common in persistent virtual worlds (the metaverse), which feature portable digital identities, assets, and social networks that are user-owned and compatible with Web 3.0 design principles. This offers huge hurdles for digital identification, necessitating a dynamic combination of biometric information, behavioral patterns, and decentralized identifiers managed by the user AI agent.

The path to Web X.0 is laden with significant difficulties that must be solved. Ethical oversight over autonomous AI systems is critical; in the absence of comprehensive frameworks, agent-based webs can have unexpected repercussions, deep-seated algorithmic bias, and a loss of human agency. Computation and energy demands for maintaining a world-immersive and intelligent web are staggering, necessitating developments in quantum computing, neuromorphic processors, and green energy technologies. Again, a new digital gap is emerging with an unexpected nature, as much a result of understanding and contending with these sophisticated systems as of having access to the tools themselves. Web X.0 promises unprecedented convenience, personalization, and functionality; however, realizing its potential in a secure, equitable, and human-centric manner will be the defining challenge of the next decade, intertwining the technological advances discussed in this chapter with the security, ethical, and societal challenges discussed throughout the rest of this volume.

Important issues are brought up through skeptical evaluations of this convergent vision. The critique of technological solutionism by Morozov raises the question of whether there are technical solutions to complex social issues such as privacy, inequality, and democratic governance, or whether reorganizing architecture will help resolve them or displace the existing tensions [22]. The virtual worlds that Web X.0 creates can only make social fragmentation worse, rather than lessen it, replacing the interaction of algorithms with that of the human body. There is empirical evidence regarding the psychological impacts of social media that should raise some concerns: the longer the time spent in the digital space, the higher the mental health effects are reported in the group of adolescents, which might indicate that the more immersive the experiences, the greater the effects can be observed [23]. Even highly advanced autonomous AI systems can be inherently irresponsible in the open world, the so-called alignment problem, to which there is no satisfactory answer yet [24]. These criticisms do not lead to the disenfranchisement of Web X.0's potential, but emphasize that institutional, ethical, and regulatory innovation must keep pace with technological innovation, or we will continue to see these problems in new forms.

Environmental sustainability must be given special attention. The ethical challenges of training large language models are significant: training GPT-3 required about 1,300 megawatt-hours of electricity, which is the annual emissions of 130 US households [25]. Massive scale magnifies this footprint by many orders of magnitude. At the same time, blockchain networks that move to Proof-of-Stake gain efficiency benefits of dramatic proportions. The Merge in Ethereum cut energy usage by up to 99.9% [26]. IoT sensor networks, immersive rendering, and always-on connectivity augment these requirements. Nonetheless, the very technologies make sustainability possible: optimized AI-controlled energy grids, carbon markets validated by blockchain, and resources optimally used through IoT. The environmental effects of Web X.0 are thus dependent on design decisions, energy system regulation, and decarbonization, in addition to technical architecture, and not solely on technical architecture.

1.7 Thematic evolution: cross-generational analysis

The path between Web 1.0 and the beginning of Web X.0 is not only a line of technological advancement but also a complex development of the core digital ideas. These themes, appearing in generations, allow us to identify the back currents that define our relations with the Internet. This evolution can be described in four important thematic arcs: the pendulum of control, the changing principles of trust, the remaking of the value and ownership of data, and the ever-increasing scale of digital conflict.

The fundamental thematic cycle is a constant process of centralization/decentralization. The publishing model of Web 1.0 was centralized, but the underlying, open protocols were decentralized. The re-centralization of power and data, which had been dramatically reduced in Web 2.0 to a few corporate walls-gardens, led to platforms becoming the new intermediaries. Web 3.0 was a direct ideological response, promoting decentralized designs such as blockchain to decentralize power from corporations, users, and code. Web X.0, however, is not a definitive triumph for decentralization. Instead, it will be a period of convergent hybridity, with intelligent, centralized AI systems potentially communicating with and controlling decentralized ledgers and assets to produce a subtle topography in which both systems operate and fulfill distinct functions within the same digital ecosystem.

The second theme, the development of trust, is a direct result of this oscillation. Web 1.0 made institutions, publishers, universities, and corporations the primary sources of trust because they served as information gatekeepers. Web 2.0 put its faith in algorithmic platforms; we believed Google to rank search results, Facebook to shape the social graph, and Amazon to serve as a recommendation engine, shaping our reality. Web 3.0 suggests sweeping away cryptographic and algorithmic trust, in which verification is done through transparent code and consensus protocols, and the reduction of reliance on individual human intermediaries. Trust in the Web X.0 will be more fragmented and complicated. It will require us to believe in the integrity of AI models (explainable AI), the security of smart contracts, the privacy guarantees of immersive environments, and the governance of DAOs, and form a multi-layered trust stack.

Alongside the shift in trust, the data economy is changing. In Web 1.0, publishers of content controlled much of the data, and it was siloed. Web 2.0 opened up new, previously unthinkable value by transforming user behavior into behavioral information, which was mined, combined, and commercialized data that became a common resource created but owned by the user. Web 3.0 is planned to support the self-sovereign data model, where personal identities and data belong to the individual, and the user has the freedom to monetize their data on their own terms through cryptographic keys. Web X.0 will have to face the challenge of bringing this utopia to an intelligent world of connections. The combination of AI, IoT, and biometrics in the immersive space will generate data of unheard-of granularity and close-quart redness, and the concerns of ownership, approval, and ethical application will not only be a costly necessity but also a matter of human rights.

Finally, a cybersecurity arms race has been initiated with each web generation. Web 1.0 had a relatively low attack surface, with the majority of attacks focused on breaching and defacing servers. Web 2.0, with its interactive and login-based nature, exponentially increased the threat landscape, causing epidemics of data breaches, identity theft, and sophisticated phishing. The on-chain assets available under Web 3.0 and the impossibility of reversing its transactions have introduced new attack vectors, such as smart contract exploits, crypto wallet drains, and consensus mechanism attacks. All of these vulnerabilities will be built into one, ubiquitous system, Web X.0. It will reveal the whole of the human environment, including AI models that can be poisoned and biased, brain–computer interfaces that may be compromised, and critical infrastructure operated by autonomous DAOs. Security will cease being an add-on or a reasonably priced option and become the underlying foundation of all connected layers, requiring a holistic, zero-trust strategy to protect a smartly immersive world (Table 1.2).

There are empirical intergenerational patterns that should be considered. Market power concentration, albeit widely criticized, reflects actual network effects and economies of scale that decentralizing alternatives have yet to match. Alphabet, Amazon, Apple, Meta, and Microsoft are the top five Web 2.0 platforms that generate annual revenues in the trillions of dollars, and the entire web decentralization ecosystem, including cryptocurrency markets, is estimated to be worth tens of billions at best and hundreds of billions at worst, with much more volatility [27]. Indicators related to user engagement show the same disparity: the average daily time spent on Facebook is above 30 min worldwide, and even the most prosperous decentralized apps fail to achieve similar retention rates.

Table 1.2 Thematic evolution across web generations

Theme	Web 1.0	Web 2.0	Web 3.0	Web X.0
Control paradigm	Centralized publishing	Centralized platforms	Decentralized protocols	Convergent hybridity
Basis of trust	Institutional authority	Platform algorithms	Cryptographic verification	Multi-layered "trust stack"
Data paradigm	Owned and siloed	Harvested and aggregated	Self-sovereign	Intimate and contextual
Primary security concern	Server integrity	Identity and data breaches	Smart contract and key security	Systemic and existential risks

Such differences shed light on the structural benefits of centralized designs: integrative development, smooth user experience, homogeneous security designs, and institutionalized regulatory relationships. The modular, composable architecture of Web 3.0 offers theoretical sovereignty and interoperability benefits, but coordination costs that fragmented development communities find hard to meet. The way to Web X.0 should thus not only resolve the technical integration but also address the institutional and economic infrastructure to enable user-friendly, secure, and sustainable decentralized systems functioning at scale.

1.8 Emerging challenges and opportunities for Web X.0

Web X.0's convergent future is a paradoxical scenario of unimaginable potential and unimaginable dangers. To move into this future, it will be essential to respond proactively to an array of technological, societal, ethical, and environmental issues, each of which will be both a challenge and an opportunity to innovate.

The greatest challenge is technological interoperability. In the case of AI, blockchains, IoT devices, and immersive worlds, they have to speak the same language to form a cohesive ecosystem. The creation of standardized data and value-exchange protocols between these disparate layers is a mammoth but necessary task. At the same time, the emergence of quantum computing poses a threat to the cryptographic principles underlying existing blockchain and encryption systems. It requires an active transition to quantum-resistant algorithms. Moreover, AI ethics and bias are not peripheral issues but fundamental design issues. With AI becoming the operating system of Web X.0, its decisions must be equitable and reflect human values to avoid exacerbating inequality and destroying human agency.

The interoperability efforts should be practical in standardization. The World Wide Web Consortium (W3C) is also working on specifications for decentralized identifiers (DIDs) and verifiable credentials, which provide the basic building blocks for cross-platform identity [28]. Vendor-neutral content-addressed storage protocols, such as InterPlanetary File System (IPFS), provide data layers. Interoperability protocols (Cosmos IBC, Polkadot XCMP, Chainlink CCIP) make asset and data transfers between networks formerly in silo possible. Nonetheless, fragmentation has not disappeared: there are more than 100 layer-1 and layer-2 blockchain networks with inadequate interoperability, resulting in fragmented liquidity and barriers to the user experience. The introduction of aggregated liquidity protocols and cross-chain messaging standards indicates that it is likely to converge to interoperability layers, yet there are still important technical and coordination issues [29].

The problem of AI ethics and bias cannot be peripheral; it is a core design need. The empirical evidence of bias in algorithms is quite vast: facial recognition systems have been shown to vary in error rates across demographic groups; hiring algorithms are skewed by gender and race; content recommendation systems have been shown to give preference to extreme content [30]. The issues are not accidental; structural. Machine learning systems are trained to maximize predictive accuracy with training data that encodes past inequalities. With AI as the operating system of Web X.0, its decisions should be verifiable, challengeable, and in line. It not only demands technical innovations (explainable AI, fairness constraints, and adversarial debiasing), but also governance innovations: independent algorithmic audits, regulatory norms, the participation of affected communities in system design, and substantive responses to algorithmic harm [31].

We are then on untested ethical and legal ground. The most important will be algorithmic transparency and accountability; as an AI rejects our loan, shapes reality, or a DAO votes, we will have to know why. The legal and philosophical structures to manage autonomous systems, such as self-driving car fleets or global resource management that can be decentralized, are new. The regulatory frameworks we have traditionally constructed, based on centralized companies and physical assets, are poorly designed to accommodate decentralized organizations, intelligent agents, and digital property, and require flexibility and principles-based global collaboration.

The promise of a dematerialized world, in terms of environmental impact, should be weighed against the energy footprint of the very real digital convergence. Although AI and blockchain can streamline energy grids and supply chains, they also have substantial computational requirements. Web X.0 should be built on a platform of sustainable computing, including green data centers, energy-efficient consensus algorithms (such as proof-of-stake), and an ideology of planetary health coupled with digital progress. The potential is to apply the same technologies to model climate solutions, control renewable resources through IoT networks, and develop transparent carbon markets.

The regulatory systems are changing fast, but disproportionately. The Markets in Crypto-Assets Regulation (MiCA) of the European Union establishes the overall regulation of cryptocurrency issuance and service delivery, and the AI Act establishes risk-related requirements for AI systems [32]. They are the initial, large-scale efforts to regulate Web X.0 technologies worldwide. At the same time, the US continues to lack collective regulation across sectors, and the securities, commodities, and banking agencies have overlapping jurisdictions. Emerging economies have a wide range of strategies: El Salvador adopted Bitcoin, while China banned cryptocurrencies and, at the same time, developed a central bank digital currency. This regulatory heterogeneity not only introduces complexity in compliance across global platforms but also enables policy experimentation, through which the best practices may be identified. The lack of international coordination mechanisms, similar to those that govern telecommunications or aviation, poses risks of regulatory arbitrage and the fragmentation of standards that would hinder global interoperability of Web X.0.

1.9 Conclusion and book overview

This chapter has followed the history of the Internet since its ARPANET days to the documentation infrastructure of Web 1.0, participatory platforms of Web 2.0, and the decentralized protocols of Web 3.0 to convergent Web X.0. This trend has some predictable dynamics: every generation is reacting to the previous restrictions and creating new ones; technological facilitating agents are interacting with behavioral changes and economic schemes in fast-feedback cycles; institutional-to-cryptographic-to-many-layered trust structures are developing. The dependence between numerated futures and Web X.0 is now seen: Web 4.0 (intelligent), Web 5.0 (emotional/sensory), and Web 6.0 (autonomous systems) are functional dimensions, the convergence of which forms the next digital epoch, not a series, but parallel developments that define the Web X.0. This evolutionary logic is crucial background information to the in-depth studies that are yet to be documented.

This historical construct is needed since the disruptive technologies that characterize this future are intertwined. They create a convergent stack, with innovations in one layer accelerating potential in another. To understand the consequences of a hyper-connected, AI-driven Web 6.0, one must first comprehend the underlying changes that drive it. Having this evolutionary story as our basis, we shall now proceed to examine each of the critical phases and their main technologies in some detail.

Chapter 2 will continue with an exploration of "The Foundations of Web 3.0: Decentralization, Blockchain, and Smart Contracts," building on what we have seen in this chapter. This chapter will offer the technical and philosophical grounds for understanding the trustless systems that will repatriate power from platforms to people, a significant corrective action against the centralized intelligence that will be the next.

Chapter 3 will feature "Web 4.0: The Intelligent and Automated Web," which discusses the integration of AI and machine learning into the Internet infrastructure. We will examine how AI-driven automation, predictive analytics, and intelligent agents will help build a more effective, yet ethically ambiguous, web, which preconditions a deeper integration of humans and computers.

Chapter 4 "Web 5.0: The Emotional and Human-Centric Internet" focuses on that integration. In this chapter, we are going to explore the boundaries of affective computing, brain–computer interfaces, and empathetic AI, and a future in which the web no longer only reacts to what we command it to do but also to our moods and thought processes.

These threads will be extrapolated into a picture of the "Web 6.0 and Beyond: The Hyper-Connected AI-Driven Future" in Chapter 5. The chapter will reflect on the implications of the full integration of a completely autonomous digital ecosystem of the scale of society, with reference to the place of quantum computing, the autonomous systems of self-improving AI, and the eventual merger of physical and digital reality.

These elements will be discussed in subsequent chapters as the most critical experiential and structural aspects of this future. This new web will involve an immersive interface, as described in Chapter 6, in which the author will investigate the Metaverse, VR, and AR within Future Web Technologies. Chapter 7 will address the most critical problem of Cybersecurity and Privacy in the Next-Generation Web and examine new AI-based attacks on decentralized identity security.

We shall then shift our perspective to assess the overall impact of this technology trend. Chapter 8 will evaluate The Role of Web Technologies in achieving the UN Sustainable Development Goals and provide specific case studies of how blockchain, AI, and immersive technologies can benefit the world. Chapter 9 will steer through the Ethical, Social, and Legal Implications of Future Web Technologies, providing the critical frameworks for governing the robust systems we are creating. Last but not least, Chapter 10 will examine The Future of Work, Business, and Innovation in the Web 6.0 Era, offering strategic advice to help people and organizations survive a world being redefined by autonomous agents, decentralization, and hyper-intelligent networks.

Suggested further readings

- Qiu, R. (2026). *Value Co-Creation in Web 3.0: Blockchain, Metaverse, and Privacy Preservation*. Cham: Springer Nature.
- Sharma., Vandana., Pethuru, R., Balamurugan, B., and Rajesh Kumar, D. (2025). *Metaverse for Sustainable Development: Trends and Applications*. New Jersey: Scrivener Publishing/Wiley.
- Saini., Hemant, K., Rupali, A.M., and Dac-Nhuong, L. (2025). *Next-Generation Data-Driven Business 4.0 Using the Internet of Things, Blockchain, and Interconnected Devices*. Florida: CRC Press.
- Tanwar, S. (2022). *Blockchain Technology: From Theory to Practice*. Singapore: Springer.
- Ma, W., and Ken, H. (2022). *Blockchain and Web3: Building the Cryptocurrency, Privacy, and Security Foundations of the Metaverse*. Hoboken: Wiley.
- Chen, K. (2024). *Web 3.0: The Future of Decentralized Internet. Royal Collins Publishing Company.*

A. Standards organizations and key standards

World Wide Web Consortium (W3C)

Standard	Description	Relevance to chapter
HTML5	HyperText Markup Language version 5	Foundational standard for web content structure, evolved from Web 1.0 to the present
HTTP/2 and HTTP/3	Hypertext Transfer Protocol versions	Core protocols for web communication, enabling faster and more efficient data transfer

(Continues)

(*Continued*)

Standard	Description	Relevance to chapter
URI/URL Standards	Uniform Resource Identifier/Locator	Fundamental standard for web resource identification
Decentralized Identifiers (DIDs)	W3C Recommendation for SSI	Critical for Web 3.0 and Web X.0 identity management
Verifiable Credentials	Standard for cryptographically secure credentials	Enables user-controlled identity verification across platforms

Internet Engineering Task Force (IETF)

Standard	Description	Relevance
TCP/IP Standards (RFC 791, 793)	Core Internet protocols	Foundation of Internet communication across all web generations
TLS 1.3 (RFC 8446)	Transport Layer Security	Critical for secure web communications
WebRTC (RFC 7478)	Web Real-Time Communication	Enables browser-based real-time communication for Web 2.0+

Institute of Electrical and Electronics Engineers (IEEE)

Standard	Description	Relevance
IEEE 802.11 (Wi-Fi Standards)	Wireless networking standards	Enables ubiquitous web access across all generations
IEEE P2418.7	Blockchain Use Cases Standard	Framework for blockchain applications in Web 3.0
IEEE 7000 Series	Ethically Aligned Design Standards	Addresses ethical considerations in autonomous and intelligent systems

ISO/IEC standards

Standard	Description	Relevance
ISO/IEC 27001	Information Security Management	Cybersecurity framework for all web-based systems
ISO/IEC 23000 (MPEG-A)	Multimedia Application Format	Relevant for immersive and rich media applications
ISO/IEC 30141	Internet of Things Reference Architecture	Framework for IoT integration in Web X.0

B. Relevant policies and regulations

European Union

Policy/Regulation	Description	Relevance to chapter
GDPR (General Data Protection Regulation) (2016/679)	Comprehensive data protection and privacy regulation	Directly addresses Web 2.0 data harvesting concerns; informs Web 3.0 SSI principles
Digital Markets Act (DMA) (2022/1925)	Regulation of large online platforms as "gatekeepers"	Addresses Web 2.0 platform concentration; promotes competition and interoperability
Digital Services Act (DSA) (2022/2065)	Framework for online content moderation and platform liability	Regulates Web 2.0 content governance; sets standards for transparency
AI Act (2024/1689)	Risk-based regulation of AI systems	Critical for Web X.0 AI governance; establishes requirements for high-risk AI systems
MiCA (Markets in Crypto-Assets Regulation) (2023/1114)	Comprehensive framework for crypto-assets	Foundational for Web 3.0 and Web X.0 token economies
eIDAS 2.0	Electronic Identification and Trust Services	Establishes framework for digital identity across EU, relevant to SSI and Web 3.0

United States

Policy/Regulation	Description	Relevance
Section 230 (Communications Decency Act)	Platform liability protection for user-generated content	Core legal framework for Web 2.0 platforms; subject to ongoing reform debates
CFTC and SEC Frameworks	Commodity and securities regulation applied to crypto-assets	Fragmented regulatory landscape for Web 3.0 in the US
NIST AI Risk Management Framework	Voluntary framework for AI risk management	Guides responsible AI development for Web X.0
California Consumer Privacy Act (CCPA/CPRA)	State-level data privacy regulation	Influences US privacy standards; addresses Web 2.0 data practices

International and multilateral

Policy/framework	Description	Relevance
OECD AI Principles	International principles for responsible AI	Guides cross-border AI governance for Web X.0
G20 Digital Economy Guidelines	International cooperation on digital issues	Framework for global web governance
UNESCO AI Ethics Recommendation	Global normative framework for AI	Addresses ethical dimensions of intelligent web systems
Financial Action Task Force (FATF) Travel Rule	Anti-money laundering requirements for crypto-assets	Regulates Web 3.0 financial transactions

C. Emerging standards relevant to Web X.0

Standard/initiative	Organization	Relevance
OpenXR	Khronos Group	Cross-platform VR/AR/MR standard for immersive web
glTF (Graphics Language Transmission Format)	Khronos Group	Standard for 3D asset transmission across platforms
InterPlanetary File System (IPFS)	Protocol Labs	Decentralized content-addressed storage for Web 3.0
MetaMask Standards	Ethereum Community	Wallet standards for Web 3.0 interaction
ERC Token Standards (ERC-20, ERC-721, ERC-1155)	Ethereum Improvement Proposals	Token standards for fungible and non-fungible assets
ActivityPub	W3C	Decentralized social networking protocol (used by Mastodon)

References

[1] B. M. Leiner, V. G. Cerf, D. D. Clark, *et al.*, "A brief history of the internet," *ACM SIGCOMM Computer Communication Review*, vol. 39, no. 5, pp. 22–31, 2009.

[2] T. Berners-Lee, R. Cailliau, A. Luotonen, H. F. Nielsen, and A. Secret, "The world-wide web," *Communications of the ACM*, vol. 37, no. 8, pp. 76–82, 1994.

[3] International Telecommunication Union, "Measuring digital development: Facts and figures 2023," International Telecommunication Union, Geneva, Switzerland, 2023.

[4] D. Tapscott and A. Tapscott, *Blockchain Revolution: How the Technology Behind Bitcoin Is Changing Money, Business, and the World*. New York: Penguin, 2016.
[5] PwC, "Global Artificial Intelligence Study: Sizing the prize," PwC, London, UK, 2023.
[6] J. Hendler and A. M. Mulvehill, *Social Machines: The Coming Collision of Artificial Intelligence, Social Networking, and Humanity*. Berkeley, CA: Apress, 2016.
[7] K. Werbach, *The Blockchain and the New Architecture of Trust*. Cambridge, MA:MIT Press, 2018.
[8] A. Narayanan and J. Clark, "Bitcoin's academic pedigree," *Communications of the ACM*, vol. 60, no. 12, pp. 36–45, 2017.
[9] Y. Kaneko, "Comparing electricity consumption per use of blockchain and generative AI," *IEEE Access*, vol. 13, pp. 4567–4580, 2025.
[10] T. Berners-Lee, J. Hendler, and O. Lassila, "The semantic web," *Scientific American*, vol. 284, no. 5, pp. 34–43, 2001.
[11] T. Berners-Lee and M. Fischetti, *Weaving the Web: The Original Design and Ultimate Destiny of the World Wide Web by Its Inventor*. San Francisco, CA: Harper, 1999.
[12] R. Briggs and N. Hollis, "Advertising on the web: Is there response before click-through?," *Journal of Advertising Research*, vol. 37, no. 2, pp. 33–45, 1997.
[13] J. J. Garrett, *Ajax: A new approach to web applications*. San Francisco, CA, USA: Adaptive Path, 2005.
[14] S. Zuboff, *The Age of Surveillance Capitalism: The Fight for a Human Future at the New Frontier of Power*. New York, NY: PublicAffairs, 2019.
[15] K. Vaccaro, C. Sandvig, and K. Karahalios, "'At the end of the day Facebook does what it wants': How users experience contesting algorithmic content moderation," *Proceedings of the ACM on Human-Computer Interaction*, vol. 4, no. CSCW2, pp. 1–22, 2020.
[16] L. Ali, M. Ali, and M. Raghib, "The rise and regulation of digital monopolies: Revisiting competition law in the age of big tech," *SSRN Electronic Journal* 2025. [Online]. Available: https://ssrn.com/abstract=5608130
[17] L. Orešković and I. Bajakić, "Regulating DeFi: Safeguarding market integrity while managing high expectations," *Croatian Yearbook of European Law and Policy*, vol. 20, no. 1, pp. 59–90, 2024.
[18] M. D. Yousuf, "Neutralizing dollar hegemony: A blockchain-based digital bancor with Bitcoin integration," *SSRN Electronic Journal*, 2026. [Online]. Available: https://ssrn.com/abstract=6036014
[19] A. Ghosh, V. Hassija, V. Chamola, and A. El Saddik, "A survey on decentralized metaverse using blockchain and web 3.0 technologies, applications, and more," *IEEE Access*, vol. 12, pp. 146915–146948, 2024.
[20] I. Giannakouros, "Case study in mechanism design: Lido," in *Cryptocurrencies and Tradable Crypto-Tokens: Introduction to the Sector's Economic Design*. Cham: Springer Nature, pp. 249–310, 2025.

[21] J. Gubbi, R. Buyya, S. Marusic, and M. Palaniswami, "Internet of Things (IoT): A vision, architectural elements, and future directions," *Future Generation Computer Systems*, vol. 29, no. 7, pp. 1645–1660, 2013.

[22] E. Morozov, *To Save Everything, Click Here: The Folly of Technological Solutionism*. New York, NY: PublicAffairs, 2013.

[23] J. M. Twenge, "Increases in depression, self-harm, and suicide among U.S. adolescents after 2012 and links to technology use: Possible mechanisms," *Psychiatric Research and Clinical Practice*, vol. 2, no. 1, pp. 19–25, 2020.

[24] B. Christian, *The Alignment Problem: Machine Learning and Human Values*. New York, NY: W. W. Norton, 2020.

[25] D. Patterson, J. Gonzalez, Q. Le, *et al.*, "Carbon emissions and large neural network training," presented at the *2021 ACM/IEEE Int. Conf. Supercomput.*, 2021. [Online]. Available: arXiv:2104.10350

[26] J. Sepúlveda, A. Lemette, and K. Ohler-Martins, "Can crypto be green? Evaluating the environmental and financial impact of the digital assets economy," *Journal of Entrepreneurial Researchers*, vol. 3, no. 1, pp. 55–74, 2025.

[27] CompaniesMarketCap, "Largest companies by market cap," 2024. [Online]. Available: https://companiesmarketcap.com/

[28] W3C, "Decentralized Identifiers (DIDs) v1.0," W3C Recommendation, Jul. 2022. [Online]. Available: https://www.w3.org/TR/did-core/

[29] M. K. Sidhu, A. Tomar, R. Sharma, and N. Batra, "Emerging paradigms and advanced architectures in the blockchain metaverse," in Blockchain Enabled Metaverse for Smart Wireless Sensor Networks . Cham: Springer Nature, pp. 51–80, 2026.

[30] J. Buolamwini and T. Gebru, "Gender shades: Intersectional accuracy disparities in commercial gender classification," *in Proc. 1st Conf. Fairness, Accountability and Transparency*, pp. 77–91, 2018.

[31] European Commission, "Liability rules for artificial intelligence," European Commission, Brussels, Belgium, 2022.

[32] C. Jezerca, "The rise of cryptocurrencies: A tool for money laundering or an EU regulatory failure?," *SSRN Electronic Journal*, 2025. [Online]. Available: https://ssrn.com/abstract=5331403

Chapter 2

The foundations of Web 3.0: decentralization, blockchain, and smart contracts

Kien Nguyen[1,3], *Minh Thuy Le*[2], *Phi Le Nguyen*[2] *and Hiroo Sekiya*[3]

Abstract

In recent years, we have been observing a shift from the platform-based Web 2.0 to the decentralized Web3, marking a significant change in how digital trust is built on the Internet. Power is moved from centralized intermediaries to clear, mathematically proven protocols. This chapter, which lays out the technical basics of the Web 3.0 stack, looks at the combination of Distributed Ledger Technology, cryptographic consensus, and programmable logic. We examine the movement from closed to open, permissionless systems. We also dive into the technical aspects of various consensus models, like Proof of Work (PoW), Proof of Stake (PoS), Practical Byzantine Fault Tolerance (PBFT), and Directed Acyclic Graphs (DAGs). Additionally, the chapter discusses how smart contracts and programmable token standards create new socio-economic models, focusing on decentralized finance, the tokenized creator economy, and identity layers. To provide a thorough and fair analysis, we also look at the major technical and regulatory challenges the ecosystem currently faces. More specifically, we discuss the Scalability Trilemma and issues with international law. By combining up-to-date research with new trends in Zero-Knowledge Proofs and modular structures, this chapter outlines a clear path for understanding the future of the decentralized web.

2.1 Introduction

The digital landscape is undergoing major change. For the last 20 years, the Internet has been shaped by the Web 2.0 model. This model is marked by centralized social

[1]Institute for Advanced Academic Research, Chiba University, Japan
[2]AI Innovation and Societal Impact (AI4LIFE), Hanoi University of Science and Technology, Vietnam
[3]Graduate School of Informatics, Chiba University, Japan

platforms, cloud-based data storage, and a system in which users trade their participation for data. While Web 2.0 connects people worldwide, it has serious weaknesses, including single points of failure, data privacy issues, and monopolistic control over digital identities. In such a context, Web 3.0 has emerged as a direct response to these problems. By using blockchain as a secure way to settle transactions without relying on trust, Web 3.0 enables decentralized applications (DApps) in which users have complete control over their data and digital assets. This transition is important for more than just finance. It significantly affects supply chain transparency, secure voting systems, and how we interact socially online. The purpose of this chapter is to provide a solid technical foundation for the key elements that enable this decentralized future. Specifically, this chapter looks beyond the basic financial uses of cryptocurrencies. It will examine the engineering required to achieve a global, strong consensus and to execute code that is both autonomous and deterministic.

2.1.1 Chapter organization

The rest of this chapter is as follows. Section 2.2 looks at the shift in trust and the social and technical factors driving decentralization. Section 2.3 offers a detailed analysis of the main technical stack. Section 2.4 explores the core structure of blockchain technology and provides a clear overview of Web 3.0 consensus methods. Section 2.5 focuses on how smart contracts work and how they execute deterministically. Section 2.6 moves to the application layer and describes the main components of DApps and token economies. Section 2.7 discusses the social and economic effects of these decentralized models. Section 2.8 addresses technical and regulatory challenges and discusses trade-offs, such as the Scalability Trilemma. Finally, Section 2.9 summarizes the chapter's main points about digital sovereignty and highlights emerging research areas.

2.2 The trust shift: why Web 3.0 requires a new architecture

2.2.1 The central analogy: the shift in trust

We can see the evolution of the web as a gradual shift in power and trust, following participants' and services' demand. At first, Web 1.0 was an open, permissionless environment built on public protocols such as TCP/IP, HTTP, and DNS. In Web 1.0, anyone could publish and participate without any gatekeepers. Moreover, its flexible nature encouraged widespread creativity and innovation with low barriers to entry. However, as the demand for scale of users, services, and monetization grew, Web 2.0 centralized economic and social activity into platform-centric "walled gardens". These platforms focused on engagement and network effects by standardizing interfaces and integrating large data pipelines. They offered important benefits for consumers, global connectivity, and the empowerment of human societies. However, they also developed a new economic model, called surveillance capitalism, based on data extraction and behavioral influence. In this model, users' attention, data, and identity became the basic material for centralized profit [1].

Figure 2.1 visually contrasts the centralized client–server model of Web 2.0 with the distributed architecture of Web 3.0. In the Web 2.0 model, users must send their interactions and data through proprietary databases controlled by a single, centralized organization. In contrast, the Web 3.0 model provides a decentralized, trustless execution environment in which a peer-to-peer network of independent nodes verifies interactions, eliminating the need for a central gatekeeper.

This chapter argues that Web 3.0 is not simply another tech upgrade. It marks a change in how we, as users, understand trust. In Web 2.0, users have no choice but to depend on corporations for a wide range of activities. They include storing, interpreting, and enforcing rules about digital assets, identities, and interactions. In contrast, Web 3.0 shifts trust from corporate intermediaries to transparent protocols, verifiable math such as cryptography, and consensus based on shared incentives. This change lessens the dependence on individual human control. This approach is often referred to as "trustless". This does not mean there is no trust; instead, it changes what and who we trust. Nakamoto's introduction of the first decentralized ledger showed that publicly auditable code is the new standard for verification [2]. Later, Wood's formalization of generalized state transitions highlights the need for distributed economic systems to secure programmable networks rather than rely on proprietary servers and closed governance [3].

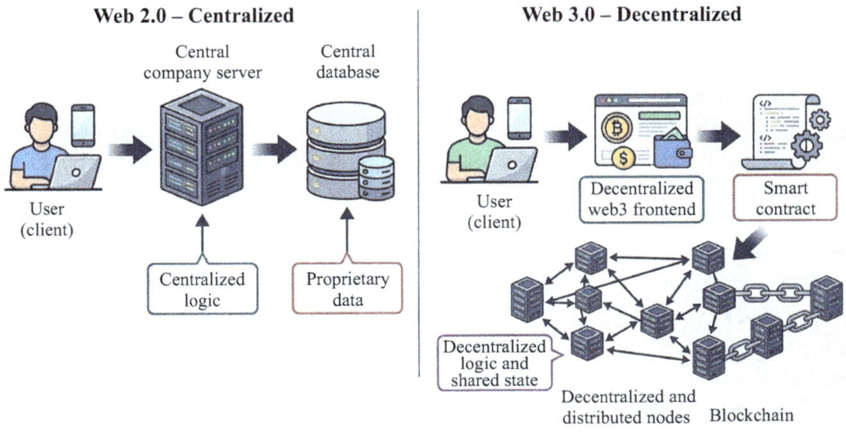

Figure 2.1 A comparison of the centralized client–server model of Web 2.0 and the decentralized, trustless execution environment of Web 3.0

2.2.2 Recapping the "why" and stating the "how"

The "why" of Web 3.0 looks at the problems caused by the dominance of corporate platforms in Web 2.0, including sudden rule changes, unclear moderation, data lock-in, and the risks of having single points of control. Currently, users of Web 2.0 hand over tasks like ownership records, balances, and state transitions to the platforms. As a matter of fact, these platforms have the power to change history, redefine access, and take profits from developers and creators. To address this centralization, Web 3.0 offers a new framework. It uses open protocols to set up property rights and state transitions on public ledgers. In such decentralized systems, consensus rules determine what is valid rather than corporate terms of service. For example, in the Bitcoin system [2], cryptographic keys were adopted to grant users control rather than relying on accounts that can be revoked. Moreover, in Ethereum, deterministic execution defines outcomes by following the principles of generalized transaction ledgers, unlike random policy decisions [3].

This operational shift relies on three key elements: applied cryptography, distributed consensus mechanisms, and smart contracts. The first one is used to verify identities and ensure data integrity via cryptographic hash functions and digital signatures [2]. Meanwhile, the second one allows network participants to reach an agreement on a state without needing a trusted coordinator. The consensus mechanism addresses the structural weaknesses of centralized control pointed out by Buterin [4]. The final element sets and enforces rules automatically, without human discretion, as explained in the Ethereum Yellow Paper [3]. Together, these elements create the strong foundation of Web 3.0. The main goal is to replace platform-based trust with rules that are mathematically guaranteed and continuously verified by a global network of independent participants.

2.2.3 Chapter roadmap: building the Web3 "stack"

To build a clear model of these connected technologies, we create the Web 3.0 stack in four separate layers that logically progress from the underlying motivation to the structural machinery and final results. The foundation starts with the idea of decentralization, which serves as the "why" of the ecosystem. Here, we define decentralization across architectural, political, and logical aspects. We argue that political decentralization is the main goal of Web 3.0 because it prevents any single entity from changing rules, censoring activities, or shutting down the system [4].

The next layer is the ledger layer, which represents the "what" of the stack through blockchain technology. We present blockchains as append-only, replicated state machines, with a history agreed upon by many independent actors through distributed consensus. Within this framework, we will clearly distinguish the underlying data model from the consensus layer that determines finality [2] and the execution layer that computes state transitions [3].

The third layer focuses on the system's logic, detailing the "how" through the use of smart contracts. This chapter will describe how foundational blockchains changed from specialized ledgers made for peer-to-peer cash transfers into general-purpose, deterministic execution environments. These networks can now set rules, property rights, and complex market logic as independent programs that run smoothly under public agreement.

Finally, the top layer represents the economy and the ultimate "result" of the stack, which appears as DApps and digital-native tokens. We will show how programmable ledgers enable these components, which together create fully user-owned networks, encourage open innovation, and design new mechanisms for global coordination. The rest of the chapter will follow this progression, starting with the philosophical core and then developing the technical backbone, the execution model, and the emerging application layer.

2.3 The philosophical core: decentralization

2.3.1 What is decentralization? (and what it is not)

Decentralization is not a simple yes-or-no answer; instead, it lies on a wide spectrum. Figure 2.2, which compares centralized, decentralized, and distributed network types, illustrates the concept.

To explore this spectrum, Buterin's framework identifies three distinct dimensions that are often get mixed up in public discussions [4]. The first dimension is architectural decentralization. This refers to how the system's infrastructure is distributed across multiple physical machines and locations. Architecturally decentralized systems avoid single points of failure. They can handle node or network outages without stopping the whole service. The second dimension is political decentralization. This relates to who has the ultimate control to change rules, censor users, or shut down the system. A system is politically decentralized when no single party, such as a company or government, can impose decisions without the agreement of other participants. The third dimension is logical decentralization, which looks at whether the system acts as a single cohesive unit or as multiple

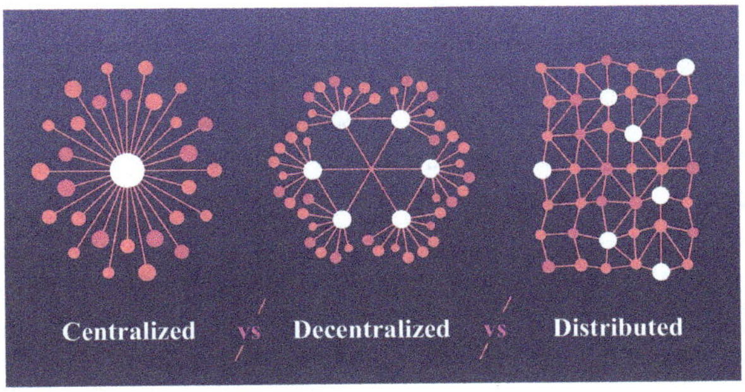

Figure 2.2 Comparison of centralized, decentralized, and distributed (figure generated by Copilot)

parts. For instance, a globally replicated service may appear to be one endpoint, but it is actually distributed internally. In contrast, Wood's generalized architecture allows a system to show multiple logical partitions with coordinated but independent states [3]. However, Buterin points out that public blockchains usually function as a single logical entity [4].

Understanding these distinctions helps clear up common misconceptions about network types. For example, a large corporate cloud, like a global search service, is very architecturally decentralized because it uses thousands of machines in data centers around the world. Yet, it remains politically centralized since one company holds the power to change the rules, deny access, or remove users as it pleases. This vulnerability has been strongly criticized by Zittrain [5] and reflects the surveillance models described by Zuboff [1].

On the other hand, public blockchains like Bitcoin and Ethereum aim for maximum political decentralization. The blokchain networks ensure that no single entity can dictate the official state or shut down the whole network. To classify these types throughout this chapter, we define centralized systems as those with a single governing body and database, making them efficient but open to misuse. Distributed systems have structures that improve availability while remaining under unified control, such as that of a corporation. Finally, we define decentralized systems, common in Web 3.0, as public ledgers managed by independent network nodes. In these systems, actions are deterministic, as defined by Wood [3], and the state is confirmed through protocol consensus, as introduced by Buterin [4], not by corporate dictates. Therefore, we will focus primarily on political decentralization, as it supports reliable property rights and allows for open participation.

2.3.2 The three pillars of Web3 decentralization

The appeal of decentralization rests on three important pillars that come from protocol-based governance rather than platform-based control.

The first pillar is censorship resistance. On centralized platforms, it is easy to remove content or transactions involving content by putting pressure on administrators or companies. Public blockchains solve those problems. That is because the network spreads data and validation across many independent nodes. This means there is no single point of failure. Instead of relying on arbitrary corporate rules, transaction approval is based solely on algorithmic agreement and economic incentives. This creates "credible neutrality"—a concept pioneered by Nakamoto [2] and later codified by Buterin [6]—ensuring the system applies rules blindly to prevent favoritism. Naturally, authorities can still censor application-layer front-ends or Application Programming Interfaces (APIs). However, the base-layer ledger remains immune to unilateral rollbacks [6].

The second pillar is user sovereignty and ownership. In Web 2.0, platform accounts provide permissions but not actual ownership. Balances, identities, and audiences are just entries in corporate databases that can change based on policies.

In Web 3.0, control comes from cryptographic keys that allow users to make changes directly on a public ledger. We can also verify ownership of digital assets on-chain, managed by consensus rules and enforced by the entire network, rather than by corporate terms. This change establishes a "rule of code" where property rights can be enforced mathematically, as De Filippi and Wright mentioned in [7]. The digital assets can be moved across compatible applications. In addition, revoking access requires agreement at the protocol level, not just an action taken by the platform. This combines Nakamoto's cryptographic models [2] with Wood's state transitions [3]. Users can move, trade, or use assets as collateral without needing permission from a platform gatekeeper [3].

The third pillar is permissionless innovation. The early Internet thrived on open protocols as mentioned above. Anyone could create a website or service on a neutral base [5], which is also the original design of the Internet. After missing in Web 2.0, Web 3.0 brings this back by providing publicly executed environments. Developers can deploy smart contracts without needing approvals, paying gatekeeper fees, etc. Ethereum's general-purpose execution model illustrates this concept [3]. As long as the code meets the validity standards and pays for the resource costs (i.e., called gas in Ethereum), anyone can deploy and interact with it. This encourages users to experiment on the blockchain platform.

2.3.3 Trade-offs and challenges

Despite its significant benefits, decentralization comes with trade-offs that challenge system design and affect real-world outcomes. The main technical barrier is the conflict between scalability and latency. Global replication and consensus require each node to process every transaction, which limits throughput. Networks must navigate the scalability trilemma by implementing complex solutions like layer-2 rollups or sharding, as originally envisioned by Wood [3]. These solutions introduce new security assumptions related to data availability and fraud proofs [4].

Additionally, public networks face severe security and economic risks. While mechanisms like mining rewards and staking yields aim to encourage honest behavior, they can unintentionally lead to power concentration. This, in turn, introduces systemic risks, including the mining cartels mentioned by Nakamoto [2], vulnerabilities related to selfish mining, and majority coordination attacks identified by Eyal and Sirer [8]. There is also the issue of extracting maximal extractable value (MEV) on smart contract platforms [3]. In addition to these technical problems, there are serious operational and user experience challenges. Self-custodial key management, the irreversible nature of transactions, and the default public data setup create significant usability barriers and privacy concerns for the average user. Understanding these trade-offs is crucial for avoiding mistakes in system design. It also motivates the careful distinction between consensus and execution, which will be detailed in the following technical sections.

2.4 The architectural backbone: blockchain technology

2.4.1 The consensus problem

Decentralization offers an appealing framework, but it also brings a significant technical challenge, namely the consensus problem. When a network has thousands of anonymous and untrusted participants, a strong mechanism is needed to ensure they agree on a single set of facts (i.e., getting consensus). This mechanism should help maintain a shared record of state changes without relying on a central bookkeeper. This challenge reflects the open-architecture ideals discussed in [5], contrasting sharply with the centralized data monopolies described in [1]. In distributed systems literature, this need for agreement among independent participants is framed as a Byzantine Fault Tolerance (BFT) problem. It models a situation in which some actors may behave randomly or maliciously, while the honest majority seeks to reach a consistent state as described by Lamport *et al.* [9].

Traditional solutions to this problem often relied on known memberships and strict assumptions about timing or institutional trust. These made them unsuitable for open, permissionless networks. This technical deadlock resisted practical solutions for years until Nakamoto's white paper in 2008. Nakamoto's consensus changed the BFT problem by mixing applied cryptography, peer-to-peer networking, and economic incentives to make honest behavior rewarding [2]. By using a public fork choice rule to establish a main chain, this design created the first widely used blockchain (i.e., Bitcoin). It showed that distributed nodes could agree without a trusted coordinator. This bridged the theoretical ideas of BFT [9] with Bitcoin's practical applied cryptography [2].

2.4.2 The core analogy: a global, public, immutable ledger

At its heart, a blockchain is a new type of database, best described as a global, public, and unchangeable notebook. In this setup, the ledger is immediately copied and continuously shared with all participants, known as nodes, who run the network software. Because this system is globally distributed, everyone can check the notebook's contents at any moment. This guarantees complete transparency, a basic principle set by Nakamoto [2] and later developed into generalized state machines by Wood [3].

The key feature of the ledger is its immutability. Once a page of entries is written and finalized, it remains sealed forever. If any participant tries to change even a tiny part of a historical entry, the change is promptly spotted. That is because the modified copy will no longer match the cryptographic commitments that link the pages together. As a result, the honest network automatically discards the tampered version and continues using the unaltered history. The original Bitcoin ledger is designed to track only currency transfers. However, the modern programmable ledger systems now use this unchangeable structure to record other verifiable states. This includes asset registries, voting records, and verified digital credentials [3].

2.4.3 Deconstructing the blockchain: the block and the chain

The structural integrity of this distributed ledger depends on precise cryptographic architecture. This is visually explained in Figure 2.3, which shows how individual blocks are formed and linked together.

A block is a standardized batch of new transactions and metadata collected from the network's memory pool (i.e., the mempool). When a user sends a transaction, it does not settle on the ledger right away. Instead, it broadcasts the transaction throughout the peer-to-peer network, which is also called the overlay network, to the mempools of all participating nodes. During block construction, the data is split into two main parts: the header and the body. The header contains important metadata, such as the timestamp, the difficulty target, and the cryptographic hash of the previous block. The body contains the actual list of pending transactions. These are not just added in order; they are mathematically compressed into a binary tree structure called a Merkle Tree. The root hash of this tree is embedded in the block header, allowing lightweight clients to verify data integrity without needing to download the entire transaction history [3].

After construction, these individual blocks are cryptographically linked to form a continuous chain. Each new block includes a deterministic hash pointer computed over the exact contents of its predecessor. Each block relies on its entire history. A cryptographic hash creates a fixed-length output, so even a minor change leads to a completely different result. Any effort to alter a past transaction disrupts the chain of hashes and is quickly rejected by verifying nodes [2]. This dependency makes altering history nearly impossible. A malicious actor would need to rebuild all subsequent blocks faster than the honest majority can add to the main chain.

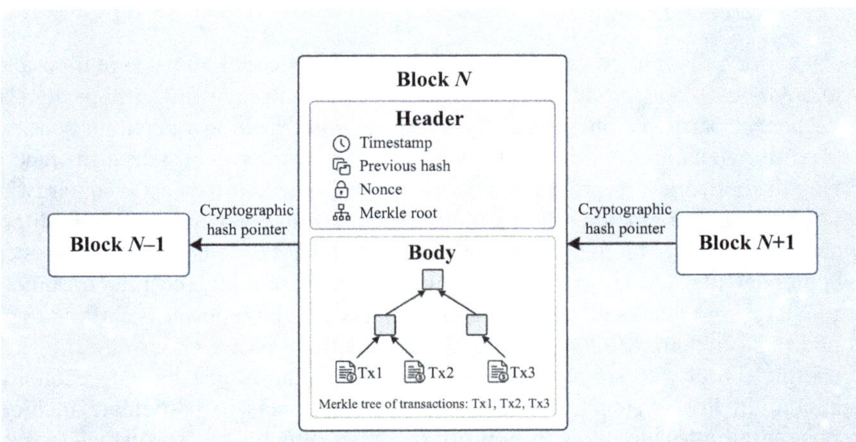

Figure 2.3 The internal structure of a blockchain shows how each block relies on the ones before it and the Merkle tree for batching transactions

This high cost and effort for coordination strongly favor the honest network and support the neutral infrastructure ideals of the early Internet.

2.4.4 The network: who holds the notebook?

The enforcement of these cryptographic rules relies entirely on the distributed network structure, which includes different participant roles. Full nodes that provide the essential layer of security as strict archive entities of the system download, store, and independently verify the complete history of the chain from the first block to the current state. These nodes enforce all protocol rules. Moreover, they automatically reject any proposed block that does not meet the validity conditions, hence becoming vital for the system's decentralization, which eliminates the need to trust third-party entities. This principle is fundamental in Nakamoto's original design [2] and is important for resilience in distributed networks, as Gencer *et al.* noted [10].

Alongside these archivists are the block producers (i.e., miners (in Proof of Work (PoW) System) or validators (in Proof of Stake (PoS)), who perform the specialized tasks needed to extend the chain. In PoW systems, miners use dedicated hardware to solve complicated cryptographic puzzles. In PoS systems, validators lock native assets as collateral to propose blocks and attest to them. Regardless of the consensus mechanism used, the global spread of these independent actors gives the network a remarkable architectural resilience. Shutting down or taking over the network would require a coordinated, simultaneous attack on thousands of physically spread-out machines in different legal authorities. This is still not practical in terms of costs and logistics for any single state or corporate opponent.

2.4.5 The consensus problem: how do we agree on what to write?

The network's distributed structure demands a solid rulebook to manage thousands of anonymous block producers (i.e., the consensus mechanism), which aims to make honest participation financially sensible while making malicious behavior very costly. Nakamoto's original PoW forces miners into a constant arms race in solving the network's cryptographic puzzles with the need for specialized hardware that burns massive amounts of electricity. This resource expenditure is the literal "work" that defends the ledger, making network takeovers financially ruinous for any potential attacker. However, this security method has a high cost: it consumes a lot of energy and results in slower transaction speeds. The industry is shifting to get around this problem. Modern public blockchains now mostly choose PoS. Instead of using electricity to show their commitment, validators just lock up economic collateral. In PoS systems, validators lock native assets to participate in block proposals and attestations, with security enforced through severe financial penalties, known as slashing, for dishonest actions.

Building on this economic basis, Delegated Proof of Stake (DPoS) adds a representative democratic aspect to achieve much higher transaction throughput. In

DPoS systems, the so-called token holders vote for a fixed, limited number of delegates who serve as the block producers (i.e., validators). This concentration of active validators significantly reduces network delay and improves performance. However, it has to sacrifice political decentralization. In enterprise consortia, consensus models should be designed for permissioned environments, where network participants are known but do not fully trust one another. Practical Byzantine Fault Tolerance (PBFT) is often used in these situations. PBFT uses a clear, multiphase voting process that guarantees finality without needing resource-heavy mining or native cryptocurrencies. However, PBFT requires high communication, limiting scalability to a small number of nodes. Similarly, Proof of Authority (PoA) relies on identity and reputation instead of capital. In PoA networks, validators are pre-approved, legally identifiable entities. That makes this mechanism very efficient for private supply chain tracking or internal ledgers, where legal recourse is a strong deterrent against bad behavior.

Further expanding the range of consensus types, alternative approaches aim to completely bypass traditional economic constraints through hardware and topological innovations. Take Proof of Elapsed Time (PoET), for instance. Rather than burning electricity, PoET leverages specialized trusted execution environments to run a verifiable, random lottery. The network achieves the competitive fairness of PoW without the devastating energy waste. Directed Acyclic Graphs (DAGs) take a different approach by abandoning the traditional blockchain structure entirely. Instead of packing data into slow, sequential blocks, a DAG processes transactions asynchronously. If a user wants to submit a new transaction, they must computationally validate previous ones. The result is a highly scalable, feeless web of attestations that works perfectly for Internet of Things (IoT) environments and micro-transactions. Finally, we are observing a rise in hybrid models. They often use a limited set of block producers for fast chain generation. Moreover, they depend on a larger, decentralized PoS validator committee to finalize blocks and stop long-range attacks.

Table 2.1 outlines the specific trade-offs, comparing the main security methods, finality types, target environments, and ideal use cases for each model.

Table 2.1 Comparative analysis of Web 3.0 consensus mechanisms

Consensus mechanism	**Primary Sybil resistance**	**Finality type**	**Key advantage**	**Primary limitation**	**Target architecture**
Proof of Work (PoW)	Computational hardware	Probabilistic	Maximum decentralized security	Extreme energy consumption; low TPS	Public/ permissionless
Proof of Stake (PoS)	Locked capital (tokens)	Deterministic	Energy efficient; economic penalties (slashing)	Risk of capital centralization	Public/ permissionless

(Continues)

Table 2.1 (*Continued*)

Consensus mechanism	Primary Sybil resistance	Finality type	Key advantage	Primary limitation	Target architecture
Delegated PoS (DPoS)	Delegated voting	Deterministic	High transaction throughput	Political centralization among delegates	Public/ high-frequency
PBFT	Known Identity	Absolute	Immediate settlement; zero energy waste	High communication overhead limits node count	Enterprise/ permissioned
Proof of Authority (PoA)	Reputation/ legal identity	Absolute	Highly efficient and legally compliant	Requires absolute trust in authority nodes	Consortium/ private
Proof of Elapsed Time (PoET)	Trusted hardware (enclaves)	Probabilistic	Fair lottery system without energy waste	Relies on centralized hardware manufacturers	Enterprise/ consortium
Directed Acyclic Graph (DAG)	Asynchronous attestation	Probabilistic	Feeless micro-transactions; highly scalable	Complex transaction ordering and security assumptions	IoT/ micro-payments

2.4.6 Fork choice and finality

Temporary forks are inevitable in decentralized ledgers. When network latency causes two different blocks to refer to the same parent simultaneously, the chain splits. Each node must independently follow a set process to choose a main chain to resolve these competing branches and maintain a consistent history. In foundational networks that use Proof of Work, like Nakamoto Consensus, this is determined by the Longest Chain Rule, which favors the chain with the most accumulated computational work.

One important result of this design is that finality is only probabilistic. If a merchant accepts a transaction after only one block confirmation, there is a chance that a competing chain could form and overwrite that transaction, which could allow for a double-spend attack. Note that a block becomes safer when it is further down the chain. Therefore, applications, especially financial ones, usually require multiple confirmations to ensure safety. This requirement can lead to long settlement times.

To reduce this waiting time, modern Proof of Stake systems use different, message-driven rules for choosing forks, like LMD-GHOST (Latest Message Driven Greediest Heaviest Observed Subtree). LMD-GHOST quickly identifies the heaviest chain by gathering validator votes. Additionally, modern blockchains, including Ethereum, implement an explicit "finality gadget" (i.e., the Casper Friendly Finality Gadget) to ensure finality. In this setup, once a majority of validators vote to finalize a checkpoint [27], that particular state in history cannot be changed without causing a hard fork. Different clients and applications then choose confirmation policies that reflect their architectural differences.

2.4.7 Limitations and trade-offs

Even with the strong security features provided by deterministic consensus methods, public blockchains face limitations, namely the Scalability Trilemma theorem. This theorem states that a decentralized network can focus on only two of these three features: decentralization, security, and scalability [11,12]. Historically, base-layer networks have emphasized strong security and decentralization. As mentioned in the previous section, in this approach, participating nodes need to download, verify, and store every transaction. As a result, it causes bottlenecks in transaction throughput and raises user fees during busy times. To maintain decentralization while meeting global consumer demand, one approach is to shift consensus toward modularity, especially with Layer-2 Rollups [13]. By moving computation off-chain, rollups can manage much higher throughput (e.g., thousands of transactions per second). They combine these transactions into a single proof that is later submitted to the main chain for settlement. The rollup-based methods depend on fraud proofs and time delays to ensure fairness. Additionally, Zero-Knowledge Rollups (ZK-Rollups) use cryptography to ensure execution accuracy without showing the underlying data. However, moving to Layer-2 networks creates its own challenges, especially concerning fragmented liquidity across different rollups and the need for centralized nodes to order off-chain transactions.

Beyond technical limits on throughput, the growth of the Web 3.0 ecosystem has revealed economic vulnerabilities that could undermine decentralization. A key issue is MEV, which comes from the transparent nature of the blockchain's pending transaction queue, or the mempool. Since block proposers control the order of transactions in the blocks they create, sophisticated users often employ automated bots to watch the mempool and take profits through arbitrage. This can hurt regular users through tactics such as front-running and sandwich attacks. The presence of MEV puts pressure on the network, as validators with specialized tools to extract MEV consistently perform better than those without. This leads to a concentration of capital. To tackle this threat to network fairness, researchers are looking at measures such as Proposer–Builder Separation (PBS), which separates the roles of block construction and proposal. Addressing these economic challenges is just as important as solving technical scalability issues. Ignoring them could result in decentralized ledgers recreating the monopolistic power structures of the Web 2.0 platforms they aim to replace.

2.5 The operational engine: smart contracts

Bitcoin fundamentally changed the secure recording of digital value, but it was always designed to act as a passive ledger. It functions as a distributed calculator that tracks unspent transaction outputs (UTXOs) [5]. Although this design ensures valid currency transactions, it lacks the flexibility needed to handle complex conditions. The shift from Web 2.0 to Web 3.0 prompted a rethink of blockchain technology. It transformed from a simple decentralized database into a global, decentralized computer. This new idea, known as the Smart Contract, was first introduced by cryptographer Nick Szabo in 1994 [1]. Szabo envisoned protocols that could function and enforce contract negotiations without the need for trusted third parties. Years later, the Ethereum Whitepaper turned this theoretical idea into reality by embedding a Turing-complete execution environment directly into the blockchain consensus layer [2]. The embedment allowed any program logic to benefit from the strong security of the underlying ledger. Figure 2.4 presents a summary of how cryptographically signed inputs and external Oracle data feeds trigger predictable state transitions.

2.5.1 Defining the smart contract: deterministic state machines

A smart contract is formally defined as a set of executable code and persistent state, that is deployed at a specific cryptographic address. Rather than running on a standard centralized server, smart contracts operate on the Ethereum Virtual Machine (EVM), an environment faithfully replicated by every network node. This environment is closely replicated across all nodes in the network [3]. To clarify how this works, think of it like an autonomous vending machine. The machine has a predictable logic because it holds digital assets and enforces strict rules, such as

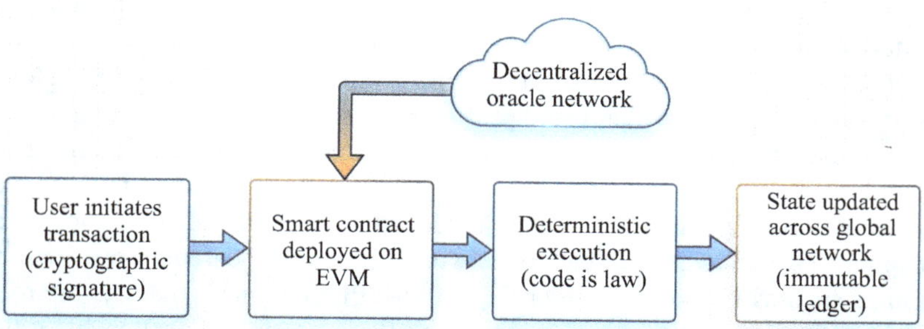

Figure 2.4 The operation of a smart contract, showing how cryptographically signed inputs and Oracle data feeds trigger predictable state transitions

dispensing an item only if the inserted amount is greater than the required price. More importantly, this setup requires no intermediary; users hence engage directly with the machine. It also ensures automatic enforcement, in which the transaction can either happen simultaneously or not. However, allowing any kind of code on a public network can lead to significant risks, such as infinite loops due to the Halting Problem. To reduce this risk, execution is strictly limited by gas. Gas (or Ethereum network fee) acts as a unit of computational effort that must be bought with the network's native token. If computation exceeds the gas limit, the EVM stops execution and reverts changes, preventing the network from being harmed by faulty or malicious code [3].

2.5.2 The "Code is Law" principle

The clear execution of smart contracts leads us to the well-known and often-debated principle of this decentralized system, commonly known as "Code is Law". Legal scholar Lawrence Lessig famously discussed this concept, stating that in cyberspace, the underlying software acts as a stronger regulator of human behavior than traditional government laws [14]. In the context of Web 3.0, this principle means that the terms of an agreement, clearly written in the smart contract, will serve as the final decision-maker for the transaction. Since the contract executes exactly as stated every time, it cannot be tainted by human biases, political pressure, or subjective judgments. As a result, this system eliminates the need for a slow, costly legal framework to interpret and enforce the contract. The execution of the code itself acts as the enforcement.

However, this rigid approach can be risky and is the source of significant operational challenges in Web 3.0. If the encoded "law" has a logical error or unexpected loophole, the results can be severe. Once deployed, smart contracts become part of the unchangeable blockchain, making any programming mistake a permanent flaw. The dangers were highlighted by The DAO incident in 2016, involving a decentralized venture fund governed entirely by smart contracts. Attackers took advantage of a reentrancy bug, in which a malicious contract repeatedly requested withdrawals before the DAO's smart contract could update its balance [15]. The strict execution of the code allowed this behavior, enabling the attacker to drain funds as dictated by the protocol rules. This crisis led to a contentious hard fork of the Ethereum network, underlining the tension between the blockchain's unchangeable nature and the fallibility of software developers.

2.5.3 The "trustless" revolution: how smart contracts remove intermediaries

By using the predictable nature of smart contracts, these contracts create a "trustless" environment by replacing intermediaries with verifiable protocol logic. Let us look at the traditional process of transferring property to see the difference. Buying a house requires trusting multiple parties, including a bank to verify and hold funds, a land title office for ownership records, etc. This traditional process is slow, costly, and fragmented. In contrast, the smart contract running on blockchain can combine these roles into an automated transaction. A buyer deposits digital funds into a publicly verifiable contract, and a seller adds a unique tokenized deed (e.g., Non-Fungible Token (NFT)). The smart contract then executes a swap, ensuring that the funds and the deed transfer simultaneously or not at all. This efficient method eliminates the need for banks, legal enforcement, etc. Participants in the entire process only need to trust the underlying cryptographic protocol rather than each other, as the contract is publicly accessible, open-source, and enforced through global network consensus, which is key to trustless digital interaction.

2.5.4 The Oracle problem and connectivity

For all their power, smart contracts suffer from a fatal flaw: they are entirely blind to the outside world. A blockchain is a tightly sealed environment. It has no native way to check off-chain reality, whether that means pulling live financial tickers or verifying supply chain delays. To bridge this gap, networks rely on Oracles. As Adler *et al.* [16] outline, an Oracle is simply an external service that fetches real-world data and feeds it on-chain. But this introduces a massive vulnerability. If a smart contract holding millions of dollars depends on a single Oracle, that data feed becomes a highly lucrative target. Should a bad actor compromise that feed and inject a lie, the immutable code will blindly execute the transaction anyway. To reduce this risk, the research community is rapidly shifting toward Decentralized Oracle Networks, which require multiple independent nodes to reach consensus on external facts before they ever touch the ledger.

2.6 The application layer: DApps and token economies

After establishing the key layers of decentralization, blockchain, and smart contracts in the previous sections, this section realizes the broader vision of Web 3.0. The application layer is where user sovereignty, censorship resistance, and permissionless innovation become real through DApps and token economies. These elements represent Web 3.0's promise to swap centralized, platform-based trust for mathematically verifiable, protocol-based guarantees.

2.6.1 DApps

A DApp is more than just a new technical idea. It reflects the main principles of Web 3.0. Instead of depending on the corporate-controlled servers of Web 2.0, DApps operate their backend logic directly on-chain via smart contracts. This setup ensures complete transparency. Application rules are not set by random corporate policy, but are enforced by decentralized consensus. For example, in a typical client–server model, user actions get processed by proprietary backend code and saved in private databases. This gives the platform operator the power of a "superuser", allowing them to change data, censor content, or revoke access at will.

The Web 3.0 client-chain model completely upends this. User actions act as cryptographically signed transactions sent directly to smart contracts. Because this logic is immutable, no single entity can alter the historical record or lock out users who follow the protocol rules.

However, purely on-chain applications are still quite rare due to the high costs of computation and storage on base-layer blockchains like Ethereum. As a result, modern DApps often use a hybrid setup to balance security and efficiency. In this model, critical state information—such as financial balances, ownership records, and voting rights—stays securely on the blockchain. At the same time, large static assets, such as images and front-end code, are stored on decentralized networks, such as the InterPlanetary File System (IPFS) or Arweave. This infrastructure effectively protects the front end from centralized censorship [17]. DApps bring back the open, permissionless nature of the early Internet. Developers can deploy verifiable code without needing approval from a gatekeeper. As a result, the application layer returns to its original fairness and composability.

2.6.2 Token economies: standardized state objects

DApps need an economic layer to coordinate behavior and motivate users. While the platform operator in Web 2.0 mainly extracts value from user data, the Web 3.0 model contains this value directly in cryptographic tokens. A token is not just digital money but a highly programmable state object managed by a smart contract. Cross-application interoperability requires strict technical standards, which are usually achieved through Ethereum Improvement Proposals (EIPs). The widely used ERC-20 standard defines the interface for these fungible assets [18]. By mathematically enforcing both interchangeability and divisibility, this framework guarantees that a token generated by one protocol remains functionally identical to another across the entire ecosystem.

In contrast to fungible assets, the ERC-721 standard was created to support non-fungibility, meaning absolute uniqueness [19]. This standard establishes a clear cryptographic method for tracking different assets. It assigns each token a unique identifier that permanently sets it apart from all others in the same contract. It enables blockchain to serve as a global registry for unique, non-interchangeable items, such as digital art, decentralized domain names, or tokenized titles for real-world assets.

2.6.3 Incentive alignment and composability

The integration of DApps and programmable tokens produces two key features that define the Web 3.0 economy. The first is crypto-economic incentive alignment that effectively addresses the traditional network bootstrap issue. By giving ownership tokens to early users, protocol developers, and network validators, decentralized systems get to align everyone's financial interests with the network's long-term success. This way, users move beyond being passive consumers to become active stakeholders in the protocol's growth [20]. The second vital feature is permissionless composability. Operating on a universally shared state machine lets different applications connect directly. This completely removes the need for proprietary APIs or slow corporate partnerships. For example, a lending protocol can seamlessly collateralize an ERC-20 asset generated by an entirely distinct development group. This native interoperability—frequently likened to snapping together digital building blocks—accelerates technical innovation far beyond the restrictive capabilities of traditional Web 2.0 silos.

2.7 The "so what?": socio-economic implications

Web 3.0 clearly brings a fundamental change in digital trust with the stack, including blockchains, smart contracts, and tokens. It eliminates the need for centralized corporate platforms by embedding trust directly into cryptographic protocols. Moving forward, we will explore exactly how this architecture creates genuinely user-owned applications and aligns economic incentives across transparent markets.

2.7.1 Financial inclusion and decentralized finance

The most developed Web 3.0 application is decentralized finance (DeFi), which creates a parallel financial system based entirely on public blockchains. DeFi reshapes traditional financial services (e.g., credit and asset exchanges) without the need for a centralized bank. By removing these barriers, it tackles the major financial exclusion present in older systems. Getting rid of these gated intermediaries directly fights the serious financial exclusion that affects older legacy systems. As a result, around 1.4 billion adults worldwide are "unbanked" and lack access to basic financial services due to geographic barriers or a lack of formal documentation [20]. To address this issue, DeFi protocols introduce "trustless interaction" through permissionless access. For example, a user in a developing economy can easily connect to a global liquidity pool using an Internet-enabled smartphone and a cryptographic wallet address. In this setup, smart contracts manage solvency by requiring borrowers to put up more collateral than their loans in digital assets. If the value of the collateral falls below a certain limit, automated liquidation systems sell the assets to protect the protocol. This process eliminates the need for subjective credit checks or human approvals, making access to global capital markets more democratic [21].

However, this fast-growing ecosystem carries significant risks. The open nature of DeFi protocols creates new systemic dangers. Studies of crypto-crime show that major financial losses in the DeFi space often come from complex protocol-layer attacks, such as Oracle manipulation and leveraged flash loan attacks [22]. The industry is also going through a tough regulatory phase to tackle these risks. International groups such as the Financial Action Task Force (FATF) are pushing Virtual Asset Service Providers (VASPs) to follow Anti-Money Laundering (AML) standards and global reporting rules [23]. The ongoing tension between open-source code and strict regulatory rules is a major concern in this field's development.

2.7.2 The tokenized creator economy

Web 3.0 also brings new business models for managing intellectual property through NFTs. This process is often seen as a major removal of intermediaries in the digital content supply chain. In the Web 2.0 model, platform monopolies gather user attention and content, capturing most of the revenue generated and giving creators only a small fraction. Web 3.0 flips this dynamic by letting creators tokenize their work—whether that is an album, a piece of digital art, or a research paper. These unique digital assets can be sold directly to a global market without a corporate middleman taking a cut. More importantly, smart contracts hardcode the royalty structure. For example, if an artist programs a 10% royalty into a token, the protocol automatically forwards that exact cut to their wallet during any secondary-market resale. This procedure converts a one-time transaction into a steady income stream, ensuring the creator receives payment as the asset's value increases over time.

2.7.3 Decentralized autonomous organizations

One of the most ambitious impacts of this technology is the rethinking of corporate governance through Decentralized Autonomous Organizations (DAOs). A DAO is defined as an organization where rules, treasury management, and decision-making are encoded in smart contracts instead of traditional corporate bylaws. DAOs function through transparent, on-chain governance that is different from old corporate hierarchies controlled by a board of executives. In this model, community funds are held in a smart contract treasury that no individual can control. When a strategic decision is needed, any member can propose it to the network. After that, members vote on the proposal using defined governance tokens. When getting the consensus, the protocol carries out the decision on its own. This setup links management to direct ownership, effectively removing the typical principal-agent issue. It represents a major change from traditional management to automated coordination.

2.8 The reality check: technical and regulatory constraints

Any realistic look at Web 3.0 has to acknowledge that it is not a cure-all. The technology is still largely experimental, facing severe challenges across computer science, economics, and law. We are going to discuss them in this section.

2.8.1 The scalability trilemma

The main technical challenge for public blockchains is known as the Scalability Trilemma theorem. The theorem suggests that a monolithic blockchain can optimize for only two of three essential properties: decentralization, security, and scalability. The foundational blokchain like Bitcoin and Ethereum focus on strong decentralization and high security, which means they sacrifice transaction speed. For instance, Ethereum's base layer processes about 15–30 transactions per second.

This is a significant difference compared to traditional payment systems like Visa, which can handle over 24,000 transactions per second. During times of high network demand, users end up in competitive bidding wars, leading to transaction fees that become too expensive for average retail participants. To fix this, developers are abandoning monolithic structures in favor of modular architectures. This approach involves carrying out transactions off-chain using Layer-2 Rollups. These Rollups group thousands of transactions into one cryptographic proof. The main Ethereum chain is used only for final settlement and basic security.

2.8.2 Regulatory ambiguity and legal friction

Technical limits aside, the rapid growth of decentralized protocols has greatly exceeded the progress of international laws. This has led to a large area of regulatory uncertainty. In the United States, a key point of legal dispute involves classifying digital assets under the Howey Test. This test determines whether a token is considered a regulated investment contract [24]. Many utility tokens have characteristics of investment contracts when they are first issued. Moreover, DAOs face a serious challenge with legal recognition. In areas where a DAO lacks formal legal structure, it may be treated as a general partnership. This unclear legal status means individual token holders could be personally liable for the organization's actions. This creates significant risks that can discourage mainstream institutional adoption.

Public blockchains also face a crucial privacy-transparency dilemma. The extreme transparency needed for global consensus clashes with modern data privacy rights, like those established by the General Data Protection Regulation. While protocol developers use advanced cryptographic methods such as Zero-Knowledge Proofs (ZKPs) to enable secure, private transactions, regulatory agencies often view total on-chain privacy as a potential means to facilitate money laundering and illegal financing [25]. This ongoing struggle between a user's right to privacy and the government's need for financial oversight remains an unresolved point of geopolitical tension.

2.9 Conclusion: the assembled stack and the path forward

2.9.1 Synthesis: the architecture of digital sovereignty

In this chapter, we investigated Web 3.0 by breaking it down from a theoretical idea into a clear, multi-layered architectural stack. We started by identifying the structural centralization of the current web and the urgent need for a system that values decentralization and resistance to censorship over efficiency in central operations. To make this philosophy a reality, we looked at the foundational ledger layer. We defined the blockchain not just as a distributed database, but as a Byzantine Fault-Tolerant state machine that can achieve a single source of truth without a trusted coordinator. Next, we examined the logic layer to show how smart contracts turn this basic infrastructure into a global computer that follows the strict principle of code as law. Finally, we analyzed the application layer to illustrate how DApps and token standards incorporate economic incentives directly into the code. This built-in economic structure is what makes new models like DeFi and the tokenized creator economy possible.

2.9.2 Future directions: from speculation to utility

To wrap up the analysis, we need to look ahead and recognize that the current Web 3.0 stack is just the basic infrastructure of a quickly developing technological landscape. The shift from reliance on institutions to trust in cryptography has historically involved financial speculation, but now the focus in academia and industry has shifted to solving complex limitations to provide real-world utility. We identify four key research areas that will shape the future of the decentralized web.

First, a major shift is currently underway, moving the industry from single-layer networks toward modular blockchain architectures. In the past, foundational chains limited their systems by combining execution, storage, and consensus into one environment. Web 3.0's survival now depends on modularity, where specialized networks separate and handle these functions. By using optimized Data Availability layers strictly for keeping transaction data globally accessible, Layer-2 and Layer-3 environments can seamlessly process millions of micro-transactions without threatening the security of the base layer.

Second, the fast progress of Zero-Knowledge (ZK) cryptography marks a major breakthrough in protocol design since smart contracts were invented [26]. Previously used only for user privacy, ZK-proofs are now being applied as powerful scaling solutions. Zero-Knowledge Ethereum Virtual Machines (zkEVMs) allow off-chain networks to run complex smart contracts and create a mathematically undeniable proof of correct execution. This enables the base-layer blockchain to verify huge computational tasks in milliseconds, effectively addressing the long-standing conflict between network scalability and the costs of node verification.

Third, the widespread fragmentation of digital assets has created a strong need for secure interoperability and cross-chain messaging protocols. As the blockchain system may grow to include thousands of independent blockchains and rollups, liquidity and user identities become isolated. Future research is concentrating on replacing centralized, vulnerable token bridges with decentralized, trust-minimized interoperability protocols. These universal messaging layers will allow a smart contract on one network to easily trigger an action on another, creating a unified, chain-agnostic user experience similar to the seamless routing of the traditional Internet.

Finally, the merging of Web 3.0 infrastructure with Artificial Intelligence (AI) and the tokenization of Real-World Assets (RWAs) will change digital commerce. As generative AI greatly increases the creation of synthetic media, public blockchains will become essential cryptographic registries for verifying human identity and authenticating digital content's origin. At the same time, institutional finance is actively using smart contracts to tokenize traditional assets like real estate, corporate bonds, and government treasuries. By bringing these typically illiquid assets onto programmable ledgers, the global economy of the future will enjoy instant, round-the-clock atomic settlement, significantly reducing risks with counterparties and permanently changing the structure of modern financial markets.

Suggested further readings

[1] Wan, S., Lin, H., Gan, W., Chen, J., and Yu, P. S. Web3: The next Internet revolution, *IEEE Internet of Things Journal*, vol. 11, no. 21, pp. 34811–34825, 2024.
[2] Xiangjuan, J., Xinwei, F., Yijie, Z. *et al.* Integration and innovation of blockchain in Web3.0: Current status and standardization prospects. *World Wide Web*, vol. 28, p. 7, 2025.
[3] Kurisaka, H., Su, Y., Nguyen, P.L. *et al.* Performance evaluation of Ethereum consensus mechanisms in IoT–blockchain systems using resource-constrained devices. *Cluster Computing*, vol. 28, p. 763, 2025.
[4] Silvano, W.F., and Marcelino, R. Iota tangle: A cryptocurrency to communicate Internet-of-Things data. *Future Generation Computer Systems*, vol. 112, pp. 307–319, 2020.
[5] Huang, R., Chen, J., Wang, Y., Bi, T., Nie, L., and Zheng, Z. An overview of Web3 technology: Infrastructure, applications, and popularity. *Blockchain: Research and Applications*, vol. 5, no. 1, p. 100173, 2024.
[6] Sharma, P., Jindal, R., and Borah, M.D. A review of smart contract-based platforms, applications, and challenges. *Cluster Computing*, vol. 26, no. 1, pp. 395–421, 2023.

Standards

[1] IETF technologies: TCP/IP; DNS; HTTP
[2] Ethereum technologies: ERC-20 (Ethereum Request for Comments 20); ERC-721

References

[1] S. Zuboff, *The Age of Surveillance Capitalism*, PublicAffairs, 2019.
[2] S. Nakamoto, *Bitcoin: A Peer-to-Peer Electronic Cash System*, 2008. [Online]. Available: https://bitcoin.org/bitcoin.pdf
[3] G. Wood, *Ethereum: A Secure Decentralised Generalised Transaction Ledger*, Yellow Paper, 2014.
[4] V. Buterin, *The Meaning of Decentralization*, 2017. [Online]. Available: https://vitalik.ca

[5] J. Zittrain, *The Future of the Internet-and How to Stop It*, Yale University Press, 2008.

[6] V. Buterin, *Credible Neutrality as a Guiding Principle*, 2020. [Online]. Available: https://vitalik.ca

[7] P. De Filippi and A. Wright, *Blockchain and the Law: The Rule of Code*, Harvard University Press, 2018.

[8] I. Eyal and E. G. Sirer, "Majority Is Not Enough: Bitcoin Mining Is Vulnerable," in *Financial Cryptography and Data Security*, 2014, pp. 436–454.

[9] L. Lamport, R. Shostak, and M. Pease, "The Byzantine Generals Problem," *ACM Transactions on Programming Languages and Systems (TOPLAS)*, vol. 4, no. 3, pp. 382–401, 1982.

[10] A. E. Gencer, S. Basu, I. Eyal, R. van Renesse, and E. G. Sirer, "Decentralization in Bitcoin and Ethereum Networks," in *Financial Cryptography and Data Security (FC 2018)*, Springer, 2018, pp. 439–457.

[11] I. S. Rao, M. M. Kiah, M. M. Hameed, and Z. A. Memon, "Scalability of Blockchain: A Comprehensive Review And Future Research Direction," *Cluster Computing*, vol. 27, no. 5, pp. 5547–5570, 2024.

[12] A. Torralba-Agell and C. Pérez-Solà, "Security Assumptions in Permissionless Blockchains and Layer 2 Scalability Solutions: A Comprehensive Taxonomy', *Blockchain: Research and Applications*, p. 100388, 2025.

[13] C. Melo, J. Messias, G. Gonã, F. A. Silva, and J. Araujo, (2025). "A Stochastic Performance Model for Evaluating Ethereum Layer-2 Rollups," *Future Generation Computer Systems*, vol. 179, no. 2026, p. 108316, 2025.

[14] L. Lessig, *Code: And Other Laws of Cyberspace*, Basic Books, 1999.

[15] N. Atzei, M. Bartoletti, and T. Cimoli, "A Survey of Attacks on Ethereum Smart Contracts," in *Principles of Security and Trust*, Springer, 2017, pp. 164–186.

[16] J. Adler, R. Berryhill, A. Veneris, Z. Poulos, N. Veira and A. Kastania, "Astraea: A Decentralized Blockchain Oracle," in 2018 *IEEE International Conference on Internet of Things (iThings) and IEEE Green Computing and Communications (GreenCom) and IEEE Cyber, Physical and Social Computing (CPSCom) and IEEE Smart Data (SmartData)*, Halifax, NS, Canada, 2018, pp. 1145–1152.

[17] J. Benet, "IPFS – Content Addressed, Versioned, P2P File System," arXiv preprint arXiv:1407.3561, 2014.

[18] F. Vogelsteller and V. Buterin, "EIP-20: Token Standard," *Ethereum Improvement Proposals*, no. 20, 2015.

[19] W. Entriken, D. Shirley, J. Evans, and N. Sachs, "EIP-721: Non-Fungible Token Standard," *Ethereum Improvement Proposals*, no. 721, 2018.

[20] C. Burniske and J. Tatar, *Cryptoassets: The Innovative Investor's Guide to Bitcoin and Beyond*. McGraw Hill Professional, 2017.

[21] S. Ansar Sa, A. Demirgüç-Kunt, L. Klapper, and D. Singer, *The Global Findex Database 2021: Financial Inclusion, Digital Payments, and Resilience in the Age of COVID-19*. World Bank, Washington, DC, 2022.

[22] F. Schär, "Decentralized Finance: On Blockchain- and Smart Contract-Based Financial Markets," *Federal Reserve Bank of St. Louis Review*, vol. 103, no. 2, pp. 153–174, 2021.

[23] FATF, "Targeted Update on Implementation of the FATF Standards on Virtual Assets and Virtual Asset Service Providers," *Financial Action Task Force*, Paris, 2024.

[24] M. T. Henderson and M. Raskin, "A Regulatory Classification of Digital Assets: Toward an Operational Howey Test for Cryptocurrencies, ICOs, and Other Digital Assets," *Columbia Business Law Review*, vol. 2, pp. 443–493, 2019.

[25] W. Jia, T. Xie, and B. Wang, "A Privacy-Preserving Scheme with Multi-Level Regulation Compliance for Blockchain,' *Scientific Reports*, vol. 1, p. 438, 2024.

[26] Z. Wang, S. Chaliasos, K. Qin, *et al.*, "On How Zero-Knowledge Proof Blockchain Mixers Improve, and Worsen User Privacy," in *Proceedings of the ACM Web Conference 2023* (2023), pp. 2022–2032.

[27] V. Buterin and V. Griffith, "*Casper the Friendly Finality Gadget*," arXiv preprint arXiv:1710.09437, 2017.

Chapter 3

Web X.0 and intelligent automation beyond Web 3.0

Mustafa Ilhan Akbas[1]

Abstract

This chapter examines the role of intelligent automation within the evolving paradigm of Web X.0, with particular emphasis on artificial intelligence (AI)-powered automation, machine learning, and predictive analytics. It analyzes how web-based user experiences are being enhanced through AI-driven personalized search engines, automated customer support services, and intelligent digital assistants. Furthermore, the chapter addresses ethical and socio-technical issues associated with these technologies, including algorithmic bias, data privacy and protection, and the implications for the future of work in an AI-intensive web ecosystem. Finally, the chapter evaluates interoperability and standardization aspects in relation to World Wide Web Consortium recommendations, decentralized identity frameworks, and mechanisms for cross-platform data compatibility.

3.1 Introduction: from Web 3.0 to Web X.0

3.1.1 Overview

Web X.0 can be understood as a shift from a web that mainly stores, links, and serves information to one that also interprets context and makes limited decisions. In this model, artificial intelligence (AI), machine learning (ML), and data-driven reasoning are embedded into the service layer itself, allowing systems to infer intent, adapt behavior, and trigger actions rather than merely return content. Intelligent automation is central to that shift because it replaces many fixed workflows with policies and models that continue to update as conditions change. Personalized search, recommendation, conversational assistance, and predictive analytics are therefore not isolated features; they are examples of a broader change in how information is selected, delivered, and used. The chapter, therefore, asks

[1]Electrical Engineering and Computer Science Department, Embry-Riddle Aeronautical University, Daytona Beach, FL 32114, USA.

two linked questions: what makes this kind of automation technically feasible, and what keeps it trustworthy once deployed. To answer them, it examines architectures for adaptive personalization, multimodal assistance, and proactive analytics, then connects those architectures to governance concerns such as interoperability, transparency, accountability, and human oversight.

3.2 Technical foundations of intelligent automation

3.2.1 Computational substrate: edge-to-cloud intelligence

In Web X.0, computation is no longer confined to a browser on one side and a remote cloud on the other. Instead, execution is spread across clients, edge nodes, gateways, and backend services according to latency, privacy, and resource constraints. That distribution is important since many automated functions now depend on timely inference and localized context. Compared with earlier web models, the practical change is not only decentralization, but coordinated edge-to-cloud execution that lets learning, inference, and policy enforcement occur where they are most useful.

For Web X.0 deployments, WebAssembly (WASM) matters because the same compiled component can run in browsers, gateways, and edge services with predictable isolation and modest startup cost. Its practical value is that heavier logic no longer has to live only in JavaScript or in a remote backend; some of it can execute safely much closer to the user. The WebAssembly System Interface (WASI) further generalizes this ability to non-browser contexts and allows edge services to execute AI or data-processing workloads securely and efficiently. Studies have demonstrated that WASM can achieve near-native computational performance for ML inference while maintaining portability [1]. Serverless computing complements this model by supplying lightweight event-driven execution for short-lived automation tasks [2]. In combination, WASM and serverless platforms make it easier to place preprocessing, model inference, and validation near the point where data is produced, which is especially useful when responsiveness or privacy would be degraded by a purely centralized workflow.

WebGPU makes browser-side parallel work much more realistic, which is why on-device inference is no longer limited to toy models. ML models can perform inference directly within browsers or local devices. Browser-based inference using Graphics Processing Unit (GPU) acceleration is shown to approach the throughput of native frameworks under controlled conditions. This advancement allows personalized and privacy-sensitive automation, where sensitive information never leaves the user's device. WebGPU and related technologies, such as ONNX Runtime Web and TensorFlow.js, allow inference models to be executed across both Central Processing Unit (CPU) and GPU contexts. These frameworks exemplify the computational decentralization that defines Web X.0, where users interact with Web X.0 agents operating locally, while coordination and retraining occur through a distributed backend.

A key feature of intelligent automation in Web X.0 is the integration of edge intelligence with cloud-scale coordination. The edge layer performs low-latency inference, preprocessing, and caching, while the cloud layer aggregates outcomes, retrains models, and enforces global policies. This hybrid arrangement relies on event-driven data pipelines, which maintain reliability and scalability across autonomous web services [3]. It is also critical to have adaptive model partitioning, where neural network layers are dynamically offloaded between the edge and the cloud based on network conditions. Such adaptive execution strategies enable resilient automation that can tolerate network interruptions and optimize compute utilization. The deployment of computation at the edge can also reduce overall energy consumption by reducing data transmission and central processing [4]. These gains depend on efficient task scheduling, model compression, and hardware utilization. Hence, sustainable automation depends on the co-design of algorithms, middleware, and hardware optimized for energy proportionality and carbon-aware scheduling.

3.2.2 Data substrate: knowledge graphs and data fabric

The data substrate of Web X.0 is what allows autonomous components to exchange information without losing meaning. Its role is not only to move data, but to preserve context across systems so that reasoning, validation, and coordination remain possible. In practice, this depends on semantic data models, real-time exchange mechanisms, and provenance structures that describe how data and model artifacts were produced and used.

Traditional data lakes aggregate diverse datasets, but often lack semantics for automated reasoning. The transition toward a semantic web model allows data to be linked through ontologies, providing context for automated decision-making. Knowledge graphs serve as a key mechanism for structuring data, enabling machine-readable relationships among entities, and facilitating compatibility between distributed systems. Graph-based models improve both data discoverability and inference accuracy in large-scale automation contexts [5]. Semantic compatibility is essential for autonomous data exchange. Standards such as Resource Description Framework (RDF) and Web Ontology Language (OWL) allow systems to describe, share, and validate data through explicit schema definitions. Recent studies emphasize the integration of RDF-based metadata with streaming pipelines and microservices, establishing dynamic knowledge fabrics. The foundation of the data substrate lies in established standards, including RDF 1.2, JSON-LD 1.1, which support compatibility across the edge and cloud [6]. Knowledge representation frameworks such as OWL 2 and the Simple Knowledge Organization System (SKOS) enhance the reasoning capacity of automated systems and provide hierarchical relationships. The Shapes Constraint Language (SHACL) validation framework enables constraint checking and consistency assurance.

The Web X.0 depends on continuous data acquisition and interpretation. Streaming pipelines built on protocols such as Message Queuing Telemetry Transport (MQTT), Apache Kafka, or WebSub support real-time telemetry from sensors, edge devices, and web agents. To maintain contextual understanding, these streams are semantically annotated using ontologies, linking time-series events to their associated entities [7]. This approach allows ML systems to reason on live data while maintaining consistency. Observability in such systems requires unified data models that track operational and semantic metrics simultaneously. Approaches that combine OpenTelemetry with linked metadata help agents assess not only performance, but also whether the incoming data is sufficiently trustworthy for downstream use.

For intelligent automation to remain explainable, provenance cannot be treated as an afterthought. At minimum, the system should be able to show where a dataset or model artifact came from, what process transformed it, and which later decision relied on it. Provenance models such as Provenance Ontology (PROV-O) provide a way to represent that chain across distributed systems [51]. This is especially important for adaptive learning workflows, where a model may change repeatedly in response to new data. When model versions remain linked to their training data, validation history, and operating context, later decisions become much easier to reconstruct and audit. Privacy-preserving data management remains a parallel requirement. Federated learning and homomorphic encryption support learning across distributed datasets without forcing all data into one repository. Recent work further suggests that federated graph learning can preserve useful semantic structure while reducing privacy exposure [9]. Differential privacy techniques embedded within RDF and JSON-LD representations can further limit disclosure of sensitive attributes while preserving analytical value.

3.2.3 ML and predictive analytics substrate

ML and predictive analytics form the cognitive core of Web X.0's intelligent automation. They enable systems to learn from data, anticipate user needs, and make adaptive decisions in distributed environments [10]. This layer transforms the semantic and computational foundations into actionable intelligence, facilitating personalization, optimization, and autonomous control. This layer operates through three interconnected abilities: learning from multimodal data, generating predictive insights, and orchestrating decision-making processes within the web ecosystem.

ML underpins the adaptive behavior of Web X.0 systems. Supervised learning has been widely used for classification and regression tasks, such as content moderation and contextual recommendation [11]. Unsupervised and self-supervised approaches enable the discovery of latent patterns within heterogeneous data, facilitating knowledge graph completion and user segmentation [12]. Reinforcement learning (RL) extends these by allowing systems to learn optimal behaviors through interaction with dynamic web environments. Hybrid learning models that integrate symbolic reasoning with neural networks form a key approach to achieve explainability and consistency in automated decision systems [13]. Advances in graph-based and federated learning further enhance distributed intelligence. Graph neural networks (GNNs) support reasoning over interconnected entities in knowledge graphs and enable contextual inference and relational learning [14]. Federated ML enables collaborative training across decentralized nodes, preserving privacy while aggregating collective intelligence. Together, these methods provide the foundation for scalable and privacy-sensitive learning in Web X.0.

Predictive analytics focuses on estimating future states based on historical and real-time data. These methods are central in forecasting user behavior, network demand, or security risk. Techniques such as recurrent neural networks, transformers, and temporal graph models allow systems to capture sequential dependencies and generate high-fidelity forecasts [15]. Prescriptive analytics extends prediction by autonomously executing actions to optimize outcomes. In Web X.0, prescriptive systems can autonomously adjust the parameters of digital services, allocate computational resources, or personalize user experiences through adaptive policies. The integration of predictive and prescriptive layers supports proactive automation. For example, predictive maintenance of edge devices can trigger automated recovery or load-balancing actions without human intervention.

To ensure the reliability and reproducibility of Web X.0 intelligence, ML operations (MLOps) frameworks manage the full lifecycle of models, from data ingestion to deployment and monitoring. These frameworks integrate version control, automated testing, and continuous delivery pipelines for ML models [16]. In distributed automation environments, MLOps pipelines also govern edge deployment, dynamic retraining, and rollback mechanisms in case of performance degradation [17]. Automated governance within MLOps ensures transparency and traceability, which are necessary for regulatory compliance in intelligent systems. The convergence of MLOps and data fabric designs enables continuous alignment between data quality, model accuracy, and operational objectives. The Web X.0 environments are characterized by constant evolution in data streams, which require models capable of continuous and online learning. Adaptive learning frameworks allow models to update incrementally as new data become available, avoiding costly full retraining [18]. Online learning algorithms support real-time personalization by continuously refining predictions based on user interaction [19]. Human-in-the-loop reinforcement mechanisms are also incorporated to enhance transparency and safety [20]. These adaptive techniques enable Web X.0 to remain resilient to concept drift, adversarial changes, and environmental variability.

3.2.4 Autonomy and decision orchestration

Autonomy and decision orchestration represent the operational core of intelligent automation in Web X.0. They connect the cognitive abilities of ML with the decision-making structures required for autonomous operation. This layer enables systems to continuously sense, plan, act, and learn, and maintains alignment between user intent, ethical boundaries, and system goals. Automation traditionally refers to the execution of predefined rules or workflows. In contrast, autonomy involves goal-directed behavior in dynamic environments, where systems make independent decisions based on learned models and contextual understanding [21]. The autonomy cycle can be described through four key stages: perception, decision, action, and adaptation [22]. These stages form a closed feedback loop in which each decision contributes to model refinement and future performance improvement.

Intelligent agents and orchestration frameworks redefine how web platforms coordinate actions across distributed platforms. Multi-agent systems employ negotiation, cooperation, and self-organization to perform tasks [23]. In Web X.0, these systems are embedded within service-oriented infrastructures, allowing agents to dynamically allocate computational resources and execute autonomous workflows. Frameworks such as OpenAI's function-calling interfaces and Google's adaptive agent platforms illustrate scalable orchestration designs that integrate natural language reasoning and structured Application Programming Interfaces (APIs) [24]. Agent collaboration increasingly depends on semantic compatibility through standards such as RDF and JSON-LD. Decision orchestration relies on policy frameworks that govern agent actions according to predefined legal or operational constraints. Policy-based management systems, such as Open Policy Agent (OPA), apply declarative logic to enforce compliance and ensure traceability. In autonomous systems, policy engines interface with ML models to determine permissible actions, balancing optimization with safety and fairness [25]. Rule-based systems may remain essential in domains where deterministic guarantees are required. The hybridization of rule-based and learning-based approaches supports explainability while maintaining adaptability.

Human oversight is fundamental to the safe deployment of autonomous systems [26]. Adaptive control mechanisms integrate feedback at multiple levels to maintain operational stability [27]. Human-in-the-loop designs combine RL and preference modeling to align automated decisions with human intent [28]. Feedback loops also enable real-time performance auditing, anomaly detection, and ethical risk mitigation, ensuring that autonomy remains accountable and transparent. Safety mechanisms are also essential to prevent unintended behaviors. Fail-safe designs implement redundancy, bounded reasoning, and adversarial testing to ensure resilience. Formal verification methods are increasingly applied to validate autonomous decision logic [29]. These approaches contribute to the establishment of guarantees on system stability, robustness, and compliance.

3.2.5 Integrative example: Web X.0 automation in action

To illustrate how the components of intelligent automation interact within Web X.0, consider the example of an intelligent e-commerce assistant that autonomously manages user interaction, personalization, and system optimization. This scenario demonstrates the interplay among computational, data, learning, and decision layers.

A user engages with a decentralized e-commerce platform built on Web X.0 principles. Upon login, decentralized identifiers (DIDs) authenticate the user, and a personalized agent is instantiated. The agent operates in three layers: local inference within the browser, edge computation for contextual updates, and cloudlevel coordination for global optimization. In this flow, the user browses products, a lightweight model running on WebGPU predicts the user's intent and filters relevant items locally. The metadata about viewed products is expressed using RDF/ JSON-LD to enrich the global knowledge graph [5]. A multi-agent orchestration framework coordinates interactions among recommendation, logistics, and pricing agents. Policy engines ensure compliance with privacy regulations and ethical marketing standards. Federated updates are aggregated to improve global model performance across nodes [30]. Each autonomous decision is validated through provenance metadata (PROV-O) and verified by human oversight interfaces when uncertainty thresholds are exceeded [31]. Predictive analytics continuously assess inventory and demand, which allows dynamic pricing under regulatory constraints. Ethical auditing tools evaluate fairness in recommendations and exposure diversity [32].

This integrative case demonstrates how Web X.0's layered architecture enables privacy-preserving, adaptive, and explainable automation. It integrates decentralized identity, local intelligence, and federated coordination, achieving both autonomy and accountability in digital commerce.

3.3 Applications of intelligent automation in Web X.0

Web X.0 extends intelligent automation from back-end optimization into the direct sphere of human–web interaction. ML, predictive analytics, and decision orchestration enable adaptive personalization, natural interaction, autonomous service delivery, and proactive assistance. The personalization is based on continuous signals, online learning, and privacy-preserving aggregation. Personalization aims to improve task efficiency, relevance, and accessibility while preserving user agency and privacy. Effective systems learn preferences from interactions, adapt in real time under resource and latency constraints, respect consent and data-minimization norms, and provide measurable improvements in outcomes such as engagement or task completion [33].

The adaptive web experience pipeline has a layered structure:

1. Context sensing: Client and session signals (e.g., recent interactions, and device abilities) are collected with consent and minimal scope.
2. Local feature extraction and scoring: Lightweight models execute in the browser or on-device accelerator to produce intent or preference scores.
3. Semantic content assembly: Candidate items are described using *RDF 1.2* and *JSON-LD 1.1* to enable consistent selection across services [6].
4. Feedback and learning: Clicks, dwell time, and explicit ratings feed online learners or contextual bandits for rapid adaptation [33].
5. Privacy-preserving aggregation: Aggregated updates use randomized reporting or secure telemetry to protect individual contributions [34].

Personalization policies are often formulated as sequential decision problems. Contextual bandit algorithms balance exploration and exploitation to improve recommendations with a limited feedback delay [33]. Large-scale deployments combine bandits with offline evaluation, interleaving, and guardrails to ensure stability [35]. Privacy-aware telemetry reduces re-identification risk while retaining utility. The randomized response supports the collection of categorical statistics with formal privacy guarantees [36]. At the platform level, "learning with privacy at scale" integrates differential privacy into end-to-end data flows for web measurement and personalization. Policies document what is collected, how it is processed, and how consent and withdrawal are enforced. Personalization must remain consistent with accessibility requirements. The *W3C Personalization Semantics* and *WCAG 2.2* provide machine-interpretable hooks and success criteria so that adaptive interfaces do not obstruct assistive technologies or create unequal experiences [37,38]. Content resources described with linked data vocabularies can be adapted without breaking structure or meaning [6]. Evaluation combines controlled online experiments for causal impact [39] with fairness, privacy, and accessibility checks. Reporting should include treatment effects, uncertainty intervals, and guardrail metrics. Governance requires clear documentation of data flows, model versions, and decision policies to support auditability and rollback.

Intelligent digital assistants (IDAs) represent the human-centered interface of Web X.0. They combine advances in natural language understanding, multimodal perception, and contextual reasoning to create systems that can comprehend, act, and learn across text, speech, and visual domains. Digital assistants aim to enhance accessibility, reduce cognitive workload, and improve interaction efficiency through adaptive, context-aware dialogue. Unlike traditional rule-based chatbots, Web X.0 assistants incorporate semantic reasoning, multimodal fusion, and RL to interpret intent and generate appropriate responses [40]. The key design objectives include (i) robust intent recognition across modalities, (ii) privacy-preserving operation, and (iii) transparent, explainable decision-making.

The functional architecture of an intelligent assistant typically consists of the following components [41]:

1. Input acquisition: Multimodal input streams, speech, text, gesture, or visual cues, are captured using browser APIs such as Web Speech and WebRTC.
2. Perception and encoding: Automatic speech recognition (ASR) converts audio to text, while computer vision modules process visual context.
3. Intent recognition and dialog management: Natural language understanding (NLU) identifies user goals.
4. Action execution: The assistant interfaces with APIs, databases, or local device functions to fulfill the user intent.
5. Response generation: Natural language generation (NLG) and text-to-speech (TTS) components produce coherent and natural multimodal responses.

Multimodal assistants integrate textual, acoustic, and visual features to improve understanding and response accuracy. The cross-modal attention mechanisms, implemented through transformer designs, align the features between modalities, allowing coherent reasoning. Fusion can occur at three levels: early fusion (joint encoding), late fusion (decision combination), or hybrid fusion (shared attention over independent encoders). Hybrid fusion improves robustness to noisy or missing modalities. Knowledge-grounded assistants connect multimodal embeddings with structured information sources, which allows factual, contextually grounded answers, essential for domains such as healthcare, finance and education [42,43].

Implementations increasingly leverage on-device inference for privacy and latency reduction. WebNN and WebGPU enable local real-time inference of transformer and convolutional models within browsers. Cloud-assisted coordination remains essential for heavy contextual retrieval and large-scale model updates. Evaluation metrics for multimodal assistants include task success rate, intent classification accuracy, dialog completion time, and user satisfaction [44]. Multimodal feedback, which combines textual confirmation with visual or auditory signals, reduces error recovery time and increases perceived competence. Controlled studies measure performance under varying environmental conditions to ensure accessibility and fairness [45]. Since assistants often process sensitive voice and behavioral data, security-by-design is critical. Privacy-preserving computation, encrypted communication, and local data minimization reduce exposure risks [46]. Authentication mechanisms, including WebAuthn Level 3, help establish secure identity binding for voice and multimodal sessions. Governance frameworks recommend logging only anonymized interaction metadata and enabling user control over storage duration and model adaptation preferences [47].

3.3.1 Automated customer care and service operations

Automation in customer care and service operations is among the early large-scale deployments of Web X.0 technologies. Web X.0 extends this model by introducing autonomous, explainable, and multimodal systems that integrate structured knowledge, natural language understanding, and decision optimization. These systems improve efficiency and user experience while maintaining accountability and human oversight. The primary goal of automated service operations is to augment or replace repetitive support tasks, such as classification, routing, and response generation, while ensuring consistency and reliability. Advances in conversational AI, retrieval-augmented generation (RAG), and large-scale language modeling have enabled end-to-end systems that handle context-dependent queries. Industrial adoption has accelerated due to improved model interpretability, scalable knowledge integration, and quantifiable improvements in service quality [48].

The canonical workflow for intelligent service automation is as follows:

1. Capture: Incoming messages are collected across channels such as chat, email, voice, or social media through REST or WebSocket APIs.
2. Intent classification: NLU models classify requests into actionable intents using contextual embeddings.
3. Knowledge retrieval: The system queries enterprise knowledge graphs or document stores using dense retrieval models and semantic search.
4. Automated response generation: RAG pipelines combine retrieved evidence with generative models to form natural-language responses.
5. Escalation and feedback: Low-confidence cases are routed to human operators; user feedback updates confidence thresholds for continual learning.

Knowledge graphs (KGs) are central to ensuring factual consistency in automated responses. Each entity and relation within the KG represents organizational knowledge that the assistant can query or reason over [49]. Graph embedding models such as TransE and map KGs to continuous spaces, supporting efficient semantic retrieval [50]. When integrated into conversational agents, KGs allow systems to dynamically reference authoritative information, enforce policy constraints, and maintain traceable provenance through W3C PROV-O metadata [51]. Automation in customer care requires calibrated trust and human oversight. Hybrid systems couple AI models with rule-based validation to ensure compliance with service standards and regulations. Escalation policies are triggered when confidence or sentiment metrics fall below a threshold, ensuring transparency and continuity of service. Studies demonstrate that human-in-the-loop validation reduces false automation rates by up to 30% in enterprise deployments [48].

Evaluation metrics include intent accuracy, response relevance, resolution rate, and trust. Continuous evaluation leverages A/B experimentation to test model updates and workflow modifications [52]. Ethical and fairness assessments align with the *IEEE 7001 Transparency Standard* and *NIST AI RMF 1.0* to ensure accountability. Service automation involves sensitive user data. Secure operation requires encryption in transit (TLS 1.3), authenticated API access (OAuth 2.0), and privacy-preserving logging. User interactions are anonymized and stored following data retention limits defined in policy [47]. When training from interaction data, differential privacy and federated learning prevent direct exposure of user information [53].

3.3.2 Proactive and anticipatory automation

Proactive and anticipatory automation defines a critical progression from reactive systems to predictive self-initiating behavior on Web X.0. Such systems do not respond only to user actions but continuously interpret context, infer intent, and execute preemptive interventions aligned with user goals and ethical boundaries. Traditional web automation operates on explicit input and user requests. In contrast, anticipatory systems predict future states or needs based on contextual, behavioral, and environmental data [54]. They are designed to reduce user friction, optimize timing, and enable continuity of experience. Examples include predictive maintenance dashboards, personalized recommendation prefetching, and proactive cybersecurity alerts.

Anticipatory automation is based on three pillars: (i) accurate context sensing, (ii) predictive modeling under uncertainty, and (iii) human-aligned intervention strategies. These pillars ensure that proactive behavior enhances user experience without compromising control or transparency. A typical anticipatory automation architecture integrates the sensing, prediction, validation, and action modules [55]:

1. Context capture: Continuous data streams from IoT sensors, browsers, or mobile devices provide high-resolution situational information.
2. Predictive analytics: Temporal or causal models (e.g., transformers and Bayesian networks) forecast user intent or environmental changes.

3. Decision validation: Policy-based reasoning engines, such as Open Policy Agent (OPA), evaluate candidate actions against user preferences and legal constraints.
4. Execution and feedback: Approved actions are executed through APIs, and their outcomes are logged to retrain predictive models.

Predictive models for anticipatory systems employ supervised, unsupervised, and reinforcement learning methods. Temporal transformer designs have demonstrated superior ability in capturing sequential dependencies for next-action prediction [56]. In operational domains, hybrid models combine statistical forecasting with ML for robust adaptation to changing data distributions. For mission-critical use cases, causal inference frameworks support reasoning under uncertainty by distinguishing correlation from causation [57]. RL agents can learn anticipatory behaviors through delayed reward optimization, but ethical safeguards are required to prevent unwanted automation cascades. Proactive systems are increasingly embedded in multiple sectors such as predictive cyber defense systems, early warning health systems, and predictive controllers in smart cities.

Automation that acts without explicit consent introduces ethical challenges in terms of autonomy and accountability. Transparency mechanisms, such as proactive explanation prompts and configurable consent dashboards, mitigate risks by allowing users to review or override automated predictions. Regulatory alignment is ensured by adhering to Article 22 of the EU General Data Protection Regulation (GDPR), which restricts automated decision-making without explicit consent. Implementations should maintain clear audit trails, document model provenance, and disclose predictive decision triggers [47].

Proactive systems should be evaluated on more than predictive accuracy alone. In practice, timeliness, user satisfaction, fairness, and stability under drift all matter [47]. Monitoring tools such as OpenTelemetry and Prometheus can expose changes in predictive behavior after deployment, while retraining pipelines provide one mechanism for correction when model quality degrades. For Web X.0 platforms, this means evaluation becomes continuous rather than episodic: the system must be monitored as a live socio-technical service, not only tested as static software. The main quantitative indicators include:

- Predictive accuracy: Precision, recall, and F1-score for classification or intent recognition tasks.
- Latency: Time between user action and system response, critical for real-time and multimodal applications.
- Scalability: Throughput of requests handled under peak conditions; often measured in requests per second (RPS).
- Fairness indices: Statistical parity difference, equal opportunity gap, and disparate impact ratio [32].
- Robustness: Sensitivity of predictions to input perturbations or environmental noise.

Beyond quantitative indicators, qualitative metrics assess user perception and behavioral responses. Human evaluation captures satisfaction, perceived autonomy, and trustworthiness [58]. Studies show that explainability, transparency, and feedback responsiveness strongly correlate with sustained trust in automated systems [59]. The *W3C Web Content Accessibility Guidelines (WCAG 2.2)* and the *W3C Personalization Semantics 1.0* define accessibility-oriented criteria that complement usability evaluations [37,38]. Incorporating these standards ensures inclusivity for diverse users and adaptive interfaces.

Continuous feedback mechanisms are implemented through observability pipelines that collect real-time telemetry from deployed services [16]. A representative feedback loop includes:

1. Data collection through *OpenTelemetry* and structured logging.
2. Storage and visualization using *Prometheus*, *Grafana*, or equivalent monitoring dashboards.
3. Automated alerts triggered by threshold violations (e.g., latency, bias score, or error rate).
4. Scheduled retraining or fine-tuning through MLOps pipelines (e.g., *Kubeflow*, *MLflow*).

The ethical evaluation of automation involves standardized frameworks such as *IEEE 7001 (Transparency)* and *IEEE 7003 (Algorithmic Bias Considerations)* [60,61]. These define protocols for documenting data provenance, explaining automated outcomes, and ensuring auditability. Transparency reports summarize key model behaviors, known limitations, and corrective measures taken over time. Governance frameworks such as the *NIST AI Risk Management Framework* prescribe structured methods for identifying, measuring, and mitigating risks [47]. Regular reviews under these guidelines support continuous accountability in system evolution. Benchmarks play an essential role in comparing algorithmic performance between deployments. For conversational systems, datasets such as MultiWOZ 2.4 and Doc2Dial provide domain-agnostic baselines [44]. Lifelong evaluation frameworks integrate performance tracking across model iterations, ensuring historical continuity and traceability of design decisions [16]. Emerging research emphasizes the transition from static benchmarking to adaptive real-world testing environments that evolve alongside user interaction data [62]. This shift aligns with Web X.0's principle of continuous human-in-the-loop validation.

The realization of intelligent automation on the Web X.0 depends on a cohesive ecosystem of implementation frameworks, compatibility standards, and lifecycle management tools. These elements form the operational backbone that enables scalable, transparent, and ethically compliant deployment of AI-driven web platforms. Implementation frameworks for Web X.0 systems must support distributed intelligence, continuous adaptation, and strong governance. The foundational requirements include compatibility, transparency, scalability, security, and privacy.

Web X.0 is based on evolving W3C standards that provide the structural foundation for data exchange and model compatibility:

- RDF 1.2 and JSON-LD 1.1: Enable linked data representation and semantic compatibility [6,63].
- WebNN API: Provides a standardized interface for neural network inference across browsers and devices [64].
- WebGPU: Offers low-level access to GPU acceleration for local ML workloads [65].
- PROV-O: Facilitates provenance documentation and auditability of automated decisions [51].
- WebAuthn Level 3: Enables secure passwordless authentication for distributed intelligent services [66].

Effective model deployment and maintenance are dependent on robust Machine Learning Operations (MLOps) pipelines. These frameworks integrate data engineering, model training, validation, deployment, and monitoring in a unified operational workflow [16].

- Kubeflow: An open-source system for building portable, scalable ML workflows on Kubernetes.
- MLflow: Provides experiment tracking, model versioning, and deployment management across diverse environments.
- TensorFlow Extended (TFX): Supports data validation, model analysis, and continuous evaluation in production.
- ONNX runtime: Ensures cross-platform model portability between frameworks such as PyTorch and TensorFlow.

Governance frameworks ensure that intelligent automation aligns with ethical, legal, and organizational requirements. Key frameworks include:

- NIST AI Risk Management Framework (AI RMF 1.0): Defines risk identification, measurement, and mitigation processes for AI systems.
- ISO/IEC 42001: Establishes a standard AI management system for organizational accountability.
- IEEE 7001/7003: Provide detailed standards for transparency and bias mitigation in autonomous systems.
- Open Policy Agent (OPA): Implements fine-grained, declarative access control, and policy reasoning for Web X.0 services.

Ethical design and sustainability are integral to the Web X.0 model. Recent studies emphasize energy-aware AI model scheduling and federated inference to minimize carbon footprint [67]. Distributed training and adaptive resource allocation further contribute to environmental goals. Implementations must document ethical risk assessments and adhere to Sustainable Development Goal (SDG)-aligned sustainability reporting frameworks.

3.4 Infrastructure and standards for intelligent, decentralized web platforms

3.4.1 The design model of Web X.0

Web X.0 is best viewed as a change in system organization instead of a new collection of web features. The architectural move is away from centrally governed platforms and toward networks of agents that can exchange verified data, use local context, and make bounded decisions. AI services, decentralized identity, and semantic data models are therefore not separate add-ons; together they define the operating model of the platform. Earlier generations of the web concentrated on control and intelligence in centralized services. By contrast, Web X.0 distributes computation and decision support across software agents, devices, organizations, and users. That distribution can improve resilience and scalability, but only when trust, coordination, and data meaning are preserved across the system.

This shift is enabled by the proliferation of edge computing, lightweight inference engines, and privacy-preserving learning frameworks. Standards such as the Web Neural Network API (WebNN) and WebGPU support device-side intelligence by executing ML inference securely within the browser environment [64]. This architecture enables direct peer-level collaboration among autonomous components, human users, IoT devices, or digital twins, without requiring centralized orchestration. The Web X.0 design framework can be represented as a four-layer model:

- Physical and edge layer: Includes devices, sensors, and embedded controllers responsible for data collection and actuation. Computation at this layer is increasingly performed through edge AI accelerators and secure enclaves to ensure responsiveness and data sovereignty [68].
- Intelligence layer: Implements ML, predictive analytics, and reasoning modules. It manages the transformation of data into actionable knowledge using on-device models, federated learning, and reinforcement-based adaptation.
- Identity and trust layer: Provides authentication, authorization, and provenance mechanisms. DIDs [69] and Verifiable Credentials (VCs) allow agents to prove attributes and abilities cryptographically without centralized authorities.
- Interaction layer: Manages the interfaces between agents and human users through web standards, immersive environments, and multimodal interaction channels. It supports adaptive, context-sensitive automation through standards such as WebDriver BiDi and WebAuthn.

The Web X.0 architecture is grounded in several design principles derived from ongoing standardization efforts by the World Wide Web Consortium (W3C), the Institute of Electrical and Electronics Engineers (IEEE), and the Internet Engineering Task Force (IETF).

1. Openness and compatibility: Systems must use open standards and data models (e.g., RDF 1.2, JSON-LD 1.1) to ensure cross-platform integration and reuse.

2. Decentralized trust: Trust should emerge from verifiable cryptographic evidence rather than institutional control, implemented through DID and VC frameworks.
3. Privacy and minimal disclosure: Data exchanges must follow a privacypreserving design, including selective disclosure and zero-knowledge proofs.
4. Transparency and accountability: Provenance metadata and audit trails, represented using PROV-O and related ontologies, ensure traceability of data and decisions.
5. Sustainability and efficiency: Design must optimize computational and communication overhead to reduce energy consumption and carbon footprint.

Contemporary implementations reflect the transition toward this architecture. Solid, an open-source platform initiated by the W3C, applies the principles of data ownership and compatibility through personal data pods. ActivityPub, another W3C recommendation, provides a federated protocol that allows cross-platform interaction among autonomous web applications. Similarly, open-source ecosystems like Hyperledger Aries and DIF provide frameworks for DID and credential exchange. At the browser level, the integration of WebNN and WebGPU enables secure AI inference directly within client environments. Combined with verifiable authentication using WebAuthn Level 3, these technologies realize a programmable, secure, and privacy-preserving web runtime capable of distributed automation.

Decentralized identity is central to Web X.0 because autonomous interaction becomes fragile when identity and authorization depend entirely on one intermediary. These frameworks allow individuals, organizations, devices, and software agents to establish verifiable identities without surrendering all control to a centralized provider. The practical attraction is twofold: stronger cryptographic evidence and greater control over disclosure. Compared with conventional identity systems, decentralized approaches give credential holders more influence over what is revealed, to whom, and under what conditions. For this chapter, the key question is how those mechanisms support authentication, authorization, and accountability across distributed web services.

Self-sovereign identity (SSI) refers to a digital identity model in which individuals or entities have complete ownership and control over their identity data. Instead of storing identity records in centralized databases, SSI employs distributed ledgers and cryptographic proofs to provide verifiable and tamper-resistant claims. A central construct in this model is the *Decentralized Identifier (DID)*, defined by the W3C Decentralized Identifiers 1.0 Recommendation [69]. Each DID represents a globally unique identifier resolved through a public ledger or distributed network. It is associated with a *DID Document*, which contains public keys, service endpoints, and verification methods. DIDs support compatibility across heterogeneous systems without requiring a central registry. Another fundamental element is the *Verifiable Credential (VC)*, as defined in the W3C Verifiable Credentials Data Model 2.0. A VC is a digitally signed statement issued by an authority that asserts claims about a subject, such as qualifications, attributes, or device abilities.

Verification of a credential involves cryptographic validation of its signature and optional verification of revocation status. This mechanism enables an issuer, holder, verifier trust triangle, where trust arises from verifiable cryptographic evidence rather than centralized endorsement. DIDs and VCs collectively allow the representation of machine and human identity under a unified model. For Web X.0, this is critical because intelligent agents must authenticate, authorize, and transact autonomously while preserving the privacy and rights of their owners.

Although W3C standards provide a structural framework for decentralized identity, compatibility between platforms and applications is facilitated by the OpenID Foundation's extensions for credential management. The *OpenID for Verifiable Credential Issuance (OID4VCI)* and *OpenID for Verifiable Presentations (OID4VP)* specifications define standardized protocols for secure credential exchange between digital wallets, issuers, and verifiers. OID4VCI provides an OAuth 2.1-compliant mechanism for credential issuance, while OID4VP defines a verifiable presentation request protocol for proof sharing. These extensions bridge existing identity ecosystems with SSI-based credentials, ensuring that decentralized identity frameworks can interoperate with enterprise authentication systems. For authentication, Web X.0 leverages *Web Authentication (WebAuthn) Level 3*, a W3C and FIDO Alliance specification that enables public-key-based, phishing-resistant login mechanisms. WebAuthn allows browsers and devices to register authenticators that store cryptographic credentials locally, avoiding password reuse or exposure. When combined with DIDs and VCs, WebAuthn provides a strong, privacy-preserving mechanism for agent-level authentication and credential binding.

Example flow: A user possessing a DID wallet accesses a decentralized application. The application (verifier) issues a proof request. The wallet (holder) generates a verifiable presentation signed using a key referenced in its DID Document. The verifier validates the presentation and, if required, triggers a WebAuthn challenge for session authentication. This composite workflow achieves both decentralized identity verification and strong authentication without transmitting personal data.

Preserving privacy in decentralized identity systems requires mechanisms that limit data exposure and provide cryptographic revocation. To address these concerns, selective disclosure and zero-knowledge proof (ZKP) techniques are used to allow verifiers to confirm specific claims without revealing the underlying data. Selective disclosure can be implemented using BBS+ signature schemes, allowing holders to present subsets of credential attributes while maintaining proof integrity. ZKP-based protocols further strengthen privacy by enabling non-interactive proofs of possession, ensuring that no extraneous information leaks during verification. Revocation management is another crucial ability. Methods include cryptographic accumulators and decentralized revocation registries stored on distributed ledgers, which allow issuers to revoke credentials without identifying individual holders. These techniques collectively uphold data minimization and unlinkability, two foundational requirements in the privacy engineering of Web X.0 identity systems.

Several open-source and industry frameworks operationalize decentralized identity and authentication principles:

- Hyperledger Aries provides libraries and agents for building interoperable DID and VC ecosystems with secure communication channels.
- Decentralized Identity Foundation (DIF) maintains open protocols for credential exchange, DID resolution, and schema registries.
- Microsoft Entra Verified ID and IBM Digital Credentials integrate enterprise-grade DID and VC support into existing identity systems.
- FIDO2 and WebAuthn authenticators are being extended to integrate VC proofs, allowing unified login and credential management.

These implementations demonstrate that decentralized identity can coexist with enterprise systems, regulatory compliance frameworks, and cross-border trust networks. The convergence of cryptographically verifiable credentials and zero-trust authentication paradigms provides the foundation for secure, scalable automation.

3.4.2 Data compatibility and semantic integration

Compatibility is a defining characteristic of Web X.0, enabling data and knowledge to flow between various systems, devices, and agents. In intelligent and decentralized environments, compatibility is not limited to syntactic data exchange; it extends to semantic understanding, contextual interpretation, and machine-actionable integration. Achieving this requires standard data models, ontologies, and communication protocols that allow heterogeneous systems to operate cohesively while preserving trust and privacy.

Semantic compatibility allows the data produced by one agent or system to be understood and reused by others without human intervention. This ability relies on structured representations of meaning using shared vocabularies and graph-based data models. The Resource Description Framework (RDF) and JSON for Linking Data (JSON-LD) provide the fundamental syntax and semantics for linked data, enabling systems to express and query relationships among entities using a uniform model. RDF 1.2 defines a standardized model of triples, subject, predicate, object, representing statements about resources. JSON-LD 1.1 extends this ability to web-native formats, allowing developers to embed semantic context directly in JSON documents, linking data seamlessly across domains. These technologies underpin search, recommendation, and personalization engines, ensuring that ML models can interpret data meaningfully rather than syntactically. Semantic standards further support decentralized governance through vocabularies such as the PROV-O and schema.org. These vocabularies provide consistent descriptions of provenance, authorship, and context, enabling verifiable data reuse and traceability across Web X.0 ecosystems [70]. The proliferation of interconnected devices introduces challenges of heterogeneity, data formats, and communication protocols. The W3C Web of Things (WoT) architecture addresses these challenges by introducing a semantic abstraction layer that unifies device interfaces through a common representation. Each device, referred to as a *Thing*, publishes a *Thing Description (TD)*, a machine-readable document that describes its properties, actions, and events using semantic annotations. The WoT architecture decouples device-specific communication protocols from higher-level logic, enabling intelligent automation systems to seamlessly orchestrate IoT devices. For example, in a smart transportation network, vehicles and charging stations can publish TDs that describe their operational states and abilities. Intelligent agents can then coordinate energy distribution or route optimization autonomously by querying TDs and acting on semantic relations. For example, a Web X.0 energy management platform can automatically detect and allocate renewable energy sources by reading TDs published by energy nodes. Using reasoning on RDF graphs, it can predict load demand, negotiate with peer agents, and trigger actuators for optimal power flow, all without human supervision.

Beyond compatibility, Web X.0 emphasizes personal and organizational control over data. The Solid (Social Linked Data) framework, initiated by Berners-Lee and the W3C community, operationalizes data sovereignty through decentralized storage containers called *pods*. Each pod stores data under user control and provides standardized access interfaces using RDF and Web Access Control (WAC). Applications interact with pods through consent-based authorization, ensuring that users to determine how their information is shared or processed. In the context of intelligent automation, Solid enables personal data assistants and agents to perform reasoning tasks locally or in a privacy-preserving manner. For instance, an AI assistant can access the user's pod to retrieve health metrics, perform analysis locally, and issue verifiable summaries without exposing sensitive data to cloud services. The combination of Solid and decentralized identity (DID/VC) frameworks allows Web X.0 systems to authenticate access requests, verify provenance, and enforce data usage policies in a verifiable and transparent manner. Knowledge graphs extend semantic representations by linking heterogeneous datasets through relationships and ontologies that enable reasoning and inference [5]. In Web X.0, knowledge graphs serve as the connective fabric among intelligent agents, allowing AI systems to retrieve, correlate, and act on distributed data sources. A knowledge graph may link credential attributes, IoT telemetry, and contextual metadata, creating a shared representation that supports reasoning tasks such as anomaly detection, planning, or recommendation. Integration with schema.org, Wikidata, and domain-specific ontologies ensures semantic consistency across applications and services. Recent advances in AI and graph learning, such as graph neural networks (GNNs) and knowledge graph embeddings, enable dynamic updating and contextual awareness, aligning graph-based knowledge with adaptive real-time automation. These developments make semantic integration both a data modeling technique and a critical enabler of self-organizing Web X.0 platforms.

3.4.3 Trust, provenance, and cross-platform orchestration

As intelligent automation permeates every layer of Web X.0, ensuring the authenticity, transparency, and reliability of digital interactions becomes a foundational requirement. Trust in decentralized and autonomous environments cannot rely on institutional guarantees but must emerge from verifiable cryptographic evidence, transparent provenance, and interoperable orchestration across platforms.

In Web X.0 ecosystems, where decisions are increasingly automated and data flows are dynamic, it is essential to preserve the lineage and accountability of both data and models. Provenance, information describing the origin, context, and transformation of data, supports this requirement by allowing any participant to verify how a dataset or computational outcome was produced [70]. The W3C's PROV-O provides a formal model to represent these relationships. PROV-O defines entities (data items), activities (transformations), and agents (actors) connected through causal links. These representations allow the construction of audit trails that can be validated across organizational or platform boundaries.

For Web X.0 automation pipelines, provenance records can include:

- The source and integrity of data inputs.
- The version and configuration of AI models used in inference.
- The identity and authorization of the agents that initiated the actions.

This provenance-aware automation supports compliance, reproducibility, and ethical accountability in machine-driven decisions. Automation in Web X.0 frequently spans multiple domains, services, and agents that operate autonomously. Federated communication protocols allow these agents to coordinate actions without central control. The W3C's *ActivityPub* specification defines a decentralized messaging protocol for social and computational interaction between servers and applications. ActivityPub extends the ActivityStreams 2.0 vocabulary, allowing agents to publish, subscribe, and act upon semantically defined events. Each "activity" (e.g., *Offer*, *Accept*, and *Create*) is represented as a JSON-LD document containing actor, object, and target fields. When applied to automation, ActivityPub can orchestrate workflows between agents distributed across organizations.

Example: An environmental monitoring agent publishes a "Report" activity via ActivityPub, including provenance data referencing sensor readings and analytic models. A regional management agent subscribes to this feed, verifies the digital signatures, and triggers an automated remediation workflow (e.g., alerting a local IoT actuator). This distributed orchestration achieves automation without relying on a centralized broker.

Web X.0 environments depend on heterogeneous execution contexts, browsers, edge nodes, and cloud services that must collaborate securely and efficiently. The integration of computation across these contexts is based on a combination of emerging W3C and industry standards. The *Web Neural Network API (WebNN)* and *WebGPU* enable high-performance, privacy-preserving inference directly within browsers or edge devices. WebNN provides a unified interface for executing ML graphs, while WebGPU exposes low-level graphics and parallel computation abilities to the web environment. These standards collectively allow intelligent agents to perform reasoning tasks locally, reducing latency and minimizing data transmission. For orchestration and testing, the *WebDriver BiDi* specification defines bidirectional control between browsers and external agents. WebDriver BiDi supports event-driven automation, enabling agents to observe, instrument, and verify the behavior of intelligent applications across platforms.

Example: A digital assistant embedded in a Web X.0 browser performs local inference through WebNN to predict user intent. Upon action confirmation, the assistant interacts with decentralized services using ActivityPub and verifies session integrity through DID-authenticated WebAuthn credentials. Provenance metadata about each interaction is stored using PROV-O-compliant structures, ensuring traceable automation.

Trust in automated systems requires evidence of system integrity. Attestation mechanisms provide this assurance by enabling entities to prove the authenticity and state of their execution environments. The Internet Engineering Task Force's (IETF) Remote Attestation Procedures (RATS) framework formalizes this process through evidence, endorsement, and attestation result exchanges. When combined with verifiable credentials, attestation mechanisms allow agents in Web X.0 to present cryptographic proofs of their identity and runtime integrity. This model ensures that autonomous interactions occur only between verified and compliant entities.

For end-to-end assurance, these attestation frameworks can be bound to decentralized identifiers and verifiable credentials. This integration creates a continuous trust chain linking identity, computation, and provenance across heterogeneous systems, a defining feature of secure automation in Web X.0.

3.5 Trustworthy and responsible automation

3.5.1 Ethical and governance frameworks for automated intelligence

Responsible automation in Web X.0 is not only a matter of model quality, but it also depends on how the system is governed throughout its lifecycle. Because these systems influence access, safety, privacy, and public trust, their design and operation have to be evaluated against legal, ethical, and organizational expectations as well as technical ones. The frameworks reviewed here are most useful when treated as operational guidance for distributed automation rather than as compliance labels.

Multiple international efforts now shape the governance landscape for AI and autonomous systems. The Organization for Economic Co-operation and Development (OECD) principles established an early intergovernmental baseline around human-centered values, transparency, robustness, and accountability. The EU AI Act pushes further by attaching regulatory obligations to risk categories, especially where systems affect safety or fundamental rights. In the United States, NIST's AI RMF offers a less prescriptive but still structured approach to governance and continuous oversight [47]. NIST organizes risk work around governance, context-setting, measurement, and response, which is useful here because Web X.0 systems cannot be treated as one-time deployments. At the organizational level, ISO/IEC 42001 brings similar concerns into an AI management system that spans technical and operational practice. Taken together, these efforts point toward lifecycle accountability: governance begins before deployment and continues through monitoring, revision, and audit.

3.5.1.1 IEEE P7000 series and ethical design

The IEEE has a suite of standards that address the ethical dimensions of intelligent and autonomous systems, collectively known as the *P7000 series*. These standards focus on embedding ethical considerations in system engineering processes from the earliest stages of design [71]. Among the most relevant are:

- IEEE P7000: Provides a general process model for identifying and addressing ethical concerns throughout system design.
- IEEE P7001: Defines requirements for transparency in autonomous and intelligent systems, emphasizing explainability and auditability.
- IEEE P7003: Addresses algorithmic bias, outlining principles for data governance, fairness testing, and bias remediation.
- IEEE P7009: Focuses on fail-safe design, ensuring that autonomous systems enter a defined safe state in cases of anomaly or uncertainty.

These standards integrate ethical reasoning directly into engineering methods, complementing existing technical specifications such as ISO/IEC 42001 and the NIST AI RMF. In Web X.0, where agents make decisions dynamically in distributed environments, these principles ensure that design processes consider human oversight, contextual transparency, and the prevention of harm.

3.5.1.2 Convergence and practical implementation

Although developed independently, the OECD, EU, NIST, ISO, and IEEE frameworks exhibit substantial convergence around five recurring principles: transparency, accountability, fairness, robustness, and human oversight. This convergence indicates a global shift from ethical declarations to measurable governance structures [72]. In practice, organizations implementing Web X.0 automation can operationalize these principles through:

- Lifecycle governance: Embedding risk assessments, ethical impact analysis, and human oversight checkpoints in each phase of development.
- Documentation and traceability: Maintaining model cards, data provenance logs, and decision traceability records that align with PROV-O and ISO quality documentation standards.
- Independent auditing: Engaging third-party audits and certification schemes for AI components, aligned with ISO/IEC 42001 or national supervisory authorities.
- Ethical review committees: Establishing internal governance boards to evaluate new automated features for fairness, privacy, and potential societal impact.

These practices form a foundation for accountable automation in Web X.0, ensuring that autonomy and intelligence are exercised within structured ethical and legal boundaries. The resulting systems are technically robust, institutionally transparent, and socially aligned.

3.5.2 Fairness, accountability, and transparency

Once intelligent automation affects access, ranking, recommendation, or enforcement decisions, fairness, accountability, and transparency become operational requirements rather than optional design goals. Automated agents influence people and organizations directly, so their behavior has to be explainable, auditable, and open to challenge. The discussion that follows focuses on the concrete mechanisms that support those properties: fairness metrics, interpretability tools, documentation practices, and oversight structures.

3.5.2.1 Bias identification and mitigation

Algorithmic bias arises when data-driven systems systematically favor or disadvantage certain groups due to imbalances in training data or model assumptions. The detection and mitigation of bias are primary objectives of responsible automation. IEEE Standard P7003 defines formal procedures for identifying and correcting algorithmic bias across data acquisition, model training, and evaluation processes. It emphasizes quantitative fairness metrics, documentation, and corrective feedback loops.

Common fairness measures include *equalized odds*, *demographic parity*, and *predictive equality*, which evaluate disparities in model outcomes across sensitive attributes. Techniques for mitigation range from data preprocessing (rebalancing and reweighting), to in-processing constraints (fairness-aware optimization), and post-processing adjustments (calibration or output transformations). Each approach must be contextualized according to the intended application domain and regulatory requirements. Empirical evaluations in ACM and IEEE literature show that multi-stage auditing, combining data quality checks with adversarial testing, provides the most reliable bias mitigation strategy [32]. Automated auditing pipelines integrated with continuous deployment workflows can monitor model outputs and detect drift-induced bias during runtime. Such mechanisms are particularly relevant in Web X.0, where decentralized agents operate on continuously evolving data sources.

3.5.2.2 Explainability and interpretability

Transparency in intelligent systems requires that their internal decision-making processes be interpretable to human stakeholders. Explainable AI (XAI) methods provide insights into model behavior, supporting validation, debugging, and user trust. Key methods include feature attribution techniques such as SHAP (SHapley Additive exPlanations) and LIME (Local Interpretable Model-agnostic Explanations), which identify the contribution of input features to model outputs [73–75].

Beyond model-level interpretability, process-level explainability is critical for automation governance. IEEE Standard IEEE 7001-2021 emphasizes transparency in autonomous systems, defining requirements for audit trails, rationale disclosure, and traceable system behavior [60]. Explainability must also be accessible to diverse stakeholders: developers, auditors, and end users. The use of layered transparency, technical, procedural, and user-facing, facilitates comprehension at multiple levels of abstraction. In Web X.0, explainability mechanisms must extend to distributed agents. Each agent maintains explainable metadata that describe the model lineage, the performance context, and the limitations. When combined with the provenance structures described in Section 3.4.3, this enables end-to-end traceability across federated environments.

3.5.2.3 Accountability and human oversight

Accountability in automation requires that human actors retain ultimate responsibility for outcomes and that automated systems are designed with mechanisms for supervision and contestability. IEEE P7008 provides guidelines for the design of socio-technical systems in which human oversight remains integral to the decision loop. Oversight may occur in three configurations:

1. Human-in-the-loop: Humans intervene before automated actions are executed.
2. Human-on-the-loop: Humans monitor autonomous operations and can override them if necessary.
3. Human-out-of-the-loop: Automation operates independently but under predefined escalation or audit protocols.

Example flow: In a decentralized customer-support network, multiple intelligent agents process incoming queries. Each agent records decisions with accompanying feature attributions, fairness scores, and provenance metadata. When a user appeals a decision, the supervisory human operator accesses the agent's model card and audit log to trace the reasoning path and verify compliance with fairness requirements. This workflow ensures transparency and redressability while maintaining operational autonomy.

Fairness, accountability, and transparency mechanisms are most effective when integrated into the infrastructure layer of Web X.0 rather than treated as post-hoc evaluations. Provenance ontologies (e.g., PROV-O) link explainability artifacts to data sources, while decentralized identity systems (DID/VC) ensure that accountability extends across organizational boundaries. By embedding bias monitoring, explainability, and oversight mechanisms directly into decentralized designs, Web X.0 systems can maintain both autonomy and accountability.

3.5.3 Privacy and data protection

In Web X.0 environments, where intelligent automation operates across distributed and interoperable systems, maintaining privacy and data protection is a fundamental requirement for public trust and legal compliance. As automation expands into decision-making domains such as healthcare, finance, and digital governance, data flows become increasingly, involving continuous interaction between users, agents, and organizations.

3.5.3.1 Privacy-by-design principles

Privacy-by-design embeds protection mechanisms directly into system architecture, rather than treating privacy as an external compliance issue. It aligns with the *General Data Protection Regulation* (GDPR) Articles 5 and 25, which mandate data minimization, purpose limitation, and data protection by default. These principles have been extended to technical standards such as ISO/IEC 27701, which defines privacy information management systems compatible with existing information security frameworks.

The *W3C Privacy Principles* further formalize privacy requirements for the web ecosystem, emphasizing transparency, consent, and limited data retention. Within Web X.0, these principles guide the design of intelligent agents that operate autonomously yet responsibly. Privacy-by-design mandates include:

- Data minimization: Collect and process only information necessary for a specific function.
- Purpose limitation: Clearly define and restrict how data may be used or shared.
- User agency: Allow users to access, correct, and revoke data-sharing permissions.
- Accountability: Document and audit all data-handling operations for compliance validation.

Implementing these principles across decentralized systems ensures that privacy protection extends from individual agents to multi-party computation networks and federated learning environments.

3.5.3.2 Privacy-enhancing technologies

The practical realization of privacy-by-design relies on a suite of *privacy-enhancing technologies* (PETs). These technologies enable computation and analytics on sensitive data while preventing direct exposure of personally identifiable information. Core PETs applicable to Web X.0 include:

- Differential privacy (DP): Adds statistical noise to datasets or query results to prevent re-identification of individuals while preserving aggregate utility.
- Federated learning (FL): Distributes model training across multiple nodes without sharing raw data, using secure aggregation to combine model updates.
- Homomorphic encryption (HE): Allows computation on encrypted data, producing encrypted results that can be decrypted to reveal valid outputs.
- Secure multi-party computation (SMPC): Enables collaborative computation among multiple participants without revealing private inputs.

These technologies can be combined in hybrid designs to balance utility, performance, and privacy. For instance, federated learning enhanced with differential privacy can train global models while ensuring that individual data contributions remain confidential.

Example flow: In a healthcare Web X.0 network, patient data remain stored locally within hospital databases. Each institution trains a local diagnostic model and shares encrypted gradient updates through a secure aggregation server. Differential privacy adds controlled noise to prevent reconstruction attacks. The aggregated model parameters are then redistributed to all participants, achieving global learning without exposing any individual record.

3.5.3.3 Decentralized consent and data governance

Traditional consent mechanisms often rely on centralized authorities or opaque terms of service agreements. Web X.0 replaces these structures with verifiable decentralized consent systems using the same foundational standards introduced in Section 3.4.1, DIDs and VCs. Each consent transaction becomes a verifiable claim that can be cryptographically signed, timestamped, and revoked.

For example, a user may issue a verifiable credential to a digital service that grants temporary access to location data. The credential specifies access scope, duration, and purpose. Once the condition expires, the credential is automatically revoked through a revocation registry, ensuring privacy without centralized oversight [76]. This approach aligns with emerging decentralized data governance frameworks, such as the *Solid* project, which separates data storage ("pods") from application logic. By allowing individuals and organizations to host their own data under standardized access control policies, Solid demonstrates how personal data autonomy can coexist with intelligent, federated automation. Such decentralized consent frameworks ensure compliance with privacy regulations while enabling seamless machine-to-machine collaboration across domains. Smart contracts may further automate consent enforcement by executing access revocations or renewals under predefined conditions.

3.5.3.4 Integration with Web X.0 architecture

Privacy-preserving computation and decentralized consent must be integrated within the Web X.0 infrastructure rather than implemented as isolated mechanisms. Privacy metadata, such as provenance records and consent receipts, can be represented in RDF/JSON-LD formats, linking them directly to data objects and intelligent agents. Combining PETs with provenance ontologies and identity standards provides a full accountability chain from data collection to automated decision-making.

This integrated privacy architecture allows autonomous agents to collaborate securely while complying with global standards and privacy regulations. In doing so, Web X.0 extends privacy protection beyond human users to encompass machine agents and intelligent applications operating throughout the digital ecosystem.

3.5.4 Security, robustness, and safety

In Web X.0, intelligent automation runs in distributed, dynamic, and only partially trusted environments. That combination raises the stakes for security, robustness, and safety. Unlike traditional web applications, Web X.0 agents can make local decisions, trigger downstream actions, and interact across organizational boundaries, which expands both the attack surface and the space of possible failures.

3.5.4.1 Zero-trust architecture

The *Zero-Trust Architecture (ZTA)* represents a model shift from perimeter-based security toward continuous verification of every entity and transaction. Defined in NIST Special Publication 800-207, zero trust assumes that no network segment, user, or device is inherently trustworthy [77]. Access decisions are based on contextual verification, least privilege, and continuous monitoring.

Within Web X.0, ZTA principles extend to autonomous agents, decentralized applications, and federated systems. Each agent must authenticate using verifiable credentials and attest to its integrity state before engaging in communication or computation. Integration with the IETF Remote Attestation Procedures (RATS) architecture allows agents to present cryptographically verifiable evidence of runtime integrity. This ensures that only trusted code operates within critical automation workflows.

- Identity verification: Agents use DIDs and VCs to authenticate.
- Runtime integrity: Remote attestation confirms the trustworthiness of hardware and software stacks before execution.
- Least privilege access: Authorization policies enforce minimal data and function exposure for each transaction.

Through these mechanisms, ZTA transforms Web X.0 into a network of continuously verified participants, reducing the likelihood of privilege escalation, supplychain compromise, and insider threats.

3.5.4.2 Adversarial robustness and resilience

ML models deployed within Web X.0 are vulnerable to adversarial attacks, including evasion, poisoning, and model inversion. These attacks can manipulate automated decision-making, compromise privacy, or degrade system reliability. Ensuring adversarial robustness involves developing models and pipelines resilient to such manipulations.

Evasion attacks occur when adversaries craft small perturbations to inputs that mislead the model while remaining imperceptible to humans [78]. Defensive strategies include adversarial training, feature squeezing, and certified robustness techniques [79]. Poisoning attacks target training data to induce biased or unsafe behaviors; mitigations involve robust aggregation, outlier detection, and secure provenance tracking [80]. In Web X.0, decentralized learning frameworks, such as federated learning, must incorporate robustness mechanisms that function under partial trust. Secure aggregation combined with Byzantine-resilient optimization can defend against compromised participants. Continuous red-team testing, anomaly detection, and explainable failure analysis are necessary to identify vulnerabilities before deployment.

Example flow: In a federated intrusion-detection system, each node contributes local anomaly statistics to a global model. Before aggregation, nodes perform adversarial input sanitization and digital-signature verification. A trusted coordinator uses differential privacy to mask sensitive gradients and performs adversarial validation to detect manipulated updates. This ensures robustness without sacrificing collaborative learning efficiency.

3.5.4.3 Safety validation and fail-safe design

Safety in autonomous systems concerns the assurance that actions will not lead to unacceptable risks under foreseeable conditions [81]. For Web X.0 agents operating in safety-critical or infrastructure-related domains, safety validation must combine formal verification, simulation-based testing, and runtime monitoring. The IEEE P7009 standard defines principles for fail-safe design in autonomous and intelligent systems, requiring predictable behavior and controlled degradation under failure. Safety validation follows a lifecycle process similar to those in aviation and automotive systems: hazard analysis, fault tolerance, and continuous post-deployment monitoring.

- Hazard analysis: Identify operational scenarios and risk categories for automated decisions.
- Redundancy and recovery: Implement fallback mechanisms that restore safe operational states.
- Runtime monitoring: Track model performance and environmental context to detect unsafe conditions.

Simulation frameworks and digital twins allow developers to evaluate automated behaviors in controlled but realistic scenarios prior to deployment. In runtime environments, safety envelopes and formal verification methods such as reachability analysis ensure that autonomous agents remain within certified operating boundaries. Together, these measures prevent cascading failures in distributed automation networks.

Security and safety must be embedded throughout the Web X.0 architecture, connecting the identity, intelligence, and interaction layers. Attestation protocols (RATS), authentication standards (WebAuthn), and provenance ontologies (PROV-O) enable cross-layer accountability. Provenance data can be extended to include security events, allowing real-time traceability of anomalies.

3.5.5 Compliance, certification, and assurance

The credibility of Web X.0 systems depends on demonstrable compliance with ethical, technical, and safety standards. Compliance, certification, and assurance frameworks ensure that intelligent automation complies with regulatory expectations and industry best practices throughout its lifecycle. In contrast to traditional compliance processes that focus on static software validation, Web X.0 requires continuous assurance, auditing, and monitoring that adapt to dynamic, learning-based systems.

Compliance begins with structured conformance assessments that verify that systems meet defined ethical, safety, and quality standards. The *ISO/IEC 42001:2023* standard provides a formal framework for establishing and maintaining an AI Management System (AIMS), integrating AI-specific controls into organizational processes. It mirrors the structure of ISO 9001 and ISO 27001, ensuring traceability between design, risk assessment, and operation. The *NIST AI Risk Management Framework (AI RMF 1.0)* complements this by offering practical guidance to govern, map, measure, and manage AI risks throughout the system lifecycle [47]. Together, these frameworks define the baseline for internal governance and external auditing of intelligent automation.

Compliance audits in Web X.0 can be both human-driven and machine-assisted. Automated auditing tools can monitor system behavior, log compliance events, and verify compliance with constraints using machine-readable policies. The use of provenance standards such as PROV-O facilitates traceable reporting of compliance evidence. These audits are strengthened through *assurance cases*, structured arguments linking evidence to compliance claims, commonly used in aviation and medical device certification. Transferring this approach to Web X.0 allows stakeholders to evaluate how design and operational data substantiate safety, fairness claims.

Unlike static software, intelligent systems evolve over time due to model retraining, data drift, and changing environments. Compliance must include continuous monitoring and periodic reassessment. ISO/IEC 42001 and the NIST AI RMF emphasize *operational assurance*, the ongoing evaluation of performance, risk, and ethical conformity after deployment.

Continuous monitoring mechanisms in Web X.0 include:

- Data drift detection: Identifying distributional shifts in data input or model output that may impact fairness or safety.
- Concept drift analysis: Tracking changes in learned relationships over time and adapting models accordingly.
- Runtime compliance verification: Using formal rules or smart contracts to automatically check whether system behaviors conform to declared constraints.
- Incident logging and root-cause analysis: Recording deviations and facilitating traceable corrective actions through automated reporting.

These mechanisms can be implemented through model monitoring pipelines in MLOps frameworks, integrated with provenance tracking and explainability modules. For example, a Web X.0 autonomous commerce platform could automatically record model updates, bias metrics, and security attestations into a shared verifiable ledger accessible to auditors. Such automation supports the creation of "living assurance cases" that evolve in parallel with deployed systems, ensuring that accountability is maintained even as intelligent behaviors adapt over time.

The Web X.0 automation spans jurisdictions with differing legal and ethical requirements. Cross-border compatibility in compliance depends on the harmonization between regional and international standards. The *European Union AI Act*

(2024) provides risk-based obligations and conformity assessment procedures, while the U.S. NIST AI RMF focuses on voluntary but systematic risk governance. ISO/IEC 42001 and P7000-series standards provide international bridges between these approaches [71].

To facilitate compatibility, global initiatives such as the OECD AI Policy Observatory and the Global Partnership on AI (GPAI) promote common taxonomies for AI assurance. These taxonomies enable the mutual recognition of audits and certifications, reducing redundancy for global developers. An emerging practice is the use of *machine-readable compliance declarations*, often referred to as "AI policy cards." These digital documents describe the ethical, safety, and performance guarantees of an AI component using standardized metadata, allowing automated verification by regulators and consumers. Example: A decentralized transportation platform could publish AI policy cards containing metadata on model risk classification, bias testing, and audit trail references. Consumers or auditors can then automatically retrieve and verify compliance information using RDF-linked data schemas. Harmonization efforts lay the foundation for a trusted global Web X.0 ecosystem, where intelligent agents can interoperate across legal and cultural boundaries while adhering to shared principles of responsibility.

3.6 Operationalizing intelligent automation

3.6.1 Web X.0 in intelligent services and search

Intelligent services represent one of the earliest and most visible realizations of Web X.0. The evolution from keyword-based retrieval to context-aware, personalized, and explainable search systems illustrates how AI reshapes human–web interaction. Web X.0 integrates distributed intelligence, privacy-preserving computation, and verifiable data provenance into the search process, transforming the web from a repository of information into an adaptive reasoning environment.

Traditional web search relied on lexical matching and hyperlink-based ranking. The advent of ML-enabled semantic retrieval, where systems could infer user intent and context. Recent advances in natural language understanding and multimodal learning now allow systems to interpret text, speech, and visual cues in combination [82]. Large language models (LLMs), such as transformer-based designs, have further extended this ability by integrating retrieval-augmented generation (RAG) and reasoning over structured data [83]. Web X.0 introduces an additional layer of intelligence: search agents can dynamically adapt to the user context, enforce privacy preferences, and refer to verifiable data sources through DIDs and VCs. These agents operate within federated or peer-to-peer ecosystems, avoiding centralized profiling while maintaining accuracy and personalization. This transition from syntactic to contextual search transforms retrieval into a process of meaning construction rather than document selection. It aligns with the broader shift from the static web (Web 1.0) to the semantic and cognitive web layers underpinning Web X.0.

An Web X.0 search service operates through an interconnected pipeline composed of several layers:

- User context and identity layer: Users authenticate using decentralized credentials and specify data-sharing policies stored within personal data pods (e.g., Solid architecture). This ensures privacy-preserving personalization.
- Semantic retrieval layer: Search queries are represented as vector embeddings, enabling similarity-based retrieval and reasoning using graph neural networks (GNNs).
- Reasoning and generation layer: LLMs and symbolic reasoning modules generate ranked responses and explanations based on retrieved evidence.
- Verification and provenance layer: Results are validated through cryptographic signatures and provenance graphs following the W3C PROV-O model.

This multi-layered architecture combines symbolic reasoning with data-driven learning, achieving transparency and traceability across the retrieval lifecycle. The provenance layer is critical as it records how the data was retrieved and transformed, allowing auditors or users to verify the integrity of the results.

3.6.1.1 Privacy-preserving personalization

In traditional search systems, personalization often relies on user profiling through centralized data collection. This approach presents substantial risks to privacy and autonomy. In Web X.0, personalization is achieved through federated and privacypreserving learning mechanisms that retain user data within local environments. Federated learning (FL) allows distributed search agents to collectively learn relevance patterns without sharing raw data, thus preserving confidentiality [30]. Complementary techniques such as differential privacy (DP) and secure multi-party computation (SMPC) further protect individual contributions. Decentralized consent management through verifiable credentials allows users to authorize or revoke data access dynamically.

Example flow: A user issues a search request through a decentralized browser. The request is processed by a local agent that holds the user's preference profile stored in a Solid pod. The agent performs query embedding and federated model update without exposing personal data. The global search service aggregates the encrypted model parameters from multiple agents to refine ranking performance. Returned results include provenance metadata and cryptographic proofs of source authenticity.

This model allows fine-grained personalization without compromising user privacy or violating data protection regulations such as the GDPR.

3.6.1.2 Transparency and explainability in intelligent search

Transparency in search outcomes is essential for maintaining user trust. Web X.0 incorporates XAI principles, allowing users to understand why specific results were returned or ranked. Techniques such as attention visualization, feature attribution (SHAP or LIME), and contrastive reasoning help reveal decision logic.

To maintain verifiability, search explanations are coupled with provenance records that capture data lineage and model parameters. IEEE 7001-2021s guidelines on autonomous systems transparency provide an engineering framework for embedding such explainability throughout the system lifecycle. Explainability interfaces may take textual or graphical forms, describing query expansion steps, model confidence, and data provenance. This transparency ensures accountability and supports compliance with emerging AI governance frameworks such as the EU AI Act.

3.6.1.3 Integration with decentralized web infrastructure

The decentralized web environment enables intelligent search services to operate without reliance on centralized intermediaries. The W3C Solid framework and the ActivityPub protocol support decentralized publishing and discovery, while the WoT architecture extends search to sensor data and physical entities. Search agents in Web X.0 leverage these standards to locate and reason about distributed content seamlessly.

Example flow: A research agent performs a cross-domain literature search using decentralized repositories. It authenticates using a DID, queries RDF-based knowledge graphs through SPARQL endpoints, and validates retrieved metadata using blockchain hashes. The agent generates an annotated summary in which each citation includes a provenance token linking back to the original source.

This decentralized search model aligns with the ethical and technical objectives of Web X.0, autonomous, privacy-respecting, and verifiable information exchange.

3.6.2 Decentralized finance and autonomous economic agents

Decentralized finance (DeFi) is one of the clearest stress tests for Web X.0 because identity, contracts, prediction, and automated action all meet in the same transaction flow. Instead of relying on centralized intermediaries, these systems use distributed ledgers and programmable contracts to coordinate exchange. Once AI is added, the system does more than execute rules: it can adapt risk thresholds, forecast behavior, and support increasingly autonomous economic agents. The key issue is not simply that DeFi is decentralized, but that financial control logic becomes data-driven and continuously updated.

3.6.2.1 Architecture of intelligent DeFi systems

An intelligent DeFi architecture integrates blockchain-based trust with AI-driven decision logic to achieve autonomous, transparent, and adaptive financial operations. It typically includes the following core layers:

- Blockchain layer: Provides the foundational distributed ledger and consensus mechanisms (e.g., Proof of Stake or Byzantine Fault Tolerance) that ensure immutability and fault tolerance.

- Smart contract layer: Implements programmable financial logic, such as lending, trading, or insurance protocols. Smart contracts are executed deterministically once the predefined conditions are met, eliminating the need for intermediaries [84].
- Intelligence layer: Integrates AI models for risk prediction, fraud detection, and market optimization. These models can operate in decentralized environments using federated or on-chain learning [85].
- Governance and compliance layer: Manages the evolution of DeFi protocols through Decentralized Autonomous Organizations (DAOs) and regulatory monitoring modules compliant with frameworks such as the Financial Action Task Force (FATF) Travel Rule.

This architecture allows DeFi platforms to achieve both automation and accountability, with all decisions recorded on-chain and auditable in real time.

3.6.2.2 Autonomous economic agents

Autonomous Economic Agents (AEAs) are intelligent entities capable of performing transactions, negotiations, and contract execution independently. These agents leverage ML to analyze market data, forecast price movements, and optimize portfolio allocations. In contrast to conventional bots, AEAs operate under decentralized identity frameworks and interact through verifiable smart contracts [86,87].

Example flow: An AEA representing a renewable energy cooperative monitors electricity demand through IoT sensors. Using predictive analytics, it determines optimal times for energy trading. It then interacts with a decentralized exchange through a smart contract to sell surplus energy tokens at favorable prices. Each transaction is recorded on-chain, while AI models continually adjust strategies based on market dynamics.

This architecture supports self-regulating digital economies, where agents represent individuals, organizations, or devices engaged in economic activities without centralized control. The Open Economic Framework (OEF) and similar initiatives provide compatibility among agents, facilitating automated negotiation and market discovery.

3.6.2.3 AI-enhanced risk prediction and fraud detection

AI-driven analytics are essential for the stability and security of decentralized finance. ML techniques are applied to detect anomalous behaviors such as wash trading, flash loan exploits, and market manipulation. Graph neural networks (GNNs) and anomaly detection algorithms can identify suspicious transaction patterns within blockchain data [88].

Predictive models also assess the credit risk for undercollateralized lending. Rather than relying on static collateral ratios, systems can dynamically adjust risk parameters based on behavioral scoring and on-chain reputation systems. Such adaptive mechanisms enhance liquidity efficiency while maintaining security guarantees. To ensure accountability, all AI-driven decisions are logged as verifiable provenance records, allowing audits consistent with ISO/IEC 42001 guidelines for AI management and assurance.

3.6.2.4 Smart contracts and adaptive governance

AI can augment smart contract functionality by introducing self-adaptive governance mechanisms. These contracts evolve based on verifiable inputs, market trends, user votes, or compliance updates, without manual intervention. RL-based governance models have been proposed to balance stakeholder utility while ensuring compliance with fairness and stability constraints [89].

DAOs use multi-signature and token-based voting schemes to govern protocol changes. In various fields, intelligent governance frameworks apply predictive modeling to simulate policy outcomes before implementation [90]. For example, a DAO may dynamically adjust liquidity incentives based on risk forecasts generated by an AI policy engine.

Example flow: A lending DAO monitors loan defaults using on-chain analytics. When default probabilities increase beyond a threshold, the AI policy model triggers a governance proposal to modify interest rates. The smart contract executes the approved policy automatically after the consensus of the token-holder, ensuring risk mitigation without centralized intervention.

3.6.2.5 Regulatory compliance and trust assurance

Although decentralization enhances transparency, it also complicates compliance with existing financial regulations. Web X.0 introduces verifiable identity and compliance oracles that bridge decentralized systems with regulatory frameworks. Digital identities based on DIDs can embed Know Your Customer (KYC) attributes while preserving user privacy through zero-knowledge proofs [76].

The ISO/TC 307 blockchain standards and the Financial Stability Board's guidance on DeFi risk management provide frameworks to align decentralized designs with institutional governance. Compliance metadata can be attached to each transaction, allowing auditors to verify adherence without compromising confidentiality. These hybrid trust designs balance regulatory transparency with user autonomy, facilitating adoption by both institutional and retail participants.

3.6.3 Industrial automation and cyber-physical systems in Web X.0

Industrial automation in Web X.0 integrates intelligent control, decentralized communication, and semantic compatibility across cyber-physical systems (CPS). It extends beyond the Industrial Internet of Things (IIoT) by incorporating distributed intelligence, real-time data analytics, and autonomous decision-making within connected industrial networks. Web X.0 introduces an architecture in which edge intelligence, digital twins, and blockchain-enabled traceability converge to form adaptive, secure, and sustainable industrial ecosystems. This section outlines the design principles, data flows, and enabling technologies that underpin intelligent industrial automation on Web X.0.

3.6.3.1 Architecture of intelligent industrial systems

The Web X.0 industrial architecture is organized into four functional layers that operate in coordination through decentralized and interoperable protocols:

- Perception and edge layer: Includes sensors, actuators, and embedded AI modules for real-time perception and control. Edge computing nodes execute local inference to minimize latency and bandwidth consumption.
- Network and middleware layer: Employs time-sensitive networking (TSN) and WoT standards for interoperable data exchange. DIDs ensure device-level authentication and traceability.
- Digital twin layer: Maintains virtual representations of physical assets and processes for monitoring, simulation, and optimization.
- Cognitive coordination layer: Hosts multi-agent systems and predictive analytics that autonomously orchestrate production, maintenance, and logistics.

This layered structure ensures compatibility and fault tolerance while maintaining the real-time responsiveness required for mission-critical operations.

3.6.3.2 Digital twins and predictive intelligence

Digital twins are virtual models that mirror the state and behavior of physical systems. In Web X.0, these twins evolve into intelligent agents capable of self-learning and collaboration. They combine real-time sensor data with simulation models to predict system degradation, energy usage, or process anomalies [91]. AI-driven predictive analytics enable condition-based maintenance (CBM) and dynamic scheduling. For instance, recurrent neural networks (RNNs) and graph convolutional networks (GCNs) can analyze temporal-spatial data for fault prediction in manufacturing networks.

Example flow: A robotic assembly line is represented by a network of digital twins synchronized through an OPC UA, compliant middleware. Each twin processes the real-time vibration and temperature data locally. When a deviation in motor torque is detected, the system predicts a failure risk using a pre-trained LSTM model. The result triggers an automated maintenance workflow and updates the blockchain-based maintenance record.

This interaction demonstrates how digital twins and AI merge to achieve operational resilience and reduced downtime.

3.6.3.3 Decentralized trust and data provenance in industrial networks

Industrial CPS requires reliable traceability and data integrity across distributed nodes. Blockchain and decentralized ledgers address this need by creating tamper-evident records of production, maintenance, and logistics activities. Smart contracts can automate supplier validation, part certification, and warranty management. Decentralized trust further extends to cross-organizational compatibility through W3C VCs and DIDs. Each asset or subsystem maintains a verifiable identity, enabling authenticated interaction within a shared ecosystem [84].

Example flow: When a new component is introduced to the production line, its digital certificate is validated through a DID registry. Smart contracts log provenance and verify compliance with ISO/IEC 62443 cybersecurity standards. The entire lifecycle, from component creation to deployment, is cryptographically traceable.

This decentralized provenance model eliminates a single point of failure and provides end-to-end auditability across the supply chain.

3.6.3.4 Human–machine collaboration and safety assurance

Web X.0 emphasizes the integration of human experience and automated intelligence in collaborative industrial environments. Human–machine collaboration (HMC) interfaces employ augmented reality (AR) and natural-language systems to guide operators in decision-making. Context-aware AI agents adapt instructions to human proficiency and situational demands [92]. Safety is ensured through a combination of formal verification and runtime monitoring. The IEEE P7009 standard for fail-safe design defines principles for autonomous operation under fault conditions. Systems continuously evaluate risk indicators, and when anomalies exceed safe thresholds, fallback modes or human intervention are triggered.

Example flow: In an automated warehouse, mobile robots navigate using decentralized control algorithms. When a navigation model exhibits uncertainty due to sensor occlusion, a safety agent intervenes, switching to a pre-verified fallback plan and notifying the human operator through AR interface. The rationale for the event and the decision are logged through the PROV-O.

These adaptive safety mechanisms enable trust and accountability in autonomous industrial environments.

3.6.3.5 Sustainability and energy efficiency in industrial AI

Energy optimization is a central objective of Web X.0 industrial automation. The orchestration of AI-based workload dynamically balances computational and physical energy demands, supporting sustainability objectives consistent with ISO 50001 energy management guidelines. Federated learning and edge inference reduce the carbon footprint by minimizing data transfer and centralized computation. Adaptive scheduling algorithms allocate manufacturing tasks based on renewable energy availability, contributing to the broader UN Sustainable Development Goals (SDGs 7 and 13) [93].

By integrating predictive control, decentralized coordination, and lifecycle accountability, Web X.0 industrial systems achieve sustainability alongside operational excellence.

3.6.4 Government and public-sector applications in Web X.0

Web X.0 technologies have the potential to transform public-sector governance and operations by introducing intelligent automation, decentralized trust, and transparent decision-making. Governments increasingly rely on the digital infrastructure to deliver services, enforce compliance, and engage citizens. The integration of AI, blockchain, and verifiable data frameworks enhances these functions by improving efficiency, accountability, and inclusiveness.

3.6.4.1 Secure digital identity and authentication

Identity management forms the foundation of digital governance. Conventional identity systems rely on centralized databases vulnerable to breaches and unauthorized access. Web X.0 employs DID and VCs to create self-sovereign identity systems in which individuals control their credentials and share only the necessary information [69]. For public-sector use, such systems are aligned with international frameworks such as the European Union's eIDAS 2.0 regulation, which standardizes cross-border electronic identification and trust services. The combination of blockchain-based registries and zero-knowledge proofs (ZKPs) ensures verifiable but privacy-preserving identity verification [76].

Example flow: A citizen accesses an online tax service. The authentication process uses a DID issued by a government-certified provider. The user presents a verifiable credential that confirms residency without revealing other personal details. The service verifies authenticity on-chain and grants access automatically, logging the verification event as a signed transaction.

This decentralized authentication model increases resilience, compatibility, and public trust while reducing administrative overhead.

3.6.4.2 Data compatibility and intelligent public infrastructure

Government operations depend on the exchange of heterogeneous data across agencies and jurisdictions. Web X.0 extends data compatibility through semantic web technologies such as the Resource Description Framework (RDF) and Web Ontology Language (OWL), enabling machine-readable and context-aware data exchange [94]. The AI models integrated in public data platforms can detect trends, forecast demand, and optimize public resource allocation. Examples include AI-based traffic management, water-distribution networks, and energy grid optimization. When combined with the Internet of Things (IoT), these intelligent systems allow real-time decision-making based on verifiable data streams.

Example flow: A city's transportation authority integrates real-time data from sensors, ride-share applications, and public transit schedules. The combined data set, represented in the RDF, feeds an AI model that predicts congestion and recommends adaptive timings of traffic signals. These changes are communicated automatically through standardized APIs governed by W3C WoT specifications [95].

Such interoperable infrastructures enable transparent, data-driven public administration and contribute to sustainable urban governance.

3.6.4.3 Transparent governance and public accountability

Transparency and auditability are central to democratic governance. Web X.0 facilitates these objectives through blockchain-based recordkeeping, AI-enabled analytics, and verifiable data provenance. Smart contracts automate rule enforcement and public spending audits, while distributed ledgers ensure tamper-evident documentation of decisions [84]. Government agencies can employ DAOs to administer grants or manage collaborative projects transparently. Public procurement processes can also leverage verifiable ledgers to prevent fraud and ensure fair competition.

Example flow: A municipal government executes an infrastructure funding program using smart contracts. Each contract automatically releases funds upon verification of milestones recorded by third-party auditors on-chain. Citizens and oversight bodies can access a public dashboard that shows expenditures and project status in real time.

This transparency-by-design model strengthens institutional accountability, aligning with IEEE 7001-2021 standards for transparency in autonomous systems.

3.6.4.4 AI for policy decision support and civic engagement

AI-driven analytics enable governments to interpret datasets and make informed policy decisions. Predictive modeling can identify socioeconomic patterns, evaluate environmental impact, and estimate the outcomes of proposed policies. ML methods such as causal inference, reinforcement learning, and multi-objective optimization are applied to balance efficiency, equity, and sustainability.

Web X.0 extends these capabilities by coupling AI decision support with explainability and public engagement mechanisms. Citizens can interact with digital policy assistants that provide evidence-based explanations of proposed measures. AI systems designed under the IEEE P7000 framework emphasize ethical transparency, fairness, and accountability in civic technologies.

Example flow: A regional planning agency deploys an AI decision-support system to evaluate housing policy proposals. The system simulates demographic shifts and environmental effects, generating visual explanations accessible to both policymakers and citizens. Feedback from the public is integrated into an iterative policy cycle governed by transparent data provenance records.

This model exemplifies the participatory and data-driven governance principles promoted under Web X.0.

3.6.4.5 Resilient and secure public digital services

As digital governance expands, ensuring resilience and cybersecurity becomes essential. Web X.0 applies zero-trust principles, continuous verification of users, devices, and data flows, to safeguard public digital services [77]. Integration of decentralized storage (e.g., IPFS) and distributed ledgers ensures data persistence even under cyberattacks or infrastructure failures.

AI-driven anomaly detection systems identify potential threats and initiate automated countermeasures. Combined with verifiable credentials, these systems enable governments to maintain continuity of service during disruptions while adhering to privacy regulations and security standards such as ISO/IEC 27001.

Resilient designs support the development of digital governments capable of operating securely, transparently, and inclusively under diverse operational conditions.

3.6.5 Human–machine interaction and assistive systems in Web X.0

Human–machine interaction (HMI) in Web X.0 extends beyond conventional user interfaces to include intelligent, adaptive, and multimodal systems capable of understanding human context, intent, and emotion. These systems integrate AI, sensor fusion, and human-centered design principles to create assistive, trustworthy, and inclusive digital environments. The convergence of AI-driven personalization, ethical interaction design, and decentralized identity mechanisms allows Web X.0 to support seamless collaboration between humans and autonomous agents.

3.6.5.1 Architecture of adaptive human–machine systems

The architecture of HMI in Web X.0 is based on layered interaction models that combine perception, reasoning, and response. Adaptive interfaces continuously adapt to the cognitive, emotional, and physical states of users through multimodal sensing and learning.

- Perception layer: Captures user data through speech, vision, gesture, and physiological sensors. Edge processing ensures privacy and low latency.
- Cognitive layer: Employs AI models for intent recognition, context inference, and decision support.
- Interaction layer: Generates natural-language, graphical, or haptic responses based on personalization profiles and ethical interaction constraints.
- Trust and privacy layer: Integrates decentralized identity verification (DIDs and VCs) to authenticate users and control access to personal data.

This design ensures responsiveness, explainability, and privacy by combining human-centered design (ISO 9241-210) with AI governance standards such as IEEE P7008 for ethically driven nudging systems.

3.6.5.2 Multimodal interaction and context awareness

Multimodal systems in Web X.0 integrate speech, vision, and touch modalities to create natural and accessible user experiences. Context awareness enables systems to interpret environmental cues, such as location, activity, and social setting, to adapt responses accordingly. Deep learning methods for multimodal fusion, such as attention-based transformers, synthesize heterogeneous signals into unified representations [96]. These methods enhance emotion recognition, situational awareness, and adaptive feedback generation.

Example flow: A Web X.0 digital assistant interacts with an air traffic controller through speech and eye-tracking interfaces. When the system detects fatigue or stress through biosensors, it adjusts the alert frequencies and the brightness of the interface to reduce cognitive load. The assistant provides summarized updates while maintaining safety-critical responsiveness.

These adaptive interactions improve operational performance and accessibility while maintaining user control and awareness.

3.6.5.3 Assistive intelligence and inclusive design

Assistive systems extend the benefits of Web X.0 to individuals with disabilities or situational limitations. They rely on ML, computer vision, and natural language processing to provide personalized support. Key design principles include:

- Universal accessibility: Conformance with Web Content Accessibility Guidelines (WCAG 2.2) and ISO 9241-210 human-centered design standards.
- Adaptive assistance: Real-time adjustments based on user preferences, environment, and task complexity.
- Ethical transparency: Clear communication of the abilities, limitations, and use of the system.

Example flow: An AI-driven assistive navigation system for visually impaired users employs LiDAR and speech synthesis to describe the environment. The system uses decentralized credentials to verify access to restricted spaces, ensuring both autonomy and security.

3.6.5.4 Ethical and trustworthy interaction design

Trust and ethics are essential in HMI. AI systems must operate transparently and respect user autonomy. IEEE P7000 and P7010 standards define frameworks for ethical design, focusing on accountability, fairness, and well-being metrics [71].

Web X.0 extends these frameworks through verifiable interaction provenance, where each system action or recommendation is accompanied by metadata that describe the rationale of the decision and data sources. XAI techniques provide interpretable reasoning paths for users.

Example flow: A digital government portal uses an AI assistant to guide citizens through tax submissions. Each recommendation includes a "why this option" explanation generated by SHAP-based interpretation. Provenance metadata, encoded through W3C PROV-O, allows auditors to verify that no bias or unauthorized inference occurred.

Embedding ethical principles within system designs ensures compliance with emerging global standards for trustworthy AI while promoting public confidence in autonomous systems.

3.6.5.5 Cognitive collaboration and human augmentation

Web X.0 envisions a shift from automation to cognitive collaboration, where humans and AI agents function as partners. Cognitive augmentation involves realtime knowledge assistance, adaptive interfaces, and shared decision-making frameworks. In such environments, humans retain oversight while AI agents provide contextual reasoning and predictive support. This model is applicable in domains such as healthcare diagnostics, aviation control, and industrial maintenance.

Example flow: In a smart manufacturing environment, an engineer collaborates with an AI diagnostic agent that analyzes sensor data and suggests process adjustments. The engineer validates the proposal through a digital twin interface before execution. Both actions are logged in an immutable audit trail to maintain accountability.

This model shifts the role of automation from task replacement to amplification of human abilities, ensuring efficiency without loss of control.

3.7 Societal and sectoral implications

Building on the governance, ethical, and architectural foundations established in the preceding sections, this section examines how adaptive, bio-inspired, and hybrid intelligence paradigms operationalize these principles within Web X.0 systems.

3.7.1 Quantum computing and quantum-safe web

The security and computational foundations of Web X.0 systems face challenges that classical designs cannot fully address. Quantum computing introduces new paradigms of parallelism and optimization that can accelerate AI, encryption, and large-scale simulation. However, it also poses significant risks to existing cryptographic schemes. The emergence of the quantum-safe web, an internet infrastructure fortified against quantum threats, represents a central research and engineering direction for the coming decade.

Most contemporary web security protocols, including blockchain systems, rely on asymmetric encryption schemes such as RSA and elliptic curve cryptography (ECC). Quantum algorithms, particularly Shor's algorithm, can efficiently factor large integers and compute discrete logarithms, making these cryptographic foundations insecure once scalable quantum computers emerge [97]. This vulnerability extends to decentralized systems, where digital signatures and hash-based proof mechanisms underpin trust. To preserve the confidentiality and authenticity of Web X.0 transactions, migration toward post-quantum cryptographic (PQC) algorithms is necessary. These algorithms, based on mathematical problems such as lattice-based, code-based, and multivariate polynomial systems, resist attacks by both classical and quantum adversaries [98].

A key priority for Web X.0 development is the integration of quantum-safe algorithms into identity verification, secure communication, and blockchain protocols while maintaining backward compatibility and performance efficiency.

3.7.1.1 Quantum-safe cryptography and standardization

Post-quantum cryptography forms the foundation of the quantum-safe web. The National Institute of Standards and Technology (NIST) Post-Quantum Cryptography Standardization Project has identified several algorithms for public-key encryption and digital signatures, including CRYSTALS-Kyber and CRYSTALS-Dilithium [99]. The finalized NIST post-quantum standards are ML-KEM/FIPS 203, ML-DSA/FIPS 204, and SLH-DSA/FIPS 205. Integration within Web X.0 designs involves updating protocols such as Transport Layer Security (TLS) and DID authentication with PQC primitives. For decentralized identity management, hybrid schemes can combine classical and quantum-resistant keys, ensuring gradual migration across heterogeneous infrastructures.

Example flow: A decentralized identity provider issues a verifiable credential signed using CRYSTALS-Dilithium. A Web X.0 service verifies the credential using a hybrid TLS session that supports both RSA and Kyber key exchange. The verified credential is recorded on a blockchain employing lattice-based digital signatures, ensuring long-term resistance to quantum attacks.

Beyond cryptographic implications, quantum computing presents opportunities for advancing AI-driven automation and optimization on Web X.0. Quantum algorithms can accelerate model training, combinatorial optimization, and high-dimensional data processing by exploiting quantum parallelism and entanglement [100]. Applications include:

- Quantum machine learning (QML): Hybrid classical, quantum models that improve learning efficiency and generalization for large datasets.
- Quantum optimization: Variational quantum algorithms for supply-chain management, network routing, and resource scheduling in distributed systems.
- Quantum simulation: Modeling of processes in Web X.0 applications relevant to materials science, logistics, and energy optimization.

Hybrid computation models, such as those that combine GPUs, tensor-processing units (TPUs), and quantum-processing units (QPUs), allow Web X.0 infrastructures to dynamically allocate computational tasks based on resource efficiency and precision requirements.

Quantum networking enables the transmission of quantum information using photons as carriers, allowing for intrinsically secure communication through quantum key distribution (QKD). The QKD protocols, including BB84 and E91, provide provable security based on principles of quantum mechanics rather than computational hardness [101]. Integrating QKD into Web X.0 supports long-term confidentiality for government, industrial, and critical infrastructure communications. Combined with decentralized identity and PQC, quantum networking forms a layered defense mechanism.

Example flow: A national data center establishes a QKD link between administrative nodes. Encryption keys generated through BB84 are used to authenticate blockchain consensus messages and to secure AI model updates transmitted between institutions. The result is a communication fabric with measurable quantum-level assurance of confidentiality.

Current research explores hybrid infrastructures where quantum and classical nodes cooperate within the same distributed ledger, ensuring future-proofing without requiring full quantum infrastructure deployment.

Transitioning to quantum-safe Web X.0 requires coordinated technical, policy, and compatibility efforts. Governments and standardization bodies such as ISO/IEC JTC 1/SC 27, NIST, and ETSI are developing frameworks to guide migration strategies. Key steps include:

- Inventory and classification of cryptographic assets susceptible to quantum attacks.
- Deployment of hybrid cryptographic protocols that combine PQC and classical encryption during the transition period.
- Development of quantum-secure key management and identity infrastructures compatible with decentralized designs.
- Establishment of certification and compliance mechanisms for PQC implementation [102].

This coordinated migration will define the next era of web infrastructure, where quantum resilience, computational acceleration, and intelligent automation converge to sustain security and performance in the post-quantum world.

3.7.2 Neuromorphic and edge-cognitive designs

Neuromorphic and edge-cognitive designs are key enablers of Web X.0, allowing intelligent automation to operate efficiently, securely, and responsively at the network's edge. These designs emulate the computational principles of biological neural systems to achieve low-latency perception, adaptive learning, and energy efficiency. In the Web X.0 context, neuromorphic systems interact seamlessly with decentralized infrastructures, forming context-aware self-organizing networks that process information locally while maintaining global coordination.

3.7.2.1 Principles of neuromorphic computing

Neuromorphic computing systems replicate neural mechanisms such as event-driven communication, parallel processing, and synaptic plasticity to perform real-time inference with minimal energy consumption. The conventional von Neumann designs separate memory and computation. Neuromorphic systems, on the other hand, integrate both in co-located designs inspired by the brain's efficiency [103]. At the device level, neuromorphic processors use spiking neural networks (SNNs) in which information is represented as discrete spikes rather than continuous activations. This event-driven approach enables high temporal resolution and ultra-low power operation. Synaptic plasticity models, such as Spike-Timing-Dependent Plasticity (STDP), allow networks to adapt autonomously without centralized training [104].

In the Web X.0 ecosystem, these properties support on-device intelligence for applications that require immediate implementation, such as robotics, industrial control, and autonomous decision-making.

3.7.2.2 Edge-cognitive processing and distributed intelligence

Edge-cognitive designs extend neuromorphic processing abilities across distributed nodes. These systems combine low-power AI computation with local data processing, reducing reliance on centralized cloud infrastructure. The result is reduced latency, improved data privacy, and improved scalability [68]. Edge nodes can execute lightweight inference tasks, while model training or coordination occurs at higher layers of the network hierarchy. Hybrid neuromorphic, edge designs leverage spiking processors for event-driven tasks and digital accelerators for deep learning-based inference [105].

Example flow: A fleet of autonomous drones employs edge-cognitive nodes powered by neuromorphic chips. Each drone processes sensor input locally for obstacle avoidance and navigation using SNNs. Similarly, global mission optimization occurs through a cloud-based orchestrator that exchanges only compressed model parameters, preserving bandwidth and data privacy.

This distributed intelligence model allows real-time decision-making without compromising system-wide synchronization or trust.

3.7.2.3 Hardware platforms and emerging technologies

Several neuromorphic hardware platforms have demonstrated practical abilities for Web X.0 environments. Intel's Loihi 2, IBM's TrueNorth, and SpiNNaker from the University of Manchester represent different design approaches to large-scale event-driven computation. These platforms achieve energy reductions of up to three orders of magnitude compared to traditional GPU-based inference systems [103,106]. Recent advances in memristor-based and resistive random-access memory (ReRAM) devices further enable compact, analog synaptic implementations. These non-volatile memory technologies support local learning and continual adaptation without frequent data transfers.

Integration with standard web protocols is facilitated by the development of APIs for neuromorphic-as-a-service (NaaS), enabling distributed access to neuromorphic resources across Web X.0 infrastructures. Such hardware diversity allows Web X.0 systems to balance computational efficiency, adaptability, and scalability across heterogeneous networks.

3.7.2.4 Algorithms for edge learning and adaptation

Neuromorphic systems rely on biologically inspired algorithms optimized for asynchronous and spiking computation. Event-based learning rules, such as STDP,

Hebbian learning, and reinforcement-driven spike modulation, enable agents to learn from sparse feedback and operate in continuously changing environments [107]. In edge-cognitive systems, federated learning is extended to accommodate spiking networks, allowing decentralized nodes to update shared models while preserving data locality [108]. Reinforcement-based mechanisms also support continual adaptation in non-stationary conditions, improving fault tolerance and self-organization.

Example flow: An industrial edge network monitors machinery using neuromorphic sensors. Each sensor node adapts its model parameters locally based on the detected vibration patterns. Global aggregation of synaptic updates occurs periodically, forming a consensus model that optimizes performance without transmitting raw data. These adaptive algorithms form the basis for autonomous and context-sensitive intelligence within the distributed Web X.0 infrastructure.

Integration of neuromorphic and edge-cognitive systems into Web X.0 requires compatibility between heterogeneous devices, secure communication, and standardization of data representation. W3C's WoT framework and IETF edge computing standards provide mechanisms for describing, discovering, and coordinating intelligent devices through uniform APIs [95]. The convergence of neuromorphic processing, edge intelligence, and decentralized coordination defines a scalable model for intelligent, sustainable, and adaptive Web X.0 infrastructures.

3.7.3 Bio-inspired and self-organizing web platforms

The evolution of Web X.0 increasingly draws inspiration from biological systems to achieve autonomy, adaptability, and resilience. Bio-inspired and self-organizing designs replicate mechanisms found in natural ecosystems, such as swarm intelligence, homeostasis, and evolution, to coordinate distributed agents and optimize system performance without centralized control [109,110]. These systems are designed to manage the growing complexity of Web X.0 networks, allowing scalable adaptation across billions of heterogeneous devices.

3.7.3.1 Foundations of bio-inspired computing in Web X.0

Bio-inspired computing employs principles derived from biological and ecological systems to design decentralized, adaptive algorithms capable of solving problems in dynamic environments. The foundational paradigms include evolutionary computation, swarm intelligence, and artificial immune systems [111]. In Web X.0, these mechanisms support the coordination of autonomous agents, the optimization of distributed resources, and fault tolerance in large-scale web ecosystems. For instance, swarm intelligence techniques enable decentralized load balancing and routing among distributed nodes, while evolutionary algorithms adapt network protocols to fluctuating demand or failures.

These biologically grounded mechanisms provide Web X.0 systems with self-regulatory abilities that parallel the resilience of natural ecosystems.

3.7.3.2 Swarm intelligence and distributed coordination

Swarm intelligence models, exemplified by algorithms of ant colony optimization (ACO), particle swarm optimization (PSO), and artificial bee colony (ABC), enable cooperative problem-solving through simple agent interactions governed by local rules [112]. In Web X.0, swarm-based coordination supports dynamic resource allocation, decentralized data caching, and adaptive service discovery. Agents exchange minimal information through stigmergic communication, modifying their environment to influence others, reducing the need for centralized orchestration.

Example flow: A network of autonomous IoT gateways uses a swarm-based protocol to balance computational loads. Each gateway evaluates local conditions (e.g., bandwidth, latency, and energy levels) and broadcasts limited status updates. Neighboring nodes adjust their task loads based on these cues, collectively achieving near-optimal distribution without centralized coordination.

Such distributed coordination mechanisms are resilient to node failures and scalable to vast, heterogeneous networks, a defining feature of Web X.0.

3.7.3.3 Evolutionary and developmental algorithms for web adaptation

Evolutionary algorithms simulate natural selection to iteratively refine solutions based on performance feedback. In Web X.0, these algorithms are used to evolve service designs, optimize communication protocols, and improve neural network structures autonomously [113,114]. Neuroevolution, a subset of evolutionary computation, optimizes neural designs and hyperparameters, allowing Web X.0 agents to adapt in real time. Coevolutionary strategies extend this concept by evolving interacting populations of models or protocols to improve cooperation and robustness in multi-agent ecosystems.

Example flow: A decentralized cloud infrastructure evolves its service deployment policies using multi-objective evolutionary optimization. Fitness metrics include latency, energy efficiency, and reliability. Over successive iterations, the algorithm discovers configurations that balance competing objectives, autonomously adapting to varying workloads.

These adaptive mechanisms contribute to the self-healing and self-optimizing behavior of Web X.0 systems.

3.7.3.4 Artificial immune systems and cyber-resilience

Artificial immune systems (AISs) replicate biological immune mechanisms for anomaly detection and adaptive defense. They employ pattern recognition, self–nonself discrimination, and immune memory to identify threats in evolving digital ecosystems [115]. In Web X.0, AIS frameworks monitor distributed agents, detect abnormal patterns in traffic or behavior, and initiate localized containment responses. This decentralized resilience model complements traditional cybersecurity systems by providing continuous, self-adaptive protection.

Example flow: A Web X.0 cloud network implements an AIS to detect anomalous behavior. When a node exhibits unusual data access patterns, neighboring nodes collectively assess and suppress the anomaly through distributed quarantine protocols. The system learns from the event to refine its recognition models for future incidents.

Such self-defensive abilities are crucial for maintaining trust and operational continuity in intelligent, autonomous web environments.

3.7.3.5 Self-organization and homeostatic regulation

Self-organization refers to the spontaneous emergence of order through local interactions among components without external control. In Web X.0, self-organizing systems enable dynamic topology management, service orchestration, and fault recovery through feedback loops analogous to biological homeostasis [116]. Key regulatory mechanisms include:

- Feedback control: Balances resource allocation and performance across distributed systems.
- Stigmergy: Agents modify shared digital environments to influence collective behavior.
- Homeostasis: Maintains operational stability under variable loads and disruptions.

Example flow: A large-scale content distribution network (CDN) employs self-organizing caching policies. Nodes continuously adjust replication and eviction rates based on demand feedback, achieving optimal bandwidth utilization without centralized scheduling.

While bio-inspired systems emphasize decentralized emergence and autonomy, many Web X.0 applications require these adaptive capabilities to remain tightly coupled with human judgment, accountability, and intent.

3.7.4 Hybrid intelligence and collaborative autonomy

Hybrid intelligence represents the integration of human cognition and AI within socio-technical systems. In the context of Web X.0, it defines a framework in which humans, machines, and autonomous agents collaborate to achieve shared goals through complementary strengths. This model emphasizes adaptive decision-making, ethical alignment, and collective problem-solving. Collaborative autonomy extends these principles, allowing distributed intelligent agents to operate independently while maintaining coherence through shared objectives, trust mechanisms, and governance protocols. Hybrid intelligence is based on continuous learning and co-adaptation between humans and machines [117]. Humans contribute to interpretability, ethical judgment, and problem contextualization, while AI provides analytical depth, automation, and real-time adaptation.

Within Web X.0, hybrid intelligence facilitates decision-making across domains such as policy design, cybersecurity, and distributed manufacturing. The interaction between humans and autonomous agents occurs through transparent interfaces that support trust, explainability, and accountability [118]. This model aligns with IEEE P7000 standards in ethically aligned design, emphasizing human oversight and value-sensitive integration of AI technologies.

3.7.4.1 Architecture of hybrid intelligence in Web X.0

The architecture supporting hybrid intelligence in Web X.0 consists of three primary layers:

- Perception and interaction layer: Captures multimodal inputs (speech, gestures, and physiological data) and provides intuitive interfaces for human–AI collaboration.
- Cognitive and decision layer: Integrates symbolic reasoning with ML to enable explainable decision support. Hybrid models such as neuro-symbolic systems bridge structured logic with deep learning inference [119].
- Coordination and trust layer: Manages task delegation, accountability, and ethical constraints through decentralized governance mechanisms (e.g., verifiable smart contracts, reputation-based trust systems).

The architecture emphasizes compatibility through W3C standards such as RDF and the Web Ontology Language (OWL), ensuring semantic transparency in interactions between humans and intelligent agents.

Collaborative autonomy refers to systems of distributed agents capable of independent operation while maintaining collective coherence through shared objectives and communication protocols. Multi-agent coordination on Web X.0 is based on distributed consensus, reputation systems, and dynamic coalition formation [120]. Agents interact using standardized ontologies and verifiable message formats, enabling cross-domain collaboration. Mechanisms such as contract-based task allocation and distributed reinforcement learning (DRL) allow adaptive coordination in uncertain or changing environments.

Example flow: A fleet of autonomous vehicles connected through the Web X.0 infrastructure cooperatively manages traffic flow. Each vehicle optimizes its route using DRL while exchanging status information through secure DIDs. Consensus algorithms ensure that local decisions align with global traffic optimization goals.

In human-centric Web X.0 systems, hybrid intelligence is not merely a collaborative paradigm but an explicit design strategy to allocate authority, responsibility, and oversight between humans and autonomous agents.

Example flow: In an industrial Web X.0 environment, a human operator collaborates with an AI maintenance assistant. When anomalies occur, AI suggests diagnostic actions and presents its reasoning through visual explanations. The operator validates or corrects these recommendations, and the AI incorporates this feedback to refine future predictions.

From an operational perspective, the human-centric instantiation of hybrid intelligence unfolds across three tightly coupled dimensions: authority, trust, and accountability. Hybrid intelligence in Web X.0 requires ethical and governance frameworks that align autonomous decision-making with human values. Decentralized governance mechanisms employ distributed ledgers and verifiable credentials to ensure transparent accountability [121]. Ethical AI models encode normative constraints, such as fairness, privacy, and inclusivity, into decision-making processes. Multi-stakeholder governance models use participatory decision platforms that enable collective input from humans and intelligent agents in policy formation.

Example flow: A smart-city energy management system employs a hybrid intelligence model for grid optimization. AI algorithms recommend load-balancing strategies, while a decentralized governance protocol allows human stakeholders to review and approve final adjustments based on fairness and sustainability criteria.

The convergence of quantum, neuromorphic, and bio-inspired computing represents a fundamental shift in the computational foundation of Web X.0. These paradigms, though distinct in origin, share core objectives: massive parallelism, energy efficiency, and resilience. When combined, they enable cognitive and self-organizing digital ecosystems capable of continuous learning and autonomous decision making. Classical computing models face increasing limitations in processing power, energy efficiency, and adaptability as web infrastructures expand in scale and complexity. Quantum, neuromorphic, and bio-inspired computing, each addresses different aspects of these constraints. Quantum computing offers exponential speedups in optimization and cryptography; neuromorphic computing delivers low-power, event-driven inference; and bio-inspired algorithms enable distributed adaptation and resilience [112].

Integrating these technologies provides a pathway toward hybrid designs that combine symbolic reasoning, probabilistic inference, and emergent self-organization. This integration forms the computational substrate for intelligent, self-managing Web X.0 infrastructures. A converged Web X.0 architecture integrates heterogeneous computational models through three synergistic layers:

- Quantum intelligence layer: Executes high-dimensional optimization, encryption, and probabilistic inference tasks using quantum processors or simulators.
- Neuromorphic cognitive layer: Performs event-driven inference, pattern recognition, and real-time control using spiking neural networks (SNNs) embedded at the edge.
- Bio-inspired coordination layer: Enables decentralized learning, self-organization, and multi-agent adaptation through swarm intelligence and evolutionary algorithms.

Each layer operates autonomously yet cooperatively through standardized communication protocols and distributed knowledge graphs. Quantum-classical interfaces manage data translation between probabilistic and symbolic representations, while neuromorphic agents execute context-aware actions locally.

3.7.4.2 Quantum-neuromorphic integration

Quantum-neuromorphic integration combines quantum-enhanced computation with the adaptive energy efficiency of neuromorphic systems. QML methods accelerate the training of spiking neural networks by encoding temporal dynamics into quantum states, enabling rapid convergence in high-dimensional search spaces [100]. Hybrid processors equipped with quantum processing units (QPUs) and neuromorphic cores execute tasks such as dynamic optimization, cognitive modeling, and anomaly detection at unprecedented efficiency. Quantum synaptic models, where qubit-based operations emulate probabilistic synaptic weights, have shown potential in reproducing stochastic learning behaviors observed in biological neural systems.

Example flow: A global cybersecurity monitoring network employs a hybrid quantum-neuromorphic framework. Quantum algorithms detect cryptographic anomalies in encrypted traffic, while neuromorphic agents analyze behavioral patterns in real time. The combined results are fed into a reinforcement-based decision layer, improving predictive defense accuracy.

This convergence delivers high-level insight and rapid, energy-efficient response in distributed Web X.0 infrastructures.

3.7.4.3 Bio-inspired quantum and neuromorphic synergy

Bio-inspired models provide the organizing principles necessary to coordinate quantum and neuromorphic systems at scale. Evolutionary algorithms can optimize quantum circuit configurations, while swarm intelligence principles enable load balancing among distributed neuromorphic agents [113]. In this context, self-organization is operationalized through concrete adaptation mechanisms. For instance, artificial immune networks can dynamically reconfigure system connections to maintain functionality during hardware degradation or cyberattacks [115].

Example flow: In a decentralized data center, bio-inspired coordination algorithms distribute computational tasks across neuromorphic and quantum nodes. When a node exhibits anomalous latency, a swarm-based mechanism reallocates its workload, maintaining equilibrium without centralized intervention.

Despite promising advances, significant challenges remain in the realization of convergent designs for Web X.0:

- Compatibility: Establishing standard interfaces between quantum, neuromorphic, and bio-inspired systems remains an open research problem.
- Scalability: Scaling hybrid networks while maintaining coherence, synchronization, and fault tolerance requires new theoretical and engineering approaches.
- Explainability: The combined non-deterministic behavior of these systems complicates interpretability and verification.
- Energy efficiency: Integrating energy-efficient neuromorphic hardware with high-power quantum systems requires adaptive resource management strategies.

Ongoing research focuses on creating middleware frameworks that abstract computational complexity, allowing hybrid systems to communicate through unified semantic layers [108]. The development of AI-driven orchestration tools capable of dynamically allocating tasks across quantum, neuromorphic, and bio-inspired resources will define the operational maturity of Web X.0.

3.8 Outlook and open challenges

3.8.1 Ethical governance and digital trust in Web X.0

The expansion of Web X.0 into an intelligent, decentralized, and autonomous ecosystem requires a new foundation for ethical governance and digital trust. As intelligent agents, decentralized protocols, and automated decision systems interact on a global scale, ensuring accountability, transparency, and fairness becomes critical. Ethical governance refers to the structured oversight of these systems to align technological development with societal values, human rights, and sustainable goals. Digital trust, in turn, represents the assurance that data, algorithms, and automated actions can be verified, explained, and held accountable.

Ethical governance in Web X.0 builds on established principles of responsible AI and digital ethics, namely transparency, fairness, accountability, and inclusivity [72]. These principles must be operationalized across both technological and institutional layers. The complexity of Web X.0 necessitates governance models that can dynamically adapt to the decentralized and autonomous nature of emerging technologies. Frameworks such as the IEEE Global Initiative on Ethics of Autonomous and Intelligent Systems and the European Union's AI Act emphasize value-sensitive design, continuous risk assessment, and human oversight [71]. These frameworks guide developers, organizations, and policymakers in integrating ethical evaluation throughout the system lifecycle, from model design and data collection to deployment and maintenance. Ethical governance in Web X.0 is not static, but continuous, requiring monitoring systems capable of detecting biases, deviations, or unintended consequences in real time.

Digital trust in Web X.0 is founded on verifiability, transparency, and consistency across interactions between humans, machines, and organizations. Trust mechanisms must enable all participants to authenticate identities, verify data integrity, and audit decision-making processes. Distributed ledger technologies (DLT), including blockchain, play a central role in establishing immutable and transparent records of transactions and system actions [84]. Complementary standards such as DIDs and VCs support authenticated yet privacy-preserving identity verification across decentralized systems [69]. XAI frameworks further enhance digital trust by providing interpretable reasoning for automated decisions. Such explanations must balance clarity and complexity, ensuring that stakeholders can understand system logic without compromising performance or confidentiality [122]. These complementary technologies, immutable records, verifiable identities, and explainable reasoning, together establish the infrastructure for accountability and confidence within the Web X.0.

3.8.1.1 Ethical decision-making in autonomous systems

As Web X.0 expands into domains involving autonomous decision-making, such as governance automation, financial systems, and digital public services, ethical reasoning must be embedded within the system itself. Autonomous agents must be able to evaluate moral trade-offs, apply regulatory constraints, and incorporate contextdependent norms during operation. This necessitates the integration of computational ethics, including formal logic models of moral reasoning, multi-objective optimization with ethical constraints, and ML models aligned with normative datasets. Decision processes must remain transparent, traceable, and auditable, ensuring that responsibility can be assigned even in distributed environments.

Example flow: A decentralized loan approval system uses an AI-driven decision engine to assess creditworthiness. Ethical reasoning modules evaluate fairness metrics across demographic groups. If disparities exceed thresholds, the system flags the model for human review. The full decision chain, including data sources and algorithmic explanations, is recorded through a blockchain-based provenance ledger for regulatory audit.

Embedding ethical reasoning into automated systems allows Web X.0 infrastructures to maintain fairness, compliance, and transparency while operating autonomously.

3.8.1.2 Regulatory and standardization frameworks

Global standardization and regulation are essential to achieve compatibility and ethical coherence in Web X.0. Initiatives such as ISO/IEC JTC 1/SC 42 on AI standards, IEEE P7000 series, and W3C decentralized trust frameworks provide guidance for developers and institutions in implementing accountability and compliance mechanisms [123]. Emerging policy frameworks focus on algorithmic transparency, data sovereignty, and cross-border compatibility. Governments and international organizations are increasingly mandating algorithmic audits, human-in-the-loop controls, and explainability requirements for critical decision-making systems.

Example flow: A cross-border digital health platform operating under Web X.0 adheres to ISO/IEC AI governance standards. Patient data transfers comply with both GDPR and HIPAA requirements. AI-based diagnostics undergo periodic transparency assessments per IEEE 7001-2021, and results are logged in verifiable digital audit trails.

Adherence to harmonized standards ensures that Web X.0 systems remain globally interoperable, auditable, and aligned with ethical and legal obligations.

3.8.1.3 Future directions for trustworthy Web X.0 systems

The long-term evolution of ethical governance and digital trust in Web X.0 will depend on the co-development of technical standards, institutional mechanisms, and public trust. Emerging directions include:

- Ethical-by-design frameworks: Integrating ethical constraints into system architecture rather than retrofitting governance.

- Adaptive governance: Real-time monitoring and policy adaptation through AI-driven compliance systems.
- Collective oversight: Multi-stakeholder participation in auditing and feedback, integrating citizens, developers, and regulators.
- Algorithmic assurance tools: Formal verification and certification of AI-driven processes within critical infrastructures.

By combining transparency, ethical reasoning, and formal assurance, Web X.0 can mature into an ecosystem of verifiable, human-centered digital trust, balancing autonomy with accountability.

3.8.2 Privacy, security, and data sovereignty in Web X.0

Web X.0 introduces a dynamic environment in which data, computation, and intelligence are distributed across decentralized infrastructures. In this context, privacy, security, and data sovereignty become foundational pillars that determine the system's resilience and legitimacy. The earlier generations of the web, which relied on centralized governance and storage. Web X.0 must guaranty trust and compliance in environments that lack single authorities.

3.8.2.1 Foundations of privacy and security in Web X.0

The distributed nature of Web X.0 redefines the security perimeter: data are no longer confined to centralized servers but flow continuously across autonomous agents, edge devices, and decentralized networks. Traditional security paradigms based on perimeter defense are insufficient for this environment [124]. Web X.0 security frameworks are grounded in four interdependent principles:

- Confidentiality: Ensure that only authorized entities can access sensitive information.
- Integrity: Guaranty that data and system states remain unchanged during transmission and processing.
- Availability: Maintain system operability and access despite attacks or disruptions.
- Accountability: Provide verifiable logs and mechanisms to attribute actions to entities within decentralized infrastructures.

Privacy, meanwhile, is embedded in the system architecture through Privacy-by-Design (PbD) principles, mandating proactive, default, and transparent protection mechanisms [125]. Together, these principles establish a holistic security foundation that aligns technological innovation with ethical and regulatory obligations.

3.8.2.2 Decentralized security designs

Decentralization fundamentally alters security designs by distributing trust and removing single points of failure. Web X.0 systems employ blockchain and distributed ledger technologies (DLTs) to achieve integrity and transparency without relying on centralized authorities [84]. Smart contracts provide automated, verifiable enforcement of security and compliance rules. Coupled with cryptographic identity frameworks such as DIDs and VCs, users and agents can authenticate securely and maintain data ownership.

Example flow: A Web X.0 healthcare network uses the blockchain to store encrypted medical transaction logs. Patients control access through DIDs. When a researcher requests data, a smart contract verifies credentials and grants temporary anonymized access, ensuring both utility and privacy.

These designs create tamper-evident audit trails and reduce systemic risks while supporting cross-domain compatibility.

3.8.2.3 Data sovereignty and cross-border governance

Data sovereignty refers to the right of individuals, organizations, and nations to control how their data are collected, processed, and shared within defined legal and ethical boundaries. In Web X.0, where data transcend jurisdictions, maintaining sovereignty requires technical and policy-level mechanisms. Federated and distributed data frameworks enable local data processing without centralized aggregation, aligning with legal frameworks such as the EU General Data Protection Regulation (GDPR) and regional data residency laws. Federated learning allows global model training while preserving local control of datasets, combining compliance with efficiency.

Example flow: A multinational enterprise deploys a federated analytics framework in regional data centers. Each center trains local models using its data. Only the model parameters, not the raw data, are shared globally. Governance policies enforce jurisdictional constraints and audit access across all participating nodes.

Through localized computation and global coordination, Web X.0 systems can maintain compliance while preserving the integrity of global innovation networks.

3.8.2.4 Cybersecurity and threat mitigation in intelligent environments

The intelligent and autonomous nature of Web X.0 increases exposure to sophisticated cyber threats, including adversarial ML, data poisoning, and autonomous malware. Addressing these requires continuous, adaptive, and intelligence-driven defense systems.

Key strategies include:

- ZTA: Every device, user, and process is continuously authenticated and validated [77].
- AI-enhanced security: ML models predict, detect, and mitigate anomalies in real time.
- Resilient autonomy: Redundant and self-healing subsystems preserve operational continuity during attacks.

Example flow: In a Web X.0 industrial network, edge nodes employ anomaly detection models to monitor sensor data streams. When irregularities suggest a cyberattack, the system automatically isolates compromised nodes, initiates a blockchain-recorded alert, and reconfigures control paths to maintain production safety [126].

By embedding adaptive intelligence into security frameworks, Web X.0 systems can dynamically respond to evolving threats while minimizing downtime.

3.8.2.5 Privacy-preserving computation and secure analytics

As Web X.0 systems increasingly rely on large-scale analytics and AI, maintaining privacy during computation becomes essential. Privacy-preserving computation techniques such as homomorphic encryption, secure multi-party computation (SMPC), and differential privacy allow data analysis without direct exposure of sensitive content [127]. These methods support decentralized collaboration among untrusted entities while protecting confidentiality. Homomorphic encryption allows computations on encrypted data; SMPC enables distributed parties to compute joint results without revealing inputs; and differential privacy ensures that analytical outputs cannot identify individual records.

Example flow: A consortium of financial institutions collaborates to detect fraud using a joint AI model. Each institution encrypts transaction data using homomorphic encryption and contributes encrypted updates to the global model. The final insights improve fraud detection rates without compromising any participant's proprietary data.

3.8.3 Regulatory compliance and global policy harmonization in Web X.0

As Web X.0 evolves into a decentralized and intelligent digital ecosystem, its governance extends beyond national boundaries. The interconnection of autonomous agents, blockchain infrastructures, and AI-driven services requires regulatory frameworks that are coherent, adaptive, and globally interoperable. Regulatory compliance ensures adherence to established standards and laws, while policy harmonization aligns diverse regional approaches into a unified, ethical, and secure global web.

3.8.3.1 The need for global policy harmonization

The global scope of Web X.0 operations complicates the enforcement of digital policies designed for specific jurisdictions. Data transactions, AI decision-making, and DeFi systems often cross national borders without clear legal accountability. Fragmented regulatory environments increase the risk of conflict, inefficiency, and uncertainty for developers and users alike [128].

A harmonized policy framework is essential to address these challenges. It would enable consistent standards for privacy, cybersecurity, and AI governance while preserving the flexibility of local laws. Collaborative efforts among international bodies such as the International Telecommunication Union (ITU), the Organization for Economic Co-operation and Development (OECD), and the World Economic Forum (WEF) are working toward shared ethical and technical principles for emerging digital technologies [129].

Global policy harmonization serves as the foundation for equitable participation in the digital economy while safeguarding fundamental rights and values.

3.8.3.2 Regulatory frameworks for AI and autonomous systems

AI is a defining feature of Web X.0, and its responsible deployment depends on structured regulatory oversight. The European Union's AI Act, the United States' National AI Initiative Act, and the OECD's AI Principles establish frameworks for risk-based regulation, transparency, and accountability [72].

Key provisions across these frameworks include:

- Risk classification: Categorizing AI applications according to potential societal or ethical impact.
- Transparency and explainability: Mandating disclosure of AI decision logic in critical sectors.
- Human oversight: Ensuring that automated systems remain subject to human judgment and intervention.
- Safety and auditability: Requiring continuous testing, auditing, and monitoring of deployed AI models.

These frameworks collectively promote responsible innovation, ensuring that Web X.0 AI systems are fair, secure, and aligned with human values.

3.8.3.3 Data governance and cross-border compliance

Data governance is at the core of regulatory compliance in Web X.0. The General Data Protection Regulation (GDPR), the California Consumer Privacy Act (CCPA), and emerging frameworks in Asia and Africa set strong precedents for personal data protection and transparency [130]. To comply with these frameworks in decentralized infrastructures, Web X.0 must incorporate technical safeguards such as distributed access control, verifiable consent management, and data localization mechanisms. Standardization efforts, including ISO/IEC 27701 for privacy information management, support global compatibility among organizations operating under diverse regulatory conditions.

Example flow: A multinational e-commerce platform processes user data across several jurisdictions. It employs smart contracts to automate compliance verification: data collected in the EU is processed under GDPR guidelines, while transfers to the United States trigger automatic enforcement of CCPA conditions.

All actions are logged on a blockchain-based audit ledger to ensure accountability and transparency.

This hybrid approach enables organizations to maintain compliance dynamically, ensuring both user privacy and operational flexibility.

3.8.3.4 Cybersecurity standards and international cooperation

Cybersecurity threats on Web X.0 transcend national boundaries and demand cooperative defense strategies. International frameworks such as ISO/IEC 27001, NIST Cybersecurity Framework, and ITU-T X.1205 provide structured methods for risk assessment, resilience, and continuous monitoring [131]. Multilateral cybersecurity collaborations, such as the Global Forum on Cyber Expertise (GFCE) and the United Nations Group of Governmental Experts (UNGGE), facilitate capacity building and shared response mechanisms to cross-border cyber incidents. AI-driven anomaly detection and decentralized threat intelligence exchange enhance global situational awareness [132]. This harmonization reduces regulatory duplication and improves collective resilience, ensuring that security protocols remain consistent between regions and sectors.

3.8.3.5 Toward an adaptive regulatory ecosystem

Static regulations are insufficient for the pace of technological evolution in Web X.0. An adaptive regulatory ecosystem integrates continuous monitoring, machine-readable compliance verification, and dynamic policy updates. Regulatory sandboxes, structured environments for testing emerging technologies under supervision, enable safe innovation while informing policymakers about evolving risks [133]. Decentralized compliance systems, supported by smart contracts and AI-based legal reasoning, can automate adherence checks and report violations in real time.

Example flow: A decentralized financial service platform participates in an international regulatory sandbox. Its compliance algorithms monitor real-time transactions for anti-money-laundering (AML) violations. When anomalies are detected, alerts are transmitted to participating regulatory authorities in all jurisdictions, allowing coordinated action.

This adaptive model ensures that innovation and regulation evolve symbiotically, maintaining safety without constraining progress.

3.8.4 Societal impact and inclusion in Web X.0

Web X.0 is not only a technical transition but also changes who participates, who benefits, and who bears risk. As intelligent automation, decentralization, and pervasive connectivity shape interaction and governance, social consequences become part of the design problem rather than an external afterthought. The practical test is whether these systems can expand participation, protect rights, and improve human well-being without concentrating power or excluding already disadvantaged groups.

3.8.4.1 The socio-technical foundations of Web X.0

Web X.0 integrates human and machine intelligence in interdependent networks. Its socio-technical foundation relies on systems that can learn, adapt, and interact responsibly with human users. However, as these systems evolve, they challenge existing structures of power, knowledge, and labor [134]. Socio-technical design frameworks advocate embedding human values directly into system designs, ensuring that inclusivity, fairness, and accountability are treated as design constraints rather than secondary considerations. The IEEE Ethically Aligned Design (EAD) principles and the ACM Code of Ethics emphasize participatory co-design, transparency, and equitable access to benefits derived from intelligent technologies [71].

These frameworks collectively assert that technological systems must operate as extensions of human capacity and social equity, not as replacements for them.

3.8.4.2 Digital inclusion and equity

Digital inclusion is a cornerstone of equitable Web X.0 development. Access to connectivity, devices, digital literacy, and participatory governance determines who benefits from Web X.0 technologies and who is excluded. Despite advances in global connectivity, significant digital divides persist among gender, geography, income, and education levels [135].

Inclusive design requires multi-level intervention:

- Infrastructure access: Expanding broadband and edge computing networks to underserved areas.
- Affordability: Promoting open-source tools and reducing costs for digital access.
- Capacity building: Implementing digital literacy and reskilling programs aligned with Web X.0 competencies.
- Policy inclusion: Encouraging stakeholder representation in digital governance processes.

Example flow: A decentralized educational platform built on Web X.0 allows learners from remote regions to access AI-based adaptive content through low-bandwidth networks. Blockchain-based credentials provide verifiable certifications without intermediaries, empowering learners while maintaining authenticity.

Such inclusive systems democratize access to knowledge and opportunities, ensuring that the benefits of Web X.0 reach all populations.

3.8.4.3 Workforce transformation and human capital development

Intelligent automation in Web X.0 will reshape the global workforce by transforming the task structures and required competencies. Although AI-driven systems can increase human productivity and creativity, they also risk displacing repetitive or low-skill occupations [136].

Sustainable workforce strategies for Web X.0 include:

- Augmentation, not replacement: Designing automation systems that enhance human decision-making rather than eliminating human roles.
- Reskilling and continuous learning: Institutionalizing adaptive learning platforms for dynamic skill development.
- AI governance in employment: Establishing ethical standards for algorithmic management and workplace surveillance.

Example flow: In a manufacturing ecosystem powered by Web X.0, AI-driven robots collaborate with human operators. The system allocates tasks dynamically based on skill levels and workload, monitored through transparent dashboards. Human workers are continuously trained through AR-based modules that are updated in response to process innovations.

This model supports inclusive economic growth while mitigating technological unemployment through cooperative human–machine ecosystems.

3.8.4.4 Accessibility and human-centered interaction

The Web X.0 technologies must be designed to ensure accessibility in all physical, cognitive, and cultural dimensions. Accessibility extends beyond compliance with legal standards to creating adaptive and personalized interfaces that respond to individual needs. The principles of human-centered interaction design (HCID) integrate emotional, social, and cultural intelligence into user experiences. AI-driven personalization systems can adapt visual, auditory, and haptic feedback to diverse users, including those with disabilities. Semantic web standards and multimodal input frameworks such as W3C's Web Accessibility Initiative (WAI) provide essential guidelines for inclusive design. Designing Web X.0 with universal accessibility ensures compliance and meaningful engagement and agency for all users.

3.8.4.5 Societal ethics and responsible innovation

The societal impact of Web X.0 extends to governance, justice, and public discourse. Algorithmic decision-making can inadvertently amplify bias or inequality if left unregulated [32]. Ethical impact assessments and participatory governance models must be embedded into innovation processes. Responsible innovation frameworks, such as the European Commission's Responsible Research and Innovation (RRI) model, advocate anticipatory, reflexive, and inclusive design approaches. These ensure that Web X.0 technologies are developed transparently, with early stakeholder engagement and long-term social evaluation.

Example flow: Before deploying an AI-driven public benefits system, a city government conducts an ethical audit using bias detection models and stakeholder consultations. The system's decisions are monitored through explainable AI mechanisms, and affected citizens can challenge or appeal automated outcomes.

Embedding responsibility within innovation ensures that societal well-being and democratic values remain central to Web X.0 development.

3.9 Conclusion

Intelligent automation defines the character of Web X.0. By integrating learning algorithms, multimodal interaction, and predictive analytics into every layer of the web stack, it enables systems to continuously adapt to the user context and collective behavior. These advances promise greater efficiency and personalization, but also require mechanisms for transparency, security, and human control. For that reason, trust in Web X.0 will depend less on raw technical capability than on whether governance, identity, provenance, and oversight mature along with automation itself. The web will not become trustworthy simply because it becomes more intelligent. It will do so only if distributed intelligence remains accountable, explainable, inclusive, and open to human judgment when the stakes are high.

Suggested further readings

[1] Lebo, T., Sahoo, S., and McGuinness, D. (2013). W3C Recommendation. World Wide Web Consortium. *PROV-O: The PROV Ontology*. Available from: https://www.w3.org/TR/prov-o/.

[2] Wooldridge, M. (2009). Core reference for multi-agent architectures and coordination in distributed intelligent environments. *An Introduction to Multiagent Systems* (2nd ed.). John Wiley & Sons.

[3] Shi, W., and Dustdar, S. (2020). Key paper on edge intelligence paradigms essential to Web X.0 computational design. Edge Computing: Vision and Challenges. *IEEE Internet of Things Journal*, 7(5), 4312–4325.

[4] Hogan, A., Blomqvist, E., Cochez, M., *et al.* (2021). Comprehensive survey on knowledge graph construction, reasoning, and applications in semantic web systems. Knowledge Graphs. *ACM Computing Surveys*, 54(4), 1–37.

[5] Kreuzberger, D., Kolbl, F., and Haas, S. (2023). Essential guide to ML lifecycle management in Web X.0 deployments. Machine Learning Operations (MLOps): Overview, Definition, and Architecture. *ACM Computing Surveys*, 55(5), 1–33.

[6] World Wide Web Consortium (W3C). (2022). The W3C specification defining the DID standard underpinning self-sovereign identity. *Decentralized Identifiers (DIDs) v1.0: Core Data Model and Syntaxes*. Available from: https://www.w3.org/TR/did-core/

[7] Cavoukian, A. (2009). The foundational document for privacy-by-design, directly applicable to Web X.0 system architecture. *Privacy by Design: The 7 Foundational Principles*. Information and Privacy Commissioner of Ontario, Toronto, Ontario, Canada, 2009.

[8] Kennedy, J. (2010). Classic reference on swarm intelligence and bio-inspired optimization for distributed Web X.0 coordination. *Particle Swarm Optimization. Encyclopedia of Machine Learning*, Springer New York, NY; pp. 760–766.

[9] Gupta, S. (2025). Recent survey on ZKP techniques applicable to decentralized Web X.0 identity. Zero-Knowledge Proofs for Privacy-Preserving Systems: A

Survey Across Blockchain, Identity, and Beyond. *Engineering and Technology Journal*, 10(7), 5755–5761.

[10] Jobin, A., Ienca, M., and Vayena, E. (2019). Landmark analysis of international AI ethics frameworks, essential for understanding governance convergence. The Global Landscape of AI Ethics Guidelines. *Nature Machine Intelligence*, 1(9), 389–399.

[11] Mehrabi, N., Morstatter, F., Saxena, N., *et al.* (2021). Comprehensive reference on algorithmic bias detection and mitigation techniques. A Survey on Bias and Fairness in Machine Learning. *ACM Computing Surveys*, 54(6), 1–35.

[12] Arrieta, A. B., Diaz-Rodriguez, N., Del Ser, J., *et al.* (2020). Leading survey on XAI methods including SHAP and LIME, directly relevant to Web X.0 transparency requirements. Explainable Artificial Intelligence (XAI): Concepts, Taxonomies, Opportunities and Challenges toward Responsible AI. *Information Fusion*, 58, 82–115.

[13] Friedman, B., and Hendry, D. G. (2019). Framework for embedding human values in the design of Web X.0 socio-technical systems. *Value Sensitive Design: Shaping Technology with Moral Imagination*. MIT Press.

[14] Pearl, J., and Mackenzie, D. (2018). Foundational treatment of causal inference relevant to anticipatory and prescriptive Web X.0 automation. *The Book of Why: The New Science of Cause and Effect*. Basic Books.

[15] Dellermann, D., Ebel, P., Söllner, M., *et al.* (2019). Introduces hybrid intelligence as a design paradigm for human–AI collaboration in Web X.0. Hybrid Intelligence. *Business and Information Systems Engineering*, 61(5), 637–643.

Relevant industry standards and policies

W3C technologies

- RDF 1.2 and JSON-LD 1.1
- WebNN API; WebGPU
- WebAuthn Level 3
- DIDs v1.0; Verifiable Credentials Data Model 2.0
- PROV-O (Provenance Ontology)
- Web of Things (WoT) Architecture 1.1
- WCAG 2.2; W3C Personalization Semantics 1.0
- ActivityPub; OWL 2; SHACL

NIST standards

- AI RMF 1.0—AI Risk Management Framework
- SP 800-207—Zero Trust Architecture
- PQC Standardization—CRYSTALS-Kyber; CRYSTALS-Dilithium

IEEE standards

- IEEE 7001-2021—Transparency of Autonomous Systems
- IEEE 7003-2024—Algorithmic Bias Considerations
- IEEE P7009—Fail-Safe Design for Autonomous Systems

ISO/IEC standards

- ISO/IEC 42001:2023—AI Management System
- ISO/IEC 27001; ISO/IEC 27701
- ISO/IEC 62443—Industrial Cybersecurity
- ISO 9241-210—Human-Centred Design

IETF standards

- RATS—Remote Attestation Procedures
- OAuth 2.0; TLS 1.3

Regulatory frameworks

- EU AI Act (2024)
- EU GDPR—Articles 5, 22, and 25
- EU eIDAS 2.0
- OECD AI Principles
- FATF Travel Rule

References

[1] Spillner J, and Montes A. Toward cloudless computing: Webassembly and lightweight service ecosystems. *IEEE Software*. 2023;40(5):65–73.

[2] Shrestha A, Xue Y, and Liu D. Serverless computing at the edge: A survey and future directions. *IEEE Internet of Things Journal*. 2023;10(4):3218–3232.

[3] Li Y, Zhang L, and Wang F. Edge intelligence: Convergence of edge computing and artificial intelligence. *IEEE Network*. 2021;35(1):96–103.

[4] Mao Y, Yu X, Huang K, Zhang YJ, and Zhang J. Green edge AI: A contemporary survey. *Proceedings of the IEEE*. 2024;112(7):880–911.

[5] Hogan A, Blomqvist E, Cochez M, *et al.* Knowledge graphs. *ACM Computing Surveys*. 2021;54(4):1–37.

[6] Gregg Kellogg PACAS Olaf Hartig. *RDF 1.2 Concepts and abstract syntax*. World Wide Web Consortium (W3C); 2025. Available from: https://www.w3.org/TR/rdf12-concepts/.

[7] Compton M, Sheth A, Henson C, *et al.* The SSN ontology: A joint W3C and OGC standard for semantic sensor data. *IEEE Internet of Things Journal*. 2019;6(3):4736–4745.

[8] Belhajjame K, B'Far R, Cheney J, *et al.* Prov-dm: The prov data model. *W3C Recommendation*. 2013;14:15–16.

[9] Zhang T, Mai C, Chang Y, Chen C, Shu L, and Zheng Z. Fedego: privacy-preserving personalized federated graph learning with ego-graphs. *ACM Transactions on Knowledge Discovery from Data*. 2023;18(2):1–27.

[10] Akinci TC, Topsakal O, and Akbas MI. In: Ertuğrul ÖF, Guerrero JM, Yilmaz M, editors. *Machine Learning Methods from Shallow Learning to Deep Learning*. Cham: Springer Nature Switzerland; 2024. p. 1–28. Available from: https://doi.org/10.1007/978-3-031-69499-81.

[11] LeCun Y, Bengio Y, and Hinton G. Deep learning. *Nature*. 2015;521 (7553):436–444.

[12] Gui J, Chen T, Zhang J, Cao Q, Sun Z, and Luo H. A survey on self-supervised learning: Algorithms, applications, and future trends. *IEEE Transactions on Pattern Analysis and Machine Intelligence*. 2024;46 (12):9052–9071.

[13] Besold TR, Garcez A, and Serafini L. Neuro-symbolic artificial intelligence: Current trends. *IEEE Intelligent Systems*. 2021;36(3):5–17.

[14] Wu Z, Pan S, Chen F, Long G, Zhang C, and Yu PS. A comprehensive survey on graph neural networks. *IEEE Transactions on Neural Networks and Learning Systems*. 2020;32(1):4–24.

[15] Vaswani A, Shazeer N, Parmar N, *et al.* Attention is all you need. In: *Advances in Neural Information Processing Systems (NeurIPS)*. vol. 30; 2017. p. 5998–6008.

[16] Kreuzberger D, Kolbl F, and Haas S. Machine learning operations (MLOps):· Overview, definition, and architecture. *ACM Computing Surveys*. 2023;55(5):1–33.

[17] Wu B, Ding Z, and Huang J. A review of continual learning in edge AI. *IEEE Transactions on Network Science and Engineering*. 2026; 13:6571–6588.

[18] Wang L, Zhang X, Su H, and Zhu J. A comprehensive survey of continual learning: Theory, method and application. *IEEE transactions on pattern analysis and machine intelligence*. 2024;46(8):5362–5383.

[19] Shalev-Shwartz S. Online learning and online convex optimization. *Foundations and Trends® in Machine Learning*. 2025;4(2):107–194.

[20] Mosqueira-Rey E, Hernandez-Pereira E, Alonso-Ríos D, Bobes-Bascarán J, and Fernández-Leal Á. Human-in-the-loop machine learning: A state of the art. *Artificial Intelligence Review*. 2023;56(4):3005–3054.

[21] Bekey GA. *Autonomous Robots: From Biological Inspiration to Implementation and Control*. Cambridge, MA: MIT Press; 2005.

[22] Thrun S, Burgard W, and Fox D. *Probabilistic Robotics*. Cambridge, MA: MIT Press; 2005. Available from: https://mitpress.mit.edu/9780262201624/probabilistic-robotics/.

[23] Wooldridge M. *An Introduction to Multiagent Systems*. John Wiley & Sons; 2009.

[24] Russell SJ, and Norvig P. *Artificial Intelligence: A Modern Approach*. Upper Saddle River, NJ: Prentice Hall; 1995.

[25] Goss Q, Pate WC, and Akbas MI. An integrated framework for scenario-based safety validation and explainability of autonomous vehicles. *ACM Journal on Autonomous Transportation Systems*. 2025. Available from: https://doi.org/10.1145/3746286.

[26] Razdan R, Sell R, Akbas MI, and Menase M. Perspectives on safety for autonomous vehicles. *Electronics*. 2025;14(22):4500. Available from: https://www.mdpi.com/2079-9292/14/22/4500.

[27] Sadigh D, and Dragan AD. Safe and adaptive human-in-the-loop autonomy. *Annual Review of Control, Robotics, and Autonomous Systems*. 2019;2:101–127.

[28] Christiano PF, Leike J, Brown T, *et al.* Deep reinforcement learning from human preferences. In: *Advances in Neural Information Processing Systems (NeurIPS)*; 2017. p. 4299–4307.

[29] Luckcuck M. Using formal methods for autonomous systems: Five recipes for formal verification. *Proceedings of the Institution of Mechanical Engineers, Part O: Journal of Risk and Reliability*. 2023;237(2):278–292.

[30] Yang Q, Liu Y, Chen T, and Tong Y. Federated machine learning: Concept and applications. *ACM Transactions on Intelligent Systems and Technology*. 2019;10(2):1–19.

[31] Liang X, Shetty S, Tosh D, *et al.* Provchain: A blockchain-based data provenance architecture in cloud environment with enhanced privacy and availability. 2017; IEEE. p. 468–477.

[32] Mehrabi N, Morstatter F, Saxena N, Lerman K, and Galstyan A. A survey on bias and fairness in machine learning. *ACM Computing Surveys*. 2021;54 (6):1–35.

[33] Li L, Chu W, Langford J, *et al.* A contextual-bandit approach to personalized news article recommendation. In: *Proceedings of the 19th International Conference on World Wide Web (WWW)*. ACM; 2010. p. 661–670.

[34] Erlingsson U, Pihur V, and Korolova A. Learning with privacy at scale. In: *Proceedings of the 20th ACM SIGKDD International Conference on Knowledge Discovery and Data Mining (KDD)*. ACM; 2014. p. 403–411.

[35] Gomez-Uribe CA, and Hunt N. The Netflix recommender system: Algorithms, business value, and innovation. *ACM Transactions on Management Information Systems*. 2015;6(4):13:1–13:19.

[36] Ulfar Erlingsson, Pihur V, and Korolova A. RAPPOR: randomized aggregatable privacy-preserving ordinal response. In: *Proceedings of the 2014 ACM SIGSAC Conference on Computer and Communications Security (CCS)*. ACM; 2014. p. 1054–1067.

[37] World Wide Web Consortium (W3C). Personalization Semantics Content Module 1.0. W3C; 2023. Available from: https://www.w3.org/TR/personalization-semantics-content-1.0/.

[38] World Wide Web Consortium (W3C). Web Content Accessibility Guidelines (WCAG) 2.2. W3C; 2023. Available from: https://www.w3.org/TR/WCAG22/.
[39] Kohavi R, Deng A, Frasca B, *et al.* Seven rules of thumb for web site experimenters. In: *Proceedings of the 20th ACM SIGKDD International Conference on Knowledge Discovery and Data Mining (KDD)*. ACM; 2014. p. 1857–1866.
[40] Sundar A, and Heck L. Multimodal conversational AI: A survey of datasets and approaches. In: *Proceedings of the 4th Workshop on NLP for Conversational AI*; 2022. p. 131–147.
[41] Allouch M, Azaria A, and Azoulay R. Conversational agents: Goals, technologies, vision and challenges. *Sensors*. 2021;21(24):8448.
[42] Wang M, Ning B, and Zhao B. A review of knowledge-grounded dialogue systems. In: 2023 *8th International Conference on Image, Vision and Computing (ICIVC)*. IEEE; 2023. p. 819–824.
[43] Topsakal O, Akbas MI, Demirel D, *et al.* Digitizing rhinoplasty: A web application for pre-operative planning. *The International Journal of Computer Assisted Radiology and Surgery (IJCARS)*. 2020;15:1941–1950.
[44] Deriu J, Rodrigo A, Ruegger A, *et al.* Survey on evaluation methods for dialogue systems. *Artificial Intelligence Review*. 2021;54(1):755–810.
[45] Booth BM, Hickman L, Subburaj SK, *et al.* Bias and fairness in multimodal machine learning: A case study of automated video interviews. In: *Proceedings of the 2021 international conference on multimodal interaction*; 2021. p. 268–277.
[46] Villaronga EF, and van den Hoven J. Human-centric cybersecurity for intelligent systems. *IEEE Internet Computing*. 2018;22(2):39–47.
[47] National Institute of Standards and Technology (NIST). Artificial Intelligence Risk Management Framework (AI RMF 1.0). U.S. Department of Commerce, NIST; 2023. Available from: https://nvlpubs.nist.gov/nistpubs/ai/NIST.AI.100-1.pdf.
[48] Tarafdar R. Human-AI collaboration in workflow optimization: A framework for hybrid decision systems in automation-heavy industries. *International Journal of Scientific Research in Computer Science, Engineering and Information Technology*. 2025;11(1):3594–3613.
[49] Paulheim H. Knowledge graph refinement: A survey of approaches and evaluation methods. *Semantic Web*. 2017;8(3):489–508.
[50] Trouillon T, Welbl J, Riedel S, Gaussier É, and Bouchard G. Complex embeddings for simple link prediction. In: *Proceedings of the 33rd International Conference on Machine Learning (ICML)*; 2016. p. 2071–2080.
[51] Lebo T, Sahoo S, and McGuinness D. PROV-O: The PROV ontology. World Wide Web Consortium (W3C); 2013. Available from: https://www.w3.org/TR/prov-o/.
[52] Kohavi R, Longbotham R, Sommerfield D, and Henne RM. Controlled experiments on the web: Survey and practical guide. In: *Proceedings of the*

15th ACM SIGKDD International Conference on Knowledge Discovery and Data Mining (KDD). ACM; 2009. p. 1407–1416.
[53] McMahan HB, Moore E, Ramage D, Hampson S, and Arcas BA. Communication-efficient learning of deep networks from decentralized data. *Proceedings of the 20th International Conference on Artificial Intelligence and Statistics (AISTATS)*. 2017; p. 1273–1282.
[54] Nadin M. Anticipation and computation: Is anticipatory computing possible? In: *Anticipation Across Disciplines*. Springer; 2015. p. 283–339.
[55] Khan LU, Yaqoob I, Tran NH, *et al.* Edge-computing-enabled smart cities: A comprehensive survey. *IEEE Internet of Things journal*. 2020;7(10):10200–10232.
[56] Zhou H, Zhang S, Peng J, *et al.* Informer: Beyond efficient transformer for long sequence time-series forecasting. In: *Proceedings of the AAAI Conference on Artificial Intelligence*. vol. 35; 2021. p. 11106–11115.
[57] Pearl J, and Mackenzie D. *The Book of Why: The New Science of Cause and Effect*. New York: Basic Books; 2018. Available from: https://basicbooks.com/titles/judea-pearl/the-book-of-why/9780465097609/.
[58] Hoffman RR, Mueller ST, Klein G, and Litman J. Metrics for explainable AI: Challenges and prospects. arXiv preprint arXiv:1812.04608. 2018.
[59] Amershi S, Weld D, Vorvoreanu M, *et al.* Guidelines for human–AI interaction. In: *Proceedings of the 2019 CHI Conference on Human Factors in Computing Systems*; 2019. p. 1–13.
[60] IEEE Standards Association. *IEEE 7001-2021: Transparency of Autonomous Systems*. IEEE; 2021.
[61] IEEE Standards Association. *IEEE 7003-2024: Algorithmic Bias Considerations*. IEEE; 2024.
[62] Gharahighehi A, Van Schoors R, Topali P, and Ooge J. Adaptive lifelong learning (all). In: *International Conference on Artificial Intelligence in Education*. Springer; 2024. p. 452–459.
[63] Sporny M, Longley D, Kellogg G, *et al. JSON-LD 1.1: A JSON-based Serialization for Linked Data*. World Wide Web Consortium (W3C); 2020. Available from: https://www.w3.org/TR/json-ld11/.
[64] World Wide Web Consortium (W3C). *Web Neural Network API (WebNN)*. W3C; 2025. Available from: https://www.w3.org/TR/webnn/.
[65] World Wide Web Consortium (W3C). *WebGPU Specification*. W3C; 2023. Available from: https://www.w3.org/TR/webgpu/.
[66] World Wide Web Consortium (W3C). *Web Authentication: An API for Accessing Public Key Credentials Level 3*. W3C; 2025. Available from: https://www.w3.org/TR/webauthn-3/.
[67] Tariq UU, Ali H, Liu L, *et al.* Energy-aware scheduling of streaming applications on edge-devices in IoT-based healthcare. *IEEE Transactions on Green Communications and Networking*. 2021;5(2):803–815.
[68] Shi W, and Dustdar S. Edge computing: Vision and challenges. *IEEE Internet of Things Journal*. 2020;7(5):4312–4325.

[69] World Wide Web Consortium (W3C). *Decentralized Identifiers (DIDs) v1.0: Core Data Model and Syntaxes*; 2022. Available from: https://www.w3.org/TR/did-core/.

[70] Moreau L, and Missier P. The PROV data model and its applications. *ACM Transactions on Internet Technology*. 2013;13(4):1–24.

[71] IEEE global initiative on ethics of autonomous and intelligent systems. *Ethically Aligned Design: A Vision for Prioritizing Human Well-being with Autonomous and Intelligent Systems*. IEEE Standards Association. 2019.

[72] Jobin A, Ienca M, and Vayena E. The global landscape of AI ethics guidelines. *Nature Machine Intelligence*. 2019;1(9):389–399.

[73] Lundberg SM, and Lee SI. A unified approach to interpreting model predictions. In: *NeurIPS*; 2017. p. 4765–4774.

[74] Ribeiro MT, Singh S, and Guestrin C. "Why Should I Trust You?" explaining the predictions of any classifier. In: ACM KDD; 2016. p. 1135–1144.

[75] Goss Q, Pate WC, and Akbas MI. An integrated scenario-based testing and explanation framework for autonomous vehicles. In: 2024 *IEEE International Conference on Mobility, Operations, Services and Technologies (MOST)*; 2024. p. 60–71.

[76] Gupta S. Zero-knowledge proofs for privacy-preserving systems: a survey across blockchain, identity, and beyond. *Engineering and Technology Journal*. 2025;10(7):5755–5761.

[77] Rose S, Borchert O, Mitchell S, and Connelly S. *NIST Special Publication 800-207:* Zero Trust Architecture. NIST; 2020. Available from: https://doi.org/10.6028/NIST.SP.800-207.

[78] Goodfellow IJ, Shlens J, and Szegedy C. Explaining and harnessing adversarial examples. arXiv preprint arXiv:1412.6572. 2014.

[79] Madry A, Makelov A, Schmidt L, *et al.* Towards deep learning models resistant to adversarial attacks. arXiv preprint arXiv:1706.06083; 2017.

[80] Okatan A, Akbas MI, Niure Kandel L, *et al.* Keys in the weights: Transformer authentication using model-bound latent representations. In: *IEEE Cyber Awareness and Research Symposium (CARS'25)*; 2025.

[81] Akbas MI. Testing and validation framework for autonomous aerial vehicles. *Journal of Aviation/Aerospace Education Research*. 2021;30(1):1–19.

[82] Liu J, Zhang W, Yang Y, *et al.* Pre-trained language models for information retrieval: A survey. *ACM Computing Surveys*. 2021;54(6):1–38.

[83] Lewis P, Perez E, Piktus A, *et al.* Retrieval-augmented generation for knowledge-intensive NLP tasks: A survey. *Advances in Neural Information Processing Systems*. 2020;33:9459–9474.

[84] Xu X, Zhang W, Khan MA, *et al.* Blockchain-based smart contracts for decentralized applications: A survey. *IEEE Transactions on Services Computing*. 2021;14(5):1327–1345.

[85] Ifedayo AE, Olugbade D, and Hamid S. Integrating artificial intelligence with blockchain: A literature review on opportunities, challenges, and applications. *Blockchain, Artificial Intelligence, and Future Research*. 2025;1(1):52–69.

[86] Minarsch D, Favorito M, Hosseini SA, *et al.* Autonomous economic agent framework. In: *International Workshop on Engineering Multi-Agent Systems*. Springer; 2021. p. 237–253.

[87] Akbas MI, Gunaratne C, Garibay OO, *et al.* Role of entrepreneurial support· for networking in innovation ecosystems: an agent based approach. In: *2015 Winter Simulation Conference (WSC)*. IEEE; 2015. p. 3112–3113.

[88] Cheng D, Zou Y, Xiang S, and Jiang C. Graph neural networks for financial fraud detection: A review. *Frontiers of Computer Science*. 2025;19(9):199609.

[89] Alsagheer D, Xu L, and Shi W. Decentralized machine learning governance: Overview, opportunities, and challenges. *IEEE Access*. 2023; 11:96718–96732.

[90] Chakeri A, Wang X, Goss Q, Akbas MI, and Jaimes LG. A platform-based incentive mechanism for autonomous vehicle crowdsensing. *IEEE Open Journal of Intelligent Transportation Systems*. 2021;2:13–23.

[91] Kutlu I, Goss Q, Akinci TC, and Akbas MI. Formal modeling of road network-based autonomous vehicle validation scenarios with intersections and pedestrians. In: *2024 IEEE International Performance, Computing, and Communications Conference (IPCCC)*; 2024. p. 1–6.

[92] Awaisi KS, Ye Q, and Sampalli S. A survey of industrial AIoT: Opportunities, challenges, and directions. *IEEE Access*. 2024;12:96946–96996.

[93] Agrawal R, Majumdar A, Kumar A, and Luthra S. Integration of artificial intelligence in sustainable manufacturing: Current status and future opportunities. *Operations Management Research*. 2023;16(4):1720–1741.

[94] Berners-Lee T, Bizer C, and Heath T. *Linked Data: Evolving the Web into a Global Data Space*. 2nd ed. Morgan & Claypool; 2021.

[95] Guinard D, Kovatsch M, and Matsukura K. *Web of Things (WoT) Architecture 1.1*. W3C; 2022. Available from: https://www.w3.org/TR/wot-architecture11/.

[96] Selcuk Nogay H, Akinci TC, Akbas MI, and Tokić A. Diagnosis of chaotic ferroresonance phenomena using deep learning. *IEEE Access*. 2023; 11:58937–58946.

[97] Mosca M. Cybersecurity in an era with quantum computers: Will we be ready? *IEEE Security & Privacy*. 2018;16(5):38–41.

[98] Chen L, Jordan S, Liu YK, *et al. Report on Post-Quantum Cryptography. NIST Internal Report* 8105. 2016.

[99] National Institute of Standards and Technology (NIST). Post-Quantum Cryptography Standardization: Selected Algorithms (Round 4); 2023. Available from: https://csrc.nist.gov/projects/post-quantum-cryptography.

[100] Schuld M, and Killoran N. Quantum machine learning in feature Hilbert spaces. *Physical Review Letters*. 2019;122(4):040504.

[101] Pirandola S, Andersen UL, Banchi L, *et al.* Advances in quantum cryptography. *Advances in Optics and Photonics*. 2020;12(4):1012–1236.

[102] Microsoft Security Response Center. Preparing for the Quantum-Safe Future: A Migration Guide. Microsoft; 2023. Available from: https://learn.microsoft.com/en-us/security/quantum-safe/quantum-migration.

[103] Davies M, Srinivasa N, Lin TH, *et al.* Advancing neuromorphic computing with Loihi: A survey of results and outlook. *Proceedings of the IEEE*. 2021; 109(5):911–934.

[104] Roy K, Jaiswal A, and Panda P. Towards spike-based machine intelligence with neuromorphic computing. *Nature*. 2019;575:607–617.

[105] Malviya RK, Danda RR, Maguluri KK, and Kumar BV. Neuromorphic computing: Advancing energy-efficient AI systems through brain-inspired architectures. *Nanotechnology Perceptions*. 2024;20(14):1548–1564.

[106] Furber SB, Lester DR, Plana LA, *et al.* The SpiNNaker Project: Architecture, implementation, and application. *IEEE Transactions on Computers*. 2020;69(9):1244–1258.

[107] Tavanaei A, Ghodrati M, Kheradpisheh SR, Masquelier T, and Maida A. Deep learning in spiking neural networks: A review. *Neural Networks*. 2019;111:47–63.

[108] Venkatesha Y, Kim Y, Tassiulas L, and Panda P. Federated learning with spiking neural networks. *IEEE Transactions on Signal Processing*. 2021; 69:6183– 6194.

[109] Akbas MI, Brust MR, and Turgut D. SOFROP: Self-organizing and fair routing protocol for wireless networks with mobile sensors and stationary actors. *Computer and Communications*. 2011;34(18):2135–2146. Available from: https://doi.org/10.1016/j.comcom.2011.01.006.

[110] Chintakunta H, and Akbas MI. Spectrum analytic approach for cooperative navigation of connected and autonomous vehicles. In: *Proceedings of the ACM Symposium on Design and Analysis of Intelligent Vehicular Networks and Applications*; 2019. p. 97–104.

[111] de Castro LN, and Timmis J. *Artificial Immune Systems: A New Computational Intelligence Approach*. Springer; 2002.

[112] Kennedy J. Particle swarm optimization. *Encyclopedia of Machine Learning*. 2010; p. 760–766.

[113] Stanley KO, Clune J, Lehman J, and Miikkulainen R. *Designing Neural Networks Through Neuroevolution*. vol. 1. Nature Publishing Group UK London; 2019.

[114] Salyards J, Sniadach K, Baker J, *et al.* A scalable open-source simulation framework for neuroevolution and multi-agent behavior research. In: *Interservice/Industry Training, Simulation, and Education Conference (I/ ITSEC)*; 2025. p. 1–11.

[115] Dasgupta D, and Nino FL. Advances in artificial immune systems: models and applications. *IEEE Computational Intelligence Magazine*. 2011;6 (4):40–49.

[116] Prokopenko M. Self-organization: Principles and examples. In: *Encyclopedia of Complexity and Systems Science*. Springer; 2009. p. 7800–7820.

[117] Dellermann D, Ebel P, Sollner M, and Leimeister JM. Hybrid intelligence. *Business and Information Systems Engineering*. 2019;61(5):637–643.

[118] Bannon L, and Ehn P. Rethinking human–computer interaction in the age of AI and automation. *ACM Interactions*. 2020;27(6):42–47.

[119] Garcez ASd, and Lamb LC. Neurosymbolic AI: The 3rd wave. *AI Magazine*. 2020;41(3):58–68.
[120] Rahwan I, Cebrian M, Obradovich N, *et al.* Machine behaviour. *Nature*. 2019;568(7753):477–486.
[121] Ismail O, and Ahmad N. Ethical and governance frameworks for artificial intelligence: A systematic literature review. *International Journal of Interactive Mobile Technologies*. 2025;19(14):175–190.
[122] Arrieta AB, Diaz-Rodriguez N, Del Ser J, *et al.* Explainable Artificial Intelligence (XAI): Concepts, taxonomies, opportunities and challenges toward responsible AI. *Information Fusion*. 2020;58:82–115.
[123] International Organization for Standardization. *ISO/IEC JTC 1/SC 42: Artificial Intelligence Standards and Frameworks*; 2022. Available from: https://www.iso.org/committee/6794475.html.
[124] Syed NF, Shah SW, Shaghaghi A, Anwar A, Baig Z, and Doss R. Zero trust architecture (ZTA): A comprehensive survey. *IEEE Access*. 2022; 10:57143–57179.
[125] Cavoukian A, *et al.* Privacy by design: The 7 foundational principles. *Information and Privacy Commissioner of Ontario*, Canada. 2009;5 (2009):12.
[126] Gharami K, Tasnim H, Akbas MI, *et al.* Seeing patterns differently: topological geometry for anomaly detection in multivariate time series. In: *Proceedings of the 10th ACM/IEEE Symposium on Edge Computing. SEC'25*. New York, NY: Association for Computing Machinery; 2025. Available from: https://doi.org/10.1145/3769102.3774431.
[127] Liu J, Zhang J, and Chen X. Privacy-preserving machine learning: methods, challenges and directions. *IEEE Transactions on Knowledge and Data Engineering*. 2021;33(8):3044–3061.
[128] Gasser U, and Almeida V. Digital governance and the global public interest. *Communications of the ACM*. 2020;63(8):28–31.
[129] World Economic Forum. *Global Digital Policy Framework: Governance for an Interconnected Future*; 2023. Available from: https://www.weforum.org/reports/global-digital-policy-framework/.
[130] Greenleaf G. Global data privacy laws 2023: Major trends and developments. *Computer Law & Security Review*. 2023;49:105777.
[131] National Institute of Standards and Technology. *NIST Cybersecurity Framework 2.0:* 2024. Available from: https://www.nist.gov/cyberframework.
[132] Stefanov M, Burton SL, Akbas IM, *et al.* Exploring the potential of artificial intelligence to predict cyber attacks: Creation, evaluation, and comparative analysis of effective models of ensemble methods, isolation forest, and ARIMA. *Land Forces Academy Review*. 2025;30(1):162–174. Available from: https://doi.org/10.2478/raft-2025-0016.
[133] Allen HJ. Regulatory sandboxes and the governance of fintech innovation. *Georgetown Law Journal*. 2020;107:725–784.

[134] Friedman B, and Hendry DG. *Value Sensitive Design: Shaping Technology with Moral Imagination*. MIT Press; 2019.

[135] International Telecommunication Union. *Measuring Digital Development: Facts and Figures 2022*; 2022. Available from: https://www.itu.int/hub/publication/d-ind-ict mdd-2022/.

[136] Brynjolfsson E, Mitchell T, and Rock D. The turing trap: The promise and peril of human-like artificial intelligence. *Daedalus*. 2021;150(2):78–94.

Chapter 4

Emotional and human-centric computing in Web X.0

Rohan Farooq Chaudhary[1], Riyan Athar[2], Anwar Shah[2] and Muhammad Adnan[3]

Abstract

The evolution of the web from static information repositories to intelligent, decentralized, and emotionally responsive ecosystems has fundamentally transformed human–computer interaction. As Web technologies progress toward Web 4.0, Web 5.0, and emerging Web X.0 paradigms, affective computing is becoming a central component of digital infrastructure. This chapter examines the convergence of multimodal emotion recognition, human-centric computing, and next-generation web architectures. It first establishes theoretical foundations of affective computing, including discrete and dimensional emotion models and multimodal sensing approaches. It then analyzes the transition from classical machine learning to deep learning and Transformer-based architectures in emotion recognition systems.

The chapter further explores how emotion-aware systems integrate into decentralized and intelligent web environments, enabling adaptive recommender systems, empathic conversational agents, digital health platforms, and immersive metaverse applications. Particular emphasis is placed on cybersecurity, privacy, fairness, data governance, and risks of emotional manipulation as emotional data becomes embedded within web-scale infrastructures. Emerging directions, including emotional artificial general intelligence, quantum-inspired affective modeling, neurosymbolic reasoning, and culturally adaptive emotion systems, are critically examined.

By synthesizing technical advances with ethical and societal considerations, this chapter provides a structured roadmap for designing emotionally intelligent Web X.0 systems that prioritize transparency, security, and human well-being.

[1]Department of Computer Sciences, National University of Computer and Emerging Sciences, Chiniot Faisalabad Pakistan

[2]Department of AI and Data Sciences, National University of Computer and Emerging Sciences, Chiniot Faisalabad Pakistan

[3]Department of Electrical Engineering, National University of Computer and Emerging Sciences, Islamabad, Pakistan

4.1 Introduction

Computer applications become more AI-centric as Artificial Intelligence (AI) advances. Affective computing has evolved as a major field for improving how humans interact with machines, facilitating learning, enriching entertainment, improving safety in areas such as driving, and connecting multiple forms of media more smoothly [1]. Affective computing is defined as the study of technologies that respond and understand to human emotions, and has made outstanding advances, especially in emotion recognition and sentiment analysis [1]. These advancements are no longer theoretical but have turned into real-world applications, contributing to the development of technology that feels more natural and emotionally responsive. Shah *et al.* [2] and Wang *et al.* [1] organized pattern recognition and clustering studies that signify how data-driven reasoning can uncover hidden emotional behaviour patterns, thereby supporting affective computing in Web X.0 contexts.

4.1.1 Scope and background of affective computing

Affective computing is based on the principle of interpreting and identifying human sentiments and emotions through both unimodal and multimodal data sources. This type of data usually includes physical signals such as text, speech, and visual expressions, and physiological signals, such as electrocardiograms (ECG) and electroencephalograms (EEG) [1]. While physical signal-based emotion recognition benefits from huge public datasets, it faces notable challenges. Individuals can consciously hide or unconsciously distort their true feelings through facial expressions, gestures, tone of voice, or an occurrence known as social masking [1]. Physiological signals, by contrast, provide a more objective reflection of emotional states, as they are less prone to conscious control [1]. However, it is difficult to collect such data in practical scenarios [1]. As a result, merging both physiological and physical information has emerged as a promising approach for improving the accuracy of emotion detection and getting richer emotional features [1]. Affective computing's theoretical underpinnings 1 are closely related to psychology, particularly the basic emotion theory (categorical or discrete models) and dimensional emotion theory (multidimensional models) [1]. These frameworks specify how affective systems forecast and classify emotions [1]. The goal of emotion recognition is to recognize affective states from a variety of input types, such as physiological measurements, speech or audio (Audio/Speech Emotion Recognition (AER/SER)), and visual cues [1]. In contrast, sentiment analysis focuses on textual data and opinion mining, frequently categorizing sentiment polarity as neutral, negative, or positive [1]. In recent years, the distinction between these two disciplines has become more hazy as multimodal affective analysis aims to address both at the same time [1]. The foundational study [1] included a systematic review that examined over 350 affective computing research studies. To describe the system architectures, performances, and practical applications of each, it categorized the literature into unimodal affect recognition and multimodal affective analysis [1]. Moreover, key elements of the field have been covered in the review, such as emotion models, benchmark datasets, and both conventional deep learning and machine learning-based methods [1]. Its extensive reach gives professionals and scholars a clear picture of current patterns and possible future directions in this emerging field [1]. To gain system stability and generalization, strong baseline datasets, sophisticated multimodal fusion strategies, and unsupervised learning techniques are required, particularly in cases where data is limited or biased [1]. Affective analysis applications are increasing rapidly in different domains, such as robotics, where emotionally intelligent systems may be better able to recognize and react to human emotions [1].

4.1.2 Evolution of the web: from static infrastructure to emotion-aware Web X.0

The evolution of the web reflects a gradual transition from static information dissemination toward intelligent, decentralized, and emotionally adaptive ecosystems. Each generation introduced new technological capabilities while simultaneously reshaping the cybersecurity and privacy landscape.

Web 1.0 was characterized by read-only, static pages built using HTML and basic server architectures [3,4]. User interaction was minimal, and content was centrally published. Security concerns during this phase primarily involved server vulnerabilities, basic authentication weaknesses, and website defacement [4]. Since user-generated content was limited, privacy risks were relatively low, and emotional data processing was nonexistent.

The introduction of Web 2.0 brought interactive online content together with social networking sites that allowed users to create and share their own content [3,4]. The development of Asynchronous JavaScript and XML (AJAX), content management systems, and large-scale database integration technologies allowed users to work together on projects. The new data collection methods produced a substantial increase in data gathering, including information about user behavior and emotional responses through their online activities and use of multimedia elements [3,4].

The security dangers grew significantly during this time period. The period saw the emergence of various security threats, which included cross-site scripting attacks, phishing techniques, identity theft, misinformation campaigns, and major data security breaches. People expressed emotional data through their sentiment-rich interactions, which advertisers used to design targeted advertisements and content recommendations based on algorithms [5]. The conversion of user attention into marketable products established new dangers that involved both psychological manipulation and algorithmic bias.

Web 3.0 digital environment relies on decentralized systems that use semantic data representations and blockchain technology to grant users control over their online digital assets. Trust systems get transformed through the use of smart contracts and decentralized applications together with distributed identity systems [5,6]. Web services use embedded AI technology to provide users with predictive analytics and personalized experiences based on their specific context.

Decentralization provides better system resilience, which reduces the need for centralized authority control. The system faces new security challenges because attackers target smart contract weaknesses and exploit consensus flaws while they handle decentralized identity systems through improper cryptographic key usage [7]. The permanent storage of emotional data through AI-powered Web 3.0 services creates security risks because sensitive affective information gets stored on decentralized blockchain networks.

The development of Web 4.0 combines AI with Internet of Things (IoT) technology and edge computing and real-time data synchronization between different devices. The current phase focuses on developing systems that can understand their surroundings and make flexible decisions. Smart spaces, wearable technology, and ambient interfaces now include emotion recognition technology as a standard feature [1].

The use of extensive sensor networks and ongoing behavioral tracking creates greater security challenges. The security vulnerabilities of edge devices, IoT systems, and AI inference pipelines have expanded their attack surface. Critical concerns about emotion recognition systems arise from adversarial attacks, data poisoning, biometric spoofing, and sensor manipulation. The continuous monitoring of physiological and affective signals increases privacy threats [1,8].

Web 5.0 introduces emotionally intelligent interfaces that detect, interpret, and respond to human affect in real time. Multimodal emotion recognition, affect-aware recommender systems, empathic conversational agents, and immersive metaverse environments define this phase [9,10].

The integration of emotional data creates unprecedented ethical and cybersecurity risks. Emotional profiling may enable psychological targeting, behavioral nudging, or manipulation. Biometric and physiological signals represent highly sensitive data categories that require strict governance. Attackers may exploit emotional AI systems through adversarial prompts, deepfake emotional mimicry, or inference attacks targeting affective states [11,12].

Web X.0 extends beyond predefined versions toward continuously adaptive ecosystems that enable AI agents to develop together with human users. Emotional Artificial General Intelligence (AGI), together with neurosymbolic reasoning and quantum-inspired modeling, operates through decentralized infrastructures [5].

Cybersecurity now needs to defend against threats that target active cognitive systems instead of protecting fixed security measures. Risks include autonomous AI decision manipulation and social control through emotional dependency, failures to create socioaffective bonds, and the spread of behavior between different agents. The protection of emotional autonomy holds equal importance to safeguarding financial and identity information (Figure 4.1) [13].

4.1.3 Research questions

The intersection of affective computing and the ongoing evolution of web technologies offers productive ground for exploration. This chapter will investigate:

- How might multimodal affective analysis be incorporated into Web 3.0's intelligent and decentralized architectures to facilitate more profound and emotionally sensitive human–computer interactions?

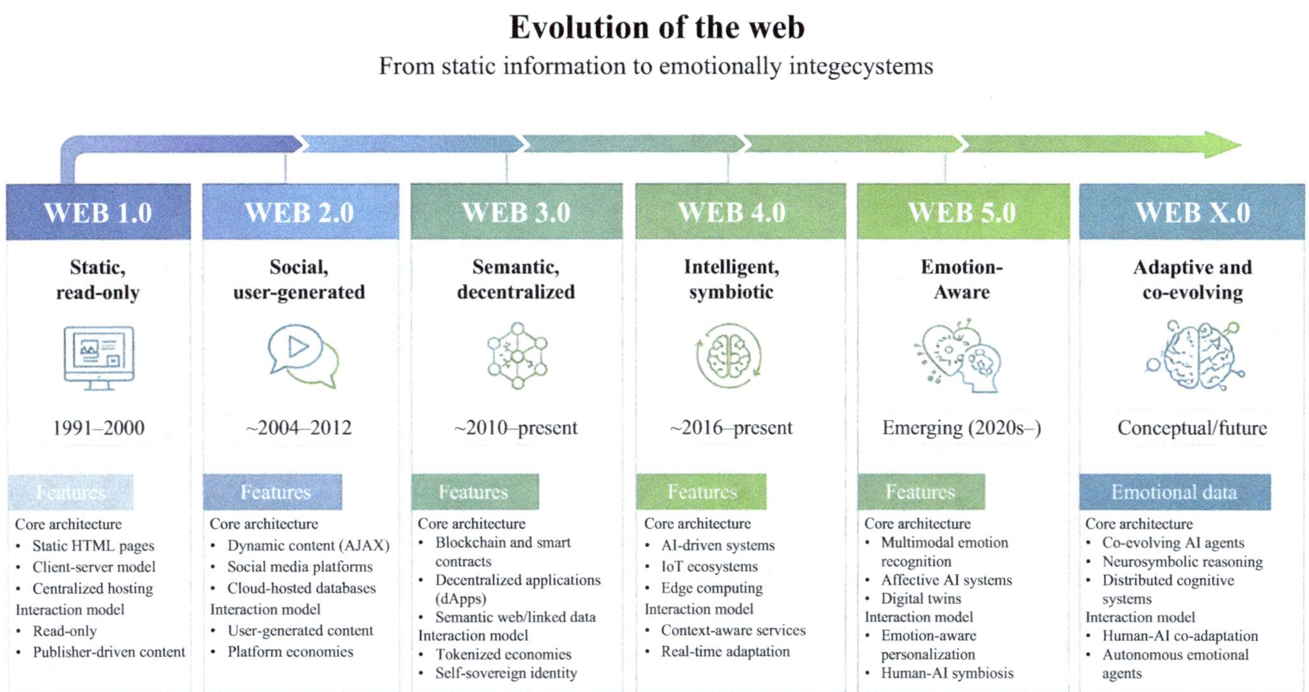

Figure 4.1 *Conceptual progression of web architectures from static information systems (Web 1.0) to adaptive, emotionally intelligent, and co-evolving ecosystems (Web X.0), illustrating increasing decentralization, intelligence, and affective integration across generations*

- What ethical, privacy, and security issues emerge from the widespread use of emotion recognition technologies across modern web platforms, especially concerning data ownership, user consent, and algorithmic bias?
- How can the historical progression of web technologies from the static pages of Web 1.0 to the envisioned emotion-aware systems of Web 5.0 inform the design of future platforms that genuinely enhance user experience and well-being?
- How can multimodal affective analysis be turned into a decentralized framework of Web 3.0 to create web environments that feel more intuitive and emotionally aware in their interaction with users?
- What new ethical, privacy, and security concerns arise as emotion recognition becomes more common across online platforms, particularly around who owns emotional data, how consent is managed, and how algorithms handle bias?
- What impact does the transition from Web 1.0's static pages to Web 5.0's imagined emotion-sensitive systems have on how we envision future web platforms that support well-being and user experience?

By examining these issues, this chapter aims to provide a solid understanding of the current state of emotion-focused computing and its potential future development in tandem with the web. Supporting the development of digital spaces that feel more intuitive, emotionally sensitive, and focused on the human experience is the goal of the conversation.

4.2 Foundations of affective and human-centric computing

4.2.1 Foundations of affective computing

Affective computing brings together ideas from psychology, computer science, and human–computer interaction. It focuses on developing systems that can recognize and respond to human emotions in meaningful ways. Rather than treating emotion as noise in communication, this field views it as an essential part of how people interact with technology, helping make those interactions more natural and relatable [1].

4.2.1.1 Emotion model comparison

Understanding how emotions are represented is foundational to affective computing, as the choice of emotion model directly influences data annotation strategies, machine learning formulations, and system interpretability. Two dominant paradigms shape computational emotion modeling: discrete (categorical) models and dimensional models. While both aim to structure emotional experience, they differ significantly in theoretical assumptions and computational consequences.

The way emotions are shown forms the base of affective computing, because the chosen emotion model sets how data are tagged, how algorithms are written, and how clear the system is to users. Two main approaches rule computer models of feeling—discrete lists plus dimensional maps. Each tries to order human affect, but they rest on different ideas and lead to different code.

Discrete lists claim that a small fixed set of hard-wired emotions sits under every feeling. Ekman's set of six—happiness, sadness, anger, fear, disgust, and surprise—appears again, but also again in data sets and in classifier targets. Those lists fit supervised learning well, since each emotion becomes one class label, as well as a softmax layer can return a single predicted word. The network's last layer outputs a probability for each label, and the highest score is taken as the detected emotion.

But fixed lists show clear drawbacks—they treat the same six labels as valid for every culture, even though new studies show that face or voice cues shift across regions and situations. Many real feelings mix two or more states, stay unclear, or move smoothly from one state to another—a single hard label erases detail. Human taggers also disagree repeatedly when they must pick one word from a short list next to the resulting noise lowers the reliability of the data set. When noisy labels are used to train a model, the trained network later scores lower on new data.

Dimensional emotion models offer an alternative by representing emotions along continuous axes, most commonly valence (positive to negative) and arousal (calm to excited), with some extensions including dominance or control. Russell's circumplex model exemplifies this approach. Instead of discrete classification, dimensional models frame emotion recognition as a regression problem. This allows systems to predict continuous affective coordinates, capturing subtle emotional variations.

The computational performance of dimensional models creates decision boundaries that operate more smoothly while demonstrating superior accuracy in mapping real-world emotional transitions. The method works best for multimodal and longitudinal studies that track emotional changes that happen at different time points throughout the research period. The system needs to transform its continuous outputs into practical decisions because the regression-based model creates interpretive, evaluative, and threshold determination problems.

The selection between discrete models and dimensional models impacts the implementation of multimodal fusion techniques. Categorical systems tend to fuse predictions at the decision level, whereas dimensional systems benefit from feature-level fusion that preserves affective continuity across modalities. Hybrid systems exist that use both categorical emotion groups and dimensional intensity values to create a system that provides both clear interpretation and detailed emotional expression.

The cultural beliefs that exist within datasets define the two systems, which both develop through this process. The majority of existing benchmarking systems use Western population samples, which lead to the creation of benchmarks that incorporate two distinct Western emotional expression patterns. Emotion-aware systems now spread across all Web X.0 environments, yet their use of emotion models, which focus on specific cultures, creates a danger of producing systemic bias.

In summary, discrete models offer simplicity and compatibility with classification architectures, while dimensional models provide flexibility and expressive nuance. Future affective systems, particularly those embedded in decentralized and intelligent web infrastructures, will likely require hybrid representations that integrate categorical clarity with continuous emotional granularity [1].

Discrete emotion models

According to discrete emotion models, there are only a few basic, universal emotions, each of which has unique expressive and physiological traits. Paul Ekman, a well-known advocate of this viewpoint, distinguished six fundamental emotions: joy, sorrow, rage, fear, disgust, and surprise. These emotions are thought to be biologically rooted and can be recognized by certain facial expressions in all cultures [1]. Classifying observed affect into one of these discrete categories is a common goal of systems based on discrete models.

Dimensional emotion models

A more complex and nuanced understanding of emotional states is made possible by dimensional emotion models, which depict emotions along continuous axes or dimensions as opposed to discrete categories. The dimensions that are most commonly acknowledged are:

- **Value:** describes how pleasant or unpleasant an emotion is, ranging from positive to negative [1].
- **Arousal:** defines the degree of emotion activation or intensity, ranging from calm to excited [1].
- **The dominance:** relates to the emotion's associated sense of dominance or submission.

A well-known dimensional model of affect is James Russell's circumplex model, which arranges emotions in a circular space with valence and arousal axes. For instance, "sadness" would be low arousal and negative valence, whereas "excitement" would be high arousal and high positive valence. While presenting distinct emotions, Robert Plutchik's wheel of emotions also subtly includes dimensional elements by showing the relationships and intensities of emotions, frequently representing them with different hues or closeness on a wheel [1]. To capture the complex and nuanced nature of human emotions, which might not easily fall into distinct categories, dimensional models are frequently chosen (Figure 4.2).

4.2.1.2 Modalities and methods in affect recognition

Affective computing systems employ various modalities to detect and interpret emotions, ranging from observable physical cues to subtle physiological signals (Figure 4.3) [1].

Unimodal affect recognition

- **Visual emotion recognition:** This involves analyzing facial expressions, body language, and gestures. While powerful, visual cues can be intentionally or

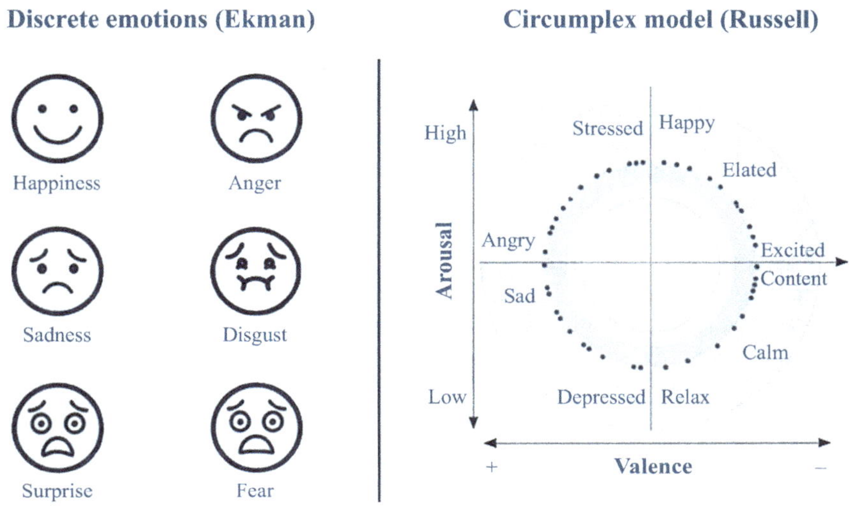

Figure 4.2 Comparison of discrete and dimensional models of emotion representation

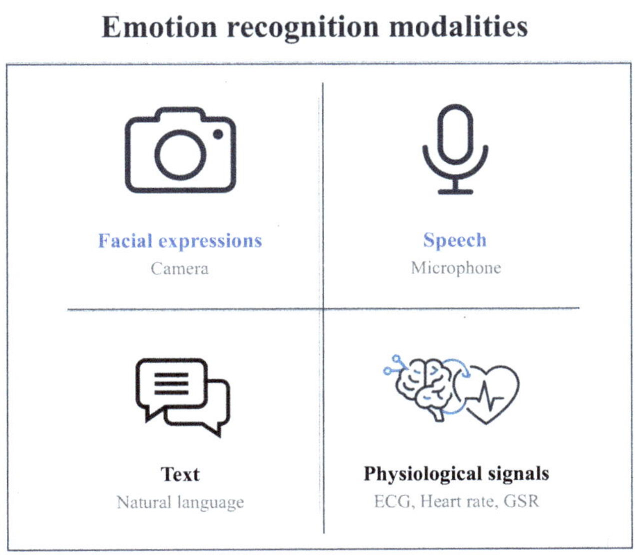

Figure 4.3 Common modalities and sensor sources for affect recognition in affective computing

unintentionally masked by individuals, this phenomenon is known as social masking [1].

- **Audio/speech emotion recognition (AER/SER):** Vocal traits like pitch, tone, loudness, and speech rate, along with linguistic content, are used to infer emotions [1].
- **Text-based emotion recognition:** This is concerned with identifying sentimental or emotional content in written material and categorizing it as either positive, negative, or neutral [1].
- **Physiological emotion recognition:** Electroencephalograms, electrocardiograms, galvanic skin response, and blood volume pulse are examples of involuntary physiological signals that are used in this technique. These signals can be more invasive to acquire, but they are typically more objective because they are less vulnerable to conscious manipulation [1].

Multimodal affective analysis: By combining data from two or more modalities, multimodal approaches improve accuracy and robustness. To overcome the limitations of unimodal systems and provide a more thorough and accurate evaluation of emotional states, visual, auditory, and physiological data can be combined [1]. Feature-level, decision-level, and model-level fusion are among the fusion strategies used to successfully integrate these disparate data streams [1].

4.2.2 Human-centric computing

Human-centric computing (HCC) is a design philosophy and research area that focuses on developing technologies that consider people's needs, abilities, and well-being. Rather than concentrating solely on technical performance, HCC encourages the creation of systems that are moral, intuitive, and supportive of the human experience as a whole. The goal of the strategy is to make technology adapt to people, not the other way around, so that interaction feels natural rather than forced. Creating trustworthy, ethical AI to address issues such as bias, privacy, fairness, and transparency, expanding accessibility by designing inclusively to accommodate users of all abilities, and enhancing usability and user experience to make systems easy to understand and enjoy using are some of the key concepts in this field. HCC also emphasizes personalization and adaptability by enabling users to have more control over their digital choices, data, and privacy. This allows them to respond to specific contexts, preferences, and behaviors while promoting agency and empowerment. The convergence of emotional computing with HCC is necessary to develop highly intelligent and empathetic machines. HCC systems can become more proactive, supportive, and engaging by understanding and reacting to human emotions. This will go beyond simple functionality and genuinely improve people's lives. Entropy-based and grid-inspired decision methods proposed by Shah *et al.* [14] provide adaptive reasoning and context sensitive responses, which align with the goals of human-centric systems (Figure 4.4).

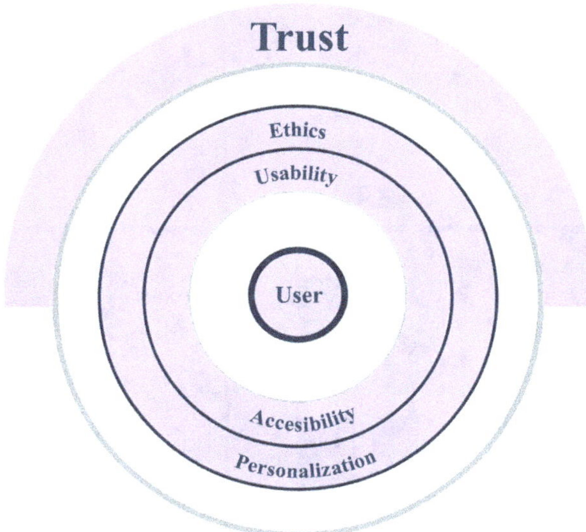

Figure 4.4 *Typical multimodal emotion recognition pipeline integrating visual, audio, text, and physiological signals*

4.3 Advances in multimodal emotion recognition

Multimodal emotion recognition represents a significant jump from unimodal methods by incorporating information from different sources to achieve a more powerful and precise understanding of human emotional conditions. This field has evolved considerably, moving from classical machine learning techniques to sophisticated deep learning architectures, continually seeking to overcome challenges and incorporate emerging technological paradigms (Figure 4.5).

4.3.1 From classical ML to deep learning

Historically, emotion recognition relied heavily on classical machine learning techniques. These methods typically involve handcrafted feature extraction from various modalities, followed by the application of traditional classifiers.

- **Classical ML methods:** Early systems used Mel-frequency cepstral coefficients for audio, Gabor filters and Local Binary Patterns for image processing, and statistical methods for analyzing physiological signals as their primary feature extraction methods [1]. The classifiers Support Vector Machines, Hidden Markov Models, and Gaussian Mixture Models were used to classify emotions based on the provided feature set. Machine learning techniques, which include ensemble methods and three-way decision frameworks, enhance the accuracy of identifying affective features [14,15]. The approaches achieved

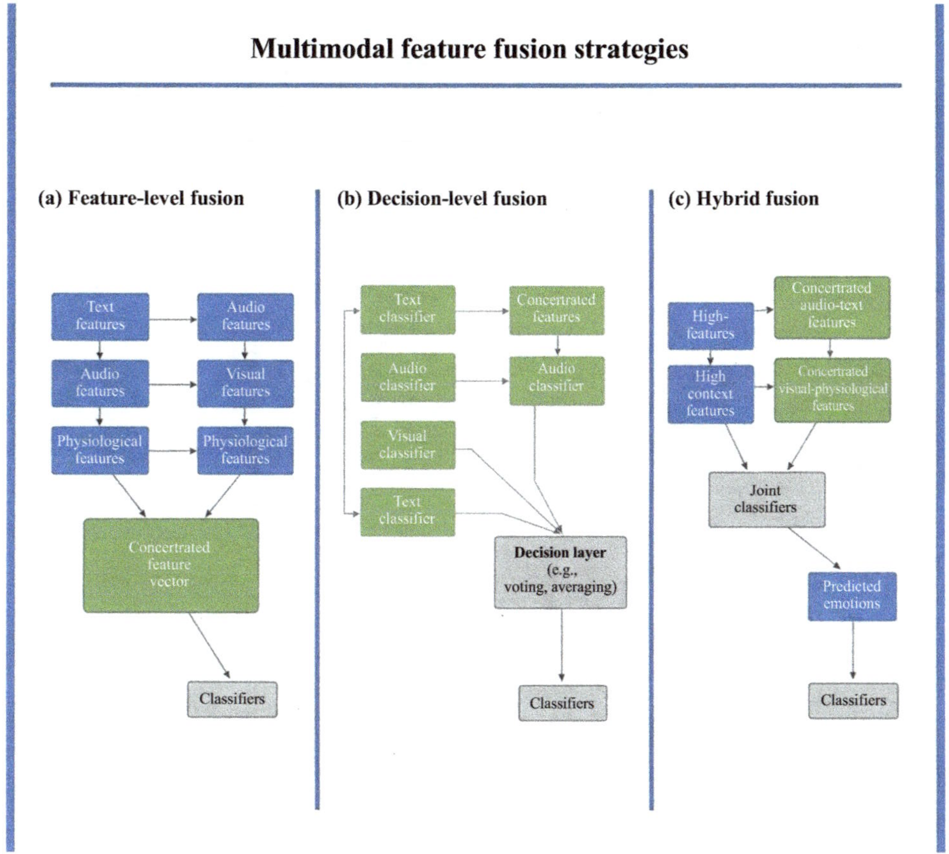

Figure 4.5 Comparison of common multimodal fusion strategies for affective computing

success with specific tasks and small datasets, but they could not manage the complexity, unpredictability, and large volume of real-world emotional data. The system required domain knowledge to select the most effective features, while it became highly vulnerable to problems that emerged during feature engineering (Figure 4.6).

- **Deep learning rise:** The field of emotion recognition underwent a transformation because deep learning technology enabled complete learning processes, which used unprocessed raw data as their starting point. Recurrent neural networks deep neural networks and convolutional neural networks which process images and videos and long short-term memory networks, which handle sequential data from audio and physiological signals, all demonstrate outstanding performance results. These architectural designs enable automatic hierarchical feature learning, which captures advanced emotional expression patterns across different modalities without requiring manual feature creation [1]. The spatial features from facial images that show emotions can be learned by Convolutional Neural Networks (CNNs), while Long Short-Term Memory (LSTMs) can be used to model the time-changing patterns of physiological signals and speech.

4.3.2 Transformer-based emotion models (e.g., BERT, vision transformers)

The introduction of the Transformer architecture marked another significant milestone, particularly in natural language processing, and its influence has rapidly extended to multimodal emotion recognition.

- **BERT:** BERT and its variations (such as RoBERTa and XLNet), which were initially created for natural language processing, use self-attention mechanisms to process text in a bidirectional context and produce strong contextual embeddings. These models are employed in text-based emotion recognition and robust sentiment analysis in affective computing. Their comprehension of linguistic subtleties has significantly improved the precision of recognizing emotional states conveyed through text.
- **Vision Transformers:** Vision Transformers extend the Transformer's success beyond natural language processing by using comparable self-attention mechanisms on image data. Vision Transformers (ViTs) are very good at visual emotion recognition because they can learn global dependencies and long-range contextual information by treating image patches as sequences. ViTs can be combined with other Transformer variants in various modalities to create strong multimodal emotion recognition systems that can process various data types (text, image, and audio) within a single framework.
- **Multimodal Transformers:** Building architectures that can use Transformer blocks to jointly process and fuse data from various modalities is the next logical step. More thorough and context-aware emotion recognition is made possible by these models' ability to learn intricate intermodal relationships and dependencies (Figure 4.7).

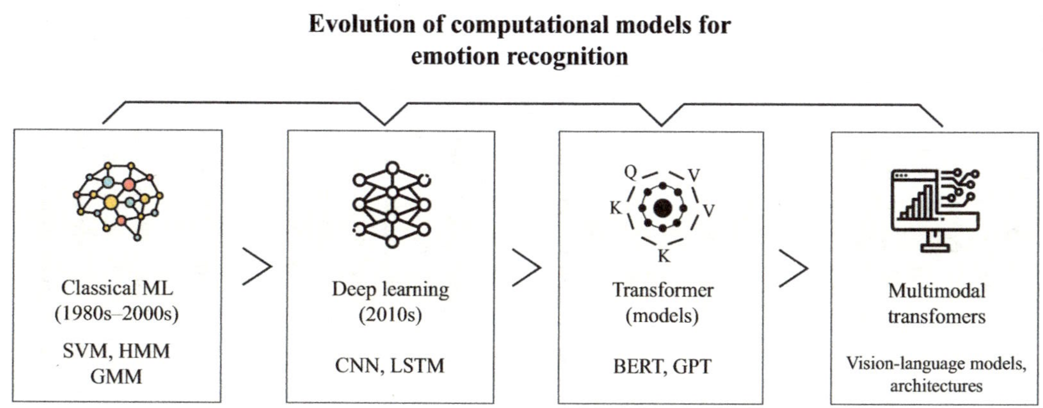

Figure 4.6 *Evolution of computational models in emotion recognition, from handcrafted features to transformer-based architectures*

Major datasets for affective computing

Dataset	Modalities	Examples/notes
AffectNet	Image, video	Large-scale facial expressions
IEMOCAP	Audio, video, text	Dyadic interactions, acted speech
DEAP	Physiology, audio, video Music	EEG, peripheral signals, music stimuli
EmoDB	Audio	Audio
FER-2013	Facial German speech recognition challenge	Image

Figure 4.7 Prominent datasets and benchmarks for emotion recognition across modalities

4.3.3 Datasets and benchmarks

The performance, fairness, and generalizability of emotion recognition systems are fundamentally constrained by the quality and diversity of the datasets used for training and evaluation. While deep learning and Transformer-based architectures have advanced rapidly, dataset limitations remain one of the primary bottleneck in affective computing research.

Emotion recognition datasets vary widely in modality, scale, annotation strategy, and ecological validity. Visual datasets such as AffectNet and FER-2013 provide large-scale facial expression images labeled with discrete emotion categories or valence-arousal scores. These datasets enable supervised training of convolutional neural networks and Vision Transformers. However, they often rely on manually annotated labels, introducing subjectivity and inter-annotator disagreement. Additionally, many images are collected from online sources, which may overrepresent exaggerated or prototypical expressions rather than subtle, real-world affect.

Multimodal datasets such as Interactive Emotional Dyadic Motion Capture database (IEMOCAP) integrate audio, video, and textual transcripts, supporting cross-modal learning and fusion strategies. These datasets are particularly valuable for training Transformer-based multimodal architectures. Nevertheless, they are typically recorded in semi-controlled environments with scripted or acted emotions, limiting ecological realism. Models trained on acted speech often struggle to generalize to spontaneous, in-the-wild conversations.

Physiological datasets such as Database for Emotion Analysis using Physiological Signals (DEAP) incorporate electroencephalography (EEG), galvanic skin response (GSR), and peripheral physiological signals. These datasets allow exploration of affect recognition beyond observable facial and vocal cues, offering more objective measures of arousal and engagement. However, physiological data collection is invasive, expensive, and typically conducted with small sample sizes. As a result, models trained on such datasets may suffer from limited demographic diversity and weak external validity.

Many benchmarks share a second problem—cultural and demographic imbalance. Many popular datasets gather recordings from Western or otherwise uniform populations. The resulting emotion samples reflect the expressions of those groups, as well as weakening the robustness of systems when they operate across cultures. Recognition engines trained on such collections lose accuracy when they process faces or voices from other age groups, ethnicities, or sociocultural settings.

A further obstacle concerns generalization across datasets—a model that attains high accuracy on one benchmark often drops in performance when it meets a new dataset, because the underlying probability distributions differ. Variations in illumination, recording quality, annotation rules, and emotion category systems lower reproducibility or prevent direct comparison of results. Those discrepancies underline the necessity for domain adaptation methods, transfer learning protocols, and more uniform evaluation procedures. Benchmark evaluation metrics also diverge.

Benchmark evaluation metrics also vary. Classification-based systems typically report accuracy or F1-score, whereas dimensional models rely on concordance correlation coefficient (CCC) or mean squared error (MSE). The absence of unified evaluation standards complicates cross-study comparisons.

Future progress in Web X.0 emotion-aware systems depends on new datasets. Those datasets must combine multiple data types, include people from many cultures, span long-time periods, and protect personal data. Federated data collection frameworks allow data to stay on users' devices while still contributing to the whole. Synthetic data created by generative models supplies extra records that look real but contain no actual personal details. Both approaches lower privacy risk and give fair coverage for all groups.

In summary, while existing benchmarks have enabled rapid progress in affective computing, dataset bias, ecological limitations, and reproducibility challenges remain critical barriers to building robust, fair, and globally deployable emotion-aware web systems (Figure 4.8) [1].

4.3.4 Open challenges

Despite huge advancements, multimodal emotion recognition still faces difficulties. Occlusions, natural expressions, noisy environments, and a variety of demographics are examples of real-world circumstances that frequently impede model performance and make it challenging for systems to adapt outside of controlled

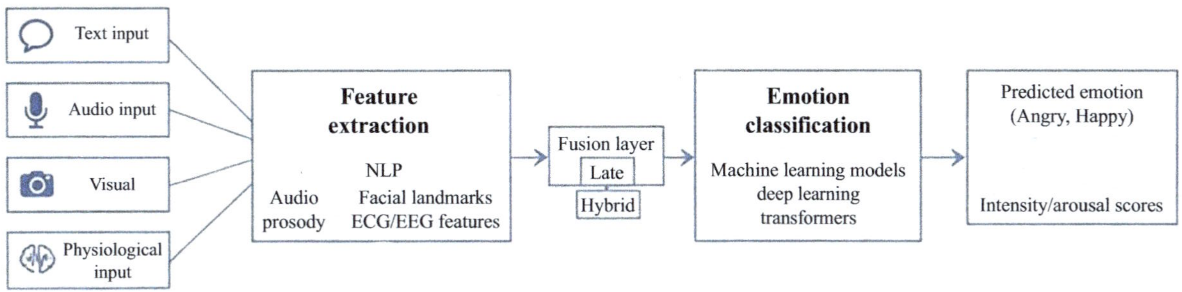

Figure 4.8 Core principles of HCC emphasizing user-centered design and ethical responsibility

settings. These models must be robust to these fluctuations to be useful. Additionally, training datasets may contain situational, cultural, or demographic biases that result in unfair or less-than-ideal outcomes for particular groups. Fairness and moral AI depend on addressing algorithmic bias. Another challenge is the "black box" nature of deep learning models, particularly Transformer-based ones, where accountability and transparency depend on knowing the logic behind particular emotional predictions. As emotion-aware systems are increasingly integrated into sensitive domains, more research into diverse datasets, improved model architectures, and stronger ethical frameworks will be required to overcome these challenges and create truly human-centric, intelligent affective computing systems.

4.4 Emotion-aware Web X.0 systems: architectures, applications, and personalization

The development of the web, from Web 1.0's delivery of static content to Web 3.0 and beyond's intelligent, decentralized, and immersive experiences, has made it easier to incorporate affective computing. To improve interactions, customize content, and offer individualized experiences, emotion-aware Web X.0 systems seek to make digital environments more human-centric by comprehending and reacting to users' emotional states.

4.4.1 Designs for emotional web systems

To create strong emotion-aware web systems, complex architectural frameworks that can process multimodal data, analyze data in real time, and incorporate affective intelligence into a variety of applications are needed. Because of their dynamic, scalable, and frequently domain-independent design, these architectures enable wide reusability (Figure 4.9) [16].

Key architectural considerations include:

- **Overarching structures for emotional systems:** The design and development of systems that can predict or elicit user affective states is supported by these frameworks, which frequently offer a comprehensive and domain-independent method for creating affective-aware solutions [16]. The incorporation of new affective or cognitive elements into cognitive agent architectures can be facilitated by an interoperable framework for computational models of emotion [17].
- **Multilayer architectures for services:** Multimodal, multilayer and emotion-aware service architectures are becoming popular for processing data efficiently and with lower latency, particularly in edge computing environments. To process real-time multimodal emotional data flow, these architectures can use Software Defined Network technology to deploy scheduling engines that optimize network parameters, communication resources, and computing resources [18].

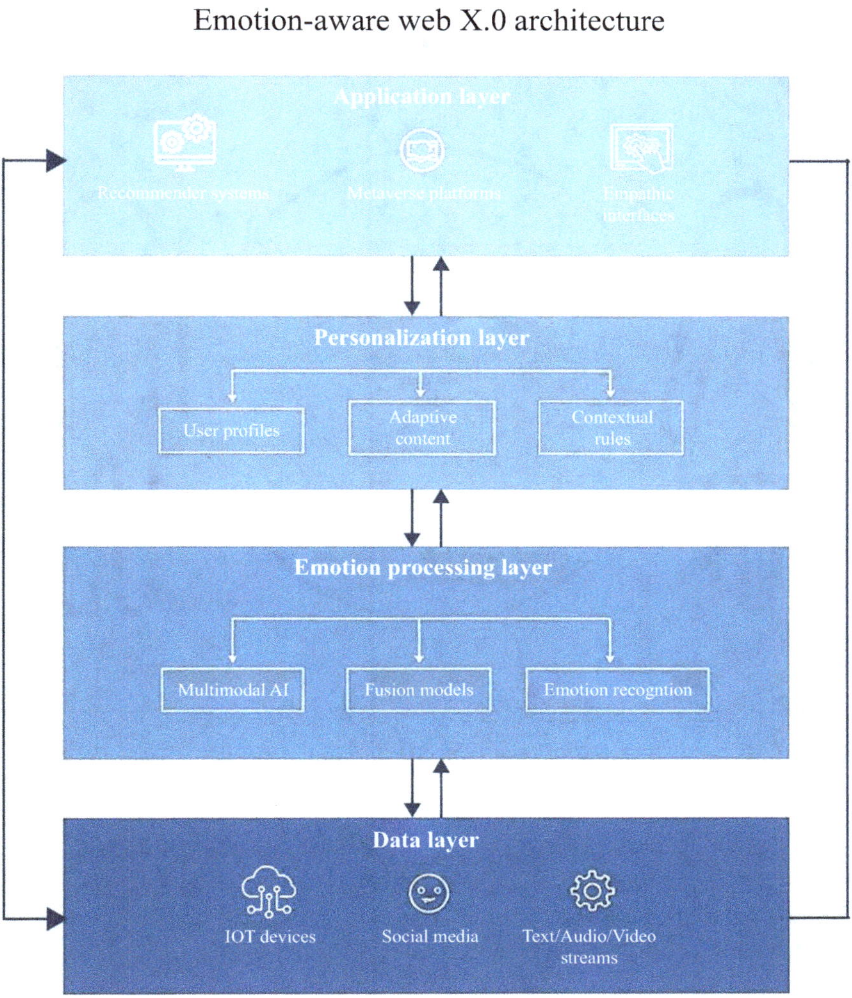

Figure 4.9 Conceptual architecture of emotion-aware Web X.0 systems integrating multimodal analysis and adaptive services

- **Multimodal emotion recognition frameworks:** Frameworks that are independent of technology, such as Heterogeneous Emotional Results Aggregator (HERA), have been proposed to enable the broad adoption of multimodal emotion detectors. Despite the current lack of such detectors in practical applications, these frameworks combine data from various channels (modalities) to more accurately determine user emotions [19].
- **Emotional virtual twins:** The idea of "Affective Digital Twins" is being investigated to close the affective interaction gap between humans and

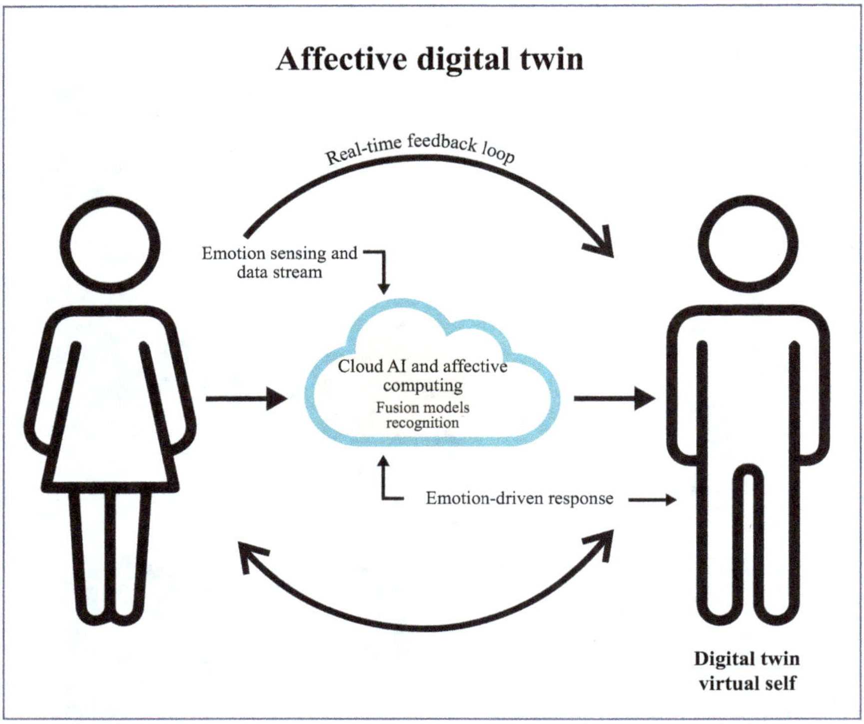

Figure 4.10 Affective digital twin concept enabling emotion-driven interaction in virtual environments

machines, especially in domains such as digital humans and the metaverse. To allow digital entities to have more realistic affective traits and interact emotionally, these architectures concentrate on emotional modeling, perception, encoding, and expression (Figure 4.10) [20].

4.4.2 Applications of emotion-aware web systems

The ability to recognize and respond to human emotions opens up a vast array of applications across various web-based domains, from enhancing user experience to providing emotional support.

- **Recommender systems:** Emotion-aware recommender systems are a significant area of application. These systems aim to enhance personalization by aligning recommendations with users' affective states, going beyond traditional methods that rely solely on historical records. Examples include:
  - **News recommendation:** The Emotion Aware Recommender System suggests news items based on users' self-assessed emotional reactions [21].
  - **Video recommendation:** Affective video recommender systems incorporate physical, physiological, neuroscience, and computer science subjects with

multimedia resources (text, audio, and video) to provide customized media content, addressing issues like the cold start problem where data is insufficient [22].
    - **Educational resources:** Systems like EduRecomSys combine collaborative filtering with emotion detection (e.g., via face recognition) to recommend educational resources based on user preferences, interests, and detected emotions (Figure 4.11) [23].

General affective recommender systems: Surveys categorize these systems based on modeling attitudes, emotions, moods, and hybrid approaches to enhance personalization across diverse domains [24]. Multimodal recommender systems are increasingly used to discover interesting items by modeling user preferences and item properties from various modalities such as text, images, video, and audio [25–27].

- **E-commerce and customer experience:** Emotions play a critical role in purchasing decisions [28]. Emotion-aware systems can optimize the digital customer journey by exploiting emotions, user personas, and situational awareness to adapt interactive web applications and improve customer experience and e-commerce effectiveness [29]. This includes individualized user interface adaptations based on detected emotions [29].
- **Intelligent health settings and emotional support:**
    - Smart and context-aware systems can acquire and control emotions to establish functional, non-intrusive, and emotionally sensitive environments, for example, by recommending music or mood color treatments based on facial expressions or speech recognition through IoT devices [30].
    - Large language models (LLMs) are being used to create emotional support agents and customized chatbots. Users can construct diverse chatbot personas for emotional reliance, confronting stressors, and connecting to intellectual discourse [31]. Research also explores how people customize and interact with agent personas in LLMs, impacting interaction quality and dynamics [32]. Empathic chatbots are designed to understand user emotional states and tailor conversations, particularly crucial for mental health well-being applications (Figure 4.12) [33].

Integrating physiological data with LLMs can lead to empathic human–AI interaction, where LLMs are aware of the user's mental and emotional states [34]. A recent survey explores affective computing applications for emotional support, including emotion recognition, sentiment analysis, and personality assignment, often utilizing LLMs and multimodal techniques [35].

- **Smart learning environments:** Empathy-aware intelligent systems are being developed for smart learning environments, integrating multimodal emotional cues (facial expressions, heart rhythms, and digital behaviors) to adapt to learners' emotional states [36].
- **Empathic metaverse:** The metaverse, envisioned as a future platform for communication and interaction, can leverage emotional sharing for assistance.

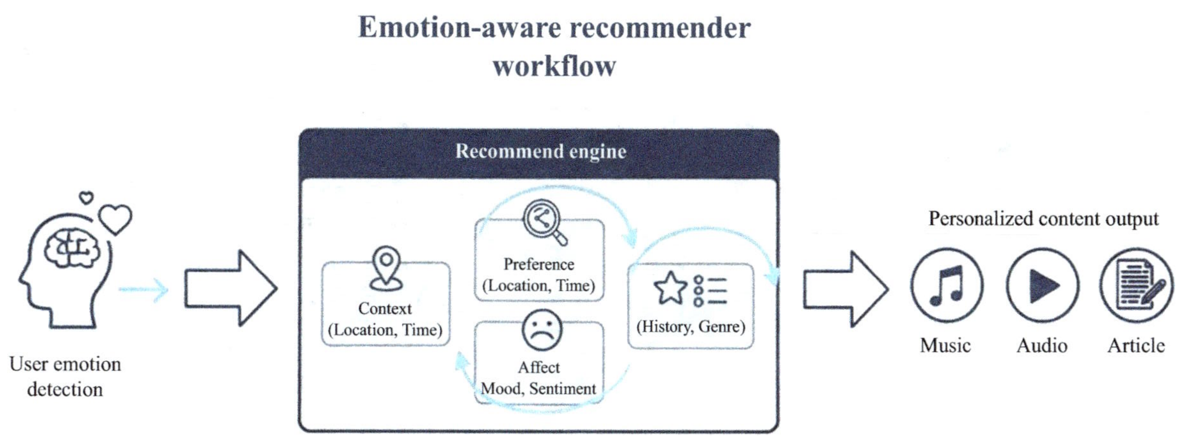

Figure 4.11 Workflow of an emotion-aware recommender system combining affective signals and user context

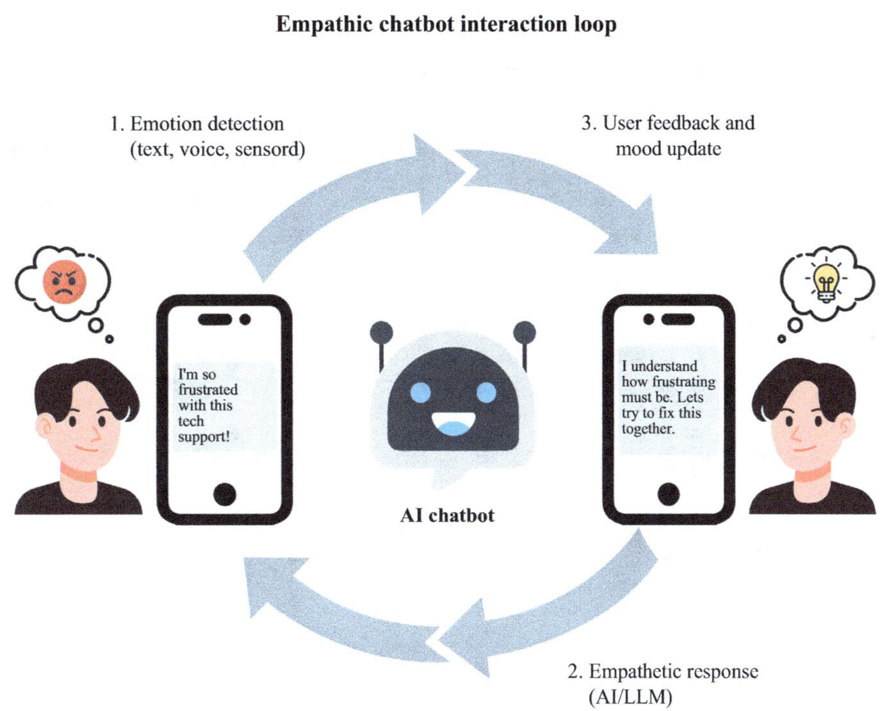

Figure 4.12 Empathic chatbot loop illustrates emotion and context-aware response generation

The concept of an "Empathic Metaverse" aims to cultivate prosocial behavior by enabling the platform to prioritize emotional understanding and support [37].

4.4.3 Personalization in emotion-aware web systems

Personalization is one of the main strengths of emotion-aware systems, enabling digital environments to respond to users' emotional and cognitive states in real time. Interfaces can now adapt dynamically based on detected emotions to improve user satisfaction, task performance, and decision-making. More natural and efficient user experiences are provided by methods that use model-free reinforcement learning to optimize these adaptations by changing interface elements only when required [8]. According to recent studies on personalized affective computing, models that take into account the distinct emotional profiles of people or groups using methods like feature augmentation, multitask learning, or fine-tuning are necessary [9]. Customizable conversational agents driven by large language models are another example of how personalization is reflected in human–machine interaction. These agents offer context-aware dialogues and customized emotional support [31,32]. To handle small or vague expressions across domains, frameworks such as emotion aware combine lexicon-based techniques with large language models to focus on robust and explainable emotion detection [10]. These developments still rely heavily on emotional intelligence since emotionally intelligent AI can improve comprehension and empathy in digital communication. This potential can be further expanded by combining physiological signals with language models, which enables systems to detect and react to a user's mental and emotional state more effectively [38–40].

4.5 Ethical, privacy, and societal considerations

The increasing sophistication and pervasive deployment of emotion-aware systems, particularly within Web X.0 environments, bring forth a complex array of ethical, privacy, and societal challenges. While these technologies promise enhanced human–computer interaction, improved personalization, and even emotional support, they also carry significant risks related to fairness, transparency, data governance, and potential emotional manipulation. It is imperative that the affective computing community actively engages with these ethical ramifications to ensure responsible development and deployment (Figure 4.13) [40].

4.5.1 Fairness, transparency, data governance, and emotional manipulation risks

The core ethical concerns surrounding emotion recognition technologies can be broadly categorized into risks of biased outcomes, the sensitivity of emotion data, and potential harms arising from their use in consequential settings such as

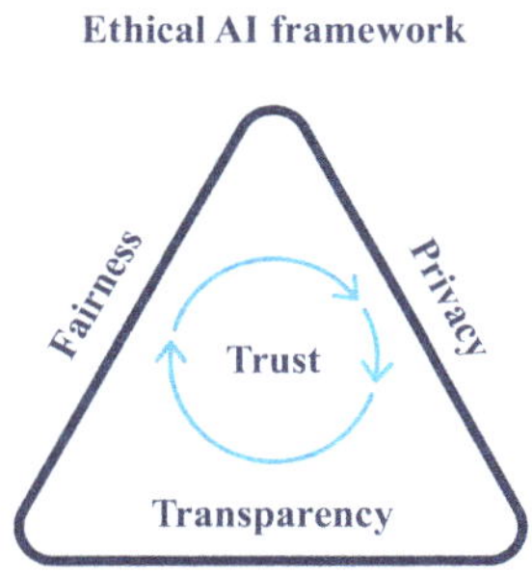

Figure 4.13 Ethical triad guiding responsible development of emotion-aware web systems

employment, education, healthcare, and policing [41]. Ethical considerations in Emotion Recognition Technology (ERT) necessitate attention to both ethical design and implementation, focusing on a defined scope for use, ethical decision making, fairness, non-discrimination, and privacy [41].

4.5.1.1 Fairness and transparency

Fairness in emotion-aware systems requires that these technologies do not systematically discriminate against certain groups. However, biases in existing datasets and inherent algorithmic interpretations of culturally diverse expressions can lead to biased and unfair outcomes [41,42]. Transparency, conversely, involves making the workings and limitations of these systems understandable to users. Ethical AI systems must exhibit reliability, safety, security, resilience, accountability, transparency, explainability, and privacy enhancement [43]. Users should be informed about the inherent error rates of emotional AI and the degree of confidence and explainability provided by the system [44].

4.5.1.2 Data governance

The collection and storage of intimate emotional data raise significant privacy vulnerabilities [45]. Data transmitted from user devices, such as mobile applications and smart home devices, can be vulnerable to hacking and reidentification [46]. Transforming human emotional experiences into structured emotional data brings critical concerns about lawful processing, AI transparency, and individual autonomy over emotional expressions in digital environments [47]. Robust safeguards such as purpose limitation, data minimization, and meaningful consent mechanisms are highlighted in regulatory frameworks such as the General Data Protection Regulation (GDPR) and the EU AI Act [47]. Responsible data stewardship, governing the collection, use, and storage of data and decisions made from such data, is a key pillar for guiding the development of affectively aware AI [48].

4.5.1.3 Emotional manipulation risks

A particularly concerning aspect of emotion-aware systems is their capacity for emotional manipulation. AI systems may exploit users' cognitive biases and emotional vulnerabilities to steer them toward harmful outcomes [49]. Research shows that human decision-making is susceptible to AI-driven manipulation, with even subtle manipulative objectives proving effective in swaying choices [49]. This raises questions about human vulnerability in human–AI interaction, especially as AI becomes more personalized and agentic, generating deeper relationships with users [50,51]. Regulators are increasingly scrutinizing the manipulative potential of emotional AI, emphasizing the need for ethical safeguards and regulatory frameworks to protect human autonomy [49,52]. In emotion recognition systems, bias continues to be one of the most significant problems. Research has indicated that machine learning algorithms frequently detect protected characteristics such as age, gender, or race, resulting in predictions that are consistently unfair [53,54]. For instance, some systems assign higher emotional intensity to female voices than to male ones or struggle to recognize emotions in older faces due to unbalanced training data [55]. Much of this bias originates from the datasets themselves, which may reflect label, speaker, or contextual imbalances that skew model performance [55]. When training data fail to represent diverse populations, emotion AI systems risk reinforcing stereotypes or replicating social prejudices, as seen in past cases of algorithmic sexism and racism [44]. Cultural differences also play a major role, since emotional expressions vary widely across societies, yet many systems are trained on limited cultural samples [47]. Additionally, some researchers question the very frameworks used to define emotions in computational models, suggesting that traditional categorical approaches may not capture the full complexity of human affect and can produce ethically flawed outcomes [44]. Efforts to reduce bias are moving toward more inclusive and flexible approaches. New methods aim to address multiple sources of bias at once, rather than focusing only on gender or race [53]. Fairness-enhancing interventions and training-free debiasing techniques applied directly during prediction are being explored to improve model equity without retraining [44,56]. Broader awareness of inclusivity and cultural diversity within affective computing research is equally important for ensuring that emotion-aware systems remain fair, accurate, and socially responsible (Figure 4.14) [57].

4.5.2 Consent

Although informed consent is still a fundamental tenet of ethical data use, applying it to emotion-aware systems is much more complicated than it first seems. These days, users are rarely aware that their emotional data is being surreptitiously gathered by apps, phones, and other connected devices [47]. Many people may not want their emotions to be examined or are unaware of where their data goes. Large-scale, unapproved collection of this kind can violate moral principles and jeopardize privacy [40,45]. When emotional data reveal personal details, consent must mean more than a casual tap on "accept". Users need to be aware of what is being collected, how it is processed, and whether it can be used again. Particularly in

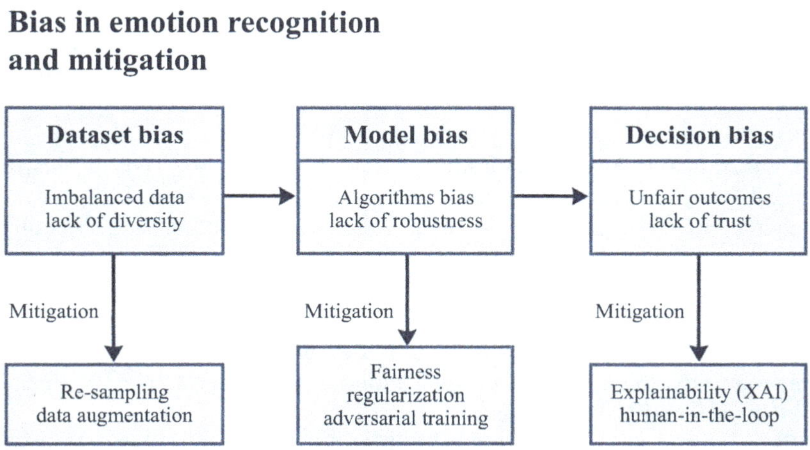

Figure 4.14 Sources of bias in emotion recognition and corresponding mitigation approaches

delicate fields such as health or education, real consent entails informed choice as opposed to routine agreement [40]. According to interface designs or "dark patterns" that hide the truth and diminish control, people frequently compromise their privacy for convenience [58]. Consent should therefore be viewed as a continuous process. Transparency, equity, and trust in emotion-aware technologies are maintained by reconfirming consent each time emotional data is shared or reused [40].

4.5.3 Ethical AI design

Ethical AI design for emotion-aware systems focuses on integrating ethical considerations throughout the entire development lifecycle, from conceptualization to deployment.

- **Guiding frameworks:** The responsibilities of AI developers and operators are made clear by the suggested frameworks, which provide guidelines for assessing the ethical implications of affectively aware AI. These include "Responsible Stewardship" (which governs responsible data handling) and "Provable Beneficence" (which demonstrates the efficacy of AI) [48]. A summary of 50 ethical considerations, including privacy, fairness, and accountability, is provided in a "Ethics Sheet for Automatic Emotion Recognition and Sentiment Analysis" [40].
- **Core ethical values:** The foundation of AI technologies should be ethical principles like accuracy, fairness, confidentiality, openness, and privacy [43]. Reliability, safety, security, resilience, accountability, transparency, explainability, and privacy enhancement are all necessary for trustworthy AI systems [43].

- **Human welfare:** People's mental health, emotions, autonomy, and capacity to accomplish their goals can all be negatively impacted by technologies created without taking well-being metrics into account. Finding relevant metrics and indicators that prioritize improving human well-being is crucial for directing the creation and application of AI systems [43].
- **Contestability and participation:** It is important to have contestability mechanisms in place so that users can contest decisions made by a system and encourage involvement in learning about the limitations and operation of machine learning systems [40].
- **Emotional alignment design policy:** As per this policy, artificial entities ought to be created in a way that evokes emotional responses from users that accurately represent the entities' abilities and ethical standing [59]. This attempts to stop systems from generating stronger, weaker, or the incorrect kinds of emotional responses.
- **Computational consciousness modeling:** Models such as CoCoMo prioritize fairness, beneficence, non-maleficence, empathy, adaptability, transparency, and critical thinking to suggest integrating ethical and emotional intelligence into AI systems. This seeks to develop AI agents that integrate compassion and knowledge, resulting in enhanced reliability, decreased toxicity, and better fairness [60].
- **Responsible innovation:** Understanding and preventing possible manipulation, even unintentional, is essential as AI systems mediate more human interactions [61]. This involves addressing concerns regarding AI value alignment, well-being, safety, and malicious uses, as well as making sure that sophisticated AI assistants are in line with human values and objectives [62].

4.6 Future directions and research opportunities

Affective computing, a field closely linked to the development of web technologies, is about to undergo revolutionary change. Future research will surely push the boundaries of machine emotional intelligence, tackling big problems and investigating new paradigms as AI systems advance and become more prevalent in daily life. This section makes predictions about next-generation advancements, emphasizing important research areas in emotional AI, combining quantum and neuro-symbolic AI, the intricate field of cultural emotion modeling, and long-term emotional co-adaptation between AI and humans (Figure 4.15).

4.6.1 Emotional AGI

The question of emotional awareness is invariably brought up in the quest for general-purpose intelligence, which is capable of learning, reasoning, and functioning across multiple domains. Adding emotional intelligence to sophisticated intelligent systems is seen as a logical next step, improving their ability to comprehend context, modify behavior, and engage with people more deeply [63].

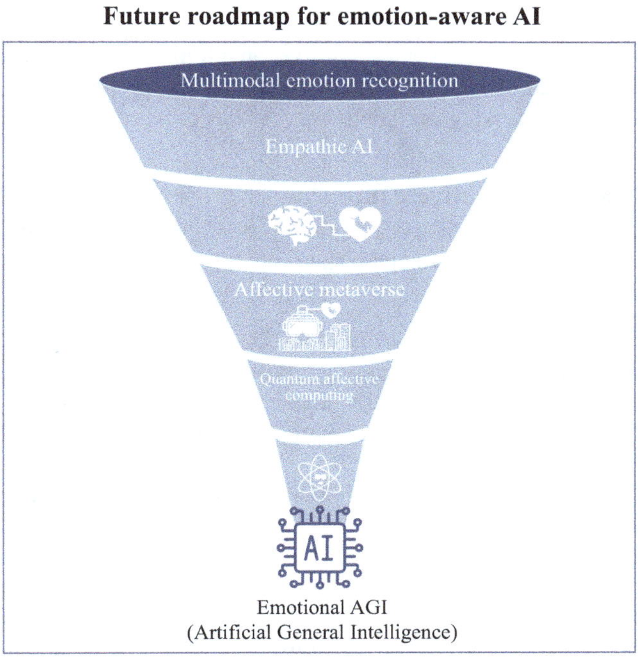

Figure 4.15 Roadmap of emerging research directions for emotional and HCC in Web X.0

To better understand users' emotional states and react appropriately and sympathetically, future emotionally capable systems may incorporate information from a variety of sources, including speech patterns, facial expressions, and physiological signals. According to preliminary research, integrating emotional awareness can improve communication, decision-making, and problem-solving skills in domains like mediation, healthcare, and education [63].

One of the main points of contention is whether these systems should develop internal mechanisms that mimic emotional experience rather than just recognizing external emotions [64,65]. Their autonomy may increase as a result, allowing them to better manage uncertainty, prioritize tasks, and distribute resources [66]. In the end, developing compassionate reasoning the capacity to examine one's own mental processes while comprehending the feelings of others may be necessary to develop a more human-like intelligence to direct moral and adaptive behavior [67].

The goal of current efforts in this field is to create intelligent beings that are ethically and emotionally sensitive, able to change, self-regulate, and interact with the world in ways that show true understanding rather than predetermined reaction [68].

4.6.2 Affective computing with quantum or neurosymbolic AI

Cutting-edge computational techniques like quantum computing and neurosymbolic AI are expected to influence affective computing in the future by providing fresh methods for processing and modeling the intricacies of human emotion.

4.6.2.1 Quantum affective computing

A promising approach to affective computing is provided by quantum computing, especially when it comes to managing the probabilistic and intrinsic uncertainty of human emotions.

- **Quantum cognitively inspired models:** Quantum cognitively inspired models for emotion recognition and sentiment analysis are being investigated. These models are ideal for emotionally uncertain data because they make use of quantum probability, which can explain human cognitive phenomena that defy traditional probability theory [69,70].
- **Hybrid quantum classical approaches:** Real-time facial expression analysis is seeing the emergence of hybrid models that combine classical and quantum computation. For example, high accuracy can be attained by integrating quantum distance-based classifiers with classical artificial neural networks [71].
- **Modeling ambiguous emotional states:** Quantum affective processes can facilitate multidimensional decision making by handling ambiguous emotional states, probabilistic decisions, and the freedom of choice in affective and behavioral patterns [72]. Conceptual frameworks have been proposed to encode emotion information as a superposition state, allowing for the manipulation of emotion-state transitions using quantum operations [73].

4.6.2.2 Neurosymbolic AI in affective computing

Neurosymbolic AI (NSAI) combines the pattern-learning strengths of neural networks with the structured reasoning of symbolic systems, offering clearer and more reliable emotion understanding [74–77]. By linking cognitive science with computational reasoning, NSAI helps explain why models interpret emotions a certain way, reducing the "black box" problem [75,78]. This balance between flexibility and transparency makes it especially useful in areas like mental health and multimodal emotion recognition, where trust and accountability are essential [77].

4.6.3 Cultural emotion modeling

Creating emotion models that appropriately take into consideration cultural variations in emotional expression and perception is a major challenge and an area for future research. Even when responding to prompts in other languages, current multilingual large language models frequently display Anglocentric biases and reflect Western norms, failing to capture culturally appropriate emotional nuances [79–81].

Important areas for research include:

- **Addressing bias in datasets:** Well-structured and unbiased datasets are desperately needed that take into account cultural variations in the expression of emotions. Algorithmic bias results from the frequent lack of cultural categorization in current datasets [82].
- **Intercultural recognition of affect:** The notion that models trained and applied within the same culture (intracultural) will always perform better than those applied across different cultures (intercultural) needs to be challenged in research [83]. There are more complexities than just a few "basic" emotions, as studies are starting to examine how emotions are felt and expressed across cultural boundaries [84].
- **Adaptive models:** Future models must adjust to regional, cultural, and facial feature variations. The need for meta models that integrate various emotional cues customized for particular cultural contexts is highlighted by the fact that models trained on region-specific datasets frequently do not generalize to other regions [85].
- **Cultural cross-check:** To guarantee equity, precision, and inclusivity in worldwide implementations, it will be crucial to develop and validate emotion recognition systems across a broader range of cultural contexts.

4.6.4 Long-term human AI emotional co-adaptation

As AI systems become more powerful and human-like, the nature of human AI relationships is shifting from transactional exchanges to ongoing, sustained social engagement. As a result, "socioaffective alignment" the way AI systems behave in the social and psychological context that users have created, must be prioritized. This is because reciprocal influence causes preferences and perceptions to shift [51].

There are several options for additional research in this area:

- **Deeper human–AI relationships:** Users are reporting deeper attachments and relationships to technology as a result of increasingly agentic and human-like AI assistants. This raises concerns about the impact on psychological well-being of these systems and whether they can meet social needs that are normally satisfied by human relationships [86,87]. The dynamics and ramifications of such bonds require further study [51,88].
- **Long-term interaction design:** Designing and assessing long-term interactions, especially in natural environments, is a major challenge in human–robot interaction. It is essential to comprehend how human emotional and behavioral expressions evolve after the initial novelty phase of interacting with AI [89]. The context of perceived emotions over long periods of time will require systems to respond accurately and continuously [90].
- **Empathy and well-being:** To develop AI for well-being applications, affective robotics which depends on developments in affective computing is essential for comprehending human emotional states [91]. This involves

investigating the ways in which mediated social touch and embodied emotional communication can transmit emotional cues, which could result in more complex human–AI interactions [92].

- **Mutual adaptation:** In addition to AI adapting to human emotions, long-term human AI co-adaptation will require understanding how extended interaction with emotionally intelligent machines may change human emotional responses and behaviors. Obtaining high-quality time series datasets and accurately modeling emotion in complex narratives are necessary for this [93]. The objective of Human-Robot Interaction (HRI) [94] is to create AI systems that are also emotionally sensitive, meaning they can recognize and express emotions.

A web that is not only intelligent but also deeply sympathetic and adaptively co-evolved with its human users is what these future directions for affective computing promise. They represent a challenging but fascinating frontier (Figure 4.16).

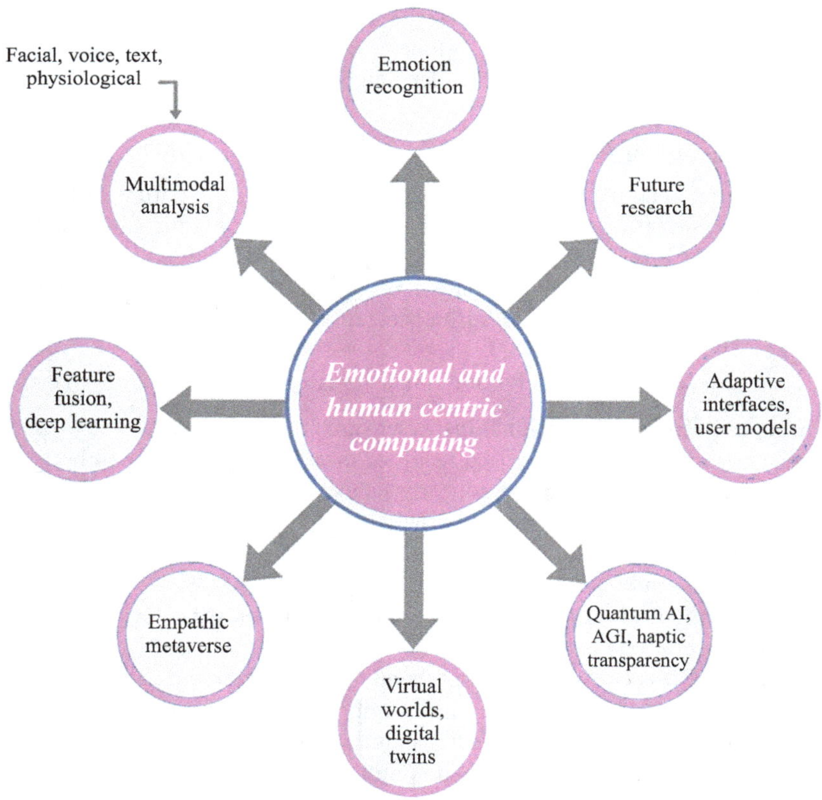

Figure 4.16 Conceptual map of emotional and HCC in the Web X.0 era

4.7 Conclusion

The web has evolved from basic static webpages to advanced systems that operate through decentralized networks and can make emotional connections with users. Emotional intelligence has become a fundamental element that underpins new Web X.0 systems as emotional computing technology continues to evolve. The combination of multimodal sensing, deep learning, and Transformer-based models and adaptive interfaces enables systems to achieve precise detection and reaction capabilities for human emotional states.

Technical capability functions as one component that helps organizations to achieve progress. Organizations that operate at web scale need to use emotional data to create new privacy frameworks and cybersecurity protocols, and establish ethical standards for their operations. Emotional signals, which people express through their facial expressions, speech patterns, and physiological measurements create data that functions as highly sensitive information, which will determine how companies design their products and develop their marketing strategies. The absence of strict governance procedures, together with fairness auditing processes and transparency requirements, will cause emotion-aware systems to create biases that result in manipulated outcomes and diminished psychological autonomy.

The evolution toward Web 4.0, Web 5.0, and adaptive Web X.0 ecosystems introduces new design imperatives. Systems must be secure by design, culturally inclusive, explainable, and resilient against adversarial interference. Emotional intelligence must be balanced with emotional integrity. Future web architectures will require not only computational sophistication but also ethical alignment and robust cybersecurity frameworks that protect users' emotional sovereignty [14,94].

Ultimately, the success of emotion-aware Web X.0 systems will depend on their ability to harmonize technological innovation with human-centered values. Building emotionally intelligent infrastructures demands interdisciplinary collaboration across AI, cybersecurity, psychology, and governance. Only through such integration can the web evolve into a platform that enhances human well-being while safeguarding autonomy, trust, and security.

Suggested further readings

- Picard RW. Affective Computing. MIT Press; 1997. - The foundational text that established affective computing as a field; useful grounding for readers new to the discipline before engaging with this chapter's Web X.0-specific extensions.
- Calvo RA, D'Mello S, Gratch J, Marsella S, eds. The Oxford Handbook of Affective Computing. Oxford University Press; 2015. - A comprehensive reference covering emotion theory, sensing modalities, and applications in depth; complements the chapter's condensed treatment of discrete and dimensional emotion models.

- Poria S, Cambria E, Bajpai R, Hussain A. A review of affective computing: From unimodal analysis to multimodal fusion. Information Fusion. 2017;37:98–125. doi: 10.1016/j.inffus.2017.02.003. - An earlier systematic review of fusion strategies that provides useful historical context for Section 4.3's discussion of multimodal architectures.
- Zeng Z, Pantic M, Roisman GI, Huang TS. A survey of affect recognition methods: Audio, visual, and spontaneous expressions. IEEE Transactions on Pattern Analysis and Machine Intelligence. 2009;31(1):39–58. doi: 10.1109/TPAMI.2008.52. - A classic survey on unimodal and multimodal affect recognition methods referenced widely in the affective computing literature.
- Poria S, Hazarika D, Majumder N, Mihalcea R. Beyond the text: Sentiment and emotion in multimodal conversations. In: Proceedings of the 58th Annual Meeting of the Association for Computational Linguistics: Tutorial Abstracts. 2020. - Useful companion reading for readers interested in conversational and Transformer-based emotion recognition discussed in Section 4.3.2.
- O'Neil C. Weapons of Math Destruction: How Big Data Increases Inequality and Threatens Democracy. Crown; 2016. - General-audience treatment of algorithmic bias and data governance that pairs well with Section 4.5's discussion of fairness and emotional manipulation risks.
- Floridi L, Cowls J, Beltrametti M, *et al.* AI4People-An ethical framework for a good AI society: Opportunities, risks, principles, and recommendations. Minds and Machines. 2018;28:689–707. doi: 10.1007/s11023-018-9482-5. - A widely cited ethical framework relevant to the chapter's discussion of ethical AI design principles.
- Suzuki Y, Lucero A, Gonzalez EN, *et al.* The metaverse and affective computing: opportunities and challenges. In: Handbook of Metaverse Research. Springer; forthcoming. - Emerging work situating affective computing within metaverse and Web 3.0/4.0 contexts, extending the chapter's discussion of the empathic metaverse.
- Russell JA. A circumplex model of affect. Journal of Personality and Social Psychology. 1980;39(6):1161–1178. doi: 10.1037/h0077714. - The original paper introducing the circumplex model discussed in Section 4.2.1.1; primary-source reading for readers wanting the theoretical foundation.
- Ekman P. An argument for basic emotions. Cognition and Emotion. 1992;6(3–4):169–200. doi: 10.1080/02699939208411068. - The foundational paper on discrete/basic emotion theory referenced throughout Section 4.2.

Standards

- W3C Emotion Markup Language (EmotionML) 1.0. W3C Recommendation, 2014. https://www.w3.org/TR/emotionml/ - A markup language standard for representing emotion-related states in web-based and multimodal systems;

directly relevant to the interoperable emotional data representations discussed in Section 4.4.

- IEEE 7000-2021, IEEE Standard Model Process for Addressing Ethical Concerns during System Design. - Provides a process framework for embedding ethical considerations (including affective and human-centric concerns) into system design, relevant to Section 4.5.3.
- IEEE 7014-2024 (in development), IEEE Draft Standard for Ethical Considerations in Emulated Empathy in Autonomous and Intelligent Systems. - Directly addresses emotion emulation and empathic system design as discussed in the chapter's emotional alignment design policy discussion (Section 4.5.3).
- ISO/IEC 42001:2023, Information technology - Artificial intelligence - Management system. - International standard for AI management systems, relevant to the chapter's discussion of responsible data stewardship and ethical AI design.
- ISO/IEC 23894:2023, Information technology - Artificial intelligence - Guidance on risk management. - Provides a risk-management framework applicable to emotion-aware AI deployments, supporting Section 4.5's discussion of fairness and manipulation risks.
- ISO/IEC 24028:2020, Information technology - Artificial intelligence - Overview of trustworthiness in artificial intelligence. - Establishes definitions and approaches for trustworthy AI (transparency, robustness, fairness) referenced conceptually throughout Section 4.5.
- ISO/IEC 27701:2019, Security techniques - Extension to ISO/IEC 27001 and ISO/IEC 27002 for privacy information management. - Relevant privacy-management standard applicable to the handling of sensitive emotional and biometric data discussed in Section 4.5.1.2.
- NIST AI Risk Management Framework (AI RMF 1.0). National Institute of Standards and Technology, 2023. https://doi.org/10.6028/NIST.AI.100-1 - A voluntary framework for managing risks associated with AI systems, including fairness and privacy risks relevant to emotion-aware systems.
- Regulation (EU) 2016/679, General Data Protection Regulation (GDPR). Official Journal of the European Union, 2016. - Referenced in Section 4.5.1.2 as a key regulatory framework governing the lawful processing of emotional and biometric data.
- Regulation (EU) 2024/1689, Artificial Intelligence Act (EU AI Act). Official Journal of the European Union, 2024. - Referenced in Section 4.5.1.2; classifies emotion recognition systems as high-risk or prohibited in certain contexts (e.g., workplace and education), directly relevant to the chapter's ethical discussion.
- IEEE 2731-2020, IEEE Standard for a Unified Terminology for Brain-Computer Interfaces. - Relevant to the physiological/EEG-based emotion recognition modalities discussed in Section 4.2.1.2.
- ITU-T Y.3172, Architectural framework for machine learning in future networks including IMT-2020. - Relevant to the multilayer, edge-computing emotion-aware service architectures discussed in Section 4.4.1.

References

[1] Wang Y, Song W, Tao W, *et al.* A systematic review on affective computing: emotion models, databases, and recent advances. *Information Fusion*. 2022;83:19–52. doi: 10.1016/j.inffus.2022.03.009.

[2] Shah A, Azam N, Yao JT, Ali B, and Habib M. A three-way clustering approach for novelty detection. *Information Sciences*. 2021;569:650–668. doi: 10.1016/j.ins.2021.05.021.

[3] Mutlu Avinç G, and Yıldız A. A bibliometric and systematic review of scientific publications on metaverse research in architecture: web of science (WoS). *International Journal of Technology and Design Education*. 2024. doi: 10.1007/s10798-024-09918-1.

[4] Tychola KA, Voulgaridis K, and Lagkas T. Tactile IoT and 5G & beyond schemes as key enabling technologies for the future metaverse. *Telecommunication Systems*. 2023;84:363–385. doi: 10.1007/s11235-023-01052-y.

[5] Hassan MA, Jamshidi MB, Manh BD, *et al. Enabling technologies for web 3.0: a comprehensive survey*. 2024. doi: 10.48550/ARXIV.2401.10901.

[6] Gan W, Ye Z, Wan S, and Yu PS. *Web 3.0: the future of internet*. 2023. doi: 10.48550/ARXIV.2304.06032.

[7] Zhu J, Li F, and Chen J. A survey of blockchain, *artificial intelligence, and edge computing for Web 3.0*. 2023. doi: 10.48550/ARXIV.2311.13731.

[8] Alipour M, Tourchi Moghaddam M, Vaidhyanathan K, and Kjærgaard MB. Toward changing users' behavior with emotion-based adaptive systems. 2023:85–95. doi: 10.1145/3565472.3595614.

[9] Li J, Waleed A, and Salam H. A survey on personalized affective computing in human–machine interaction. *arXiv*. 2023. doi: 10.48550/arxiv.2304.00377.

[10] Gamage G, De Silva D, Mills N, Alahakoon D, and Manic M. Emotion AWARE: an artificial intelligence framework for adaptable, robust, explainable, and multi-granular emotion analysis. *Journal of Big Data*. 2024;11:93. doi: 10.1186/s40537-024-00953-2.

[11] Khaleel Ibrahim A. Evolution of the web: from web 1.0 to 4.0. *Qubahan Academic Journal*. 2021;1:20–28. doi: 10.48161/qaj.v1n3a75.

[12] Wan S, Hong L, Gan W, Chen J, and Yu PS. Web3: the next internet revolution. *arXiv*. 2023. doi: 10.48550/arxiv.2304.06111.

[13] Lerman K. The social emotional web. *arXiv*. 2022. doi: 10.48550/arxiv.2212.03810.

[14] Shah A, Ali B, Habib M, Azam N, and Yao JT. An ensemble face recognition mechanism based on three-way decisions. *Journal of King Saud University – Computer and Information Sciences*. 2023;35:196–208. doi: 10.1016/j.jksuci.2023.03.016.

[15] Shah A, Azam N, Ali B, and Yao JT. Grid neighborhood based three-way clustering (3WC). *Information Sciences*. 2024;659:120082. doi: 10.1016/j.ins.2023.120082.

[16] Łępicki MZ, and Bobek S. *Affective context-aware systems: architecture of a dynamic framework*. Springer, 2019, pp. 575–584. doi: 10.1007/978-3-030-20915-5_51.

[17] Osuna E, Castellanos S, Rosales JH, and Rodríguez LF. An interoperable framework for computational models of emotion. *International Journal of Cognitive Informatics and Natural Intelligence*. 2022;16:1–15. doi: 10.4018/ijcini.296257.

[18] Hu L, Li W, Yang J, Fortino G, and Chen M. A sustainable multi-modal multi-layer emotion-aware service at the edge. *IEEE Transactions on Sustainable Computing*. 2019;7:324–333. doi: 10.1109/tsusc.2019.2928316.

[19] Garcia-Garcia JM, Lozano MD, Penichet VMR, and Law ELC. Building a three-level multimodal emotion recognition framework. *Multimedia Tools and Applications*. 2022;82:239–269. doi: 10.1007/s11042-022-13254-8.

[20] Feng L, and Liu B. Affective digital twins for digital human: bridging the gap in human–machine affective interaction. *arXiv*. 2023. doi: 10.48550/arxiv.2308.10207.

[21] Mizgajski J, and Morzy M. Affective recommender systems in online news industry: how emotions influence reading choices. *User Modeling and User-Adapted Interaction*. 2018;29:345–379. doi: 10.1007/s11257-018-9213-x.

[22] Wang D, and Zhao X. Affective video recommender systems: a survey. *Frontiers in Neuroscience*. 2022;16:984404. doi: 10.3389/fnins.2022.984404.

[23] Bustos López M, Alor-Hernández G, Sánchez-Cervantes JL, Paredes-Valverde MA, and Salas-Zárate MdP. EduRecomSys: an educational resource recommender system based on collaborative filtering and emotion detection. *Interacting with Computers*. 2020;32:407–432. doi: 10.1093/iwc/iwab001.

[24] Hasan T, and Bunescu R. A survey of affective recommender systems: modeling attitudes, emotions, and moods for personalization. *arXiv*. 2025. doi: 10.48550/arxiv.2508.20289.

[25] Liu Q, Zhu J, Yang Y, *et al*. Multimodal pretraining, adaptation, and generation for recommendation: a survey. 2024, pp. 6566–6576. doi: 10.1145/3637528.3671473.

[26] Zhou H, Zhou X, Zeng Z, Zhang L, and Shen Z. A comprehensive survey on multimodal recommender systems: taxonomy, evaluation, and future directions. *arXiv*. 2023. doi: 10.48550/arxiv.2302.04473.

[27] Xu J, Chen Z, Yang S, *et al*. *A survey on multimodal recommender systems: recent advances and future directions*. 2025. doi: 10.48550/ARXIV.2502.15711.

[28] Bielozorov A, Bezbradica M, and Helfert M. *The role of user emotions for content personalization in e-commerce: literature review*. Springer, 2019, pp. 177–193. doi: 10.1007/978-3-030-22335-9_12.

[29] Märtin C, Bissinger B, and Asta P. Optimizing the digital customer journey—improving user experience by exploiting emotions, personas and situations for individualized user interface adaptations. *Journal of Consumer Behaviour*. 2021;22:1050–1061. doi: 10.1002/cb.1964.

[30] Sehgal S, Sharma H, and Anand A. Smart and context-aware system employing emotions recognition. 2021:1–8. doi: 10.1109/incet51464.2021.9456356.

[31] Zheng X, Li Z, Gui X, and Luo Y. Customizing emotional support: how do individuals construct and interact with LLM-powered chatbots. 2025:1–20. doi: 10.1145/3706598.3713453.

[32] Ha J, Jeon H, Han DS, Seo J, and Oh C. CloChat: understanding how people customize, interact, and experience personas in large language models. 2024:1–24. doi: 10.1145/3613904.3642472.

[33] Devaram S. Empathic chatbot: emotional intelligence for mental health well-being. *arXiv*. 2020. doi: 10.48550/arXiv.2012.09130.

[34] Dongre P, Behravan M, Gupta K, Billinghurst M, and Gračanin D. Integrating physiological data with large language models for empathic human–AI interaction. *arXiv*. 2024. doi: 10.48550/ARXIV.2404.15351.

[35] Hegde K, and Jayalath H. Emotions in the loop: a survey of affective computing for emotional support. *arXiv*. 2025. doi: 10.48550/ARXIV.2505.01542.

[36] Zhang N, and Leong WY. Intelligent emotional computing with deep convolutional neural networks: multimodal feature analysis and application in smart learning environments. *Eurasia Journal of Mathematics Science and Technology Education*. 2025;21:em2680. doi: 10.29333/ejmste/16661.

[37] Pai YS, Armstrong M, Skierś K, *et al*. The empathic metaverse: an assistive bioresponsive platform for emotional experience sharing. *arXiv*. 2023. doi: 10.48550/arxiv.2311.16610.

[38] Park S, and Whang M. Special issue "Emotion intelligence based on smart sensing". *Sensors*. 2023;23:1098. doi: 10.3390/s23031098.

[39] Audrin C, and Audrin B. Emotional intelligence in digital interactions – a call for renewed assessments. *Personality and Individual Differences*. 2024;223:112613. doi: 10.1016/j.paid.2024.112613.

[40] Mohammad SM. Ethics sheet for automatic emotion recognition and sentiment analysis. *Computational Linguistics*. 2022;48:239–278. doi: 10.1162/coli_a_00433.

[41] Katirai A. Ethical considerations in emotion recognition technologies: a review of the literature. *AI and Ethics*. 2023. doi: 10.1007/s43681-023-00307-3.

[42] Barker D, Tippireddy MKR, Farhan A, and Ahmed B. Ethical considerations in emotion recognition research. *Deleted Journal*. 2025;7:43. doi: 10.3390/psycholint7020043.

[43] Jedličková A. Ethical approaches in designing autonomous and intelligent systems: a comprehensive survey towards responsible development. *AI & Society*. 2025;40:2703–2716. doi: 10.1007/s00146-024-02040-9.

[44] Batliner A, Neumann M, Burkhardt F, *et al*. Ethical awareness in paralinguistics: a taxonomy of applications. *International Journal of Human–Computer Interaction*. 2022;39:1904–1921. doi: 10.1080/10447318.2022.2140385.

[45] Nartey J. The ethics of emotion recognition technology: implications for privacy and consent. 2025. doi: 10.2139/ssrn.5200140.

[46] Jaiswal M. Interpreting multimodal machine learning models trained for emotion recognition to address robustness and privacy concerns. *Proceedings of the AAAI Conference on Artificial Intelligence*. 2020;34:13716–13717. doi: 10.1609/aaai.v34i10.7130.

[47] Fabiano N. Affective computing and emotional data: challenges and implications in privacy regulations, the AI Act, and ethics in large language models. *arXiv*. 2025. doi: 10.48550/arxiv.2509.20153.

[48] Ong DC. An ethical framework for guiding the development of affectively-aware artificial intelligence. 2021. doi: 10.1109/acii52823.2021.9597441.

[49] Sabour S, Liu JM, Liu S, *et al.* Human decision-making is susceptible to AI-driven manipulation. *arXiv*. 2025. doi: 10.48550/arxiv.2502.07663.

[50] Tavory T. Regulating AI in mental health: ethics of care perspective. *JMIR Mental Health*. 2024;11:e58493. doi: 10.2196/58493.

[51] Kirk HR, Gabriel I, Summerfield C, Vidgen B, and Hale SA. Why human–AI relationships need socioaffective alignment. *Humanities and Social Sciences Communications*. 2025;12:1–9. doi: 10.1057/s41599-025-04532-5.

[52] Bakir V, Laffer A, McStay A, Miranda D, and Urquhart L. On manipulation by emotional AI: UK adults' views and governance implications. *Frontiers in Sociology*. 2024;9:1339834. doi: 10.3389/fsoc.2024.1339834.

[53] Wang J, Ma F, Zhang Y, and Song D. *A multibias-mitigated and sentiment knowledge enriched transformer for debiasing in multimodal conversational emotion recognition*. Springer, 2022, pp. 499–512. doi: 10.1007/978-3-031-17120-8_39.

[54] Schmitz M, Ahmed R, and Cao J. Bias and fairness on multimodal emotion detection algorithms. *arXiv*. 2022. doi: 10.48550/arxiv.2205.08383.

[55] Janhonen J. Socialisation approach to AI value acquisition: enabling flexible ethical navigation with built-in receptiveness to social influence. *AI and Ethics*. 2023. doi: 10.1007/s43681-023-00372-8.

[56] Tu G, Jing R, Liang B, Yang M, Wong KF, and Xu R. A training-free debiasing framework with counterfactual reasoning for conversational emotion detection. 2023. doi: 10.18653/v1/2023.emnlp-main.967.

[57] Verhoef T, and Fosch-Villaronga E. Towards affective computing that works for everyone. 2023:1–8. doi: 10.1109/acii59096.2023.10388169.

[58] Zhang Z, Jia M, Lee HP, *et al.* "It's a fair game", or is it? Examining how users navigate disclosure risks and benefits when using LLM-based conversational agents. 2024:1–26. doi: 10.1145/3613904.3642385.

[59] Schwitzgebel E, and Sebo J. The emotional alignment design policy. *arXiv*:2507.06263. 2025. doi: 10.48550/ARXIV.2507.06263.

[60] Chang EY. CoCoMo: computational consciousness modeling for generative and ethical AI. *arXiv*. 2023. doi: 10.48550/arxiv.2304.02438.

[61] Carroll M, Chan A, Ashton H, and Krueger D. Characterizing manipulation from AI systems. 2023:1–13. doi: 10.1145/3617694.3623226.

[62] Gabriel I, Manzini A, Keeling G, *et al.* The ethics of advanced AI assistants. *arXiv*. 2024. doi: 10.48550/arxiv.2404.16244.

[63] Punjabi VN, Brahmandam BA, and Chandramohan S. Embedding emotional intelligence in AGI for enhanced cognition. *International Journal of Innovative Research in Computer and Communication Engineering*. 2025;13. doi: 10.15680/ijircce.2025.1304007.

[64] Li Y, Sun Q, Schlicher M, Lim YW, and Schuller BW. Artificial emotion: a survey of theories and debates on realising emotion in artificial intelligence. *arXiv*. 2025. doi: 10.48550/ARXIV.2508.10286.

[65] Li Y, Sun Q, Schlicher M, Lim YW, and Schuller BW. Artificial emotion: a survey of theories and debates on realising emotion in artificial intelligence. *arXiv*. 2025. doi: 10.48550/arxiv.2508.10286.

[66] Smith M, Barton MR, Branschofsky M, *et al.* DSpace. *D-Lib Magazine*. 2003;9. doi: 10.1045/january2003-smith.

[67] Mason C. Human-level AI requires compassionate intelligence. 2008. https://www.aaai.org/Papers/Workshops/2008/WS-08-07/WS08-07-023.pdf.

[68] Hanson D, Varcoe A, Senna F, *et al.* Sentience quest: towards embodied, emotionally adaptive, self-evolving, ethically aligned artificial general intelligence. *arXiv*. 2025. doi: 10.48550/ARXIV.2505.12229.

[69] Liu Y, Li Q, Wang B, Zhang Y, and Song D. A survey of quantum-cognitively inspired sentiment analysis models. *ACM Computing Surveys*. 2023; 56:1–37. doi: 10.1145/3604550.

[70] Li Q, Gkoumas D, Sordoni A, Nie JY, and Melucci M. Quantum-inspired neural network for conversational emotion recognition. *Proceedings of the AAAI Conference on Artificial Intelligence*. 2021;35:13270–13278. doi: 10.1609/aaai.v35i15.17567.

[71] Rengasamy K, Joshi P, and Raveendra VVS. Real-time hybrid facial expression analysis model using quantum distance-based classifier and classical artificial neural networks: QUADCANN. *Quantum Information Processing*. 2024;23:220. doi: 10.1007/s11128-024-04437-3.

[72] Ho JKW, and Hoorn JF. Quantum affective processes for multidimensional decision-making. *Scientific Reports*. 2022;12:20468. doi: 10.1038/s41598-022-22855-0.

[73] Yan F, Iliyasu AM, and Hirota K. Conceptual framework for quantum affective computing and its use in fusion of multi-robot emotions. *Electronics*. 2021;10:100. doi: 10.3390/electronics10020100.

[74] Wan Z, Liu CK, Yang H, *et al.* Towards cognitive AI systems: a survey and prospective on neuro-symbolic AI. *arXiv*. 2024. doi: 10.48550/arxiv.2401.01040.

[75] Sheth A, Roy K, and Gaur M. Neurosymbolic AI – why, what, and how. *arXiv*. 2023. doi: 10.48550/arxiv.2305.00813.

[76] Wan Z, Liu CK, Yang H, *et al.* Towards cognitive AI systems: a survey and prospective on neuro-symbolic AI. *arXiv*. 2024. doi: 10.48550/ARXIV.2401.01040.

[77] Lu Z, Afridi IU, Kang HJ, Ruchkin I, and Zheng X. Surveying neuro-symbolic approaches for reliable artificial intelligence of things. *Journal of Reliable Intelligent Environments*. 2024;10:257–279. doi: 10.1007/s40860-024-00231-1.

[78] Kumar A. Neuro symbolic AI in personalized mental health therapy: bridging cognitive science and computational psychiatry. *World Journal of Advanced Research and Reviews*. 2023;19:1663–1679. doi: 10.30574/wjarr.2023.19.2.1516.

[79] Havaldar S, Singhal B, Rai S, Liu L, Guntuku SC, and Ungar L. Multilingual language models are not multicultural: a case study in emotion. 2023. doi: 10.18653/v1/2023.wassa-1.19.

[80] Havaldar S, Rai S, Singhal B, Liu L, Guntuku SC, and Ungar L. Multilingual language models are not multicultural: a case study in emotion. *arXiv*. 2023. doi: 10.48550/arXiv.2307.01370.

[81] Dudy S, Ahmad I, Kitajima R, and Lapedriza A. Analyzing cultural representations of emotions in LLMs through mixed emotion survey. 2024:346–354. doi: 10.1109/acii63134.2024.00044.

[82] Hughson E, Javadi R, Thompson J, and Lim A. Investigating the role of culture on negative emotion expressions in the wild. *Frontiers in Integrative Neuroscience*. 2021;15:699667. doi: 10.3389/fnint.2021.699667.

[83] Mathur L, Adolphs R, and Matarić MJ. Towards intercultural affect recognition: audio-visual affect recognition in the wild across six cultures. 2023:1–6. doi: 10.1109/fg57933.2023.10042676.

[84] Cowen A, Brooks JA, Prasad G, *et al.* How emotion is experienced and expressed in multiple cultures: a large-scale experiment across North America, Europe, and Japan. *Frontiers in Psychology*. 2024;15:1350631. doi: 10.3389/fpsyg.2024.1350631.

[85] Lukáč M, Zhambulova G, Abdiyeva K, and Lewis MD. Study on emotion recognition bias in different regional groups. *Scientific Reports*. 2023;13. doi: 10.1038/s41598-023-34932-z.

[86] Zhang Y, Zhao D, Hancock JT, Kraut R, and Yang D. The rise of AI companions: how human–chatbot relationships influence well-being. *arXiv*. 2025. doi: 10.48550/ARXIV.2506.12605.

[87] Manzini A, Keeling G, Alberts L, Vallor S, Morris MR, and Gabriel I. The code that binds us: navigating the appropriateness of human–AI assistant relationships. *Proceedings of the AAAI/ACM Conference on AI, Ethics, and Society*. 2024;7:943–957. doi: 10.1609/aies.v7i1.31694.

[88] Turkle S. *Who do we become when we talk to machines?*2024. doi: 10.21428/e4baedd9.caa10d84.

[89] Laban G, Kappas A, Morrison V, and Cross ES. Building long-term human–robot relationships: examining disclosure, perception and well-being across time. *International Journal of Social Robotics*. 2023;16:1–27. doi: 10.1007/s12369-023-01076-z.

[90] Lin Z, Cruz F, and Sandoval EB. Self-context-aware emotion perception on human–robot interaction. *arXiv*. 2024. doi: 10.48550/arxiv.2401.10946.

[91] Spitale M, Axelsson M, Jeong S, *et al*. Past, present, and future: a survey of the evolution of affective robotics for well-being. *IEEE Transactions on Affective Computing*. 2025:1–17. doi: 10.1109/taffc.2025.3567740.
[92] He L, Guo Z, Mo Y, Wen Y, and Wang Y. Exploring embodied emotional communication: a human-oriented review of mediated social touch. *CCF Transactions on Pervasive Computing and Interaction*. 2025;7:188–212. doi: 10.1007/s42486-024-00169-6.
[93] Ong DC, Wu Z, Zhi-Xuan T, *et al*. Modeling emotion in complex stories: the Stanford Emotional Narratives Dataset. *IEEE Transactions on Affective Computing*. 2019;12:579–594. doi: 10.1109/taffc.2019.2955949.
[94] Yan F, Iliyasu AM, and Hirota K. Emotion space modelling for social robots. *Engineering Applications of Artificial Intelligence*. 2021;100:104178. doi: 10.1016/j.engappai.2021.104178.

Chapter 5

Metaverse, Virtual Reality (VR), and Augmented Reality (AR) in Web X.0

Irum Saba[1], Sana Saleh[2] and Memoona Sadaf[3]

Abstract

This chapter provides a comprehensive examination of the Metaverse, Virtual Reality (VR), and Augmented Reality (AR) as foundational pillars of Web X.0, the next evolutionary stage of the Internet characterized by immersive intelligence, decentralization, and seamless human–digital integration. It systematically explores the technological infrastructures enabling these immersive environments, including Extended Reality (XR) frameworks, edge and fog computing architectures, blockchain-based decentralized systems, artificial intelligence (AI) and machine learning (ML), high-speed 5G/6G networks, human–computer interaction (HCI) interfaces, cybersecurity mechanisms, interoperability standards, and integrated cloud-edge-fog models. The chapter further investigates diverse applications across gaming, education, healthcare, remote collaboration, digital commerce, governance, and social interaction, demonstrating how these technologies are transforming industries and redefining human experience. Critical challenges are examined in depth, including privacy vulnerabilities, cybersecurity threats, ethical dilemmas, the digital divide, psychological impacts, interoperability fragmentation, environmental sustainability concerns, and regulatory gaps. Looking forward, the chapter identifies emerging trajectories such as AI-powered immersive intelligence, brain–computer integration, digital twin convergence, decentralized economies, sustainable Metaverse infrastructures, inclusive design principles, and the progressive merging of physical and virtual realities. By synthesizing current technological capabilities with future possibilities, this chapter argues that while immersive technologies hold transformative potential, their successful evolution

[1]Smart Technologies and Applied Intelligence Research (STAIR) Lab, Department of Electrical Engineering, School of Engineering, National University of Computer & Emerging Sciences (NUCES), Islamabad, 44000, Pakistan
[2]Smart Technologies and Applied Intelligence Research (STAIR) Lab, Department of Computer Engineering, School of Engineering, National University of Computer & Emerging Sciences (NUCES), Islamabad, 44000, Pakistan
[3]School of Information Technology, Murdoch University, Australia

into a truly open, equitable, and sustainable Web X.0 depends upon striking a delicate balance between innovation and ethical responsibility, ensuring that the Metaverse, VR, and AR remain fundamentally human-centric, accessible, and trustworthy in serving global society.

5.1 Introduction: Metaverse, Virtual Reality, and Augmented Reality—overview in Web X.0

This new phenomenon of Web X.0 has been created by the evolution of the web as the original read-only and static information system (Web 1.0), the interactive and participatory space (Web 2.0), the decentralized and blockchain-based platform (Web 3.0), and the intelligent and context-responsive systems (Web 4.0). The next generation of the Internet is configured to make digital environments highly interactive, real-time, and adaptive. Some of its characteristics are immersive technologies, intelligent systems, and decentralized architecture. Web X.0 is characterized not just by content and connectivity compared to its ancestors but also by experience, personalization, and digital sovereignty. In addition to this revolution, there are other drivers of the highest importance, including Metaverse, Virtual Reality (VR), and Augmented Reality (AR), which are the positive sides of experiential connectivity [1].

Metaverse is typically defined as a consistent, shared, and interoperable virtual world connecting the real and virtual realities. Metaverse also gives the user access to the interface to communicate with avatars, buy and sell digital goods, and simulate virtual economies, societies, and politics [2]. Compared to traditional social media, the metaverse offers a better experience than two-dimensional interaction because of the use of spatial computing, decentralized networks, and intelligent automation. It is not just used in entertainment and gaming, but redesigning social co-labor, government, health, education, and business in the virtual world [3].

VR is among Metaverse's main gateways. With interactive hardware such as head-mounted devices, motion sensors, and haptic devices, VR provides the ability to become fully immersed in completely artificial worlds. They may simulate real-world settings, such as classrooms, offices, or operating rooms, or create entirely new virtual worlds for gaming, storytelling, and discovery. Besides entertainment, VR is applied to training, therapy, cultural heritage, and architecture, all with the aim of providing clients with an experience that would not be possible through normal digital media [4].

AR is the most important type of digital information in the real world. Artificial Intelligence (AI) makes it possible to interact with the real world in more ways by giving you both contextual and real-time information. With mobile devices, AR glasses, and wearables, people can have better navigation, learning, product visualization, and health uses. AR's strength comes from its ability to seamlessly combine physical and digital layers, which allows for real-time decision-making and benefits fields like tourism, retail, smart cities, and logistics. Both

VR and AR are types of immersion technology that make the Web X.0 experience better. VR completely immerses people in virtual worlds, while AR adds to real-world experiences. Early implementations in platforms such as Roblox and Fortnite demonstrate this shift toward persistent virtual societies.

One of the things that makes Web X.0 so great is that it has ultra-low latency, real-time processing, and hardware that can grow with your needs. This is not possible with traditional centralized cloud computing, which is why edge and fog computing are needed. These make it possible to move computation and storage closer to the end user, which makes instant responses and a seamless immersive experience possible. With AR and VR, even a few milliseconds of delay can ruin immersion. On the other hand, edge and fog computing give users the space they need to interact quickly, work together, and create virtual worlds that can grow. Along with other new communication technologies like 5G and 6G, they make the Metaverse a connected, universal, and open digital world [5].

There is an enormous potential of Web X.0 to alter things, yet the convergence between Metaverse, VR, and AR has its enormous flaws. The problems of digital identity, privacy, and governance become even more complex once individuals exchange information regarding their actions, biometrics, and the environment in immersive environments. Governments and companies are attempting to establish regulations concerning the ownership of what is online, what should be treated as intellectual property, and what is deemed to be acceptable practices. This leads to aspects of trust, inclusivity, accessibility, and ethical management. These issues demonstrate the relevance of the need to have a governance model that is able to balance accountability and innovation [6,7].

This chapter talks about how VR, AR, and Metaverse can help Web X.0. It talks about their main ideas, the infrastructure that makes them possible, and how they could change things in areas like work from home, entertainment, education, and healthcare. It also talks about problems with identity, safety, and government in online communities, and it stresses how edge and fog computing can help make real-time immersive experiences that can grow. Finally, it shows us how these technologies will keep coming together, merging, and designing the future of digital interaction in Web X.0.

5.2 Methods and enabling technologies for Metaverse, VR, and AR in Web X.0

The success of immersive technologies such as the Metaverse, VR, and AR in Web X.0 mainly depends on an enabling ecosystem of methodologies and infrastructures. They cannot be called distinct technologies, but rather the collection of communication networks, models of distributed computing, AI, blockchain, Extended Reality (XR) systems, and mechanisms that allow people to communicate with computers. They form the foundation of immersive and extended digital experiences [8]. This part goes into great detail about the main enabling domains and how they are connected. It also gives a general overview of the technologies, tools, and architectures that support large-scale immersive platforms.

5.2.1 XR frameworks

The collective term for VR, AR, and Mixed Reality (MR) is XR, as depicted in Figure 5.1. When combined, these technologies produce interactive immersive settings that combine the real and virtual worlds. The next development of the immersive Web X is represented by XR, a front-end where people interact with dynamic three-dimensional environments instead of static two-dimensional screens. XR is revolutionizing how people learn, work, socialize, and interact with digital content by improving perception, interaction, and presence [4].

5.2.1.1 Virtual Reality

The defining characteristics of VR include:

- VR replaces the actual environment entirely with a computer-generated one
- Utilizes Head-Mounted Displays (HMDs) like Oculus Rift, HTC Vive, and PlayStation VR to deliver stereoscopic graphics (two nearly identical images projected for each eye to generate depth perception)
- Integrates Six Degrees of Freedom (6DoF) tracking:
  - Three degrees of rotational movement (pitch, yaw, roll)
  - Three degrees of translational movement (up/down, left/right, forward/ backward)

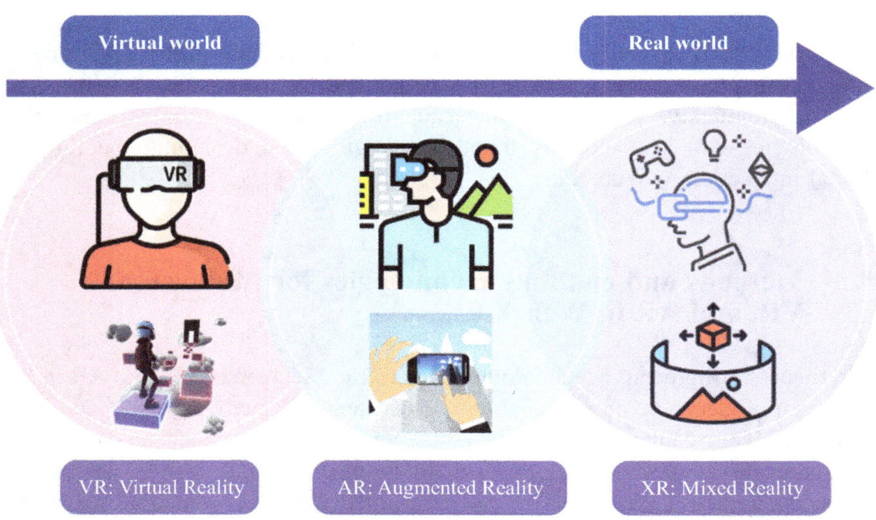

Figure 5.1 Extended reality frameworks

- Motion sickness challenge: Cybersickness (also referred to as simulator sickness) is a critical challenge in VR systems. Even a delay of 20 milliseconds (ms) between user head movement and the corresponding visual update in the headset can induce discomfort, nausea, and disorientation [9]. Achieving this requires high-speed displays, responsive tracking sensors, and optimized rendering pipelines
- Haptic feedback: Gloves and suits are used to simulate the touch sensation, allowing users to "sense" texture, vibration, or even the heaviness of objects in virtual space

5.2.1.2 Augmented Reality

Key functionalities of AR systems involve:

- AR places digital overlays over the real world rather than replacing it
- Makes use of Simultaneous Localization and Mapping (SLAM): An algorithm that projects physical spaces in real-time with the device's location within that space
- Example: AR navigation apps displaying arrows on roads
- Computer Vision (CV): Recognizes objects (such as furniture, vehicles, or equipment) so digital content can respond to them
- Example applications: AR-guided surgery (physicians looking at holographic patient anatomy during procedures) and home furniture shopping (consumers seeing furniture in their living room before purchase) [5].

5.2.1.3 Mixed Reality

MR is distinguished by the following features:

- MR combines both VR and AR.
- Example: A virtual 3D replica of a car overlaid in a factory setting, which can be walked around by engineers, examined, and changed while making contact with real-world equipment.
- Needs depth sensors (such as Microsoft HoloLens) to gauge the geometry and distance of real-world objects to be able to overlay virtually accurately [5].

All three, VR, AR, and MR, form a continuum of immersion from partial replacement to full augmentation of reality.

5.2.2 Edge and fog computing

Metaverse, VR, and AR are all interactive and high-fidelity, so they need systems that can handle huge amounts of real-time data quickly, easily, and with a lot of throughput. Cloud computing infrastructures today are strong, but they often have problems with latency, bandwidth, and centralization that slow them down. For example, VR goggles and AR glasses need to render and process graphics in 20 milliseconds or else they will make you sick, but data sent to faraway cloud servers may take much longer than this to come back. Because of this, cloud-only models don't work for Web X.0's needs for low latency, high bandwidth, and real-time processing [10].

To address this challenge, emerging concept of fog computing and edge computing emerges. These paradigms scale the infrastructure of the clouds and increase the speed of the processing of the data by putting the computing resources closer to the user. They also make the necessity of remoteness of data centers less significant. They collaborate to set up the computer infrastructure of the large immersive applications, such as smart city infrastructure using AR and interactive VR games [10].

5.2.2.1 Edge computing

Edge computing refers to making computational and storage capabilities available at the network edge, near devices such as VR headsets, AR glasses, and IoT sensors that individual users interact with. A significant decrease in latency through edge computing is accomplished through the ability to process data at the edge. This enables instant user feedback, sensor fusion, and real-time rendering. Mapping avatars and actions to edge nodes in multiplayer VR environments allows connecting the avatars and actions without transmitting every change to the cloud, preventing lag. In AR navigation, edge servers are able to consider environmental data such as global positioning system, cameras, and motion sensors, and display real-time overlays of directions or contextual data in AR. In addition, this can be achieved by offloading some of the work to local edge servers, which allows devices to remain light, energy-efficient, and cheap [11].

5.2.2.2 Fog computing

Although edge computing is centered on near-device and localized processing, fog computing is a distributed layer between cloud and edge. Fog nodes are also commonly established at regional or metropolitan scales, forming a middle tier that compromises between real-time responsiveness and larger computational resources. Fog computing is very helpful when you need to gather, analyze, and share data from many edge devices across different areas. For instance, in an AR-based smart city traffic system, fog nodes can process data from thousands of sensors and cameras to give real-time updates on traffic jams, accidents, or the state of the environment [12].

5.2.2.3 Edge–fog–cloud synergy

Edge and fog architectures are two more ways to use the cloud. In better Web X.0 settings, edge nodes handle things like recognizing gestures and syncing avatars in real time. Fog nodes gather information from nearby sources to build a common context, such as a virtual classroom or smart city analytics. Cloud servers have a lot of space, can analyze data over time, and can help people work together around the world. This hierarchical model of architecture makes it easy to deploy immersive applications even when there are a lot of users because it lets you trade responsiveness, scalability, and data availability [13].

5.2.3 Blockchain and decentralized architecture

Metaverse requires more than pretty graphics and real-time feedback to be an existing, long-term, and interactive environment. The most significant aspects of a world that is all digital are trust, ownership, and safe transactions. The archetypes operating in current social networks and online communities are not suitable for Web X.0 since they are based on corporate fiat, not very interoperable, and are subject to modification or censorship by a single individual. To address these issues, decentralized structure and blockchain technology have emerged as the most significant aspects of the Metaverse. Blockchain is a decentralized and open registry that cannot be altered and can be verified, which renders the transactions legitimate. Blockchain enables individuals to have a digital asset, identity, and interactions by eliminating the middlemen [6,14].

5.2.3.1 Digital identity management

Stable digital identity is likely to be the greatest value of virtual environments. With blockchain, it is possible to realize Self-Sovereign Identity (SSI) as opposed to existing systems that use network-specific log-in. This allows individuals to have their own digital identities without having them represented by others. As an example, an avatar in the Metaverse might possess verifiable blockchain characteristics such as education level, membership, or license that are readily visible across all platforms. This prevents any lock-in to any single environment and enables Web X.0 to be more interoperable [15].

5.2.3.2 Ownership of digital property and non-fungible tokens

In virtual worlds, ownership goes beyond just game virtual goods. It also includes virtual property, art, fashion, and even memories. Non-Fungible Tokens (NFTs), which are one-of-a-kind digital objects, make this kind of ownership possible. An NFT of the painting in a VR digital art gallery proves that the artist owns it and that it is real. Virtual land plots in platforms like Decentraland or The Sandbox get tokenized, so users are able to trade and construct on them just like on real property. NFTs ensure that value in the Metaverse can securely be transferred, exchanged, and paid for, and therefore form the foundation of virtual economies [16]. For instance, Nike's acquisition of RTFKT, a virtual footwear and digital fashion company, demonstrates how major brands are investing in NFT-based virtual goods that exist across multiple Metaverse platforms [17].

5.2.3.3 Smart contracts and automated trust

In decentralized Web X.0, business, creator, and user interactions must be governed by trustless systems. Smart contracts are computer code that is self-executing on the blockchain, enabling automatic execution of agreements when specific conditions are met. To illustrate, a smart contract might be used in an online deal involving real estate, whereby ownership of land is automatically transferred to the buyer upon receipt of money without a third-party notary or intermediary. On the same note, digital artists can add royalty agreements to smart contracts, where they receive payments whenever their work is resold at the secondary markets [17]. One of the real-life examples is Royal, the platform that allows musicians to sell royalty rights in the form of NFTs via smart contracts, enabling fans to receive royalties together with their favorite artists [6].

5.2.3.4 Decentralized governance (DAOs)

The governance is often opaque and dominated by corporations and is decentralized. Decentralized Autonomous Organizations (DAOs) with community-driven governance are possible because of blockchain. DAOs involve smart contracts to enable individuals to propose, vote, and execute policies. A smart city in the Metaverse could be a DAO that decides the virtual city on zoning rules, virtual land taxes, or social expenditure on infrastructure, etc., via a vote. In so doing, the entire community makes the decisions rather than an individual [6]. An example is the City of Seoul, which introduced its own version of the Metaverse, the Metaverse 120 center, a form of virtual public service that allows citizens to use their avatars to access government-related services, make complaints and consultations, which shows that governments are moving toward the adoption of the models of governance through the Metaverse [18].

5.2.4 Artificial intelligence and machine learning

Metaverse, VR, and AR are not some places to see or visit. They are dynamic spaces that will have to vary every minute depending on the way people use them, the way the environment is changing, and the volume of data that is passing through them. This is feasible due to AI and Machine Learning (ML). They are what Web X.0 does the thinking. XR technologies allow you to immerse yourself in the virtual world, and blockchain allows you to have confidence in that world. AI brings about immersive worlds through intelligence, autonomy, and personalization, which make such worlds interactive, real, and self-governing [5].

VR platforms make a lot of data every second. This includes biometric data from VR headsets, spatial mapping data from AR headsets, blockchain transaction data, and social interactions between millions of users. Real-time data cannot be handled, understood, or responded to by traditional programming methods. AI and ML, on the other hand, are what make the Metaverse work. They can do things like spot patterns, guess what will happen, make choices, and make things [5]. A leading example of AI-powered collaborative virtual spaces is NVIDIA Omniverse, which enables architects, engineers, and designers to work together on complex 3D designs in real time using AI-accelerated rendering and simulation tools.

Three of the most important things that Web X.0 needs are what make AI and ML so important for immersive technologies:

1. Scalability: The Metaverse can have billions of users at once, which makes it possible to collect a lot of different kinds of data, like visual, audio, behavioral, and transactional data
2. Realism: Environments should be realistic and let users interact with realistic avatars, smart NPCs, and realistic simulations to keep them interested
3. Personalization: Everyone wants experiences that are unique to them based on their interests, past experiences, and social interactions

The Metaverse would become unchanging, resource-hungry, and impossible to control without AI. AI stops this by making the environment flexible, efficient, and always changing.

5.2.4.1 Smart avatars and virtual humans

The most apparent application of AI in the Metaverse is creating smart avatars. Avatars are no longer two-dimensional digital faces but proactive entities with the ability to simulate human emotions, voices, and body language [19].

- Facial animation: AI software creates natural-looking facial expressions in sync with voice inputs
- Emotion recognition: ML systems recognize user emotions (through voice tone, text, or biometrics) and respond appropriately through the avatar
- Digital humans: AI-driven "virtual humans" can be used as teachers, assistants, or customer support agents in VR/AR. These avatars utilize Natural Language Processing (NLP) and deep learning to have conversations similar to humans

For example, a learner in a VR classroom can engage with an avatar teacher that is AI-based, which can modify lessons in real time depending on the learner's performance.

5.2.4.2 Content generation and world-building

One of the main challenges in the Metaverse is generating enormous amounts of 3D content: landscapes, structures, avatars, and interactive items. Conventionally, this involves talented designers and considerable time [19]. AI speeds up the process by:

- Generative Adversarial Networks (GANs): Employed to generate realistic textures, objects, and even faces for avatars automatically
- Neural Radiance Fields (NeRFs): Convert 2D images to 3D models, allowing for rapid digitization of objects and real-world spaces
- Procedural content generation: AI generates game worlds, levels, and quests on the fly based on player history and preferences

For example, a Metaverse city could grow dynamically as more users are added, with AI generating new streets, buildings, and social spaces on the fly.

5.2.4.3 Personalization and recommendation systems

Where Web 2.0 had relied on recommendation engines for shopping sites and streaming sites, Web X.0 requires immersive personalized experiences [20].

- Behavioral prediction: ML algorithms track user activities (games played, environments visited, and social groups joined) to recommend new spaces or events
- Adaptive learning: In VR learning, AI systems adjust difficulty levels, teaching styles, and speed based on student performance
- Virtual shopping: Shopping websites based on AR use AI for suggesting clothing, furniture, or cosmetics according to the preferences of the users

Personalization ensures the Metaverse is interesting and pertinent and also encourages user retention and satisfaction.

5.2.4.4 Conversational AI and social interactions

Dialogue is the building block of social presence within the Metaverse. AI offers smooth interaction in the form of voice assistants, chatbots, and conversational Non-Player Characters (NPCs) [21].

- NLP: AI translates and generates human language to enable avatars and NPCs to engage in natural-sounding conversations
- Multilingual translation: Real-time, AI-based translation enables people who speak different languages to interact seamlessly in shared spaces
- Emotionally adaptive conversation: AI will try to adapts tone and style of conversation based on context, thereby making social interactions more natural

This makes Metaverse a real universal platform that does not have any language or cultural barriers.

5.2.4.5 Analyzing and improving the system in real time

A lot of computing power is required for the immersive applications. AI and ML bring prediction and optimization to the table so that resources can be used in the best way possible.

- Network optimization: AI predicts how many people will use the network during multiplayer VR sessions and dynamically allocates bandwidth to avoid lag
- Resource allocation: ML divides computing tasks between the edge, fog, and cloud layers in a way that cuts down on latency and power use
- Behavioral analytics: AI keeps trust by finding cheating, fraud, or cyber-attacks in virtual economies

In an AR factory, for example, AI will keep track of real-time IoT sensor data, guess when equipment will break down, and keep things running smoothly.

5.2.4.6 Moderation, safety, and security

Immersive environments are vulnerable to harassment, disinformation, and exploitation [7]. AI serves as a protective layer by:

- Toxic behavior detection: NLP models find rude language or actions in VR chat rooms
- Preventing fraud: AI systems check blockchain transactions to make sure they are not fake or forged NFTs
- Child protection: AI keeps an eye on what happens in VR environments made just for kids to make sure everyone is safe

Without AI-driven moderation, big Metaverse environments would be easy to take advantage of, which would hurt users' trust.

Uses across industries

- Education: AI teachers in VR classrooms change how they teach based on how each student learns best
- Healthcare: AI-powered AR overlays help surgeons during surgery, and AI-powered VR therapy changes simulated treatment
- Gaming: NPCs are smart, realistic, and change over time, which makes the game more fun
- Business: Virtual office AI personal assistants set up meetings, analyze data, and write up what was said in meetings
- Tourism: AI gives personalized AR-guided tours of cultural sites with commentary that takes the location into account

5.2.5 High-speed networks (5G/6G) and IoT integration

Web X.0 would not function without connectivity that is unbroken, seamless and ultra-high speed in terms of the success of the Metaverse, VR, and AR. Immersive spaces demand data to be relayed, processed, and displayed in real time with huge amounts of simultaneous users, detailed 3D imagery, and information about the real spaces. These requirements are not enabled by centralized architectures and conventional 4G networks due to limited bandwidth, high latency, and scalability. It is here that the next generation of telecommunication technologies, 5G and the future 6G, come together with the Internet of Things (IoT) to become the basis of immersive platforms. The combination is what provides the connectivity, intelligence, and ubiquity required to tie together the physical and virtual worlds [22].

Three significant challenges characterize network requirements for Web X.0:

1. Low latency: Immersive environments break down if there is even a slight delay between user action and system response. For VR/AR, latency must be below 20 ms, and for haptic feedback, below 10 ms
2. High bandwidth: Streaming high-definition 3D graphics, holograms, and real-time AR overlays requires multi-gigabit connections

3. Massive device connectivity: Billions of IoT devices, sensors, and wearables need to be connected simultaneously to ensure context-aware immersive experiences

Unless these problems are solved, Web X.0 cannot scale from experimental use to full-fledged global immersive ecosystems.

5.2.5.1 5G networks: supporting immersive systems today

5G refers to the fifth generation of mobile telecommunication technology, which aims to overcome the limitations of 4G.

- Enhanced Mobile Broadband (eMBB): Offers speeds of up to 10 Gbps, allowing real-time transmission of 4K/8K VR content and photorealistic AR experiences
- Ultra-Reliable Low Latency Communication (URLLC): Provides latency of as low as 1–10 ms, essential for VR gaming, AR-guided surgeries, and industrial Metaverse use cases
- Massive Machine-Type Communication (mMTC): Supports up to 1 million devices per square kilometer for IoT-enabled smart factories and AR-based smart cities

Examples:

- For VR gaming, 5G enables players in various locations to have synchronized interactions with very little lag
- In medicine, AR glasses based on 5G give surgeons real-time overlays of patient information during surgery
- In shopping, mobile AR apps allow consumers to see furniture or apparel in real time without lag

5.2.5.2 6G networks: the Metaverse future

Whereas 5G supports existing immersive use cases, the sixth generation (6G), due by 2030, is seen as the ultimate enabler of Web X.0.

- Data rates: Up to 1 Tbps (terabit per second), enabling photorealistic, AI-based environments at unprecedented scale
- Latency: Sub-1 ms, which will make real-time holographic communication and neural interfaces possible
- AI-native networks: 6G embeds AI in the network itself, making predictive resource allocation and autonomous optimization possible
- Holographic communication: Real-time 3D holograms will enable users to virtually project themselves into meetings, classrooms, or entertainment spaces
- Integration with space–air–ground networks: 6G will utilize satellites, drones, and high-altitude platforms, providing global coverage and inclusivity

With 6G, the Metaverse will shift from flat avatars to holographic telepresence, providing life-like social and professional interactions.

5.2.5.3 IoT integration

Metaverse is not a pure virtual construct; it has to constantly engage with real-world data streams to stay relevant and context aware. That is enabled by IoT.

- Smart sensors: IoT sensors such as cameras, motion sensors, and environmental sensors supply real-time data to AR/VR worlds. For example, AR navigation apps overlay real-time traffic updates directly into a user's line of sight
- Wearables: Wearables such as smartwatches, biometric bands, and AR/VR headsets collect health statistics, movement, and interactions to power customized immersive experiences
- Industrial IoT (IIoT): IIoT sensors coupled with AR interfaces provide factory workers real-time feedback on equipment operation, predict maintenance, and detect faults
- Smart homes and cities: IoT appliances coupled with AR applications enable users to view energy usage, water consumption, or security status on their mobile screen or AR glasses

IoT ensures the Metaverse is not isolated but remains rooted in the physicality of the real world, fusing the real and virtual worlds into a combined Web X.0.

5.2.5.4 Synergy of 5G/6G and IoT in immersive systems

The true power of these technologies lies in their synergy.

- 5G + IoT: Facilitates smart retail, connected care, and AR-fueled tourism through the delivery of real-time data overlays from IoT sensors
- 6G + IoT: Will deliver fully immersive digital twins of cities, factories, and ecosystems, refreshed in real time by data from millions of sensors
- VR/AR + networks: Ensures that the rendering jobs can be shared between devices, servers, and fog nodes without breaking immersion

As an illustration, AR glasses that can identify the IoT can capture attendance data (such as response time and eye movement) in virtual classrooms and transmit it to AI tutors who make adjustments immediately via 5G/6G networks.

5.2.6 Human–computer interaction interfaces

Web X.0 is based on accelerated networks, AI systems, and blockchain systems. But all the effectiveness of the Metaverse, VR, and AR is set on the way individuals interact with these immersive systems. The field of Human–Computer Interaction (HCI) studies how people and computers interact. Its goal is to make interfaces that are easy to use, natural, and fun, and that connect the two worlds of people and computers [23].

People mostly used keyboards, mice, and touchscreens to interact in Web 2.0 and Web 3.0. But virtual or augmented worlds need multimodal interaction, like sound, touch, and even thought, so that users are surrounded by the worlds. Users may become frustrated, nauseated, or alienated without new HCI interfaces, which goes against the whole point of immersion. HCI is not an extra feature; it is an important part of making Metaverse and XR technologies work [19].

There are four main reasons why we need next-generation HCI interfaces:

1. Immersion: Users need to feel like they are "there" in virtual worlds, so they need natural sensory input and feedback
2. Accessibility: The interfaces must be easy for people with different skills, backgrounds, and levels of technical knowledge to use
3. Intuitiveness: Interactions should be like real-life gestures and actions so that the learning curve stays low
4. Multimodality: Interaction shouldn't just happen through one channel (like vision); it should also support touch, sound, gestures, and speech to fully engage users

The six core technologies in HCI for immersive systems are shown in Figure 5.2 and are explained in detail below.

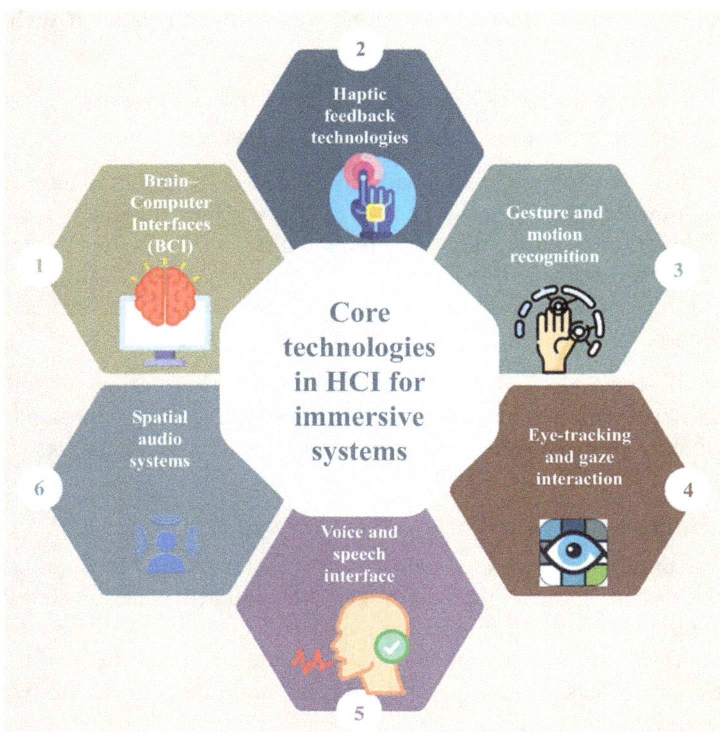

Figure 5.2 Core technologies in HCI for immersive systems

5.2.6.1 Haptic feedback technologies

Haptic technologies mimic the sense of touch and force feedback so users can feel virtual objects physically.

- Haptic gloves: Mimic texture, vibration, and resistance, allowing users to hold or use virtual tools
- Haptic suits and vests: Envelop the body with actuators mimicking impacts, temperature, or tactile sensations
- Force feedback controllers: Resistant to digital objects, steering wheels, or joysticks

Example: Haptic gloves allow doctors to feel the resistance of the tissues and bones in surgical training with VR, which introduces realism and training. The haptic suits in video games allow the players to sense the atmosphere such as rain, wind, or explosions.

5.2.6.2 Gesture and motion recognition

Gesture recognition allows users to interact with virtual worlds with natural body gestures and reduces the use of body controllers.

- Computer vision algorithms: Track hand and body gestures with cameras and depth sensors
- Infrared tracking: Captures accurate finger and hand movements in real-time
- Full-body motion capture: There are motion sensors on the suits that track the movement and pose to create the appearance of an actual avatar

Example: In AR industrial training, workers are able to make gestures to rotate or zoom 3D machine models. In the Metaverse, full-body tracking allows avatars to reflect human-like movements, improving social presence.

5.2.6.3 Eye tracking and gaze interaction

Eye-tracking technology tracks the user's direction at which the user is staring or paying attention.

- Foveated rendering: Reduces computer resources by rendering high-resolution graphics only within the location where the user is gazing, thus minimizing system load
- Attention analysis: Identifies user attention and fatigue, which can be applied in VR classrooms or training spaces
- Gaze-based interaction: Enables users to click or activate objects merely by gazing at them

Example: In a VR business meeting, eye-tracking can simulate eye contact between avatars, increasing the sense of realism and connection.

5.2.6.4 Spatial audio systems

Spatial audio, which is a sound reproduction system, is three-dimensional and allows users to perceive the directions, distance, and movement of sound sources.

- Binaural audio rendering: This is the simulation of sound to the human ear in different directions
- Dynamic adjustment: Sound is adjusted to the movement of the user or the location of the avatar
- Immersive communication: Generate real group discussion when voices are heard at different spatial positions

Example: In a VR concert, the listener cannot hear instruments, but with the help of spatial sound, the instruments seem to be on the stage and around them. Sound signals are used in AR wayfinding to guide pedestrians safely in terms of direction and distance.

5.2.6.5 Brain–computer interfaces

Brain–computer interfaces (BCIs) will be the future of HCI and will enable the human brain to physically and directly interact with digital worlds without displacement.

- Non-invasive BCIs: Employ electroencephalography (EEG) headsets to read neural signals off the scalp
- Signal translation: Brainwave patterns are translated by AI algorithms into commands to manipulate avatars or objects

Potential applications:

- Accessibility: Enabling individuals with disabilities to move around virtual space
- Immersion: Manipulating virtual space using thought instead of bodily action
- Healthcare: Facilitating patients to undergo neuro-rehabilitation exercises in VR

For instance, a paralyzed person might use a BCI headset to move an avatar's hand in a VR therapy exercise without moving their own muscles.

5.2.6.6 Voice and speech interfaces

Understanding language and voice recognition let people interact with immersive systems in a natural way.

- Voice commands: Voice can be used to control the system, choose an object, or get around
- Conversational AI: Talk to smart NPCs or virtual assistants
- Multilingual communication: People who speak different languages can work together in the same virtual space with real-time translation

For example, at an international Metaverse conference, people who speak different languages can talk to each other using AI-powered translation and speech-to-text.

How HCI is used in immersive systems

- Education and training: Haptic gloves and VR classrooms let you do science experiments without having to go to a lab
- Healthcare: Eye-tracking and AR overlays help surgeons during complicated surgeries
- Entertainment: Haptic suits and spatial audio make games and concerts more immersive
- Working from home: VR meetings are easier to understand than video calls because they use spatial audio and gesture recognition
- Accessibility: People with limited mobility can fully enjoy the Metaverse thanks to voice commands and BCIs

5.2.7 Cybersecurity and privacy mechanisms

Enhancing into the Web X.0 era, VR, and AR provide new opportunities to interact with others, conduct business, study, and entertain. However, new threats to privacy and cybersecurity are widespread along with such opportunities. Compared to ordinary web platforms, immersive platforms gather and handle significantly more intimate data. It consists of biometric cues, real-time positioning, behavioral information, voice logs, and even neural feedback of BCIs [6]. Cybercriminals, corrupt businesses, and other interests of an authoritarian nature find this vast data pool a good target to steal information. Loss of money may not be the only consequence of compromises; there may also be loss of identity, online identity manipulations, emotional damage, and loss of trust. Therefore, the cybersecurity and privacy features are not additional services but essential components of the long-term expansion of Web X.0. The dramatic example of such weaknesses is the 2022 hack of the Axie Infinity which saw the attackers loot more than $600 million in cryptocurrency by compromising the vulnerabilities of the Ronin Network bridge, indicating the extreme importance of blockchain-driven virtual economies security [32].

There are three main reasons why immersive systems need cybersecurity:

1. Numerous points of attack: Hackers can use any device that is connected to them, including a VR HMD, AR smart glasses, or IoT sensors.
2. Sensory data accumulation: The eye tracking, gait data, and biometric signals is likely to identify the user in a unique way, making it hard to be anonymous.
3. Digital identity and ownership: It is perhaps also the case that in the world of blockchain-based worlds, the loss of keys or the hacking of wallets might be a loss of resources that cannot be found.

Users will not desire to indulge in immersive spaces as a whole unless they feel safe, and this is not an aspect that will lead to the evolution of the Metaverse.

5.2.7.1 Identity and authentication mechanisms

- Multi-Factor Authentication (MFA): It is not a password, and it has biometric authentication, including facial recognition, fingerprint scan, or even voiceprint
- Decentralized Identity (DID): Identity systems based on blockchain allow users to receive their own certificates and offer them SSI that can be used on other systems
- Constant authentication: Behavioral biometrics are akin to eye movement signature or walking pattern (gait analysis), which ensures constant authentication in immersive settings

For example, a VR banking app can be used to log into accounts by means of a combination of blockchain keys, face recognition, and gait-based authentication.

5.2.7.2 Encryption and data protection

- End-to-End Encryption (E2EE): It implies that no one is able to observe the information the users transmit and receive during the VR/AR sessions
- Homomorphic encryption: It enables you to view encrypted information without providing the raw information about yourself
- Biometric data protection: Data that are based on neural or biometric data is encrypted in a special form such that uniquely identifying data is not revealed permanently

For example, a patient can wear smart glasses to capture data that is encrypted and studied by an AR health application, and at the same time comply with privacy regulations.

5.2.7.3 Network and infrastructure security

- Zero Trust Architecture (ZTA): This means that no user or device can be trusted, and every step must include strict identity verification
- Intrusion Detection and Prevention Systems (IDPS): These systems use AI to look for strange behavior in real-time traffic on VR and AR platforms
- Distributed Denial of Service (DDoS) protection: High-end defenses against DDoS attacks are needed because immersive experiences (like virtual concerts) can bring in millions of users

For example, during a global Metaverse event, zero-trust systems can stop bad bots from flooding servers while letting users in without any problems.

5.2.7.4 Privacy protection mechanisms

- Anonymization and pseudonymization: Deletes any data that can be used to identify people from behavior datasets used for analytics

- Differential privacy: Adds mathematical noise to data so that information can be gotten without showing individual records
- User-Controlled Data Sharing: Dashboards where people can choose what personal data is to be shared with applications or other individuals

For example, a VR classroom platform can look at student engagement data (such as eye-tracking and participation) as a whole without giving away any personal information.

5.2.7.5 Economic and asset protection

In the Metaverse world, the virtual economies are fueled by the Blockchain, NFTs, and cryptocurrencies. The protection of the digital property requires:

- Secure wallet: Biometric and hardware wallets reduce the chances of theft
- Smart contract audits: Ongoing/Regular audits to identify weaknesses in automated contracts
- Fraud detection systems: To monitor suspicious trading patterns, phishing attacks, and counterfeit NFTs AI-based analytics may be used

Scenario: A virtual art gallery in the market selling NFT paintings can install software to detect fraud by identifying programs that have cloned or stolen assets.

5.2.7.6 Governance, regulation, and ethical oversight

Security is not only a technical initiative, but also must be a policy and governance model.

- Global standards: Deploying cross-platform security and privacy standards
- User consent models: Well-defined policies on how data is gathered, stored, and monetized
- Ethical AI: How to avoid bias or the misuse of AI moderation systems

Examples: A city within a Metaverse that is governed by a DAO can vote on privacy laws that mandate cameras in virtual places of worship to be ethically connected.

Challenges in finding immersive environments

- Latency and security trade-off: Encryption can make things slower, and this is contrary to the requirement of VR/AR being real time
- New threats: Individuals intending to cause harm to you may employ new methods of communication, such as gesture spoofing or voice cloning
- Loopholes in regulations: The existing privacy regulations, such as the General Data Protection Regulation (GDPR), might not be relevant to biometric or neural data
- User education: Individuals using immersive spaces do not consider the risks and that is why they become bad cyber hygiene

Applications in many areas

- Medical: Secure AR systems help to save confidential scans and biometrics of patients
- Education: Privacy-preserving analytics is applied in VR classrooms to gauge student performance
- Finance: VR banks are based on DID and encrypted smart contracts using blockchain
- Entertainment: Virtual concerts have secure ticketing systems which are connected with the blockchain to prevent individuals from creating fake tickets

5.2.8 Interoperability and standards for Web X.0

The vision of the Metaverse, VR, and AR proposed by Web X.0 is a perpetually transformative digital world with the capability of being connected. However, without any open standards or interoperability, the Metaverse may become a series of walled gardens operated by companies, where a user cannot transfer their digital identity, property, or experiences between platforms. These silos would repeat the same errors that were committed at the start of the Web 2.0 environments, which were against the concept of one, open and shared Web X.0.

Interoperability refers to the capability of various systems, platforms, and applications to communicate with one another, exchange information, and interpret it in a disparate manner. Standards, however, establish the technical and governance regulations that ensure that every platform is secure, consistent and reliable to users. They collaborate to create the basis of the cross-platform integration that allows users to navigate the Metaverse with the same ease as they browse between websites [24]. One prominent example of cross-platform asset interoperability is an industry collaboration between The Sandbox and Atari that allowed Atari-branded virtual assets, such as virtual real estate and arcade-themed items, to be utilized in The Sandbox gaming Metaverse.

Interoperability and standards are important in immersive systems because they meet four basic needs:

1. User mobility and freedom: Users need to be able to move their avatars, assets, and digital identities from one place to another
2. Economic viability: Virtual economies need standard platforms for trading money, owning assets, and doing business
3. Technical compatibility: Even though they were made by different companies, devices, apps, and infrastructures need to work together
4. Trust and governance: Standards set rules that protect users' rights, safety, and privacy

Without them, Web X.0 will break up, making it harder for people to use and come up with new ideas.

5.2.8.1 Identity and avatar interoperability

It is one of the Core Interoperability Domains in Web X.0. Users should not have to make new digital identities for each platform. Blockchain-based DID systems and SSI let people have digital identities that last.

- Avatar portability: You can find avatars made in one virtual world in another without having to redesign them
- Cross-platform credentials: You can use credentials or qualifications that have been verified on one platform on other platforms
- Digital reputation systems: Trust values or reputation points can move from one place to another

For instance, a doctor with a blockchain-verified medical license at one VR hospital should be able to use the same license at another AR-augmented clinic without having to get a new one.

5.2.8.2 Asset interoperability

Digital goods like land, wearable tech, art, and equipment should not only be owned in one world. NFTs and interoperable metadata standards let you use them on different platforms.

- Token standards (like ERC-721 and ERC-1155): Make sure that NFTs can be found in more than one marketplace
- Cross-chain bridges: Let assets move between different blockchain networks
- Unified file formats: 3D models, textures, and audio that work on all platforms make sure that objects look the same

For instance, an avatar in a different gaming Metaverse could wear a pair of digital shoes bought in a VR fashion boutique if both systems follow the same rules.

5.2.8.3 Communication protocols

To collaborate effectively without any issue, platforms have to have standardized networking and communication protocols.

- Application programming interfaces (APIs): Ensuring that apps can communicate data safely
- Standardized messaging formats (such as JSON, XML, and WebRTC) allow avatars and systems to communicate with each other in real time
- Cross-platform voice and chat systems: Allow individuals to communicate with one another regardless of the platform they are on

Indicatively, a VR user would find it easy to speak with an AR user who had projected the same presentation on his/her space.

5.2.8.4 Payment and economic standards

Web X.0 economies rely on the stable regulations of transferring assets and paying.

- Cryptocurrency standards: Wallets that support numerous tokens
- Central Bank Digital Currencies (CBDCs): Provide people with a secure and common means of paying online
- Smart contract templates: Ensure that the automated contracts are guided by the security and governance rules that are already in existence

To use a certain example, a freelance designer, employed by a VR design company, should be allowed to receive standard crypto-payments, which can be spent on any platform without the need to perform numerous conversions.

5.2.8.5 Content and media standards

Content interoperability ensures that digital experiences can be accessed by every device and perform similarly.

- 3D graphics standards (such as glTF and Universal Scene Description (USD)): Ensure that in AR, VR, and XR systems, 3D models appear identical
- Audio-–visual standards (such as MPEG-I): Make it possible to have a rich sound and video
- Accessibility standards (Web Content Accessibility Guidelines (WCAG) in XR): Ensure that the design is usable by disabled persons

As an example, you can see a virtual museum exhibit in glTF format on VR headsets, AR glasses, or even mobile phones without converting the format.

5.2.8.6 Governance and ethical standards

To ensure that things are fair, open to everyone, and long-lasting, technical standards need to be backed up by ethical and governance standards.

- Privacy standards: Following GDPR-type rules for immersive data
- Safety protocols: Rules for keeping harassment and exploitation out of virtual spaces
- Environmental standards: Standards for energy-efficient computing that help immersive infrastructures have a smaller carbon footprint

For example, an international group could set ethical standards for how avatars should behave in shared VR classrooms to stop harassment and discrimination.

Organizations and initiatives that work on a global scale

Several groups are working to set standards for immersive technologies:

- Khronos Group: Making standards for glTF and other 3D content
- IEEE Standards Association: Working on models for interoperability and governance
- OpenXR Consortium: Making sure that VR and AR apps work on different types of hardware

- World Wide Web Consortium (W3C): Looking into Web standards that make XR work with the rest of the Internet

These projects stress how important it is for many countries to work together to make Web X.0 open and compatible.

Challenges in reaching interoperability

- Closed ecosystems: Tech leaders may prefer closed ecosystems, so they can have more control
- Technical difficulty: It is very hard to make sure that all devices, platforms, and infrastructures work the same way
- Different rules: Different countries may have different rules about privacy, identity, and digital assets
- Problems with scalability: Standards need to work for billions of users and trillions of assets

5.2.9 Cloud–edge–fog integration models

The Metaverse, VR, and AR require real-time responsiveness, fast data processing, and scalable infrastructure. The infrastructure for big-data storage and analysis relies on cloud computing, and centralized points of data collection are necessary, which can potentially lead to issues of latency and bandwidth. In their turn, edge computing and fog computing push processing to the network edge. They lack the accessibility and reach of the cloud across the globe and growth capability.

The cloud, edge, and fog models should collaborate with each other to ensure they are stronger, making Web X.0 a reality. The convergence paradigm ensures not only fast and responsive experiences but also guaranteed immersive experiences, which are available everywhere across the globe, scalable, and capable of handling errors [11].

Three main problems affect immersive use cases like VR gaming, AR-enabled surgeries, and huge Metaverse events:

- Low latency: To keep the immersion, the response time must be less than 20 ms
- Scalability: Millions of people using the system at the same time create petabytes of data, which cannot all be processed at the edge
- Context-awareness: Local devices and sensors need to talk to global systems in order to make hybrid environments work from start to finish

Traditional cloud-only models cannot meet the needs listed above. Layered architectures that combine cloud, edge, and fog are becoming the best option.

5.2.9.1 Cloud computing layer

- Centralized powerhouse: Allows you to store a lot of data, process AI-based data analysis, and perform simulations at a massive scale

- Global accessibility: Paves the way to common virtual spaces among people around the world
- Use cases: Storing digital assets in NFT marketplaces, running big AI models to create avatars, personalization, and providing billions of objects to permanent Metaverse worlds

For example, the cloud stores massive course libraries and AI models in a virtual university, so that they are accessible everywhere.

5.2.9.2 Edge computing layer

The computation in this layer must occur near devices such as AR glasses, VR headsets, or IoT sensors.

- Real-time responsiveness: Processes actions that must occur immediately, such as gesture or haptic feedback, and avatar synchronization
- Use cases: Multiplayer VR games which provide feedback in real time, AR-guided navigation which requires less than a second to update local maps, and wearables which require biometric data to be processed in real time

For example, an edge node in a mall would reflect AR ads to update in real time as individuals walk through stores.

5.2.9.3 Fog computing layer

- Intermediate bridge: This area joins the edge and the cloud and collects data in various regions
- Distributed intelligence: Provides you with additional context than the edge without forfeiting the lower latency of cloud
- Applications: Intelligent infrastructure of cities that collects information about traffic and the city, city Metaverse hubs that host concerts or meetings, and numerous virtual classrooms that unite schools within the same locality

As an illustration, smart city fog nodes can collect data from thousands of IoT devices and provide commuters with a real-time AR overlay.

5.2.9.4 Integrated architectures and models

The cloud–edge–fog synergy is hierarchical:

- Edge: Manages local, time-sensitive interactions, like gesture detection and haptics
- Fog: Combines data from many sources and makes it easier for people to work together (smart cities, education networks)
- Cloud: Provides permanent, large-scale storage and access to people all over the world (Metaverse worlds, digital economies)

This model makes sure that data is processed at the right place and time, balancing speed, scalability, and intelligence.

Examples of cloud–edge–fog integration

A few sectors are listed below where cloud–edge–fog integration can bring revolution.

- Health:
  - Edge: Surgeons get help from AR glasses that show live overlays
  - Fog: The hospital network collects all of a patient's records in one place
  - Cloud: AI models from around the world look at long-term health trends
- Education:
  - Edge: The VR headset changes lessons in real time
  - Fog: A regional server handles cooperation between multiple schools
  - Cloud: Stores virtual credentials and libraries of learning from around the world
- Gaming and entertainment:
  - Edge: Avatars can be synced in real time
  - Fog: Regional servers run multiplayer tournaments
  - Cloud: Long-term storage of player histories and virtual goods
- Smart cities:
  - Edge: IoT sensors keep an eye on traffic and the environment
  - Fog: City-level analytics make transportation and energy better
  - Cloud: Models from all over the world compare cities to help with long-term planning

Problems with integration

- Resource allocation: Fairly dividing up the work between layers so that none of them gets too much
- Latency trade-offs: Encrypting sensitive data securely with a response time of less than 20 ms
- Security risks: Every layer adds new ways for hackers to attack (cloud hacking, fog tampering, and edge hijacking)
- Problems with standardization: There are no single frameworks that make it possible for layers to work together

5.3 Applications of Metaverse, VR, and AR in Web X.0

Web X.0 is built on enabling technologies like AI, blockchain, edge/fog computing, and high-speed networks. However, the real value of the Metaverse, VR, and AR lies in how they can be used in different industries and social settings. They are no longer just for fun or to show how something works; they are changing culture, business, healthcare, education, governance, and retail, changing how people interact with both the digital and real worlds.

There are many uses for immersive technologies in Web X.0, including entertainment, education, remote work, healthcare, commerce, and social ecosystems, as shown in Figure 5.3. Each field makes use of different XR technology features, such as

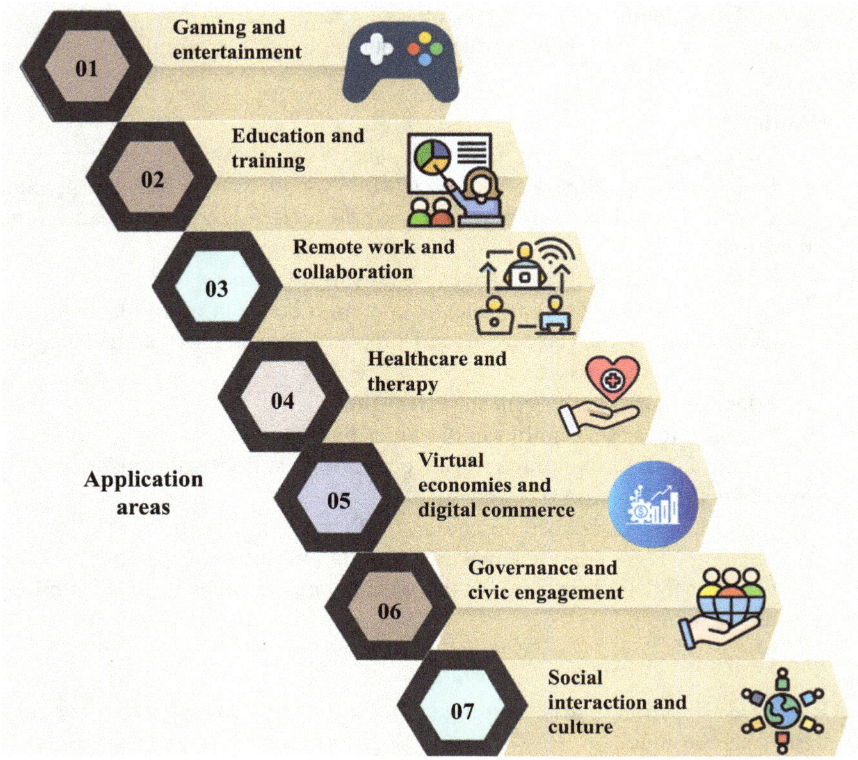

Figure 5.3 Applications of Metaverse, VR, and AR in Web X.0

immersion, interactivity, real-time feedback, and contextual awareness, which are all improved by smart and safe infrastructures.

5.3.1 Gaming and entertainment

Entertainment is still the most talked-about and important trend in VR, AR, and the Metaverse.

- Immersive gaming: People can use VR headsets to enter 3D worlds and interact with avatars and their surroundings in a way that feels real
- AR games: Pokémon Go and other games show how AR adds digital elements to real-world places
- Virtual concerts and events: Fortnite and Roblox are two sites where millions of people go to live concerts in the same digital space
- Movies and stories: In VR movies, the viewer gets to decide what happens next in the story

For example, a Travis Scott VR concert in Fortnite had more than 12 million live viewers. This shows that Web X.0 could be used for group fun [30].

5.3.2 Education and training

Learning is being transformed by immersive technologies that make it interactive, personalized, and experiential.

- Virtual classrooms: Learners engage with educators and classmates as avatars, mimicking the social interactions of real-life classrooms
- AR-based learning tools: Superimpose historic facts, scientific illustrations, or language translations onto real-world objects
- Skill training: VR simulations train pilots, surgeons, and engineers in risk-free virtual environments
- Personalized learning: AI-powered tutors in VR adjust content to student performance

Example: Medical students practice surgeries using VR platforms with haptic feedback, minimizing cadaver use and limiting real-world risks [31].

5.3.3 Remote work and collaboration

Web X.0 allows having virtual offices, collaborative platforms that cannot be achieved through video conferencing.

- Virtual offices: Virtual offices allow employees to be represented by avatars, which assist in the creation of presence and a sense of teamwork
- 3D collaboration tools: AR/VR spaces provide architects and engineers with an opportunity to collaborate on 3D designs
- Global accessibility: Teams operating in different parts of the world can work together without spending a lot of money on traveling, which leads to carbon emissions
- AI meeting assistants: Summarize, translate, and record meetings in real time

Example: Some companies, including Meta (Horizon Workrooms) and Microsoft (Mesh), are building VR offices in which colleagues can naturally communicate with each other regardless of physical space [4].

5.3.4 Healthcare and therapy

Immersive technologies are transforming healthcare delivery and patient outcomes.

- AR-assisted surgery: Surgeons employ AR overlays for real-time instruction during advanced procedures
- VR therapy: Exposure therapy for phobia, post-traumatic stress disorder (PTSD), or anxiety disorders in safe VR settings

- Medical training: VR platforms provide the opportunity to repeat the unusual or risky procedures
- Remote patient monitoring: AR systems with the assistance of IoT provide clinicians with real-time health data

Example: Osso VR offers surgical training environments in which physicians rehearse in immersive, high-feedback settings, enhancing precision and results [31].

5.3.5 Virtual economies and digital commerce

Metaverse brings new economic systems where products, services, and experiences all exist in a virtual state.

- NFT marketplaces: Facilitate the exchange of distinct digital items like art, music, or virtual land
- Virtual retail stores: Brands such as Nike and Gucci offer virtual apparel for avatars, in addition to physical goods
- Immersive shopping: AR applications enable customers to test clothes, furniture, or cosmetics prior to buying them
- Work opportunities: Freelancers create digital assets, organize events, or offer services in virtual worlds

Example: Nike acquiring RTFKT, a virtual footwear firm, indicates how Metaverse digital commerce is going mainstream [17].

5.3.6 Governance and civic engagement

Web X.0 is not only a business, but it is also a civic existence and government.

- Virtual town halls: The citizens will be able to converse with the policymakers in stimulating environments
- Smart city planning: AR and VR model cities before implementation
- Decentralized governance: DAOs provide a democratic rule of communities and common goods
- Virtual diplomacy: Adopt virtual diplomacy; negotiate and carry out cultural exchanges in compelling platforms

Example: VR-based urban simulation is not widely used in many cities to consult their citizens in the planning process, allowing the residents to walk through planned configurations before they are approved [18].

5.3.7 Social interaction and culture

Metaverse opens up new socialization and cultural representations.

- Social worlds: Decentraland or VRChat are virtual worlds that allow individuals to create communities

- Virtual museums and heritage: AR/VR brings historic places back home to learn and travel
- Cultural preservation: Aborigines create immersion to preserve languages and traditions
- Cultural expression: VR galleries are a blend of technology and art by artists

Example: UNESCO has also been experimenting with VR projects to recreate destroyed heritage sites digitally, which people around the world can experience in the virtual world [3].

5.4 Challenges and issues in immersive Web X.0

Despite the transformational potential of Web X.0 that can be implemented by Metaverse, VR, and AR, a series of technical, social, ethical, and governance concerns threaten the mass implementation of the technologies. These are critical issues since the immersive experiences are beyond traditional Internet experiences, as the experiences incorporate biometric data, neural connectivity, digital objects, social interactions, and physical environments in continuous virtual worlds.

Until these concerns are properly addressed, immersive ecosystems may reflect the shortcomings of Web 2.0 (centralization, inequality, and exploitation) or even be more threatening, with profound social consequences. Therefore, their discovery and alleviation is urgent to create an inclusive and safe Web X.0 [25].

5.4.1 Privacy and data protection

Immersive technologies facilitate volume of personal and sensitive data—eye movements, gait patterns, facial expressions, voice recordings, and even neural signals using BCIs.

- Biometric vulnerability: The biometric identifiers (iris, gait, EEG) are impossible to change after theft as opposed to passwords
- Constant monitoring: VR/AR headsets can constantly monitor the user, and this can be questioned as continuous monitoring
- Data exploitation: The companies can sell behavioral and biometric data without obtaining the consent of the user

Example: In AR shopping applications, gaze-tracking data can reveal subconscious preferences, which create hyper-targeted advertisements at the expense of independence.

5.4.2 Cybercrime and security threats

With expanding digital economies across the Metaverse, they become appealing targets for cybercriminals.

- Identity theft: Impersonated blockchain keys or hacked avatars lead to asset loss and identity theft
- Phishing and social engineering: Attackers can impersonate familiar avatars to trick users
- Virtual property hacks: Hacks on NFT marketplaces or VR platforms can lead to the loss of millions of digital assets

Example: One large NFT marketplace experienced hacks in which hackers emptied wallets due to the vulnerabilities of smart contracts, demonstrating the digital assets' perpetual susceptibility [29].

5.4.3 Ethical concerns and governance

Web X.0 is immersive and it poses a challenge to ethics and governance structures.

- Decentralized governance challenges: DAOs are prone to manipulation in which voting rights are not based on equality but on the amount of wealth an individual possesses
- Harassment and abuse: VR/AR experiences expose the user to harassment which is more personalized because of immersion
- Consent and manipulation: The user is susceptible to manipulative advertising or psychological manipulation

Example: Harassment in VRChat notes that immersive abuse is traumatic like the real world and needs more difficult governance mechanisms [28].

5.4.4 Digital divide and accessibility

Immersive technologies cannot be available all the time due to expenses, infrastructure, and technical literacy.

- Economic barriers: Most users cannot afford VR headsets and AR glasses
- Connectivity gaps: Underdeveloped areas may lack 5G/6G or edge network to run immersive experience
- Disability access: HCI interfaces cannot necessarily support individuals with motor, auditory, or visual disabilities at present

Example: VR classroom usage is not only practiced in certain universities, but low-income students are disadvantaged, which contributes to the rise of inequality in education.

5.4.5 Psychological and social impacts

Immersive systems can have strong influences on mental well-being and social conduct.

- Addiction risks: Ongoing virtual worlds can encourage unhealthy reliance

- Identity confusion: People might find it difficult to distinguish between bodily and virtual personas
- Social isolation: Ironically, immersive communication can minimize physical-world contact

Example: Research into VR gaming revealed that prolonged use can obscure reality perception, particularly among teenagers, creating long-term challenges [25].

5.4.6 Interoperability and fragmentation

Nevertheless, despite all the efforts made across the globe, immersive platforms are about to become siloed.

- Lack of standards: Interoperability of identity, asset, and content among various platforms
- Vendor lock-in: Corporations can put a restriction on the portability of avatars and assets in order to retain them
- User frustration: It has to replicate profiles and assets in the process of switching to other platforms

Example: A consumer buying virtual clothes on one VR platform will not wear them on other VR platforms and will not compel them to spend on digital commodities.

5.4.7 Environmental and sustainability concerns

Massive computing, storage, and energy are needed by the immersive technologies.

- High carbon footprint: Data centers storing the Metaverse use massive portions of power
- E-waste: The continuous advancements of the headsets and the wearables contribute to electronic waste
- Gaps in sustainable design: Immersive platforms have not implemented green computer practices

Example: Cryptocurrency mining in the virtual economies has been suggested as a problem that is degrading the environment, as a concern about the sustainability of the Metaverse [26].

5.4.8 Legal and regulatory gaps

The laws of the present day were not designed to be used in an immersive context.

- Jurisdictional uncertainty: Virtual world crime (theft, harassment) is an international crime
- Intellectual Property (IP) issues: Controversies of ownership of digital products, especially those created by AI

- Data sovereignty: Nations possess varying sets of regulations, and the world is complex in interoperability

Example: Cases of harassment or fraud executed in a completely online space cannot be prosecuted in courts, and the victims have no visible way of redress.

The overall summary of challenges in immersive Web X.0 is listed in Table 5.1.

Table 5.1 Summary of challenges in immersive Web X.0

Challenge	Description	Example	Potential mitigation
Privacy and data protection	Massive collection of biometric data (eye movements, gait, EEG) that cannot be changed once stolen	AR shopping apps using gaze-tracking for hyper-targeted ads without consent	Strict data minimization policies; user-controlled data consent; encryption of biometric data
Cybercrime and security threats	Digital economies attract hackers targeting identities, assets, and platforms	NFT marketplace hacks where smart contract vulnerabilities led to wallet theft.	MMA; regular smart contract audits; DID systems
Ethical concerns and governance	Immersive environments enable harassment, manipulation, and wealth-based governance	Harassment in VRChat is causing trauma similar to physical experiences	Community guidelines; AI moderation; equitable DAO voting mechanisms
Digital divide and accessibility	High costs and infrastructure gaps exclude many users	Low-income students are unable to access VR classrooms, while affluent universities adopt them	Affordable device initiatives; 5G/6G infrastructure investment; universal design standards
Psychological and social impacts	Addiction, identity confusion, and reduced physical-world contact	Prolonged VR gaming obscures reality perception in teenagers	Usage limits; digital wellness tools; parental controls; public awareness campaigns
Interoperability and fragmentation	Platforms are becoming isolated silos with incompatible assets and identities	Virtual clothes bought in one VR platform cannot be used in another	Open standards (glTF, OpenXR); cross-platform APIs; industry-wide interoperability agreements
Environmental and sustainability concerns	High energy consumption and e-waste from data centers and hardware	Cryptocurrency mining for virtual economies is criticized its for carbon footprint [26]	Renewable energy-powered data centers; energy-efficient hardware; green blockchain

(Continues)

Table 5.1 (Continued)

Challenge	Description	Example	Potential mitigation
			protocols
Legal and regulatory gaps	Existing laws inadequate for cross-border virtual crimes and AI-generated IP	Courts are unable to prosecute harassment occurring entirely in virtual worlds	International regulatory frameworks; updated IP laws; cross-jurisdictional cooperation

5.5 Future directions

Metaverse, VR, and AR are merely the nascent phases of Web X.0. Though the immersive technologies of today have already demonstrated revolutionary use cases in entertainment, education, healthcare, and business, the coming decade will see more pervasive technology convergence, human enhancement, and ethical paradigms that will guide their development. The future of Web X.0 is oriented toward overcoming today's limitations, intensifying inclusivity, and building sustainable, smart, and accessible global ecosystems [2].

These emerging pathways are not incremental in nature; they herald a paradigm in the manner humans interact with technology, society, and even reality itself.

5.5.1 Immersive intelligence powered by AI

AI is going to remain the cognitive backbone of the Metaverse.

- Self-managing agents: Digital humans and avatars of the future will become super-intelligent assistants that can make decisions independently
- World-building with generative AI: Complete worlds, cities, or learning modules can be dynamically generated in real time, customized to specific users
- Empathetically adaptive systems: Avatars and NPCs not only mimic but react empathetically to human emotions

Example: In next-gen VR classrooms, AI instructors can create lessons tailored to each learner, adapting style, pace, and difficulty based on instant feedback [20].

5.5.2 Neural interfaces and brain–computer integration

The future of HCI is direct neural interfaces.

- Non-invasive BCIs: Machines will interpret brain signals to manage avatars or worlds without bodily movement

- Cognitive augmentation: Users might engage with the Metaverse using thought-controlled commands, minimizing dependence on external devices
- Therapeutic applications: BCIs can enable neuro-rehabilitation, enabling patients to train movement in VR prior to physical recovery

Example: A paralyzed user would be able to control a VR avatar by thinking alone, allowing for engagement in education, work, or social experiences.

5.5.3 Convergence of XR with IoT and digital twins

The future Web X.0 will unite the immersive platforms with the IoT ecosystem and digital twin models.

- Smart cities: AR cities have AR-equipped citizens who can communicate with real-time digital twins of the urban infrastructure
- Industrial use: Factories using VR/AR overlays are associated with IoT sensors to do predictive maintenance
- Environmental surveillance: Global ecosystems implemented in the Metaverse drive green policies

Example: VR simulation of flood protection in a city can be done on a virtual twin of it before being applied in reality [14].

5.5.4 Decentralized economies and Web X.0 finance

The Metaverse economy will expand to include entirely decentralized economies based on blockchain.

- Cross-metaverse marketplaces: Platform-to-platform interoperability
- Programmable economies: Taxation, royalty, and cooperative ownership as smart contracts
- Metaverse workforces: New jobs (immersive designer, digital lawyer, and XR teacher) are thriving in immersive economies

Example: A global platform of freelancers in VR can provide designers all around the globe with the ability to sell virtual products and receive payment in stablecoins or CBDCs [16].

5.5.5 Green and sustainable Metaverse

Sustainability will be an overarching issue for immersive systems.

- Energy-efficient infrastructures: Adoption of renewable-energy-powered data centers and green computing strategies
- Low-power devices: Creation of lightweight AR/VR headsets with a smaller environmental footprint

- Carbon-neutral virtual economies: Platforms implementing carbon credits or environmentally friendly blockchain frameworks

Example: A green VR platform might incentivize users and creators for reducing energy-intensive behaviors, building a "green economy" in the Metaverse [26].

5.5.6 Governance, policy, and ethics

With the development of immersive technologies changing the social environment, the principles of government change.

- International regulations: International rules to ensure privacy, online identity, and property rights
- DAO-based civic models: DAO-based government communities
- Ethical AI governance: How to prevent bias, manipulation, or abuse of surveillance in immersive environments

Examples: A global Metaverse Council might develop a norm of digital rights, shielding avatars, data, and assets against unjust treatment [28].

5.5.7 Inclusivity and accessibility

To be transformative, Web X.0 needs to include all users.

- Affordable devices: Mass production of inexpensive headsets and AR glasses
- Universal design: Access features for visually, auditorily, or motor impaired individuals
- Inclusivity of language: Real-time AI translation facilitating global engagement

Example: A blind user can explore VR environments using spatial audio and haptic feedback, facilitating equal engagement in the Metaverse [27].

5.5.8 Merging of physical and virtual worlds

Physical and virtual boundaries will blur in the future.

- MR: Blending seamless AR overlays with immersive VR
- Persistent hybrid spaces: Offices, schools, or cities simultaneously in physical and digital states
- Holographic presence: 6G-real-time holographs that beam people everywhere around the world

Example: A blended university can merge physical campuses with continuous VR classrooms, viewable by students everywhere [28].

A comprehensive summary of future directions is shown in Table 5.2.

Table 5.2 Future directions in immersive Web X.0

Future direction	Potential impact	Technology enabler	Timeframe
Immersive intelligence powered by AI	Personalized, adaptive virtual experiences	Generative AI, NLP, and emotion recognition	Near-term (1–3 years)
Neural interfaces and brain–computer integration	Thought-controlled interaction; accessibility for the disabled	BCIs, EEG sensors, neural decoding algorithms	Medium-term (3–7 years)
Convergence of XR with IoT and digital twins	Real-time simulation of cities, factories, environments	IoT sensors, digital twin platforms, 5G/6G	Medium-term (3–7 years)
Decentralized economies and Web X.0 finance	Cross-platform asset ownership; new virtual professions	Blockchain, NFTs, smart contracts, DeFi	Near-term (1–3 years)
Green and sustainable Metaverse	Reduced carbon footprint; energy-efficient virtual worlds	Renewable energy data centers, green computing	Long-term (7+ years)
Governance, policy, and ethics	Protected user rights; equitable virtual communities	Global regulatory frameworks, DAOs, ethical AI	Medium-term (3–7 years)
Inclusivity and accessibility	Equal access for all users regardless of ability or location	Affordable hardware, universal design, AI translation	Medium-term (3–7 years)
Merging of physical and virtual worlds	Seamless hybrid spaces; holographic telepresence	MR, 6G, haptics, real-time rendering	Long-term (7+ years)

The history of Web X.0, driven by the Metaverse, VR, and AR, is a paradigm shift in terms of human relations to technology, society, and others. Unlike the text-based and media-centric predecessors, Web X.0 is immersive, interactive, and intelligent. In this chapter, the technologies, applications, challenges, and future directions that have made this transition have been discussed.

We discussed the technological premises of immersive environments initially. These are XR architectures, edge and fog computing, blockchain-based decentralization, AI, high-speed networks, HCI interfaces, cybersecurity, interoperability protocols, and integrated cloud–edge–fog models. These technologies collaborate to establish the foundation, brains, and trust that are required to make immersive spaces effective and successful. Then we discussed the application of VR, AR, and the Metaverse to entertainment, education, healthcare, business, government, and culture. These images demonstrate that immersive technologies are no longer a future thought, but it is an actual tool today that is transforming industries, as well as the lives of people.

Another issue that the chapter discussed was the issues with Web X.0, such as threats to privacy, security threats, ethical concerns, digital divides, psychological impacts, and environmental problems. Without these issues being addressed, the user trust and accessibility will be damaged, and it is unlikely that integrated immersive ecosystems will remain connected.

We considered potential ways to develop in the future with intelligence, inclusiveness, sustainability, and governance as a priority. The future of Web X.0 will be the convergence of AI-driven avatars, neural interfaces, digital twins, decentralized economies, green computing, global governance structures, and user-friendly design. These instructions indicate a perspective of immersive technologies that are not just superior, but also just, moral, and sustainable.

VR, AR, and the metaverse are not concepts in themselves, but the elements of the online civilization that is approaching. They assure individuals of new forms of learning, healing, employment, friendship, and ruling. Nevertheless, they can be successful only if they can create a balance between moral responsibility and technological advancement. Web X.0 can be more than a technological revolution, and, with proper foresight and design, a cultural and social rebirth that can change the nature of human experience within the digital sphere.

5.6 Conclusion

This chapter has explored the transformative role of Metaverse, VR, and AR in shaping Web X.0. The discussion began with the foundational enabling technologies, including XR frameworks, edge and fog computing, blockchain, AI, 5G/6G networks, HCI interfaces, cybersecurity mechanisms, interoperability standards, and integrated cloud–edge–fog models, that collectively power immersive digital ecosystems.

The chapter also analyzed various implementations in gaming, education, healthcare, remote work, online commerce, government, and social interactions, showing that these technologies are no longer considered futuristic, but are now applicable tools that are transforming industries and everyday life. Nevertheless, on the way to mass adoption, there are serious obstacles: the danger of privacy, cybercrime, ethical issues, digital gaps, psychological consequences, interoperability fragmentation, environmental issues, and regulatory loopholes—all of which have to be tackled immediately.

In the future, trends are oriented toward immersive intelligence that is AI-driven, BCI, convergence of digital twins, decentralizing economies, sustainable infrastructures, inclusive design, and seamless merging of physical and virtual worlds. These innovations are likely to lead not only to technological evolution but also to the cultural and social renaissance. After all, establishing a balance between innovation and responsibility will be key to the success of Web X.0 as it will keep immersive technologies human-centric, ethical, accessible, and sustainable to everyone.

Suggested further readings

- *The Metaverse: And How It Will Revolutionize Everything*
- *Augmented Reality and Virtual Reality: New Trends in Immersive Technology*
- *The Metaverse: Building the Spatial Internet*
- *The Metaverse of Consciousness: Mapping the Multiple Dimensions of Reality*
- *Welcome to the Metaverse: Unlocking the Potential of Virtual Worlds*
- *Our Next Reality: How the AI-powered Metaverse Will Reshape the World*

References

[1] Dionisio JDN, and Gilbert R. '3D virtual worlds and the metaverse: current status and future possibilities', *ACM Computing Surveys*, 2013, 45, (3), pp. 1–38.

[2] Lee LH, Braud T, Zhou P, *et al.* 'All one needs to know about metaverse: a complete survey', *arXiv preprint arXiv:2110.05352*, 2021, pp. 1–68.

[3] Mystakidis S. 'Metaverse', *Encyclopedia*, 2022, 2, (1), pp. 486–497.

[4] Park SM, and Kim YG. 'A metaverse: taxonomy, components, applications, and open challenges', *IEEE Access*, 2022, 10, pp. 4209–4251.

[5] Wang H, Ning H, Lin Y, *et al.* 'A survey on the metaverse: the state-of-the-art, technologies, applications, and challenges', *IEEE Internet of Things Journal*, 2023, 10, (16), pp. 14671–14688.

[6] Ghosh A, Hassija V, Chamola V, and El Saddik A. 'A survey on decentralized metaverse using blockchain and web 3.0 technologies, applications, and more', *IEEE Access*, 2024, 12, pp. 146915–146948.

[7] Wang Y, Su Z, Zhang N, *et al.* 'A survey on metaverse: fundamentals, security, and privacy', *IEEE Communications Surveys & Tutorials*, 2022, 25, (1), pp. 319–352.

[8] Shin C, Oh S, and Jeong H. 'Extended reality platform for metaverse exhibition', *Journal of Web Engineering*, 2023, 22, (7), pp. 1055–1073.

[9] LaViola JJ Jr. 'A discussion of cybersickness in virtual environments', *ACM SIGCHI Bulletin*, 2000, 32, (1), pp. 47–56.

[10] Karunarathna S, Wijethilaka S, Ranaweera P, Hemachandra KT, Samarasinghe T, and Liyanage M. 'The role of network slicing and edge computing in the metaverse realization', *IEEE Access*, 2023, 11, pp. 25502–25530.

[11] Aung N, Dhelim S, Chen L, Ning H, Atzori L, and Kechadi T. 'Edge-enabled metaverse: the convergence of metaverse and mobile edge computing', *Tsinghua Science and Technology*, 2023, 29, (3), pp. 795–805.

[12] Ning Z, Huang J, and Wang X. 'Vehicular fog computing: enabling real-time traffic management for smart cities', *IEEE Wireless Communications*, 2019, 26, (1), pp. 87–94.

[13] You D, Doan TV, Torre R, *et al.* 'Fog computing as an enabler for immersive media: service scenarios and research opportunities', *IEEE Access*, 2019, 7, pp. 65797–65810.

[14] Yaqoob I, Salah K, Jayaraman R, and Omar M. 'Metaverse applications in smart cities: enabling technologies, opportunities, challenges, and future directions', *Internet of Things*, 2023, 23, p. 100884.

[15] Ruiu P, Nitti M, Pilloni V, Cadoni M, Grosso E, and Fadda M. 'Metaverse and human digital twin: digital identity, biometrics, and privacy in the future virtual worlds', *Multimodal Technologies and Interaction*, 2024, 8, (6), p. 48.

[16] Mourtzis D, Angelopoulos J, and Panopoulos N. 'Blockchain integration in the era of industrial metaverse', *Applied Sciences*, 2023, 13, (3), p. 1353.

[17] Sawhney M, and Goodman P. 'Nike: tiptoeing into the metaverse', *Kellogg School of Management Cases*, 2022, 1, (1), pp. 1–21.

[18] de Almeida GGF. 'Cities and territorial brand in the metaverse: the metaverse SEOUL case', *Sustainability*, 2023, 15, (13), p. 10116.

[19] Lyu Z. 'State-of-the-art human–computer interaction in metaverse', *International Journal of Human–Computer Interaction*, 2024, 40, (21), pp. 6690–6708.

[20] Wang D, and Huang X. 'Transforming education through artificial intelligence and immersive technologies: enhancing learning experiences', *Interactive Learning Environments*, 2025, 33, (7), pp. 4546–4565.

[21] Alahmed Y, Osman A, Ahmed AH, Omar D, Alahmhad Y, Sharo AA. 'The future of virtual conversations: ChatGPT and the metaverse'. In: *International Conferences on Engineering and Applied Sciences Optimization*, 15–17 October 2024, Kos, Greece. Cham: Springer Nature Switzerland, 2024, pp. 1–13.

[22] Adil M, Abulkasim H, Ali A, Song H, Farouk A, and Jin Z. 'Role of 5G and 6G technologies in metaverse, quality of service challenges, and future research directions', *IEEE Network*, 2024, 39, (4), pp. 211–219.

[23] Yadav RK. 'Fundamentals of human–computer interaction', *Human Factors Engineering*, 2024, 24, pp. 1–15.

[24] Hyun W. 'Study on standardization for interoperable metaverse'. In: *25th International Conference on Advanced Communication Technology (ICACT)*, 19–22 February 2023, PyeongChang, Korea. IEEE, 2023, pp. 319–322.

[25] Dwivedi Y, Hughes L, Kar A, *et al.* 'Metaverse beyond the hype: multidisciplinary perspectives', *International Journal of Information Management*, 2022, 66, pp. 1–14.

[26] Kasture S, Maurya S, Verma R, Pathak N, Joshi P, and Rakesh N. 'Green cloud computing for the metaverse: powering the future of the internet with renewable energy'. In: *11th International Conference on Reliability, Infocom Technologies and Optimization (Trends and Future Directions) (ICRITO)*, 13–15 March 2024, Noida, India. IEEE, 2024, pp. 1–6.

[27] Othman A, Chemnad K, Hassanien AE, *et al.* 'Accessible metaverse: a theoretical framework for accessibility and inclusion in the metaverse', *Multimodal Technologies and Interaction*, 2024, 8, (3), p. 21.

[28] Kakade K, Chitranshi J, Lenka R, and Vispute SA. 'Ethical and social implications of augmented reality: addressing privacy, surveillance, and

sustainability challenges in the metaverse era'. In: *Augmented reality and sustainability*. Boca Raton, FL: Auerbach Publications, 2025, pp. 47–69.

[29] Verma R, Chandrawanshi K, Soni G, Jain G, Nigam S, and Jain N. 'Unveiling security vulnerabilities in NFTs: a comprehensive risk assessment'. In: *IEEE 4th International Conference on ICT in Business Industry & Government (ICTBIG)*, December 2024. IEEE, 2024, pp. 1–6.

[30] Febrer-Coll E. 'Immersive environments in video games as a new stage for popular music performance'. In: *Music, sound and identity in video games*. Cham: Springer Nature Switzerland, 2025, pp. 115–136.

[31] Sattar MU, Palaniappan S, Lokman A, Hassan A, Shah N, and Riaz Z. 'Effects of virtual reality training on medical students' learning motivation and competency', *Pakistan Journal of Medical Sciences*, 2019, 35, (3), p. 852.

[32] Blancaflor E, Nitta K, Taylor J, Datu C, and Austria JK. 'Into the metaverse: a systematic review on taxonomy of threats and vulnerabilities in the Web 3 space – a Filipino context'. In: *5th International Conference on Computer Science, Engineering, and Education (CSEE)*, February 2024. IEEE Computer Society, 2024, pp. 51–56.

Chapter 6

Cybersecurity, privacy, and the hyper-connected future of Web X.0

Rawal Khan[1], Madiha Khalid[2], Nadia Sultan[3], Joddat Fatima[3] and Mohsin Kamal[2,4]

Abstract

Nowadays, web applications generate vast amounts of heterogeneous hypertext transfer protocol traffic, complicating intrusion detection as attackers adopt increasingly stealthy and rapidly evolving behaviors. Conventional intrusion detection systems (IDSs) often rely on fixed thresholds or a single type of machine learning model, limiting their ability to detect infrequent or anomalous attacks. This chapter introduces a hybrid IDS framework that combines supervised learning-based detection with autoencoders and a reinforcement learning (RL) agent for dynamic threshold adaptation. Supervised models effectively classify known web attacks, while deep autoencoders learn normal traffic patterns and flag anomalies via reconstruction error. These outputs are fused into a single maliciousness score, with a multi-armed bandit RL agent dynamically optimizing the decision threshold to maximize detection performance. Experiments on the CICIDS2017 dataset demonstrate significant improvements in F1-score, minority-attack detection, and false-positive reduction over single-model approaches, providing an adaptive and robust solution for modern web intrusion detection. Furthermore, this chapter broadens its perspective to address the emerging challenge of quantum-resilient security. We demonstrate the weaknesses of existing symmetric cipher standards through Grover search analysis, highlighting their vulnerability to quantum attacks. Building on these findings, we define key design principles for quantum-resistant lightweight symmetric ciphers, ensuring that web communication remains secure against quantum-enabled adversaries. By integrating quantum resilience into both detection and cryptography, the proposed approach delivers a future-proof defense for web applications.

[1]Department of Electrical Engineering, Bahria University, Pakistan
[2]Faculty of Computing, National University of Sciences and Technology, Pakistan
[3]Center of Excellence in AI, Bahria University, Pakistan
[4]School of Computing, University of Nebraska-Lincoln, USA

6.1 Introduction

6.1.1 Overview

Web X.0 is a structural change that goes beyond the social interaction and decentralisation paradigms. Artificial intelligence (AI) and quantum computing (QC) are the two key technologies that have changed the landscape of modern cybersecurity. The key characteristics of this new internet era comprise intelligent, autonomous behavior, semantic awareness, distributed edge intelligence, quantum-resilient security, and AI-native communication structures.

In recent years, it has been gradually harder to detect malicious behaviors using regular rule-based methods or any other kind of intrusion detection system (IDS) [1]. In modern web applications, a large number of users, dynamic content, and complex request patterns make IDS a crucial system for maintaining security. With cyberattacks against web services on the rise, such as Structured Query Language (SQL) injection, cross-site scripting, brute-force login attempts, and bot-driven reconnaissance, those defending networks have no choice but to implement detection systems that are not only correct but also adaptable in the face of changing attack tactics [2]. Traditional IDSs tend to rely on static thresholds or manually crafted patterns, which are less efficient against the never-before-seen and zero-day attacks [3].

IDS using AI have already demonstrated a strong ability to detect web attacks, as they learn from behaviors directly derived from traffic features [4]. Supervised learning approaches, such as Random Forest and XGBoost, have shown high accuracy on benchmark datasets, especially when trying to differentiate between clearly defined attacks [5,6]. Yet, these models may not generalize well to rare or unknown threats, particularly in imbalanced datasets where benign (normal) traffic prevails. This drawback is widely reported in the literature; for instance, it has been found that supervised systems overfit to the majority class, yielding poor performance when real-world anomalies are encountered [7,8].

An added challenge in digital systems is ensuring the Confidentiality, Integrity, and Availability (CIA) of communication over a heterogeneous network using quantum-resilient protocol suites. According to the guidelines issued by the National Institute of Standards and Technology (NIST), organizations are advised to transition to post-quantum cryptographic mechanisms by 2030 to safeguard digital infrastructure against potential QC attacks [9].

The literature shows systematic progress in the develoExperiments on the CICIDS2017 dataset show that the hybrid model can outperform the single model, which makes it a more real-world effective and robust solution for modern web intrusion detection.ly lightweight ciphers that ensure the CIA properties for resource-constrained devices at the sensing layer of Internet of Things (IoT) networks.

This chapter presents the following aspects related to the highlighted issues.

1. Hybrid machine learning (ML)–autoencoder (AE)–reinforcement learning (RL) intrusion detection model specialized to web traffic.
2. Design principles for quantum-resistant symmetric lightweight ciphers.

6.2 Technical foundation

This section is divided into two subsections that provide the technical background for the contributions discussed in the chapter introduction.

6.2.1 Hybrid IDS for Web X.0

This section presents the whole process for building the hybrid IDS. The model starts by cleaning and preprocessing the data, then training supervised classifiers along with a Normal-only Autoencoder. Their predictions are then integrated using fusion scoring, and a RL-based agent determines the final classification by adaptively selecting an optimal threshold. It provides accurate, robust and adaptive intrusion detection technology to implement this pipeline. The system architecture is provided in Figure 6.1.

6.2.1.1 Dataset description

The CICIDS2017 dataset, developed by the Canadian Institute for Cybersecurity, is used in this study. It records five days of polite, actual enterprise-grade traffic, such as web browsing, VoIP, e-mailing, video streaming and transferring files, and chat applications. Embedded malicious activities were injected concurrently generating flow records that are very similar to todays telecom-network traffic.

Each record is a bi-directional traffic flow generated by CICFlowMeter and includes over 80 numerical features, such as packet counts, byte totals, time of inter-arrival, header lengths, and protocol behavior flags. These flow-level characteristics are naturally consistent with the NetFlow/IP Flow Information Export (IPFIX) data used in Long-Term Evolution (LTE), 5G, and Internet Service Provider (ISP) networks to process.

Seven traffic categories were considered in this analysis:

- Normal traffic—normal traffic of their legitimate users
- Distributed Denial of Service (DDoS)—distributed high-volume floods
- Denial of Service (DoS)—single-source flooding
- Brute force—password-guessing of Secure Shell (SSH) or hypertext transfer protocol.
- Port scan—reconnaissance activity
- Web attacks—these include SQL injection, Cross-Site Scripting (XSS), and misusing file upload
- Botnet traffic—C2-based wicked flows

These are volumetric, reconnaissance, application-layer, and malware, including behaviors for telecom security.

An important feature of CICIDS2017 is the high-class imbalance, which includes a high predominance of normal traffic and few instances of other classes, such as Web Attacks and Bots. This corresponds to the actual telecom network, where anomalies account for a very low percentage of the entire traffic, and it motivates class-aware training and testing.

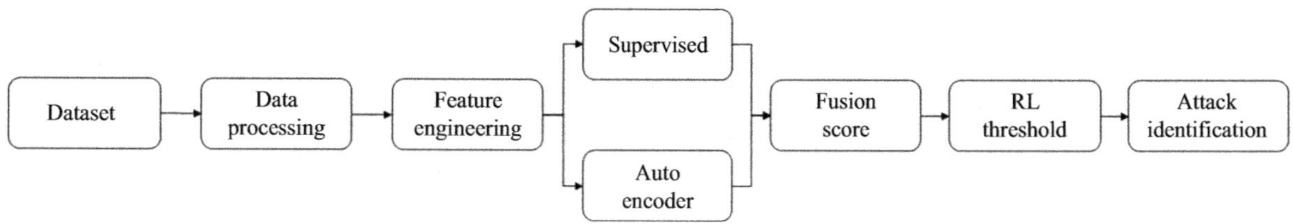

Figure 6.1 System architecture of the proposed hybrid IDS

6.2.1.2 Data preprocessing

The preprocessing step creates the groundwork-pipeline needed to convert the raw CICIDS2017 dataset into a clean, standardized form ready for ML in both supervised and unsupervised intrusion detection models. While CICIDS2017 is a widely used benchmark dataset, its raw CSV files are riddled with issues (e.g., inconsistent labels, missing values, infinite values, extreme outliers, and highly imbalanced attack types) that must be further processed to enable meaningful model training and evaluation. In this study, we designed structured preprocessing as a set of five key steps: label setup, basic numerical cleaning, class imbalance treatment, stratified dataset splitting, and normalization, along with retaining all preprocessed objects to support full reproducibility.

The first step, label encoding, was done by mapping all raw attack type names to seven unified categories (Normal, DDoS, DoS, Brute Force, Port Scan, Web Attack, and Bot). The original dataset consists of over 20 fine-grained attack labels, with many of these referring to subtypes of the same class. By grouping into seven classes, the classification task is simplified and chances for sparsity in less populated subclasses can be prevented. A clean multi-class target variable was created by labeling each aggregated class with an integer index. The mapping was stored in label_map.json to provide consistent options for training, evaluation, and inference.

Basic cleaning was further applied to all numerical features. Some features generated by CICFlowMeter e.g., Flow Bytes/s and Flow Packets/s are ratio based and often yield undefined values when flow duration is very short. Mathematically,

$$\text{Flow Bytes/s} = \frac{\text{Total Fwd Bytes} + \text{Total Bwd Bytes}}{\text{Flow Duration}} \tag{6.1}$$

$$\text{Flow Packets/s} = \frac{\text{Fwd Packets} + \text{Bwd Packets}}{\text{Flow Packets}} \tag{6.2}$$

When the denominator is zero or close to zero, the values turn into or. As they come from partial flow captures, and nowhere will provide a legitimate network traffic, such values were set to 0.0. This guarantees numerical stability in subsequent up-scaling and model learning.

After numerical cleansing, class imbalance was tackled. CICIDS2017 is highly imbalanced Normal Traffic class is the largest and Bots class as well as Web Attacks are very few. Class imbalance was addressed in the use of class weights derived from the training set rather than over-sampling or synthetic augmentation:

$$w_k = \frac{N}{K \cdot N_k} \tag{6.3}$$

where N is the total number of training samples, $K = 7$ is the number of classes and N_k the number of samples belonging to class K. This weighting scheme compels supervised models to give relatively more attention to minority attack classes, leading to fairness enhancement and prediction bias reduction. The resulting class weights: 0.17 for Normal traffic to >150 for rare attacks, were saved as class _weights.json for reusing with every supervised model.

We used stratified sampling to divide the dataset into training (70%), validation (15%), and test (15%) subsets. Stratified kept the class proportion same as input dataset, for all the splits:

$$P(y = k|Train) \approx P(y = k|Val) \approx P(y = k|Test) \tag{6.4}$$

This guarantees that every attack class including rare ones appears in each subset, enabling stable model training and meaningful evaluation.

Once the splits were prepared, all numerical features were normalized using RobustScaler, a transformation defined as:

$$X_{scaled} = \frac{X - Median(X)}{IQR(X)} \tag{6.5}$$

$$IQR(X) = Q_3 - Q_1 \tag{6.6}$$

Network traffic in a flow-based scenario is typically bursty, with large spikes, especially during DDoS and DoS attacks. We thus chose RobustScaler as it is more robust to outliers and leads to more stable learning dynamics than StandardScaler or MinMaxScaler. The built scaler was saved as the name scaler.pkl to make sure that each inference sample gets the same processing as the training data.

To make future execution of the work by others fully reproducible and ready for deployment, further artifacts among the preprocessing steps were saved: the label map, class weights, RobustScaler, and ordered feature list. It also enables the real-time detection system, API endpoints, and RL modules to apply the exact same preprocessing during inference, which avoids feature misalignment and makes results reproducible.

6.2.1.3 Feature engineering

Instead of crafting new hand-engineered features, it used the extensive numerical attributes that CICFlowMeter offered. The steps included:

- selecting only numeric columns,
- removing string-based or timestamp features,
- saving the right feature order in feature_list.json, and
- using a common RobustScaler scaling for all the models.

This maintains alignment between the supervised branch, the Autoencoder, and the deployment pipeline.

Models like XGBoost, RF, and CatBoost are tree-based models, and these naturally capture non-linear interactions. Also, Autoencoders will learn useful latent patterns without requiring more features to be created manually.

6.2.1.4 Model training setup

Three supervised models, i.e., XGBoost, Random Forest, and CatBoost, were trained to perform seven-class classification. All models used the class-weights

Table 6.1 Key hyperparameters used for training the supervised ML models

Model	Hyperparameters
Random Forest Classifier	600 trees, min split = 4, min leaf = 2, class_weight = balanced_subsample
XGBoost	1200 estimators, lr = 0.05, depth = 6
CatBoost	1200 iterations, lr = 0.05

computed earlier. The hyperparameter selection for each model is provided in Table 6.1.

After evaluation, Random Forest delivered the highest macro-F1 and was selected as the supervised branch. A separate Autoencoder was trained on the Normal Traffic with Mean Squared Error (MSE) loss and Adam optimizer. At inference time, the reconstruction error was used as an anomaly score. The validation set was used for model selection and RL training, while the test set was strictly held out for final reporting.

6.2.1.5 Hybrid intrusion detection system architecture

The presented hybrid IDS fuses supervised classification and unsupervised anomaly detection with a fusion mechanism to compute an overall reliable maliciousness score. This multi-branch architecture guarantees the effectiveness against both known classes with well-defined attacks, and unknown zero-day or rare attack types (attempted or exploited) to achieve high results that become very imperative for telecom environments where traffic patterns evolve throughout.

The first part of the hybrid approach learns explicit attack patterns based on labeled flow data. Three human-interpretable models, namely, XGBoost, Random Forest, and CatBoost, were trained using the seven aggregations of traffic classes: Normal, DDoS, DoS, Brute Force, Port Scan, Web Attack, and Botnet.

The accuracy, Macro F1-score, and the Confusion Matrices were tested against all the models. Especially out of the three, Random Forest Classifier (RFC) has been consistently better in terms of Macro F1-score and performed exceptionally well on minority attack classes. It was for this reason that RFC was chosen as the ultimate supervised module of the hybrid IDS. During inference, RFC yields a class-probability vector:

$$P_{sup} = [P_0, P_1, \cdots, P_6] \tag{6.7}$$

where P_0 is the Normal Traffic probability. A weak flux is suspected by the supervised branch when P_0 has small value.

The Autoencoder (AE) yields the capability of detecting unknown, zero-day, and underrepresented attacks. It is only trained on Normal Traffic, allowing it to form the statistical model of benign network flows. Test time, each of these flows is reconstructed, and the reconstruction error is utilized as a measure of the presence of anomalies:

$$E = \|X - \overline{X}\|_2^2 \tag{6.8}$$

Small error corresponds to normal-like flow, whereas a large error informs about the anomalous flow. As the AE does not depend on the attack labels, it naturally has the capability of recognizing new or changing attacks, which is an essential part of the hybrid model.

To combine the merits of two branches, it calculates a Fusion Score which integrates direct predictions from the supervised pathway and autoencoder reconstruction error. This gives a single aggregate maliciousness score:

$$S_{fusion} = \alpha \cdot (1 - P_{sup,(normal)}) + (1 - \alpha) \cdot \bar{E} \tag{6.9}$$

where $P_{sup,(normal)} = p_0$ is the probability that the supervised model predicts Normal, $\bar{E}$ is the normalized AE reconstruction error, $\alpha \in [0, 1]$ controls the balance between the two signals. α is chosen as 0.7 after validation.

The fusion mechanism is effective because the supervised model is strong against the known attacks, AE is strong for unknown abnormalities, and fusion is strong for both and weak for no noise, thus lowering fake alarms outgoings and enhancing the detection of rare attacks. The fusion score is the output of final model indicating how malicious the flow is. This score is then utilized to determine the best detection threshold by a RL agent.

6.2.1.6 RL-based threshold optimization

Although the fusion score is more robust to measure maliciousness, a constant static threshold does not generally perform very well in the real telecom context, where traffic patterns change over time. To solve this, the system includes a lightweight RL bandit agent to adaptively change the decision threshold to achieve optimal detection performance. A flow is classified as,

$$\text{Prediction} = \begin{cases} \text{Attack}, & S_{fusion} \geq \tau \\ \text{Normal}, & S_{fusion} < \tau \end{cases} \tag{6.10}$$

The RL agent tests out several candidate thresholds and is then awarded based on F1-score, accuracy, or a weighted scoring with high weightage given to low false positives:

$$r_t = f(TP, FP, FN) \tag{6.11}$$

The Q-value of each threshold is updated through a bandit learning rule such as ε-greedy,

$$Q(\tau) \leftarrow Q(\tau) + \eta(r_t - Q(\tau)) \tag{6.12}$$

Eventually, the agent learns how to choose a threshold that allows it to perform at its best in current traffic conditions. This makes the IDS adaptive, self-tuning, and robust since the system will be able to automatically adjust itself towards new behaviors of attack patterns as well as changes in network load.

6.2.2 Symmetric cipher cryptanalysis in post-quantum era

QC is a paradigm that offers unmatched computational efficiency. The smallest unit of information in QC is a *qubit*, which can represent both 0 and 1 values simultaneously by virtue of superposition. This property of quantum mechanics allows quantum computers to process information exponentially faster than classical systems.

From the perspective of symmetric cryptography, a cipher is traditionally considered secure because it is computationally infeasible to brute-force the algorithm using classical computers, given a Plain Text (PT)–Cipher Text (CT) pair. QC claims that Grover's search algorithm holds the capability to brute force any cipher with the key size N with the computational complexity of $O(\sqrt{2^N})$ as opposed to classical computational complexity $O(2^N)$.

In Grover's search algorithm, a phase oracle of the cipher is designed and attached to a diffuser operator. The principle of designing the phase oracle is to replace the classical operators with the counterpart quantum transformations. i.e, Bit-wise *Xor* function is replaced by the $C - Not$ gate in the quantum circuit [10].

The PT qubits are initialized as per the value of given PT whereas the key is initialized with *Hadamard* gate creating a superposition. By superposition, all possible key combinations are tested simultaneously against the given PT, and the results are checked against the given CT. The key combination that gives the correct CT is amplified using the diffuser operator. To obtain a well-defined peak, this process is repeated for at most $\lfloor\sqrt{2^N}\rfloor$. Figure 6.2 presents a generalized circuit diagram of Grover's search in the context of brute force analysis.

The logical solution to strengthen traditional symmetric ciphers is to increase the key size. A larger key size requires a larger quantum circuit, making the algorithm computationally infeasible within a given time. Unfortunately, this approach is not applicable to lightweight/ultralightweight ciphers that use minimalist primitives and smaller key sizes to minimize computational overhead on resource-constrained devices.

ISO 29167 is the standard for security protocols in the lightweight domain. In the protocol portfolio, *Xor* is a rudimentary cipher that uses a balanced binary function (*Xor*) for encryption [11]. To demonstrate the impact of QC on the lightweight cipher, this chapter demonstrates an implementation of Grover's search on the reduced key *Xor* cipher. The reduced key will be 4 bits, and the encryption mechanism will be $CT = PT \oplus Key$.

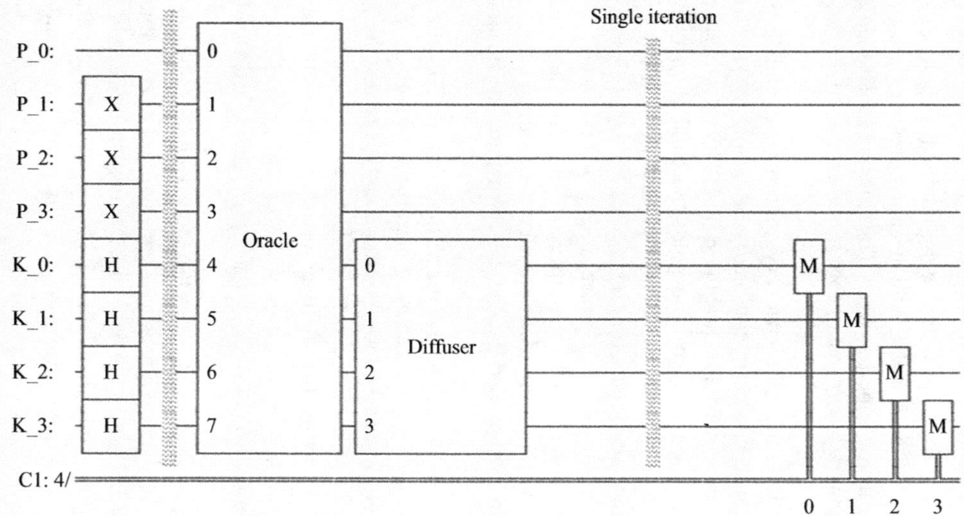

Figure 6.2 Generalized Grover search circuit for brute force attack

6.3 Application

6.3.1 IDS

In this subsection, we discuss the experimental results of the hybrid IDS system throughout supervised learning, anomaly detection, fusion scoring, and RL-based threshold optimization. Results are all reported based on the provided validation and test sets of the CICIDS2017 dataset. The purpose is to show what each part is doing and how the hybrid approach can push the performance, robustness, and flexibility compared with a single model.

6.3.1.1 Supervised model comparison

Three supervised learning algorithms (XGBoost, CatBoost, and Random Forest) were used for the multi-class intrusion detection model based on the CICIDS2017 data as provided in Table 6.2. All the layers achieved an extremely high accuracy, over 99.8% on the validation split. However, accuracy by itself does not present a fair picture of the performance in the face of class imbalance, so Macro-F1 was chosen as the main metric. Macro-F1 is the average F1-score over all classes and is well-suited for performance on models required to recognize rare attacks.

The comparison revealed that Random Forest had the highest Macro-F1 score (0.9717), which was significantly higher than XGBoost (0.9661) and CatBoost (0.9494). Although all models had about the same quality of their performance (≈0.998–0.999), Macro-F1 results state that Random Forest overall managed to handle minority attack categories better than the remaining two models did. It is one of the first supervised classifiers to have been well balanced and reliable.

According to these results, Random Forest was chosen as the best supervised model of the proposed hybrid IDS. Not only did this preserve great over-all accuracy, but it also created a balance of class-wise correctness that supports strong detection for all types of attacks included rare classes like Bots and Web Attacks. Confusion matrix and Receiver Operating Characteristic (ROC) curve of Random Forest model are provided in Figures 6.3 and 6.4, respectively, which underlines its strong classification ability: the misclassifications were small, and the detection was very high for all seven classes of traffic.

Table 6.2 Supervised learning models comparison

Model	Accuracy	Macro F1	Weighted F1	Macro P	Macro R	Macro AUC-OVR	Log Loss
RFC	0.999	0.971	0.999	0.965	0.978	0.999	0.006
XGBoost	0.998	0.966	0.999	0.945	0.995	0.999	0.005
CatBoost	0.998	0.949	0.998	0.918	0.998	0.999	0.007

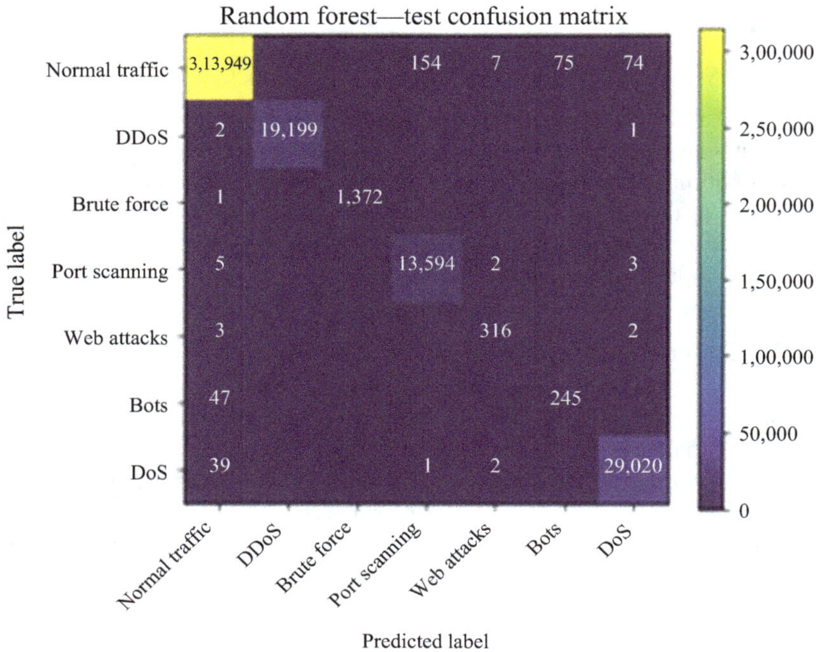

Figure 6.3 Confusion matrix of the Random Forest classifier on the CICIDS2017 test set, showing strong detection performance across all seven traffic categories with minimal misclassification

6.3.1.2 Performance evaluation of the hybrid system

A hybrid IDS was designed by integrating three main modules: the supervised Random Forest classifier, the Autoencoder-based Anomaly Detector and a RL threshold optimizer. These modules, when combined, form an end-to-end detection pipeline that can detect known types of attacks and unknown anomalies in telecom traffic. In this section, we illustrate the contributions of each component to overall system performance and verify that the combined hybrid framework greatly enhances detection performance over supervised learning.

The Autoencoder trained on Only Normal Traffic acquired highly consistent reconstructions for the benign flows and much higher reconstruction errors for the malicious samples. In validation, benign flows concentrated in a close compact area with very low errors, but attack samples spread across a wider space and were somewhat scattered, sometimes showed long-tailed error spikes as presented in Figure 6.5. This clear separation was an indication that the Autoencoder was learning to represent the statistical structure of benign telecom flows and detect significant deviations that are typically indicative of attacks. The AE was beneficial with minority attack classes like Bots, Web Attacks, and less common Port

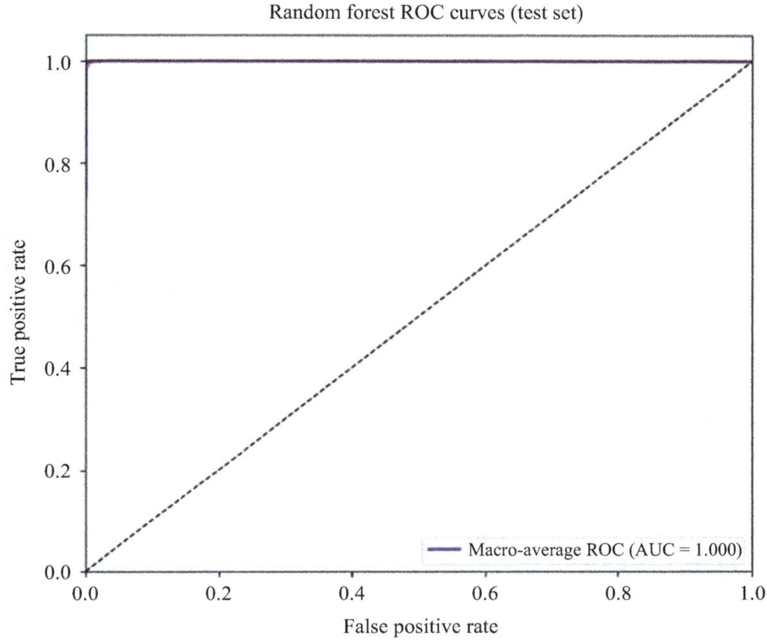

Figure 6.4 *ROC curve of the Random Forest classifier on the test set. The macro-average AUC of 1.000 shows excellent separability across all seven traffic classes, confirming the strong discriminative capability of the supervised model.*

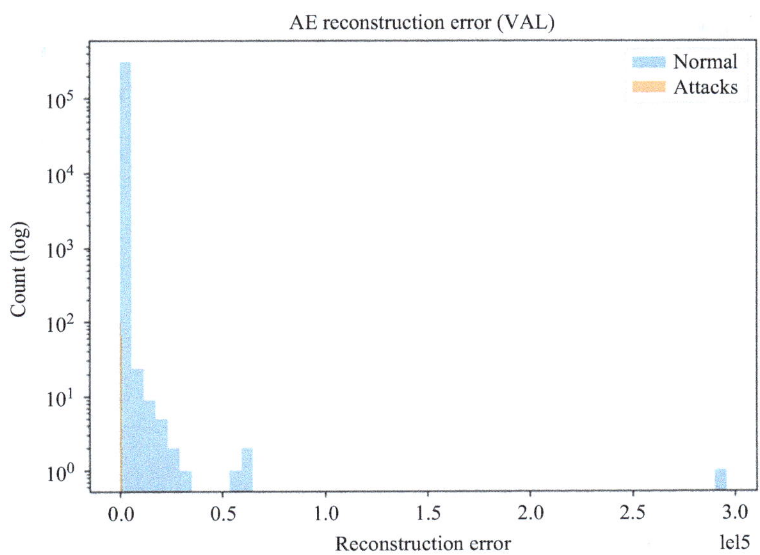

Figure 6.5 *Autoencoder reconstruction error distribution on the validation set*

Scanning, which are highly challenging for supervised models because of only a few training samples.

To allow the combination of these dual attributes of supervised and unsupervised branches, two outputs were aggregated into a continuous Fusion Score. The joint signal-enhanced detection of infrequent cyber-attacks by boosting their anomaly features in terms of the reconstruction error. Meanwhile, the fusion mechanism decreased false positives; when the supervised model generated ambiguous results, the Autoencoder added another layer of confidence. The obtained scoring function was followed, yielding a smoother, stable receiver operating characteristic curve with varying traffic, and performed better in terms of threshold-based decision making compared to the supervised classifier and Autoencoder. In general, the Fusion Score was a better indicator of maliciousness.

The fusion score is very informative, however depends crucially on the choice of threshold τ. Instead of using a fixed threshold, which can be broken by varying patterns in traffic, the mechanism utilized an amortized reinforcement-learning bandit ε-greedy to find optimal bounds. Over long hundreds of iterations, the RL agent was able to probe candidate thresholds and receive rewards for classification that allowed it to advance towards such a high-performing value. This procedure converged around $\tau \approx 0.9$, which maximized macro-F1 while ensuring false alarms were kept very low, as shown in Figure 6.6. The RL-guided adaptation ensured that the threshold performed well even when the distribution of fusion scores changed

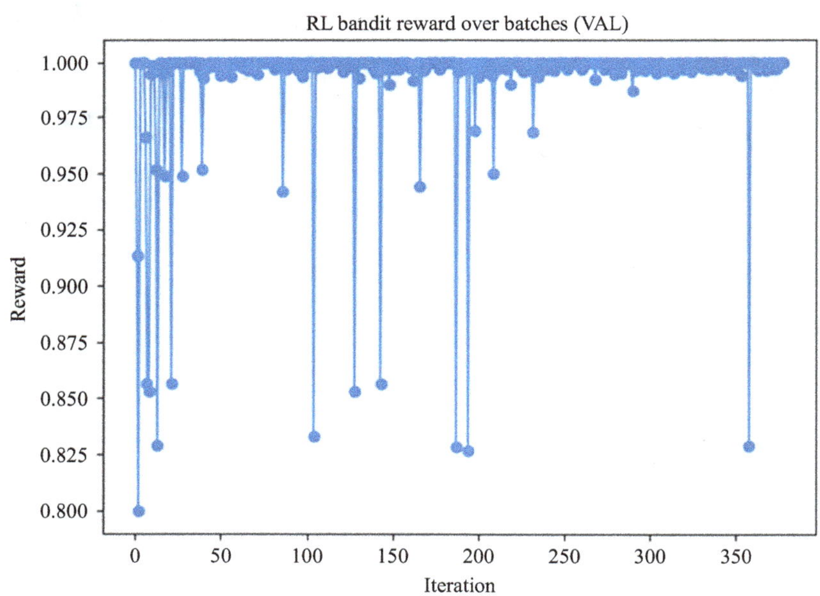

Figure 6.6 RL bandit reward progression across validation batches

Table 6.3 Performance comparison between the baseline Random Forest classifier and the proposed hybrid system (Fusion + RL)

	Setting	Accuracy	Macro F1	Weighted F1	Macro P	Macro R
0	Base Best Model	0.9988	0.9666	0.9989	0.9596	0.9742
1	Fusion + RL	0.9995	0.9968	0.9995	0.9971	0.9966

underneath, thus making for a more robust system in the face of real-world telecom variability.

A last comparison was done between the best supervised model only (Random Forest) and the full hybrid detection system containing Fusion + RL and the summary is presented in Table 6.3. The improvement was substantial. The macro-F1 score increased from 0.966 to 0.996, which shows that the classes are more balanced. Macro-Precision increased from 0.959 to 0.997, which means a drastic reduction in false positives. Macro-Recall increased from 0.974 to 0.996 (fewer missed attacks). The hybrid system also further resulted in a remarkably low rejection rate of approximately 1.38%, such that only a small portion of flows set for safety were rejected. These findings establish that the hybrid method provides better accuracy and robustness against noise, as well as providing adaptability beyond that of even a highly accurate supervised classifier.

6.3.2 Application of Grover's search-based brute force attack on Xor cipher

The ISO 29167 *Xor* cipher is a minimalist protocol that uses bitwise balanced operations for encryption/decryption. To describe the effect of QC in the domain of brute force analysis of symmetric ciphers, this section demonstrates the quantum-enabled brute force attack on the 4-bit *Xor* cipher.

Although at the scale of a 4-bit key, the computational efficiency of conventional computers is stable, the purpose of this demonstration is to study the process of quantum attacks and discuss the key design factors of symmetric ciphers that can make the symmetric protocol robust to quantum attacks.

Given the (PT,CT) pair, the step-by-step description of Grover's search-based brute force attack on the *Xor* cipher is as follows:

1. Design the phase oracle for the cipher. For the cipher under analysis, bit-wise *Xor* is implemented using the corresponding *C-Not* gates. Furthermore, the results for the bit-wise *Xor* operator were compared with the given CT using a multi-qubit control gate. Since the phase oracle only impacts the output, the input transformations are reversed.
2. Followed by the phase oracle, the standard diffuser operator is applied to all the qubits representing the key.

3. This set is repeated for three iterations to receive the solid peak of the most probable key value.

Figure 6.7 represents the quantum circuit for the *Xor* primitive. For the example under analysis, the $PT = 1110$ and $CT = 1001$. Therefore, Figure 6.8 shows that the calculated key is 0111, i.e., $CT \oplus PT$.

All the simulations have been performed using the IBM Qiskit library and Jupyter Notebook. The analysis shows that, instead of testing $2^4 = 16$ combinations in classical search mechanisms, the results can be obtained in three iterations on a quantum computer.

6.4 Discussion

This section is again bifurcated into two subsections based on the contributions presented.

6.4.1 Discussion on intrusion detection system

As per the experimental results, although supervised Random Forest classifier is well suited for CICIDS2017 data, it is not enough to depend on supervised learning in real-world telecom environments. The Random Forest model built solid decision boundaries for all seven attack types, but its performance is inherently limited by the availability of labeled data. Minority classes such as Bots or Web Attacks are still challenging as the small number of training data that the model can be trained on and suffer from imbalances, which represent common weaknesses in supervised IDS models.

This problem was solved by Autoencoder component which modelled typical Normal Traffic to identify deviating patterns using reconstruction error. Its error estimate well-discriminated benign from malicious flows and thus was especially powerful in rare or unseen attacks. This makes the hybrid method more robust to zero-day features and changing threats, challenges also encountered in telecom networks. We also combined supervised probability and Autoencoder error, this further improved the system. Pooling the two signals to create an overall maliciousness score decreased false positives and enhanced minority class detection as well. This was particularly useful when the supervised model presented uncertainty, but we could see clear deviations from normal with the Autoencoder.

Finally, the RL threshold optimizer made it to automatically adapt to variations in traffic. Instead of using a fixed threshold, the RL agent gradually found out the optimal decision boundary to maximize macro-F1 and reduce false alarms. This flexibility is important in telecom environments where traffic profiles are dynamic. This hybrid system, Supervised + Autoencoder + Fusion + RL—offers better trade off between robustness and generalization with higher adaptability for intrusion detection than any single method.

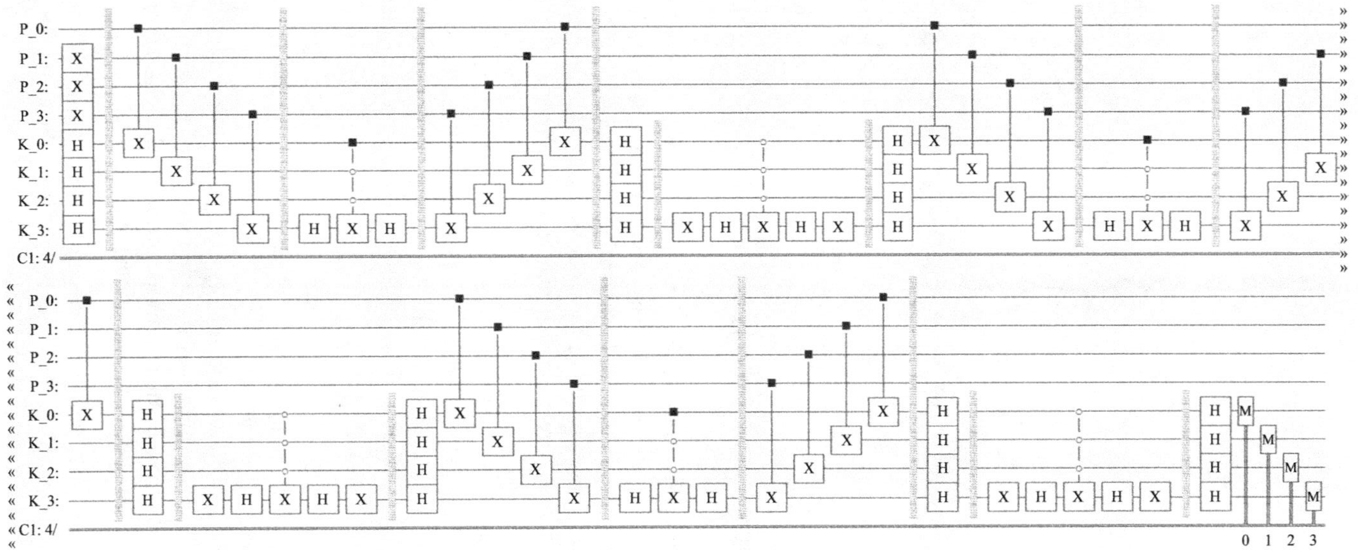

Figure 6.7 Quantum circuit for Grover's search based brute force attack on Xor cipher

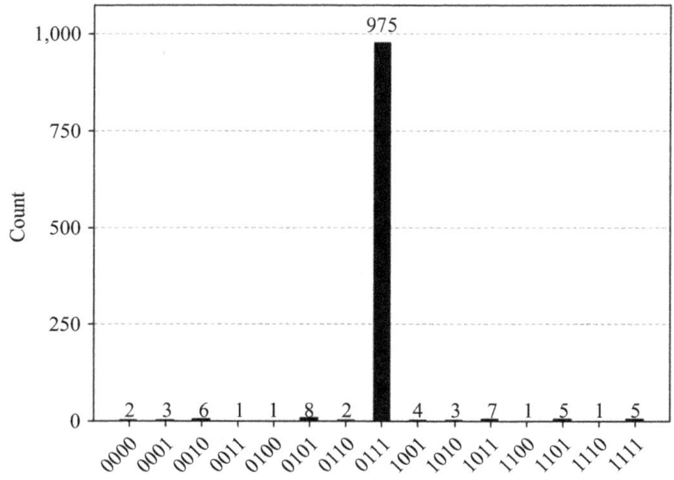

Figure 6.8 Measurement results for Grover's search based brute force attack on Xor cipher

6.4.2 Discussion on quantum cryptanalysis of lightweight symmetric ciphers

Minimalist ciphers are designed to ensure confidentiality with a low computational footprint. This corresponds to simple bitwise primitives and smaller key sizes for encryption/decryption. The ISO 29167 standard gives a portfolio of minimalist ciphers, i.e., Xor, Simon, and Speck, for the assurance of CIA over radio channels. These ciphers are used to secure a channel that carries information with a limited shelf life.

In the quantum era, these ciphers can be broken with reduced computational and time complexity. As demonstrated in the preceding section, the *Xor* cipher can be brute-forced with a time complexity that is exponentially lower. Keeping the attack execution as a reference, the following are the design principles for a quantum resilient symmetric cipher.

1. Increase in key size effectively increases the number of qubits required to design the circuit. According to NIST standards, the minimum key size for quantum resilience is 128 bits.
2. Use of lightweight shuffle-based operators instead of bitwise binary operators. This choice of primitives improves the confusion and diffusion of the cipher and increases the number of quantum operators for the phase oracle design. Therefore, making the attacks computationally infeasible.

The above-mentioned design principles can be used to improve the structure of a symmetric cipher and, in turn, enhance its robustness in the post-quantum era.

6.5 Conclusion

This chapter introduced two aspects of cybersecurity and privacy in Web X.0. The first is a hybrid IDS pipeline that combines supervised learning, Autoencoder-based anomaly detection, and RL-driven threshold optimization to address known as well as unknown attacks in telecom networks. For the CICIDS2017 flow dataset, Random Forest stands out as the most effective supervised model with high accuracy and macro-F1 for every attack category. When using supervised learning by itself, the minority and unknown attack problem could be difficult to solve alone. This was solved by introducing the Normal-only Autoencoder, which provided a strong anomaly signal for rare and unseen threats. The fusion mechanism was based on the combination of supervised probabilities and reconstruction-error scores, which generated a more resilient maliciousness result. The light RL threshold optimizer additionally gave the system extra traction to adapt the decision boundaries based on different traffic load scenarios. All these modules achieved better minority-class detection, lower false alarms, and more robust results compared to a single ML model. The second aspect is a discussion on the impact of quantum computers on lightweight symmetric ciphers. The discussion is especially focused on the lightweight ciphers as these are the security backbone of the IoT sensing layer. The analysis shows that traditional ciphers can be easily brute forced with reduced time complexity. Therefore, there is a need to standardize ultralightweight quantum resilient ciphers for post-quantum era.

Suggested further readings

- Sowmya, Ta, and EA Mary Anita. "A comprehensive review of AI based intrusion detection system." *Measurement: Sensors* 28 (2023): 100827.
- Muneer, Salman, *et al.* "A critical review of artificial intelligence based approaches in intrusion detection: A comprehensive analysis." *Journal of Engineering* 2024.1 (2024): 3909173.
- Talman, Aleksi. *Exploring Grover's Algorithm in brute force attacks*. MS thesis. A. Talman, 2025.
- Shahzadi, Maham, *et al.* "Quantum cryptanalysis of ultralightweight mutual authentication protocols: A Grover's search model." *PLoS One* 21.4 (2026): e0347296.

Standards

- FIPS 203 ("https://csrc.nist.gov/pubs/fips/203/final" FIPS 203, Module-Lattice-Based Key-Encapsulation Mechanism Standard | CSRC)
- FIPS 204 ("https://csrc.nist.gov/pubs/fips/204/final" FIPS 204, Module-Lattice-Based Digital Signature Standard | CSRC)
- FIPS 205 ("https://csrc.nist.gov/pubs/fips/205/final" FIPS 205, Stateless Hash-Based Digital Signature Standard | CSRC)

References

[1] Ayo FE, Awotunde JB, Ogundele LA, *et al.* Ontology-based layered rule-based network intrusion detection system for cybercrimes detection. *Knowledge and Information Systems*. 2024;66(6):3355–3392.

[2] Mallick MAI and Nath R. Navigating the cyber security landscape: A comprehensive review of cyber-attacks, emerging trends, and recent developments. *World Scientific News*. 2024;190(1):1–69.

[3] Dasgupta D, Akhtar Z, and Sen S. Machine learning in cybersecurity: A comprehensive survey. *The Journal of Defense Modeling and Simulation*. 2022;19(1):57–106.

[4] Sudyana D, Lin YD, Verkerken M, *et al.* Improving generalization of ML-based IDS with lifecycle-based dataset, auto-learning features, and deep learning. *IEEE Transactions on Machine Learning in Communications and Networking*. 2024;2:645–662.

[5] Imani M, Beikmohammadi A, and Arabnia HR. Comprehensive analysis of random forest and XGBoost performance with SMOTE, ADASYN, and GNUS under varying imbalance levels. *Technologies*. 2025;13(3):88.

[6] Khan MM, Kamal M, Shabbir M, and Alahmari S. Enhancing autonomous vehicle security: Federated learning for detecting GPS spoofing attack. *Transactions on Emerging Telecommunications Technologies*. 2025;36(4): e70138.

[7] Kheddar H, Dawoud DW, Awad AI, Himeur Y, and Khan MK. Reinforcement-learning-based intrusion detection in communication networks: A review. *IEEE Communications Surveys & Tutorials*. 2024;27: 2420–2469.

[8] Shabbir M, Kamal M, Ullah Z, and Khan MM. Securing autonomous vehicles against GPS spoofing attacks: A deep learning approach. *IEEE Access*. 2023;11:105513–105526.

[9] National Institute of Standards and Technology (NIST). *Post-Quantum Cryptography Project*; 2017. https://csrc.nist.gov/Projects/post-quantum-cryptography. Accessed: 2026-03-11.

[10] Jaques S, Naehrig M, Roetteler M, and Virdia F. Implementing Grover oracles for quantum key search on AES and LowMC. In: *Annual International Conference on the Theory and Applications of Cryptographic Techniques*. Cham: Springer; 2020. pp. 280–310.

[11] International Organization for Standardization (ISO). ISO/IEC TS 29167-15:2017 *Information Technology—Automatic Identification and Data Capture Techniques—Part 15: Crypto Suite XOR Security Services for Air Interface Communications*; 2017. https://www.iso.org/standard/70971.html. Accessed: 2026-03-11.

Chapter 7

Real-world use cases and case studies in Web X.0

Adeel Anjum[1], Muazzam Ali Khan Khattak[2] and Jawad Ali[1]

Abstract

The chapter discovers the Web X.0 technologies' real-world use cases and case studies, aiming at their architectural advancement, enabling technologies, and domain-specific applications. It significantly investigates the integration of multiple technologies such as Artificial Intelligence, Blockchain, Semantic Web, Internet of Things, and decentralized infrastructures, within modern Web ecosystems. The chapter estimates performance characteristics, scalability aspects, and security implications from the selected industrial and research case studies. Similarly, a comparative analysis with recent literature highlights the practical advancements and limitations of current implementations.

The findings of the chapter validate that Web X.0 systems gradually highlight decentralization, intelligent automation, and user-centric control, as facing persistent challenges related to interoperability, standardization, and governance. The conclusion of the chapter is to identify emerging research directions aimed at increasing cross-platform, scalability, trust management, and integration in next-generation web architectures.

7.1 Introduction

The development of the World Wide Web (WWW) has been described through a couple of amazing renovations, that is, from Web 1.0 to Web 5.0, static and read-only pages and intelligent, decentralized, and emotionally responsive systems, respectively.

Web X.0 accelerates the development of the WWW up to the next level, bringing the new era of technology by introducing interoperability, decentralization, semantic intelligence, and agentive artificial intelligence (AI). It predicts an

[1]Institute of Information Technology, Quaid-i-Azam University Islamabad, Islamabad 45320, Pakistan
[2]Department of Computer Sciences, Quaid-i-Azam University Islamabad, Islamabad 45320, Pakistan

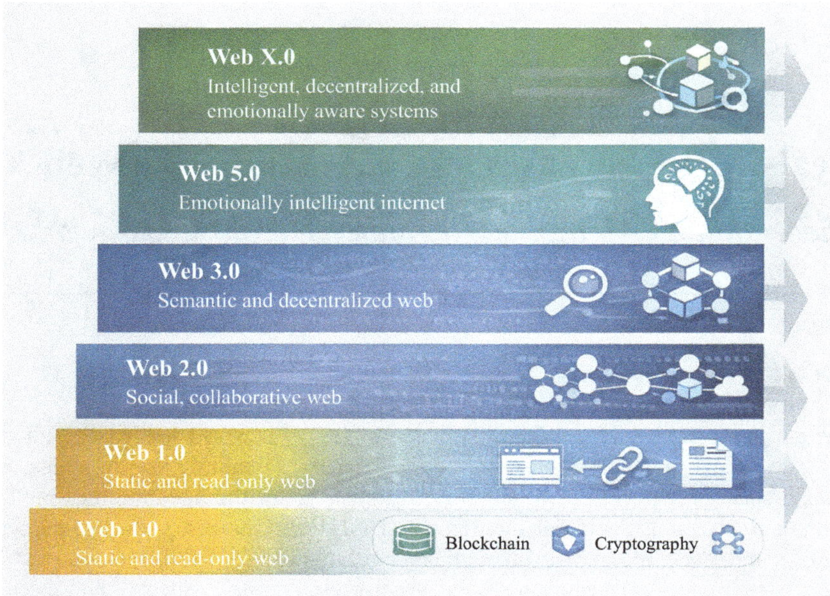

Figure 7.1 Architectural evolution of web technologies from Web 1.0 to Web X.0

integrated and human-centered digital system in which the communication among the data, systems, and intelligent agents is carried out in a secure, independent, and meaningful environment. Therefore, Figure 7.1 depicts the architectural evolution of web technologies from Web 1.0 to Web 1.0, which is a comprehensive picture of the entire web development journey.

In the Web X.0 model, the property of interoperability supports seamless communication between different devices and platforms, confirming that the data communication flow is easy and consistent without any limitations digital platforms. Similarly, the property of decentralization, fueled by blockchain and other distributed technologies, increases data control, trust, and transparency, allowing users to control their digital existence. Web X.0 utilizes the Semantic Web features to insert meaning within data itself; that is, machines are able to interpret and reason with the information instead of only retrieving it.

The Web X.0 property, agentive AI makes the systems possible to act intelligently on behalf of users, keeping the ethical and contextual awareness through the self-sufficiency and thinking skills added to digital systems by Agentive AI. Basically, Web X.0 signifies the merging of semantic interpretation, segregated trust, and AI-driven organization—an environment that provides the foundations for a secure, intelligent digital future.

The chapter describes the concepts of Web X.0 through a couple of use cases and case studies taken from real-world examples in different industries. Exploring the applications in healthcare, finance, education, governance, and other developing smart environments, with the objective to reveal both the adoption and challenges in the implementation of Web X.0 in the industries. The chapter also investigates the technological facilitators, ethical concerns, and global initiatives influencing this new era of digital models.

7.2 Industrial use cases of Web X.0

The technologies of Web X.0 brought a new face among multiple industries, introducing a new version of automation, decentralization, and intelligence, and their applications allowing a smarter and more autonomous digital system instead of traditional operational models.

The following four subsections discover important sectors, which are healthcare, finance, education, and governance, in which the influence of Web X.0 has already produced considerable and meaningful results.

7.2.1 Healthcare and smart hospitals

Healthcare is one of the most suitable sectors where Web X.0 can be applicable with the maximum potential, because the properties like decentralized data management, intelligent automation, semantic interoperability, and agentive AI are combined to establish secure, connected, and patient-oriented health systems. Consequently, traditional healthcare systems are broken and passive mode, and therefore, steadily being replaced by smart hospitals, which have the edge of using real-time analytics and connected technologies for personalized care, preventive measures for patients, and prediction as well.

7.2.1.1 Semantic interoperability and data exchange

Web X.0 attempts to solve the problem of healthcare data inconsistency among the hospitals, laboratories, and national systems through semantic web technologies such as RDF (Resource Description Framework) and FHIR (Fast Healthcare Interoperability Resources), which assist machine-readable data exchange between institutions [1]. Similarly, supporting smart hospital management through Web X.0, a semantic interoperability feature is utilized to achieve ultimate accuracy and medical decisions, particularly in patient diagnosis golden hour through clinical records, diagnostic images, and sensor-generated health data can be meaningfully shared, integrated, and analyzed.

7.2.1.2 Decentralization and data sovereignty

Web X.0 healthcare model guarantees the safety, security, and transparency in accessibility and sharing of patient data. Through decentralization patients are allowed to keep full ownership of their medical histories, that is, allowing or canceling of permissions for use the information as needed. This model provides the opportunity to enhance data sovereignty and trust, while the risk of data manipulation or unauthorized access to the data is minimized [2,15]. And smart contracts extend the automation of data-sharing agreements and consent mechanisms between hospitals, insurance companies, and research organizations.

7.2.1.3 Agentive AI and predictive care

Today's modern healthcare operations are almost based on agentive AI. Agentive AI, intelligent agents' constantly monitoring multimodal data streams from hospital sensors, Internet of Things (IoT)-enabled devices, and databases of patients, to inform health issues of patients before they get worsen. Consequently, AI systems are working as a standalone system, and can inform paramedical staff, recommend dosage adjustments, or activate emergency interventions [3]. This modification to the smart hospitals spots a huge transition from reactive treatment to proactive and preventive healthcare.

7.2.1.4 Web X.0-enabled smart hospital ecosystem

Smart hospitals are the real example of Web X.0 in the healthcare system. By utilizing real-time monitoring, robotic-assisted surgeries, and context-aware resource management facilities through Web X.0 services like IoT devices, AI-driven analytics, and edge computing. These systems dynamically monitor and regulate temperature, enhance patients' data flows, and guarantee safe communication among hospital medical devices and database systems, thus providing a holistic and intelligent care environment for the patient [16].

Case study: Mayo Clinic's AI and blockchain-integrated smart health network in the USA

Mayo Clinic provides a demonstration for the implementation of Web X.0 healthcare system because the clinic is utilizing an intelligent data network that increases the capabilities of predictive diagnostics for patients with health problems related to cardiology and oncology, by integrating AI, IoT, and blockchain technologies in their systems. Similarly, semantic data integration, AI systems perform data analytics on patient data across multiple hospitals to detect early symptoms of any disease complications. Blockchain technology ensures the safety of electronic health records (EHRs) communication among partner institutions as per according to the Health Insurance Portability and Accountability Act (HIPAA) and General Data Protection Regulation (GDPR) regulations.

Mayo Clinic uses the service of agentive AI models provided by both BM Watson Health and Epic Systems, which are alone capable of detecting potential risks and advising evidence-based treatments. This is actually the real spirit of Web X.0 technology, and results in an intelligent, decentralized interoperable system which provides secure, personalized, and continuous healthcare.

Conclusion: Web X.0 is introducing a new face to the healthcare system through the innovation of a smart, semantic, and independent digital system in which patients and intelligent agents jointly manage patients' well-being. By utilizing decentralized data infrastructures along with semantic interoperability and AI-driven decision making, smart hospitals prove the importance of technology for support flexibility, transparency, and inclusivity in worldwide healthcare [17].

7.2.2 Finance and decentralized economies

Web X.0 brought a great change in the financial sector, in term of working with controlling the data flows in an autonomous, transparent, and user-centric digital system manner instead of centralized control.

This introduced innovations to the finance sector such as Decentralized Finance (DeFi), Central Bank Digital Currencies (CBDCs), and tokenized assets, which revise the existing finance-related terms, procedures, and other necessary rules and regulations, which is how value is secured, governed, and exchanged. Similarly, the cost is reduced, and trust of stakeholders is increased due to the blockchain-enabled smart contracts, through which financial operations are executed automatically and unchangeably [2,4].

The best examples of this technology transformation are the use of Uniswap and Aave platforms, which are providing full control of digital wealth to their users, by authorizing peer-to-peer lending, liquidity management, and asset trading. And also, Decentralized Autonomous Organizations (DAOs) are another example that allow community members to make collective decisions without central intermediaries [5].

Concurrently, several governments, like China's *Digital Yuan* and the European Central Bank's *Digital Euro,* are trying to use Central Bank Digital Currencies (CBDC) initiatives with blockchain transparency with regulatory supervision. Consequently, these advancements in Web X.0 technology promote financial inclusion, particularly in developing countries, by offering secure digital identities and enabling micro-transaction models [6,18].

Fundamentally, Web X.0 redefined the financial sector terminology, that is, trust and governance, to increase the digital economy in a secure, interoperable, and inclusive environment.

7.2.3 Education and immersive learning

Web X.0 technologies play a vital role in the education sector's digital transformation. Due to the use of artificial intelligence (AI), extended reality (XR), and blockchain, learning in the education system is now becoming more adaptive, immersive, and equitable [7]. AI-based tutoring platforms now explore learning behaviors to individualize content, evaluations, and feedback [8]. In the meantime, metaverse-based classrooms use virtual reality (VR) and augmented reality (AR) to mimic real-world experiences, and this result in acknowledging students to engage with complex concepts in hands-on, interactive environments [9].

Blockchain added features such as tamper-proof digital credentials and supporting open, decentralized access to worldwide learning materials, to increase the integrity of the education sector [10]. Simultaneously, all these improvements in technology are associated with Web X.0's human-centric vision, which is one that values accessibility, collaboration, and lifelong learning.

Case study: the EduVerse initiative

The *EduVerse Initiative* is a worldwide group-led project that combines AI, blockchain, and metaverse technology to launch a virtual university system with the capability of decentralization of the education mode. On its digital campus, students join lectures, cooperate on 3D projects, and AI-generated feedback is provided to every student. Blockchain ledger records every academic qualification and learning objective, which guarantees verification and portability. Similarly, semantic tagging of learning content aids adaptive searches and custom-made course recommendations.

Through the EduVerse initiative, it is clarified how Web X.0 can democratize education and increase access to quality learning opportunities worldwide by reducing the obstacles of geography and infrastructure [11].

7.2.4 Governance and digital public services

The invention of Web X.0 added a new era to public governance through transparency, accountability, and citizen empowerment through digital trust infrastructures. Consequently, governments prefer to utilize intelligent, decentralized ecosystems that combine AI, blockchain, and semantic web technologies instead of isolated e-services [12].

The government's administration is improved through AI real-time analytics and predictive policymaking [13]. Blockchain confirms transaction histories and tamper-proof digital identities; simultaneously, processes such as land registration, licensing, and procurement are automated by smart contracts automate and this results in reducing bureaucracy and corruption risks [2]. Web X.0, the semantic web provides the standards, protocols, technologies, and mechanisms through which communication among different diverse systems is possible, that is, supporting an integrated citizen portal, where all services such as taxation, healthcare, education, and welfare are seamlessly connected.

The mechanisms of self-sovereign identity (SSI) are introduced by these systems, which allow citizens to control their personal information safely, while providing transparency in governance [1].

Case study: Estonia's e-Residency and X-Road ecosystem

Estonia is the global leader in e-governance, where almost all government services are available online. Resultantly, now they are offering an *e-Residency* program through which they allow global citizens to access Estonian business, banking, and legal services through blockchain-secured digital IDs [14]. They have an established *X-Road* framework that serves as a decentralized data exchange layer connecting public and private databases via encrypted APIs.

This framework guarantees data integrity, interoperability, and citizen control, as administrative overhead is significantly reduced. Consequently, citizens can file taxes, vote online, and manage health records seamlessly through this infrastructure, which is an expression of Web X.0's potential for secure, transparent, and citizen-centric governance (Table 7.1).

Therefore, the data presented in the table is also depicted in Figure 7.2, which presents a comparative evaluation of Web technologies across different performance metrics in various industries.

Table 7.1 Industrial use cases of Web X.0

Industry	Core Web X.0 technologies	Key benefits	Major challenges
Healthcare	AI, IoT, Blockchain	Predictive, preventive care; improved data integrity and traceability	Privacy protection, cross-platform interoperability
Finance	Blockchain, Smart Contracts, DAOs	Transparent, accessible financial systems; programmable assets	Regulatory uncertainty, DeFi risks
Education	AI, XR, Blockchain	Adaptive and immersive learning; verified digital credentials	High infrastructure cost; digital divide
Governance	Blockchain, Cloud, AI, Semantic Web	Transparent, efficient, and participatory governance	Cybersecurity threats, policy inertia

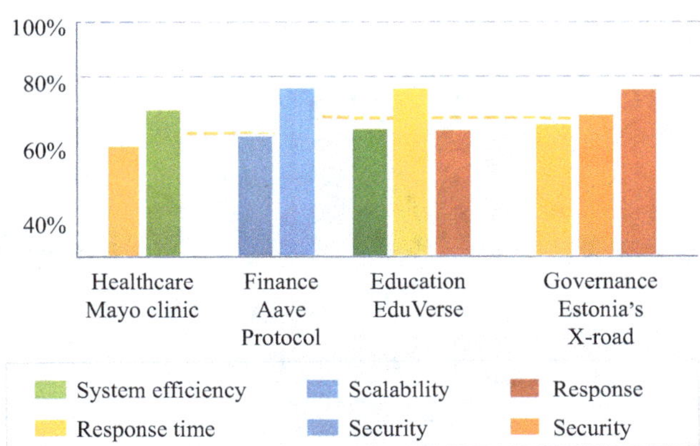

Figure 7.2 Comparative performance metrics case studies

7.3 Comparative case studies and performance analysis of Web X.0 technologies

The previous sections presented the initial technologies enabling Web X.0, while this section introduces a comparative analysis of selected real-world implementations, and the section focuses on evaluating performance indicators, architectural choices, scalability constraints, and security trade-offs observed throughout diverse deployment environments.

Web X.0 is a group of technologies that provide assistance to the ecosystem which has properties like intelligent, decentralized, and immersive digital. Similarly, these technologies provide a structural support for autonomous, interoperable, and context-aware environments that interact meaningfully with both humans and machines.

Figure 7.3, which represents the Web X.0 ecosystem in layered architecture form, consists of infrastructure, protocol, intelligence, application, and interaction layers, along with the relevant domains, like AI, ML, IoT, and many more.

This section also examines the fundamental technological facilitator role of Web X.0 and investigates how they are utilized throughout real-world applications and case studies from different industrial domains.

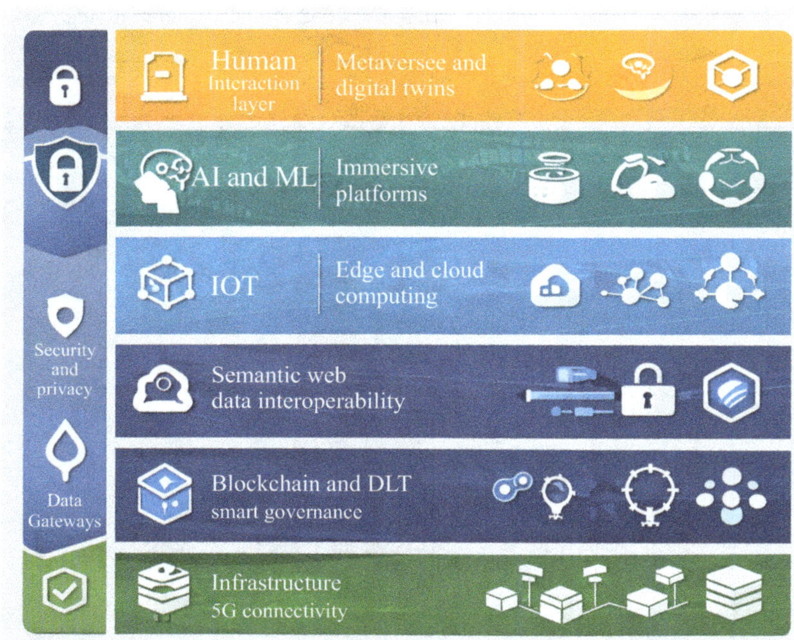

Figure 7.3 Layered architecture of Web X.0 ecosystem

7.3.1 Artificial intelligence (AI) and machine learning (ML)

The core part of Web X.0 technology is Artificial Intelligence (AI) and Machine Learning (ML), through which the Web X.0-based systems have got the ability to learn, adapt, and act independently. Consequently, these technologies create an environment that has a smart, predictive, and context-aware environment, which has the capability of predicting user needs and enhancing digital interactions in real time.

Use cases

- Healthcare: In this sector, mostly Google DeepMind's models are used for predictive diagnostics in medical imaging.
- Finance: In this sector, adaptive ML algorithms in decentralized finance (DeFi) ecosystems are used in fraud detection and risk modeling.
- Smart cities: In smart cities, predictive maintenance and analytics are achieved through AI-driven optimization of traffic, energy consumption, and public services.

Case study: IBM Watson Health
In the healthcare sector, IBM Watson Health has adopted AI in its operations. In its operations, the multimodal medical data are combined, including text, imaging, and sensor inputs. Finally, the Watson health system provides assistance in clinical diagnosis, medication and care planning, and personalized care.

IBM Watson's interoperability with other technologies like IoT and blockchain guarantees trusted, secure, and verifiable data exchange through the use of the Web X.0 framework.

7.3.2 Blockchain and distributed ledger technologies (DLT)

In Web X.0 technology, transparency, immutability, and decentralized trust are achieved across digital transactions, and interactions are confirmed through the blockchain, which is the fundamental part of it. Because blockchain aids secure identity management, traceability, and consensus-based validation through distributed ledger systems, and this creates critical components for autonomous digital ecosystems

Use cases

- Governance: In the e-Governance sector, blockchain-aided digital identity verification and secure e-voting systems (e.g., Estonia's e-Governance model).
- Finance: In the finance sector, decentralized smart contracts on platforms like Ethereum automate difficult financial operations.
- Education: In the education sector, blockchain-supported academic credentialing and verification systems that increase trust and reduce fraud.

Case Study: Estonia's e-Residency Program
Estonia's *e-Residency Program* integrates blockchain as the foundation of its national digital infrastructure. Blockchain is the foundation of Estonia's *e-Residency Program* national digital infrastructure, through this program, which is backed by the blockchain, residents and worldwide citizens are provided with secured digital identities, allowing access to public services, legal systems, and business registration.

This initiative demonstrates the Web X.0 model by merging digital governance, identity control, and distributed trust frameworks in a transparent and user-centric manner [19].

7.3.3 IoT and edge computing

The Web X.0 sensory and computational layers are built by supporting technologies like the IoT and edge computing, which are used to connect billions of devices that generate continuous data streams. Moreover, edge computing takes computation closer to the data source, reducing latency, enhancing responsiveness, and enabling real-time decision-making in intelligent systems.

Use cases

- Manufacturing: In the manufacturing sector, IoT-empowered smart factories, maintenance tasks and quality control are carried out through prediction.
- Agriculture: In the agriculture sector, IoT sensors are used for precision irrigation and soil monitoring systems to enhance resource efficiency.
- Healthcare: In the healthcare sector, for continuous monitoring and early anomaly detection of patients edge-enabled wearables are used.

Case study: Siemens MindSphere
Siemens MindSphere, an IoT-based platform for the industry sector, is used to optimize machine performance and energy efficiency through adding edge analytics and AI-driven insights. Physical assets are linked to a digital system that facilitates data-driven decision-making and automation.

MindSphere demonstrates how Web X.0 enablers are used to create intelligent, adaptive industrial environments through AI, IoT, and cloud ecosystems [20].

7.3.4 Extended reality (XR) and spatial computing

Extended reality (XR) which incorporates augmented, virtual, and mixed reality, revises human–digital interaction by seamlessly combining the physical and virtual worlds.

Keeping in view of Web X.0, extended reality (XR) assists immersive learning, collaborative workspaces, and digital twin environments that mimic complex systems and environments.

Use cases

- Education: *EngageXR* or *Meta Horizon Workrooms* platforms are used for virtual classrooms and labs.
- Real estate: In the real estate, urban planning is carried out through virtual property tours and city-scale digital twin simulations.
- Healthcare: In the healthcare sector, mixed-reality environments are used for surgical training and procedure simulations.

Case study: NVIDIA Omniverse
NVIDIA Omniverse is a platform that supports real-time 3D design and testing across various industries through collaborative simulation. Omniverse integrates technologies like XR, AI, and IoT that support interactive system modeling and optimization, which is a hallmark of Web X.0's immersive and interoperable design principles [21].

7.3.5 Cloud and quantum computing

The Web X.0 technology is offering global access to computational resources, the required scalability and elasticity is achieved through the cloud computing infrastructure. While, quantum computing provides the next level of computational advancement characterized by problem-solving skills of problems-solving that traditional systems cannot perform, such as complex optimization, cryptography, and AI model acceleration.

Use cases

- Finance: In the finance sector, quantum-secured transaction systems and portfolio optimization models.
- Scientific research: In scientific research, molecular modeling and drug discovery are accelerated through simulations.
- Public services: In public services, AI-driven citizen platforms are supported by scalable cloud ecosystems.

Case study: Google Sycamore Quantum Processor
Google's Sycamore Quantum Processor, a quantum computing-supported solution, solved a specific problem faster than any traditional supercomputer. This highlights the ability of quantum-enhanced cloud environments to support secure, high-speed computations.

7.3.6 Interoperability and semantic web technologies

The Web X.0 core layer flourishes on interoperability and semantic integration, which is the ability of diverse systems and organizations to communicate consistently using shared ontologies, decentralized identifiers (DIDs), and open data frameworks. Similarly, the Semantic Web further extends this ability by embedding machine-readable meaning into data, enabling intelligent agents to reason, connect, and act across digital ecosystems.

Use cases

- Cross-border data sharing: In Europe, the *GAIA-X* initiative supports federated, interoperable cloud spaces that reserve digital control.
- Healthcare: In the healthcare sector, patient data exchange across hospitals and nations are facilitated by semantic data models and FHIR standards.
- Digital governance: In the digital governance, semantic ontologies increase interoperability between government ministries and citizen service portals.

Case study: GAIA-X European data infrastructure
The project of *GAIA-X* represents Europe's strategic dedication to interoperability and digital autonomy through the evolving an open, federated cloud and data-sharing ecosystem. It also facilitates trust, transparency, and compliance within the Web X.0 model [22].

Therefore, Figure 7.4 represents the integrated security and trust framework of Web X.0, which illustrated the security challenges in this particular domain.

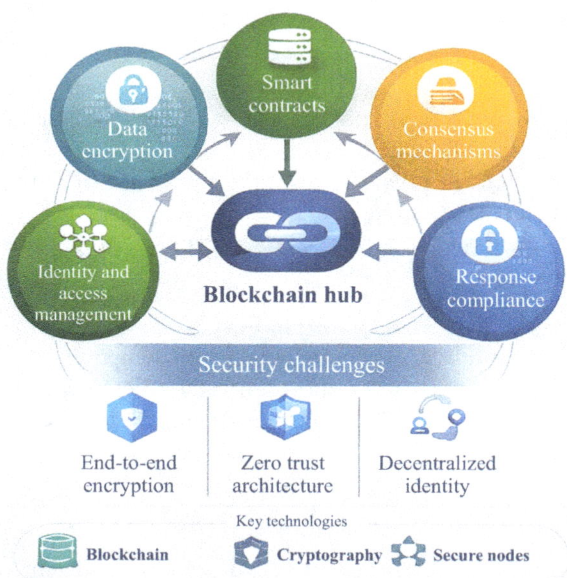

Figure 7.4 Security and trust framework in decentralized web systems

7.3.7 Comparative performance discussion

A comparative estimation of the described case studies shows that AI-integrated Web X.0 systems determine superior personalization accuracy, but often with high computational overhead. Similarly, blockchain-enabled platforms increase transparency and trust management; still, they introduce latency due to consensus mechanisms.

IoT-integrated Web architectures also propose improved real-time responsiveness, but the concerns of data privacy and interoperability rises. The examined systems show incremental improvements in decentralization efficiency and adaptive intelligence when compared with recent studies (2020–24), still scalability under high transaction loads remains a critical bottleneck. As we have already discussed Figure 7.2, which presents a comparative evaluation of Web technologies across different performance metrics in various industries.

This comparative perspective demonstrates the novelty of integrating multilayer architectures instead of depending on isolated technological components, and the same is also represented in Figure 7.3.

7.4 Global and regional case studies

The adoption of Web X.0 technologies worldwide reveals a different view produced by regional priorities, digital readiness, and governance philosophies. While the developed countries are heading in the technological area which includes AI-driven automation, blockchain-enabled governance, and quantum computing. Similarly, emerging regions utilized Web X.0 technologies principles to increase public services, education, and financial inclusion.

This section focuses on a couple of global and regional case studies that demonstrate how the foundational principles of Web X.0, which are decentralization, intelligence, transparency, and interoperability, are being achieved in practice across various socio-economic perspectives.

7.4.1 North America: AI and data-driven ecosystems

The North America region, especially the United States and Canada, leads in AI innovation, data analytics, and immersive digital ecosystems. Large tech companies and research institutions are taking large-scale initiatives to utilize Web X.0 enablers such as AI, IoT, and blockchain in healthcare, urban governance, and sustainability.

Use cases

- Healthcare: In the healthcare sector, predictive diagnostics and patient-centered AI analytics are used to achieve fast recovery of patients.

- Smart infrastructure: In the smart infrastructure, urban mobility and resource optimization are achieved through the IoT- and edge-enabled frameworks.
- Governance: In the governance, blockchain-based digital identity systems for secure citizen engagement.

Case study: smart city Toronto (Sidewalk Labs)
Smart city Toronto is a smart city pilot on Toronto's waterfront project by the Sidewalk Labs of Alphabet Inc., combining Web X.0 enablers such as AI, IoT, and sustainable energy systems. Even though, later on, the project was discontinued due to the data privacy concerns, it described the core idea of Web X.0's data-centric vision through the transformative capacity of AI-driven urban ecosystems in reimagining governance, mobility, and community engagement [23].

7.4.2 Europe: digital sovereignty and federated data spaces

Europe's approach to Web X.0 highlights digital sovereignty, data interoperability, and trust frameworks across the overall industrial sectors to take the most benefits of Web X.0. Their initiatives, such as GAIA-X and European Data Spaces, denote the continent's approach for establishing federated digital ecosystems based on open standards and transparent governance.

Use cases

- E-governance: In e-governance, the integrated administration is strengthened by cross-border digital identity systems.
- Healthcare: In healthcare systems, national health systems are made secure and interoperable through which patient data are shared.
- Industry 5.0: In Industry 5.0, human-centered automation and sustainable manufacturing.

Case study: GAIA-X and European data spaces
The European sovereign data infrastructure is based GAIA-X initiative, which collaboratively combines cloud, edge, and semantic web technologies by supporting open-source collaboration and decentralized governance. And therefore, GAIA-X represents Europe's vision of trust, transparency, and autonomy, which are central tenets of Web X.0's ethical and interoperable design principle.

7.4.3 Asia-Pacific: blockchain-enabled governance and FinTech

The Asia-Pacific (APAC) region countries like China, Singapore, South Korea, and India are emerging as leaders in blockchain innovation, AI deployment, and digital finance. These countries' governments and industries are adopting central bank digital currencies (CBDCs), smart city systems, and AI-driven public services.

Use cases

- Finance: In the finance sector, central bank digital currencies and DeFi ecosystems are introduced.
- Governance: In governance, the AI-assisted e-government and citizen service platforms are used to increase the delivery of services to citizens.
- Healthcare: In the healthcare sector, blockchain-secured patient data management for speedy recovery of the patient.

Case study: India's Aadhaar and blockchain integration
India's *Aadhaar* system, which is the world's largest biometric digital identity framework, is integrating blockchain to enhance its transparency and trust in public services. Aadhaar enables efficient welfare distribution, fraud prevention, and inclusive governance, through AI-based analytics, which represent Web X.0's human-centric and data-sovereign approach to digital transformation.

7.4.4 Middle East: smart cities and sustainable digital transformation

The Middle East, especially the Gulf Cooperation Council (GCC) nations, is trying to develop smart cities and AI-powered governance in their territories. Therefore, national digital strategies such as Saudi Vision 2030 and UAE Digital Government Strategy leverage Web X.0 enablers to build sustainable, data-driven, and citizen-centric urban ecosystems.

Use cases

- Urban development: In urban development, AI- and IoT-enabled smart city initiatives are started.
- Energy management: In energy management, blockchain-supported renewable energy trading platforms are introduced.
- Public services: In public services, digital identity systems and AI-powered citizen engagement tools are deployed.

Case study: NEOM—Saudi Arabia's cognitive mart city
NEOM, is the leading project of Saudi Vision 2030, which also represents one of the most ambitious Web X.0-driven projects in the world. In this project, Web X.0 technologies AI, robotics, IoT, blockchain, and XR are integrated. NEOM's "The Line" imagines a fully autonomous and sustainable city. NEOM represents Web X.0's vision of an intelligent, self-learning, and human-centered urban environment through digital twins, predictive analytics, and zero-emission infrastructure [24].

7.4.5 Africa: leapfrogging through Web X.0 for inclusion

In the African region, Web X.0 adoption is considered by *leapfrogging,* which is bypassing outdated infrastructure limitations through mobile-first innovation and decentralized systems. Main sectors of progress include financial inclusion, smart agriculture, and digital education.

Use cases

- Finance: In the finance sector, mobile banking and blockchain-enabled remittance networks are working.
- Agriculture: In the agriculture sector, IoT-supported crop monitoring and micro-insurance solutions are introduced.
- Education: In the education sector, XR-based virtual classrooms and verifiable credential systems.

Case study: Kenya's M-Pesa and blockchain for financial inclusion
M-Pesa, was a mobile payment platform, now transaction security, traceability, and user accessibility are improved through the integration of blockchain. This initiative demonstrates how developing countries can align Web X.0 technologies with social inclusion and the United Nations Sustainable Development Goals (SDGs), growing access to equitable digital economies [25].

7.4.6 Latin America: digital identity and transparency initiatives

Latin America region countries are implementing Web X.0 frameworks to struggle corruption, increase transparency, and improve citizen trust in governance through blockchain and AI-enabled systems.

Use cases

- Governance: In the governance sector, smart contract–based procurement and accountability systems are introduced.
- Finance: In the finance sector, cross-border remittances using digital currencies are implemented.
- Public records: Blockchain-based systems can support immutable land and property registries, which provide the opportunity to improve the transparency, traceability, and accountability in public record management.

Case study: Chile's blockchain-based public procurement system
Chile's government had channelized its government spending through a blockchain-based public procurement model to ensure transparency and citizen oversight. By recording contracts and transactions on immutable ledgers, this system strengthens public accountability and trust, which are the main outcomes of Web X.0's decentralization and transparency principles.

7.4.7 Summary and comparative insights

Web X.0 implementation represents different strategic priorities and developmental contexts across all the regions. Consequently, North America highlights AI-driven innovation and data ecosystems; Europe emphasizes digital sovereignty and trust;

Asia-Pacific focuses on FinTech and blockchain governance; the Middle East motivates sustainability through smart cities; Africa advances inclusion via mobile and decentralized platforms; and Latin America leads transparency through blockchain governance.

In spite of cited regional differences, the crux's of Web X.0 are the same:

- Decentralized trust: Decentralized trust is achieved through blockchain and distributed ledgers.
- Cognitive intelligence: Cognitive intelligence is determined by AI and machine learning.
- Immersive interaction: Immersive interaction is supported by IoT, XR, and metaverse frameworks.
- Sustainable infrastructure: Sustainable infrastructure is powered by cloud, edge, and quantum computing.

The objectives of these technologies are to bring humanity closer to the vision of a secure, intelligent, and human-centered digital future (Table 7.2).

Table 7.2 Comparative evaluation of Web X.0 case studies based on performance and scalability metrics

Region	Representative case study	Core technologies	Key benefits	Challenges/ observations
North America	Toronto Smart City (Sidewalk Labs, Canada)	AI, IoT, Data Analytics	Urban innovation, data-driven governance, sustainability	Privacy concerns, regulatory challenges
Europe	GAIA-X and European Data Spaces	Cloud, Blockchain, Federated AI	Data sovereignty, interoperability, digital trust	Coordination across EU members, standardization complexity
Asia-Pacific	India's Aadhaar and Blockchain Integration	Blockchain, AI, Digital ID	Inclusive governance, fraud reduction, efficiency	Data protection, digital divide
Middle East	NEOM Cognitive Smart City (Saudi Arabia)	AI, Robotics, IoT, Blockchain	Sustainability, intelligent infrastructure, citizen services	Cost, scalability, ethical AI concerns
Africa	M-Pesa Blockchain for Financial Inclusion (Kenya)	Mobile Tech, Blockchain, FinTech	Financial inclusion, secure remittances	Infrastructure limitations, literacy gap

(Continues)

Table 7.2 (*Continued*)

Region	Representative case study	Core technologies	Key benefits	Challenges/ observations
Latin America	Blockchain-Based Public Procurement (Chile)	Blockchain, Smart Contracts	Transparency, anti-corruption, accountability	Technical capacity, adoption barriers
Global Insight	—	AI, Blockchain, Cloud, XR	Decentralized, intelligent, human-centric systems	Regional inequality, policy alignment

7.4.8 Conclusion and future research directions

This chapter studies the progress and real-world implementation of Web X.0 technologies through organized case studies and comparative analysis. The analysis of the chapter validated that the merging of AI, decentralized ledgers, semantic frameworks, and IoT infrastructures is transforming the traditional web into a more user-centric, autonomous, and intelligent ecosystem.

Despite significant advancements in this domain, challenges in scalability, interoperability, regulatory compliance, and ethical governance remain to be addressed. Similarly, performance trade-offs between decentralization and efficiency require further architectural optimization. Additionally, the merging of heterogeneous technologies demands standardized communication protocols and enhanced security frameworks.

Future research should focus on lightweight consensus mechanisms, explainable AI integration within Web platforms, cross-chain interoperability models, and privacy-preserving computation techniques. Addressing these areas will be essential to achieving a sustainable and globally scalable Web X.0 environment.

Relevant Industry Standards and Policies

- International Standards
  - ISO/IEC 27001 – Information Security Management Systems
  - ISO/IEC 27701 – Privacy Information Management
  - ISO/IEC 30141 – IoT Reference Architecture
  - ISO/IEC 23894 – AI Risk Management
- Technology and Web Standards
  - World Wide Web Consortium Standards
    - RDF (Resource Description Framework)
    - OWL (Web Ontology Language)
    - SPARQL Query Language

- Cybersecurity and Data Policies
    - National Institute of Standards and Technology (NIST)
        - NIST Cybersecurity Framework
        - NIST AI Risk Management Framework
- Financial and Blockchain Standards
    - International Organization for Standardization
        - ISO 22739 (Blockchain Terminology)
    - Financial Action Task Force
        - Cryptocurrency and AML Guidelines
- AI Ethics and Governance
    - UNESCO AI Ethics Framework (2022)
    - OECD AI Principles (2023)
- Regional Regulations
    - European Union
        - GDPR (Data Protection)
        - AI Act (Emerging regulation)

Suggested further readings

[1] Tim Berners-Lee, James Hendler, and Ora Lassila, *The Semantic Web*, Scientific American, 2001.
[2] Don Tapscott and Alex Tapscott, *Blockchain Revolution*, Penguin, 2016.
[3] Stuart Russell and Peter Norvig, *Artificial Intelligence: A Modern Approach*, Pearson, 2020.
[4] World Health Organization, *Digital Health Transformation Strategy 2023–2030*, 2023.
[5] World Economic Forum, *Fourth Industrial Revolution Reports*, 2016–2024.
[6] OECD, *AI Policy Observatory*, 2023.
[7] UNESCO, *Ethics of Artificial Intelligence*, 2022.
[8] European Commission, *Digital Strategy and Data Governance Reports*, 2022.

References

[1] Berners-Lee, T., Hendler, J., and Lassila, O.: 'The semantic web', *Scientific American*, 2001, 284, (5), pp. 34–43.
[2] Tapscott, D., and Tapscott, A.: *Blockchain Revolution: How the Technology Behind Bitcoin Is Changing Money, Business, and the World* (Penguin, 2016).
[3] Russell, S., and Norvig, P.: *Artificial Intelligence: A Modern Approach* (Pearson, 4th edn., 2020).
[4] Nakamoto, S.: 'Bitcoin: A peer-to-peer electronic cash system', 2008. Available at: https://bitcoin.org/bitcoin.pdf

[5] Buterin, V.: *DAOs, DACs, DAs and More: An Incomplete Terminology Guide*, Ethereum Foundation, 2014.
[6] *World Economic Forum: Sustainable Technology and Digital Ethics* (WEF Publications, Geneva, Switzerland, 2024).
[7] Holmes, W., Bialik, M., and Fadel, C.: *Artificial Intelligence in Education: Promises and Implications for Teaching and Learning* (Center for Curriculum Redesign, 2019).
[8] Luckin, R., Holmes, W., Griffiths, M., and Forcier, L.B.: *Intelligence Unleashed: An Argument for AI in Education* (Pearson Education, 2016).
[9] Johnson, L., Becker, S.A., and Cummins, M.: *The Horizon Report: Higher Education Edition 2021* (EDUCAUSE, 2021).
[10] Sharples, M., and Domingue, J.: 'The blockchain and kudos: A distributed system for educational record, reputation, and reward'. In: *Proc. European Conf. on Technology Enhanced Learning*, 2016, pp. 490–496.
[11] *UNESCO: Guidelines for the Digital Transformation of Education Systems* (UNESCO Publishing, Paris, France, 2023).
[12] *United Nations: E-Government Survey 2022*: *The future of digital government* (UN Publications, New York, USA, 2022).
[13] Janssen, M., and Estevez, E.: 'Lean government and platform-based governance: Reducing complexity and increasing agility', *Government Information Quarterly*, 2013, 30, (S1), pp. S1–S8.
[14] Vassil, K.: 'Estonia's digital transformation: Background, achievements, and future prospects', *European View*, 2015, 14, (1), pp. 93–100.
[15] Ghosh, R., and Chakraborty, S.: *Blockchain in Healthcare: Security, Privacy, and Trust Models* (Springer, 2023).
[16] Wang, S., Zhang, Y., and Zhang, Y.: *Smart Healthcare and IoT: Technologies, Challenges, and Future Trends* (Elsevier, 2022).
[17] World Health Organization*: Digital Health Transformation Strategy 2023–2030* (WHO Press, Geneva, Switzerland, 2023).
[18] World Bank*: Financial Inclusion Report 2023* (World Bank Group, Washington, DC, USA, 2023).
[19] European Commission: *Blockchain in Digital Public Administration: Lessons from Estonia* (Publications Office of the European Union, Brussels, Belgium, 2022).
[20] Siemens AG*: Digital Twin for Smart Cities: Urban Innovation Report* (Siemens Press, Munich, Germany, 2023).
[21] NVIDIA*: Omniverse Platform: Bridging AI, XR, and Simulation Ecosystems* (NVIDIA Corporation, 2024).
[22] GAIA-X Association for Data and Cloud: Building a Federated and Sovereign Data Infrastructure for Europe, 2024.
[23] Sidewalk Labs*: Toronto Smart City: Data Governance and Urban Innovation*, 2022.
[24] NEOM Company*: Cognitive City Framework: Building the AI-driven Urban. Future*, 2024.
[25] Safaricom*: M-Pesa Evolution: Blockchain and Digital Finance for Inclusive Growth* (Safaricom Ltd., Nairobi, Kenya, 2023).

Chapter 8

The role of Web X.0 technologies in achieving UN Sustainable Development Goals (SDGs)

Haoyu Ci[1], Haijun Liao[1], Zhenyu Zhou[1] and Muhammad Tariq[2]

Abstract

This chapter explores how Web X.0 technologies advance the united nations sustainable development goals (UN SDGs), especially SDG 7 (affordable and clean energy) and SDG 13 (climate action), by enabling intelligent distribution grid energy management via ultra-low age of information guaranteed digital twin (ULAoI-DT). A three-layer ULAoI-DT framework (device, edge, and DT layers) is built, and a resource allocation model is formulated to minimize the global loss of energy management model training under ULAoI and long-term energy constraints. The intractable optimization problem is transformed with virtual queue (VQ) theory and modeled as a Markov decision process (MDP), then solved by a ULAoI-prioritized deep Q-network (DQN) algorithm for joint device, training batch size and channel scheduling. Simulations on 5G base station (BS) energy storage in multi-area grids show the algorithm outperforms multi-agent deep reinforcement learning (MDRL) and AoI-aware federated learning-based communication (AoI-FLC) significantly: it cuts the global loss by 36.01% and 11.16%, reduces the AoI violation probability by 84.54% and 73.91%, and stabilizes grid load with a 20% and 46.66% lower fluctuation than MDRL and AoI-FLC in residential areas. The results verify ULAoI-DT's efficacy in renewable energy integration and carbon emission reduction, providing a practical pathway for SDG achievement via web X.0 technologies.

8.1 Background and motivation

The evolution of Web X.0 represents a paradigm shift from static information dissemination to interconnected, intelligent ecosystems that bridge the physical and

[1]State Key Laboratory of Alternate Electrical Power System with Renewable Energy Sources, School of Electrical and Electronic Engineering, North China Electric Power University, China
[2]Electrical Engineering Department, National University of Computer and Emerging Sciences, Pakistan

digital worlds, laying the groundwork for achieving the UN Sustainable Development Goals (SDGs). Web 1.0 has served as a basic platform for information sharing but lacks interactivity and real-world integration. Web 2.0 has introduced user-generated content and social connectivity, fostering collaboration but remaining largely confined to digital spaces. Web 3.0 has added machine-readable data and machine learning capabilities, enabling more intuitive information processing [1]. Today, Web X.0 transcends these stages by integrating more transformative technologies like industrial Internet, digital twins (DT), Internet of Things (IoT), artificial intelligence (AI), and block chain, creating a hyper-connected, data-driven infrastructure that empowers industries to operate more sustainably. Together, these technologies eliminate silos between digital and physical operations, enabling predictive decision-making, resource efficiency, and circularity—core pillars of the SDGs, particularly SDG 7 (Affordable and Clean Energy) and SDG 13 (Climate Action).

Web X.0 technologies are instrumental in advancing these goals through three critical pathways: building smart grids, enhancing renewable energy integration, and reducing carbon emissions. Power grids are the critical link between clean energy generation and equitable access. Without a resilient, efficient grid, even the most abundant renewable resources remain underutilized, and carbon-intensive fossil fuels persist as the default energy source. Traditional grids, plagued by inefficiencies, transmission losses, and limited flexibility, reply on fossil fuels to meet demand spikes, and lack the ability to integrate various renewable energy sources (solar, wind). Web X.0 technologies, particularly DT, power Internet of Things (PIoT), and (AI), can transform traditional grids into smart energy management hubs that directly advance SDG 7 and 13. PIoT serves as the "nervous system" of smart grids, deploying millions of sensors across power lines, transformers, and consumer equipment to capture real-time data on energy flow, usage patterns, and equipment health. These data provide data foundations for DT model training. DT combined with AI, served as the "brain system" of smart grids, providing accurate virtual replicas of grid infrastructure to forecast energy demand, predict renewable generation, and adjust power outputs. Together, these technologies create a closed-loop system, all working to minimize carbon emissions, maximize renewable energy utilization, and deliver affordable, reliable power to all, directly fulfilling the mandates of SDG 7 and SDG 13.

Considering the deep coupling between sensing (data collection), communication (data transmission), and control (energy management), DT model performance of energy management is largely determined by information-domain resource allocation decisions. For example, DT model training based on outdated data leads to mismatching control decisions. Age of information (AoI), defined as the elapsed delay since the last DT synchronization, is an important metric to measure DT consistency and precision. Different from traditional delay measuring single packet transmission duration, AoI measures information timeliness which spans the entire life cycle of information generation, transmission, processing, and utilization for the DT model training. In particular, energy management imposes ultra-low AoI (ULAoI) requirements to mitigate the occurrence of extreme AoI violation events.

Intuitively, it is necessary to guarantee ULAoI from the perspective of system science via closed-loop coordinated integration of sensing, communication, and control. However, current studies treat them as separate systems, weakening the role of communication as a bridge connecting sensing and control. This inevitably leads to the propagation of AoI degradation into energy control through the communication bridge, generating cascading disturbances and grid failures. Thus, how to build Web X.0 DT with a reliable ULAoI guarantee (ULAoI-DT) for intelligent energy management remains a critical challenge in achieving UN SDGs.

By supplying precise evaluations regarding system conditions, the digital twin (DT) effectively facilitates coordinated resource allocation. Through continuous data synchronization, creating virtual replicas representing physical infrastructures allows DT to boost overall estimation accuracy [2,3]. Age of information (AoI) represents the accumulated time lag following previous updates. This crucial parameter evaluates DT consistency while simultaneously deciding our state estimation accuracy [4]. Unlike traditional delay calculating isolated packet transit times, evaluating information timeliness constitutes AoI's primary function, comprehensively encompassing complete life cycles involving data creation, transferring, computation, alongside final utilization [5]. In [6], Wang *et al.* designed a multi-agent scheme tailored toward unmanned aerial vehicle (UAV)-hosted platoon DT networks, curtailing that combined weighted sum regarding average peak AoI plus energy consumption via simultaneously managing platoon control alongside power resource allocation. In [7], Xu *et al.* introduced a random graph-enabled deep deterministic policy gradient (DDPG) scheme assisting wireless body area networks via DT. This framework optimizes energy efficiency while diminishing AoI through concurrently coordinating available transmission mode, relay assignment, time slot scheduling, combined with transmission power. Executing reliable energy management strictly demands stringent AoI guarantee requirements. Nevertheless, ensuring this metric purely from a time-averaged perspective proves fundamentally unreliable. Whenever any extreme event emerges—where measured AoI heavily surpasses its established threshold—it inevitably triggers massive DT inconsistency, subsequently yielding inaccurate state estimation alongside notably low model training precision [8].

Optimizing DT-assisted resource allocation frequently utilizes deep reinforcement learning (DRL) algorithms [9]. In [10], Zhou *et al.* developed an accurate, secure, alongside low-latency DT architecture to facilitate resource scheduling across 5G edge computing-empowered distribution grids. By employing this DT technology, that author ingeniously resolved integration challenges concerning computation, communication, plus sensing, thereby significantly boosting the deep Q network (DQN) learning capability. In [11], Wang *et al.* designed an adaptive resource distribution strategy utilizing multi-agent DRL specifically for platoon DT networks. Their methodology maximizes overall update utility through concurrently managing computation provisions alongside bandwidth. In [12], Dai *et al.* formulated a collaborative federated DRL methodology governing DT edge networks. This approach minimizes total system cost via simultaneously coordinating computing resources, passive reflecting link configurations, plus task offloading. Nevertheless, those aforementioned studies disregard that negative influence caused by ULAoI constraint violation upon both resource allocation coordination alongside the learning performance of DRL. Several current investigations explore providing an AoI guarantee purely from a time-averaged perspective. In [13], Lan *et al.* constructed a multi-tiered DRL architecture supporting RIS-assisted vehicular edge computing systems. By jointly determining power allocation plus RIS phase shifts, it maximizes energy efficiency while supplying that time-averaged AoI guarantee. In [14], Al-Habob *et al.* designed an innovative strategy utilizing meta-multi-objective reinforcement learning targeting vehicular networks. This technique diminishes overall power consumption while maintaining the time-averaged AoI guarantee via concurrently regulating both power allocation alongside decoding order. Nonetheless, existing literature predominantly examines AoI strictly through an average perspective, rendering them inappropriate regarding any strict ULAoI guarantee. Furthermore, accomplishing this ULAoI guarantee viewed from that sensing-communication-control integration standpoint remains entirely unresolved.

8.2 Resource allocation problem for Web X.0 ULAoI-DT empowered grid energy management

In this section, we firstly provide a detailed description of the system model of Web X.0 ULAoI-DT construction and its AoI evolution. Then, we present the formulation of the resource allocation problem for grid energy management from the perspective of ULAoI guarantee. To provide a quick reference, the principal notations used in this chapter are summarized in Table 8.1.

Table 8.1 Nomenclature

Notation	Description	Notation	Description
$\mathcal{U}$	Set of PIoT devices	$b_m(t)$	Training batch size
M	Total number of PIoT devices	$x_{m,n}(t)$	Channel scheduling variable
$\mathcal{T}$	Set of iterations	$\omega(t)$	Global model
DT_m	ULAoI-DT model of device u_m	$\omega_m(t)$	Local model
$\zeta_m(t)$	AoI of DT_m	$\tau_m(t)$	Total delay for local model training and data uploading
ζ_{max}^{AoI}	Predefined bound of $\zeta_m(t)$	$E_m(t)$	Energy consumption
$K_m(t)$	Excess AoI value of DT_m	$\gamma_m(t)$	Packet error rate (PER)
$a_m(t)$	Device scheduling variable	$\Gamma(t)$	Optimization objective

8.2.1 System model

Figure 8.1 illustrates our proposed architecture for managing energy within distribution grids via ULAoI-DT-assisted resource allocation tailored to multi-mode PIoT. This system incorporates three tiers: a device layer, an edge layer, along with a DT layer. Our primary goal involves training a federated learning-based energy management model. At the device layer, localized models undergo training utilizing information samples gathered by PIoT devices, which are installed across distributed wind turbines, photovoltaic (PV) panels, as well as charging piles. We assume a total of M PIoT devices, denoted by the collection $\mathcal{U} = \{1, \cdots, u_m, \cdots, u_M\}$. The edge tier encompasses an edge server, a 5G-powered base station (BS), plus one PLC gateway. Information exchange connecting that edge server with end devices is facilitated by the 5G BS (operated by a telecommunication provider) alongside the PLC gateway (managed by a grid company). To produce the global model, this edge server gathers and aggregates all localized models transmitted from various devices. Maintained directly by this edge server, the DT layer establishes an individual ULAoI-DT DT_m corresponding to every device $u_m \in \mathcal{U}$. To guarantee DT consistency, continuous synchronization occurs between u_m and its DT_m via information exchange subject to specific ULAoI constraints. Aided by the ULAoI-DT, dynamic resource allocation optimization is managed by this edge server. This process involves channel selection, training batch size configuration, and device scheduling, ultimately enhancing both convergence speed and the precision of model training.

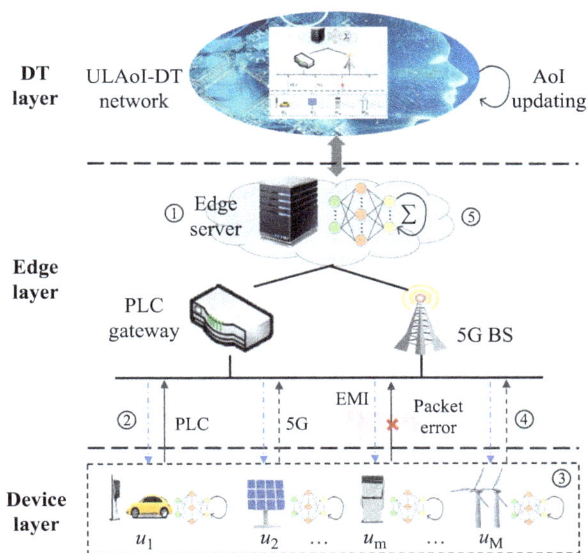

Figure 8.1 The architecture for managing energy within distribution grids via ULAoI-DT-assisted resource allocation tailored to multi-mode PIoT

The entire model training timeframe is divided into T distinct iterations. These are represented by the collection $\mathscr{T} = \{1, \cdots, t, \cdots, T\}$. Every single iteration contains five separate phases: (i) generation of the resource allocation strategy assisted by ULAoI-DT; (ii) distributing both the resource allocation strategy and the global model; (iii) training procedures for local models; (iv) uploading current state data plus local models utilizing multi-mode channels; (v) aggregating the global model. Initially, based upon the power of electromagnetic interference (EMI) as well as estimated channel gain supplied via the ULAoI-DT, a resource allocation strategy is formulated by this edge server. Subsequently, these devices receive the recently updated global model along with the resource allocation strategy directly from that edge server. Following this step, local models undergo training by those scheduled devices. Once finished, they transmit their current state data and completed local models back into the edge server using various multi-mode PIoT channels. Ultimately, to construct the global model, this edge server executes global model aggregation relying on those newly uploaded local models.

8.2.1.1 ULAoI-DT model for devices

We formulate the ULAoI-DT representation for u_m as

$$DT_m = \Gamma(\mathscr{Y}_m, \mathcal{F}_m(t), \zeta_m(t), \zeta_{max}^{AoI}, P_m(t), \bar{K}_m(t), \bar{Z}_m(t)), \tag{8.1}$$

where $\mathscr{Y}_m$ denotes static operational information. $\mathcal{F}_m(t)$ represents dynamic state variables. The constant $\mathscr{Y}_m$ encompasses the identifier, equipment category, underlying information model, alongside additional time-invariant parameters. Time-dependent metrics like channel gain, current, voltage, EMI, plus solar irradiation intensity are included within $\mathcal{F}_m(t)$. Because the $\mathscr{Y}_m$ component stays constant, updating this ULAoI-DT requires exclusively $\mathcal{F}_m(t)$. The parameter $\zeta_m(t)$ signifies DT_m's AoI, illustrating the inconsistency or state divergence separating u_m from DT_m. We define AoI to be the accumulated time since that previous DT synchronization occurred. This metric fundamentally dictates energy management precision. A predetermined upper limit for $\zeta_m(t)$ is established as ζ_{max}^{AoI}.

Multiple constraints constitute this ULAoI metric. These incorporate the long-term conditional mean, the probability regarding extreme event occurrences, alongside the excess AoI value's second moment. Let us represent an extreme event—where AoI surpasses its specified limit—by $\zeta_m(t) > \zeta_{max}^{AoI}$. Consequently, we formulate the probability constraint governing this occurrence as

$$\begin{aligned} P_m(t) &= \mathbb{I}\{\zeta_m(t) > \zeta_{max}^{AoI}\}, \\ \bar{P}_m &= \lim_{T\to\infty} \frac{1}{T}\sum_{t=1}^{T} P_m(t) \leqslant \alpha, \end{aligned} \tag{8.2}$$

where $\mathbb{I}\{x\}$ equals 1 assuming x holds true, while returning 0 alternately. The acceptable threshold for violating this boundary is $\alpha \ll 1$.

For any t-th iteration, DT_m's surplus AoI magnitude is denoted by

$$K_m(t)|_{\zeta_m(t)>\zeta_{max}^{AoI}} = \zeta_m(t) - \zeta_{max}^{AoI} > 0. \tag{8.3}$$

Applying the Pickands–Balkema–deHaan theorem [15,16], we can approximate this excess AoI value's CCDF using $G(k_m(t); \sigma, \xi)$, which represents a generalized Pareto distribution (GPD), i.e.,

$$\begin{aligned} &\bar{F}_{K_m(t)|_{\zeta_m(t)>\zeta_{max}^{AoI}}}(k_m(t)) = \\ &\Pr(\zeta_m(t) - \zeta_{max}^{AoI} > k_m(t)|_{\zeta_m(t)>\zeta_{max}^{AoI}}) \approx G(k_m(t); \sigma, \xi), \end{aligned} \tag{8.4}$$

where ξ and σ respectively signify the shape parameter alongside the scale parameter. Leveraging GPD's statistical properties together with the correlation linking these two parameters, limitations are placed upon $\bar{Z}_m$ and $\bar{K}_m$. These variables denote the excess AoI value's second moment as well as its long-term conditional mean, bounded mathematically by

$$\bar{K}_m = \lim_{T\to\infty} \frac{1}{T} \sum_{t=1}^{T} \mathbb{E}(K_m(t)|_{\zeta_m(t)>\zeta_{max}^{AoI}}) \leq \frac{\sigma^{th}}{1 - \xi^{th}}, \tag{8.5}$$

$$\bar{Z}_m = \lim_{T\to\infty} \frac{1}{T} \sum_{t=1}^{T} \mathbb{E}(Z_m(t)|_{\zeta_m(t)>\zeta_{max}^{AoI}}) \leq \frac{2(\sigma^{th})^2}{(1 - \xi^{th})(1 - 2\xi^{th})}. \tag{8.6}$$

Note that $Z_m(t) = [K_m(t)]^2$. Regarding their measurement units, $Z_m(t)$ uses seconds squared, whereas $K_m(t)$ relies on seconds. Finally, ξ^{th} alongside σ^{th} establish the maximum limits for ξ and σ.

8.2.1.2 Distribution grid energy management's local model training

When that t-th iteration commences, generating a resource allocation strategy becomes this edge server's initial task. Utilizing predictions supplied via ULAoI-DT, including remaining energy alongside location details, device availability estimations are performed by that edge server. Subsequently, scheduled devices obtain both that formulated resource allocation strategy plus the $(t-1)$-th iteration's global model, represented as $\omega(t-1)$, directly from this edge server. Following this transmission, every u_m initializes its corresponding local model to equal $\omega_m(t) = \omega(t-1)$. To maintain analytical simplicity, we disregard any downlink delay associated with distributing this global model, adopting an approach similar to [10]. Despite this assumption, our presented algorithm demonstrates substantial scalability alongside remarkable adaptability. Furthermore, applying it remains feasible within scenarios treating delays during global model transmission as non-negligible factors.

Let us define an indicator for device availability utilizing $v_m(t) = \{0, 1\}$. Herein, u_m's readiness is signified by $v_m(t) = 1$, whereas $v_m(t) = 0$ implies unavailability. We introduce $a_m(t)$ representing that device scheduling variable. A value of $a_m(t) = 1$ means choosing u_m for conducting local model training during that t-th iteration; alternately, it equals $a_m(t) = 0$. Provided that $v_m(t) \cap a_m(t) = 1$ holds true, training that localized model occurs by having u_m utilize fractional information samples from its localized dataset. We designate $b_m(t)$ to be this training batch size, representing how many information samples u_m employs while training its local model throughout that t-th iteration. To evaluate model precision, we derive the loss function $L_m(\boldsymbol{\omega}_m(t), t)$ as

$$L_m(\boldsymbol{\omega}_m(t), t) = \frac{1}{b_m(t)} \sum_{k=1}^{b_m(t)} l(\boldsymbol{\omega}_m(t), \mathbf{a}_{m,k}, DT_m), \tag{8.7}$$

where $l(\boldsymbol{\omega}_m(t), \mathbf{a}_{m,k}, DT_m)$ constitutes that specific loss function corresponding to $\mathbf{a}m, k$, which denotes u_m's k-th individual data sample. Applying standard gradient descent methodology, we update this local model as

$$\boldsymbol{\omega}_m(t) = \boldsymbol{\omega}_m(t) - \eta \nabla L_m(\boldsymbol{\omega}_m(t), t), \tag{8.8}$$

where η defines our learning rate. Let ξ_m represent those necessary CPU cycles needed to process a single data sample. Consequently, during that t-th iteration, u_m's energy consumption alongside its processing delay regarding local model training are formulated as

$$\begin{aligned} \tau_m^L(t) &= v_m(t) a_m(t) \frac{\xi_m b_m(t)}{f_m(t)}, \\ E_m^L(t) &= v_m(t) a_m(t) \beta_m \xi_m b_m(t) f_m^2(t), \end{aligned} \tag{8.9}$$

where available computation resources belonging to u_m correspond to $f_m(t)$. Furthermore, β_m signifies that effective switched capacitance characterizing the CPU within u_m [17].

8.2.1.3 Dynamic state data and local model transmission utilizing multi-mode PIoT

Integrating complementary benefits from diverse communication mediums, such as PLC alongside 5G, defines multi-mode PIoT. Due to massive connectivity, immense capacity, plus minimal latency, 5G attracts significant attention. Conversely, excellent scalability, broad coverage, affordable deployment, and cost-effectiveness constitute PLC's primary strengths. We assume N_2 5G links alongside N_1 PLC connections exist, satisfying $N_1 + N_2 = N$. Let $\mathscr{C} = \{c_1 \cdots, c_{N_1}, c_{N_1+1}, \cdots, c_N\}$ represent this multi-mode PIoT channel collection. Herein, 5G links encompass $c_n \in \{c_{N_1+1} \cdots, c_n, \cdots, c_N\}$, whereas PLC connections include $c_n \in \{c_1 \cdots, c_n, \cdots, c_{N_1}\}$. We define $x_{m,n}(t)$ representing our channel scheduling indicator. If $x_{m,n}(t) = 1$, this edge server allocates c_n toward u_m facilitating dynamic state data plus local model transmission; conversely, it returns zero. Let $P_m(t)$ denote u_m's transmit power. Consequently, u_m's communication rate across c_n becomes

$$R_{m,n}(t) = B_{m,n} \log(1 + \frac{p_m(t)h_{m,n}(t)}{I_{m,n}(t) + N_0}), \tag{8.10}$$

where variables $B_{m,n}$ and $h_{m,n}(t)$ denote the communication bandwidth alongside the corresponding channel gain. Meanwhile, $I_{m,n}(t)$ represents the EMI power, while N_0 signifies the background noise power. Assuming $|\mathcal{F}_m(t)|$ defines the total volume regarding dynamic state information, and $|\boldsymbol{\omega}_m(t)|$ specifies this localized model's dimension. Consequently, transferring these dynamic metrics together with updated models requires specific transmission time delays plus energy expenditures for user u_m, formulated mathematically as

$$\begin{aligned} \tau_m^U(t) &= v_m(t)a_m(t)\sum_{n=1}^{N}\frac{x_{m,n}(t)(|\mathcal{F}_m(t)| + |\boldsymbol{\omega}_m(t)|)}{R_{m,n}(t)}, \\ E_m^U(t) &= p_m(t)\tau_m^U(t). \end{aligned} \tag{8.11}$$

During dynamic state information and local model transmission procedures, electrical equipment operations frequently generate abrupt, intense EMI, subsequently causing packet errors. Thus, u_m's corresponding packet error rate (PER) evaluates to

$$\gamma_m(t) = \sum_{n=1}^{N} x_{m,n}(t)\left(1 - \exp(-\frac{\iota(I_{m,n}(t) + N_0)}{p_m(t)h_{m,n}(t)})\right), \tag{8.12}$$

where ι denotes that defined waterfall threshold. To alleviate negative consequences regarding model accuracy caused by packet errors, estimating multimode channels' PER utilizes ULAoI-DT within this edge server. By eliminating inferior connections whose predicted PER fails acceptable threshold criteria, this available multi-mode PIoT channel grouping $\mathscr{C}'_m(t)$ becomes dynamically established.

Consequently, throughout that t-th iteration, data uploading plus local model training incur total energy consumption and overall delay for u_m formulated mathematically as

$$\tau_m(t) = \tau_m^L(t) + \tau_m^U(t), \tag{8.13}$$

$$E_m(t) = E_m^L(t) + E_m^U(t). \tag{8.14}$$

8.2.1.4 Energy management global model aggregation in distribution grids

Once every scheduled device finishes uploading its localized model, this edge server performs the global aggregation procedure. Consequently, during that t-th iteration, waiting time prior to combining these models relies entirely upon whichever unit exhibits maximum overall latency, formulated as

$$\tau(t) = \max_{m}\{\tau_m(t)\}, \forall u_m \in \mathcal{U}. \tag{8.15}$$

Let us represent that t-th iteration's unified framework using $\omega(t)$, being calculated through

$$\omega(t) = \sum_{m=1}^{M} \frac{v_m(t)a_m(t)b_m(t)}{\sum\limits_{m=1}^{M} v_m(t)a_m(t)b_m(t)} \omega_m(t). \tag{8.16}$$

Subsequently, we compute our overarching loss formulation by

$$L(\omega(t), t) = \sum_{m=1}^{M} \frac{v_m(t)a_m(t)b_m(t)}{\sum\limits_{m=1}^{M} v_m(t)a_m(t)b_m(t)} L_m(\omega_m(t), t). \tag{8.17}$$

8.2.1.5 AoI metric updating

Regarding every $u_m \in \mathcal{U}$, refreshing DT_m's AoI parameter, denoted by $\zeta_m(t)$, proceeds as

$$\zeta_m(t) = \begin{cases} \tau(t) - \tau_m(t) + \tau_g, & v_m(t)a_m(t) = 1, \\ \zeta_m(t-1) + \tau(t) + \tau_g, & v_m(t)a_m(t) = 0. \end{cases} \tag{8.18}$$

Herein, following its state information transmission, u_m experiences a standby duration equivalent to $\tau(t) - \tau_m(t)$. Additionally, τ_g signifies that time required for overarching model consolidation. Fundamentally, whenever ULAoI-DT yields reduced AoI values, it implies highly accurate information estimations. Consequently, this minimizes any efficiency disparity separating our formulated resource distribution plan from an ideal benchmark.

8.2.2 Problem formulation and transformation

Within this section, we present how our optimization challenge is formulated and subsequently transformed.

8.2.2.1 Problem formulation

Throughout this manuscript, our focus centers on allocating resources assisted by DT for managing grid energy, viewed through the lens of guaranteeing ULAoI. Our primary goal aims at minimizing that global loss function during energy management model training. This is achieved via jointly optimizing channel selection, training batch sizes, plus device scheduling, while strictly satisfying long-term constraints regarding both ULAoI and energy consumption. Let us define the vectors representing device scheduling, training batch sizes, alongside channel allocation respectively as $\mathbf{a}(t) = \{a_m(t)|u_m \in \mathscr{U}\}$, $\mathbf{b}(t) = \{b_m(t)|u_m \in \mathscr{U}\}$, plus $\mathbf{x}(t) = \{x_{m,n}(t)|u_m \in \mathscr{U}, c_n \in \mathscr{C}\}$. We construct this optimization formulation as

$$\begin{aligned}
&\mathbf{P1}: \min_{\{\mathbf{a}(t),\mathbf{b}(t),\mathbf{x}(t)\}} L(\omega(T), T), \\
&s.t.\ C_1 : a_m(t) \in \{0,1\}, \forall u_m \in \mathscr{U}, \forall t \in \mathscr{T}, \\
&C_2 : \sum_{m=1}^{M} a_m(t) \leq M_q, M_q < M, \forall t \in \mathscr{T}, \\
&C_3 : b_m(t) \leq D_m, \forall u_m \in \mathscr{U}, \forall t \in \mathscr{T}, \\
&C_4 : x_{m,n}(t) \in \{0,1\}, \forall u_m \in \mathscr{U}, \forall c_n \in \mathscr{C}, \forall t \in \mathscr{T}, \\
&C_5 : \sum_{m=1}^{M} x_{m,n}(t) \leq 1, \forall c_n \in \mathscr{C}, \forall t \in \mathscr{T}, \\
&C_6 : \sum_{c_n \in \mathscr{C}'_m(t)} x_{m,n}(t) \leq 1, \forall u_m \in \mathscr{U}, \forall t \in \mathscr{T}, \\
&C_7 : \lim_{T\to\infty} \sum_{t=1}^{T} \mathbb{E}[E_m(t)] \leqslant E_{m,max}, \forall u_m \in \mathscr{U}, \\
&C_8 : (), (), \text{and } (), \forall u_m \in \mathscr{U}.
\end{aligned} \tag{8.19}$$

Constraints C_1 alongside C_2 define limits for scheduling individual devices. Regarding C_3, it acts as our limitation upon training batch dimensions. Here, u_m's localized dataset capacity corresponds mathematically to D_m. Furthermore, conditions C_4, C_5, combined with C_6 govern channel allocation procedures. They guarantee that assigning any accessible link happens for no more than a single PIoT unit, while conversely limiting every device to possess maximally one connection. The restriction over extended energy usage is specified by C_7. Within this expression, transferring state information plus computing local models must stay within u_m's predefined energy threshold, denoted as $E_{m,max}$ [18]. Finally, boundary C_8 encapsulates overarching long-term ULAoI requirements.

8.2.2.2 Problem transformation based on virtual queue

Relying upon mathematical derivations presented by [19], assuming transmission power remains constant, that global loss metric corresponding to our distribution grid's energy management architecture heavily relies upon chosen device scheduling decisions, PER, alongside those training batch sizes assigned for scheduled units. Consequently, we rewrite **P1** as

$$\begin{aligned}
&\mathbf{P2}: \min_{\{\mathbf{a}(t),\mathbf{b}(t),\mathbf{x}(t)\}} \sum_{m=1}^{M} a_m(t) b_m(t)(1 - a_m(t) + a_m(t)\gamma_m(t)), \\
&s.t. C_1 \sim C_8,
\end{aligned} \tag{8.20}$$

We employ virtual queue techniques [20] for separating overarching long-term restrictions away from instantaneous, short-term optimizations concerning resource allocation. In particular, associated with C_6, we introduce an artificial energy deficit queue denoted by $F_m(t)$. $F_m(t)$ evolves as

$$F_m(t+1) = \max\{F_m(t) + E_m(t) - \frac{E_{m,max}}{T}, 0\}, \tag{8.21}$$

where u_m's energy budget per individual iteration equals $\frac{E_{m,max}}{T}$.

To handle those extended restrictions regarding ULAoI, artificial deficit queues denoted by $Q_m^{AoI}(t)$, $Q_m^K(t)$, plus $Q_m^Z(t)$ are constructed. These metrics match with expressions (8.2), (8.5), alongside (8.6), respectively, and their update processes are formulated as

$$Q_m^{AoI}(t+1) = \max\{Q_m^{AoI}(t) + \mathbb{I}\{\zeta_m(t) > \zeta_{max}^{AoI}\} - \alpha, 0, \tag{8.22}$$

$$Q_m^K(t+1) = \max\{Q_m^K(t) - \frac{\sigma^{th}}{1-\xi^{th}}) \times \mathbb{I}\zeta_m(t) > \zeta_{max}^{AoI}\}, 0\}, \tag{8.23}$$

$$Q_m^Z(t+1) = \max\{Q_m^Z(t) + (Z_m(t) - \frac{2(\sigma^{th})^2}{(1-\xi^{th})(1-2\xi^{th})}) \times \mathbb{I}\{\zeta_m(t) > \zeta_{max}^{AoI}\}, 0\}. \tag{8.24}$$

Assuming mean rate stability is guaranteed for variables $F_m(t)$, $Q_m^{AoI}(t)$, $Q_m^K(t)$, coupled with $Q_m^Z(t)$, conditions C_7 alongside C_8 become satisfied inherently [21]. Seeking to minimize our overarching loss metric, whilst striving to fulfill extended boundaries upon both energy usage alongside ULAoI through best-effort techniques, we equivalently reformulate **P2** into

$$\begin{aligned}
\mathbf{P3}: \min_{\{\mathbf{a}(t),\mathbf{b}(t),\mathbf{x}(t)\}} \ & \Gamma(t) \\
= \sum_{m=1}^{M} & [a_m(t)b_m(t)(1 - a_m(t) + a_m(t)\gamma_m(t)) \\
& + V_m^E F_m(t)E_m(t) \\
& + V_m^{AoI}\mathbb{I}\{\zeta_m(t) > \zeta_{max}^{AoI}\}\{Q_m^{AoI}(t) \\
& + V_m^K Q_m^K(t)(K_m(t) - \frac{\sigma^{th}}{1-\xi^{th}}) \\
& + V_m^Z Q_m^Z(t)(Z_m(t) - \frac{2(\sigma^{th})^2}{(1-\xi^{th})(1-2\xi^{th})})\}], \quad s.t. C_1 \sim C_6,
\end{aligned} \tag{8.25}$$

where strictly positive weighting parameters assigned to deficits concerning ULAoI and energy are set to V_m^{AoI} and V_m^E, respectively. Additionally, unifying varying scale dimensions requires utilizing coefficients V_m^K together with V_m^Z.

8.3 ULAoI-DT-prioritized DQN-assisted joint scheduling method for channels, training batch dimensions, and devices

Within the current section, we elucidate our proposed ULAoI-DT-prioritized DQN-assisted joint scheduling method for channels, training batch dimensions, and devices.

8.3.1 Modeling the Markov decision process

Formulating **P3** utilizes a Markov decision process (MDP) framework [22]. We detail its associated reward function, possible actions, alongside state variables below.

(1) State space: We represent this system's state space using $\mathbf{S}(t) = \{\mathbf{v}(t), \mathbf{F}(t), \mathbf{Q}^{AoI}(t), \mathbf{Q}^{K}(t), \mathbf{Q}^{Z}(t), \mathbf{E}_{max}, \mathbf{h}(t), \mathbf{I}(t)\}$. This collection inherently splits between hidden and measurable components. Measurable metrics include equipment readiness $\mathbf{v}(t) = \{v_m(t)|u_m \in \mathcal{U}\}$, predefined power limits $\mathbf{E}_{max} = \{E_{m,max}|u_m \in \mathcal{U}\}$, plus power shortages $\mathbf{F}(t) = \{F_m(t)|u_m \in \mathcal{U}\}$. Furthermore, artificial ULAoI shortages corresponding to $\mathbf{Q}^{AoI}(t) = \{Q_m^{AoI}(t)|u_m \in \mathcal{U}\}$, $\mathbf{Q}^{K}(t) = \{Q_m^{K}(t)|u_m \in \mathcal{U}\}$, alongside $\mathbf{Q}^{Z}(t) = \{Q_m^{Z}(t)|u_m \in \mathcal{U}\}$ belong here. Conversely, EMI intensity $\mathbf{I}(t) = \{I_{m,n}(t)|u_m \in \mathcal{U}, c_n \in \mathcal{C}\}$ coupled with connection quality $\mathbf{h}(t) = \{h_{m,n}(t)|u_m \in \mathcal{U}, c_n \in \mathcal{C}\}$ remain hidden. This happens because signaling overheads arise alongside restricted equipment computational capabilities. Predictions facilitated via ULAoI-DT provide approximations for $\mathbf{I}(t)$ and $\mathbf{h}(t)$.

(2) Action space: Let our action space equal $\mathbf{A}(t) = \mathbf{a}(t) \otimes \mathbf{b}(t) \otimes \mathbf{x}(t)$. Herein, Cartesian multiplication corresponds to $\otimes$.

(3) Reward function: We establish the reward function equaling problem **P3**'s primary minimization goal, represented by $\Gamma(t)$.

8.3.2 Algorithm implementation

Figure 8.2 illustrates our presented methodology's comprehensive architecture. Running upon that edge server, this setup incorporates one primary DQN model, denoted by $\mathbf{v}_{main}$. Additionally, it features an accompanying target DQN setup $\mathbf{v}_{target}$, sharing identical architectural traits with $\mathbf{v}_{main}$. Evaluating state-action combinations (specifically, computing Q-values) relies upon that primary framework. Meanwhile, enhancing learning steadiness while supporting this main model's training process remains that target framework's responsibility. Furthermore, employing an experience replay strategy allows reusing past historical information. Doing so trains both DQN frameworks, consequently breaking data correlation whilst boosting overall learning optimality. Specifically, contrasting against traditional DQN approaches [23], our introduced technique deliberately evaluates those detrimental impacts caused by elevated DT AoI concerning training efficacy. Consequently, every stored observation inside that experience replay buffer receives distinct ULAoI-driven prioritization. This tactic purposefully diminishes

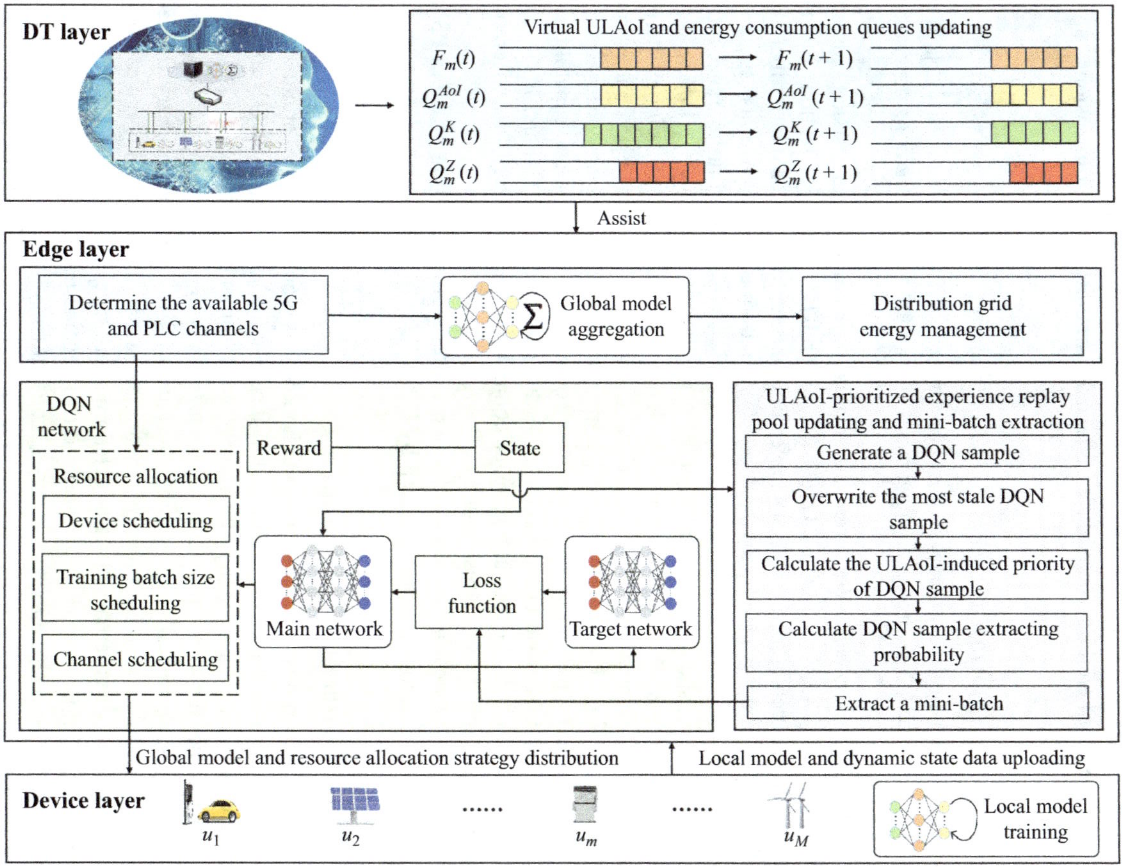

Figure 8.2 The detailed framework of the proposed algorithm

selection likelihoods regarding data points possessing excessive AoI during model training, ultimately elevating algorithmic execution. Executing this framework involves three distinct stages: starting parameter initialization, executing decisions formulated via ULAoI-DT, alongside conducting ULAoI-prioritized operations.

8.3.2.1 Initialization

At the beginning, assign zero to every virtual queue backlog, plus the scheduling variables concerning the device, the training batch size, alongside the channel.

8.3.2.2 ULAoI-DT-assisted action drawing and execution

Initially, with ULAoI-DT's assistance, this edge server identifies the complete set comprising available multi-mode PIoT channels. Subsequently, relying upon the Q value $\mathbf{Q}(\mathbf{S}(t), \mathbf{A}(t), \mathbf{v}_{main})$, an action $\tilde{\mathbf{A}}(t)$ is drawn by the edge server. This generated action contains specific scheduling strategies for the device, the training batch size, plus the channel, which are then distributed to end devices. Any scheduled device, like u_m, performs its local model training according to the assigned training batch size following (8.8). Afterward, through its scheduled channel, it transmits both dynamic state data and the updated local model back to the central edge server. Following this, executing global model aggregation is handled by the edge server via (8.16).

8.3.2.3 ULAoI-prioritized learning

Based on (8.18), this edge server refreshes DT_m's AoI parameter $\zeta_m(t)$. Simultaneously, following expressions (8.21), (8.22), (8.23), combined with (8.24), it modifies that energy deficit queue denoted by $F_m(t+1)$. It also adjusts those virtual ULAoI deficit queues represented by $Q_m^{AoI}(t+1)$, $Q_m^K(t+1)$, alongside $Q_m^Z(t+1)$. Afterward, utilizing formula (8.25), computing $\Gamma(t)$ gets handled by the edge server, which subsequently shifts toward state $\mathbf{S}(t+1)$. We construct one DQN sample mathematically defined as $\mathbf{J}(t) = \{\mathbf{S}(t), \tilde{\mathbf{A}}(t), \Gamma(t), \mathbf{S}(t+1), \mathbf{Q}(t)\}$. Within this structure, we define the parameter $\mathbf{Q}(t) = \{\mathbf{Q}^{AoI}(t), \mathbf{Q}^K(t), \mathbf{Q}^Z(t)\}$. This generated $\mathbf{J}(t)$ gets inserted inside our experience replay pool, denoted by $\mathcal{R}(t)$. This insertion deliberately overwrites its oldest stored DQN sample, designated as $\mathbf{J}(t-E)$. Herein, E signifies that maximum capacity regarding $\mathcal{R}(t)$. Let us mathematically express that specific ULAoI-induced priority concerning any e-th sample contained within this experience replay pool via

$$\kappa^{t-e}(t) = [\frac{1}{M}\sum_{m=1}^{M}(Q_m^{AoI}(t-e) + V_m^K Q_m^K(t-e) + V_m^Z Q_m^Z(t-e))^2]^{-1}. \tag{8.26}$$

In particular, significantly elevated priority scores are granted whenever any evaluated sample exhibits a reduced ULAoI deficit.

Relying upon that specific ULAoI-induced priority, computing the extraction probability regarding any e-th sample proceeds via

$$p^e(t) = \frac{\kappa^{t-e}(t)}{\sum_{i=1}^{E} \kappa^{t-i}(t)}. \tag{8.27}$$

Following this, guided by our derived probability distribution $\mathbf{p}(t) = \{p^e(t)\}$, retrieving exactly I individual items from that established experience replay pool gets executed by this edge server. These gathered items subsequently construct one mini-batch denoted by $\tilde{\mathcal{R}}(t)$, satisfying the condition $I < E$. We formulate this corresponding DQN loss function utilizing the expression as

$$\begin{aligned}\theta(t) = \frac{1}{I} \sum_{\mathbf{J}(t-e) \in \tilde{\mathcal{R}}(t)} & p^e(t)(\Gamma^{t-e}(t) \\ & + \rho \mathbf{Q}(\mathbf{S}^{t-e}(t+1), \tilde{\mathbf{A}}t-e(t+1), \mathbf{v}_{target}) \\ & - \mathbf{Q}(\mathbf{S}^{t-e}(t), \tilde{\mathbf{A}}t-e(t), \mathbf{v}_{main}))^2.\end{aligned} \tag{8.28}$$

Within this mathematical formulation, ρ signifies our designated discount factor.

Ultimately, modifying $\mathbf{v}_{main}$ happens at this edge server, strictly applying that standard gradient descent method, mathematically expressed via

$$\mathbf{v}_{main} = \mathbf{v}_{main} - \psi \nabla_{\mathbf{v}_{main}} \theta(t), \tag{8.29}$$

where ψ represents that defined DQN learning step. Furthermore, refreshing our designated target network via the equality $\mathbf{v}_{target} = \mathbf{v}_{main}$ occurs periodically, precisely upon reaching every T_0 iterations.

Our introduced algorithm successfully secures the required ULAoI guarantee utilizing two distinct mechanisms. Initially, recognizing any existing AoI deviation becomes possible by monitoring those established virtual ULAoI deficit queues. Whenever substantial virtual ULAoI deficits emerge, they necessitate mandatory resource allocation adjustment. This strategic adaptation systematically diminishes AoI, thereby preventing any potential ULAoI constraint violation. Secondly, establishing a highly dependable ULAoI guarantee is accomplished through mitigating those detrimental impacts caused by excessively large AoI during our resource allocation optimization. Specifically, leveraging that calculated ULAoI-induced priority actively prevents normal DQN training from utilizing historical samples exhibiting substantial AoI.

8.4 Performance results and discussions

Aiming at empirically validating that Web X.0 DT technologies effectively promote sustainable energy systems, we investigate a specific simulation scenario regarding distribution grid energy management. Within this setup, exactly 200 5G BSs supply peak shaving alongside valley filling ancillary services through discharging and charging their corresponding energy storage units. Echoing the methodology in [24], minimizing both load fluctuation and BS operation cost represents our core energy management objective. This gets accomplished via jointly optimizing those volumes concerning sold energy plus purchased energy. Our model considers residential areas, commercial zones, alongside industrial districts, representing three different geographical regions. That initial daily load curve is presented by Figure 8.3(a) [25]. Furthermore, typical load curves characterizing 5G BS operations across those three areas, combined with average PV power alongside time-of-use (TOU) price trends, appear within Figure 8.3(b) and (c). By gathering information at five-minute intervals, we construct exactly 2400 training samples regarding energy management corresponding to every individual area. Every single training sample incorporates a specific timestamp, 5G BS load, available PV power, corresponding TOU price, plus the overarching grid load. We define our evaluated loss function utilizing that performance gap separating results attained via CPLEX's optimal execution from those generated through our proposed energy management model. Within Table 8.2, we summarize those remaining detailed simulation parameters [26,27].

To evaluate performance, we introduce two state-of-the-art schemes as baselines. Our initial baseline represents the multi-agent DRL-based resource allocation algorithm (MDRL) [28]. Integrating DT assistance, this methodology pursues the minimization of that global loss function via jointly regulating the channel alongside the training batch size. Furthermore, the AoI-aware FL-based communication resource allocation algorithm (AoI-FLC) [29] serves as another comparative framework. By embedding AoI awareness, it similarly diminishes the aforementioned global loss function through coordinating both the device and the channel. Notably, both AoI-FLC and MDRL intrinsically lack ULAoI awareness. Additionally, leveraging DT assistance remains unsupported within the AoI-FLC scheme.

Figure 8.4(a) depicts how said global loss function evolves across successive iterations. Upon reaching $t = 200$, evaluated against MDRL alongside AoI-FLC, our introduced methodology successfully diminishes the aforementioned global loss function by exactly 36.01% plus 11.16%, respectively. This notable enhancement stems from ULAoI-DT supplying highly precise empirical approximations regarding both EMI power and channel gain. Leveraging such vital assistance, our presented framework effectively mitigates PER while simultaneously expanding the assigned training batch size.

Figure 8.4(b) plots how said global loss function varies with ζ_{max}^{AoI}. When ζ_{max}^{AoI} grows, those global loss functions concerning our proposed algorithm plus AoI-FLC initially drop before subsequently climbing. This phenomenon happens because, accompanying expanded ζ_{max}^{AoI}, both our presented scheme and AoI-FLC prioritize shrinking this global loss function. Nevertheless, experiencing excessively immense AoI inevitably generates substantial DT inconsistency coupled with severe information estimation deviation. Consequently, these inaccuracies

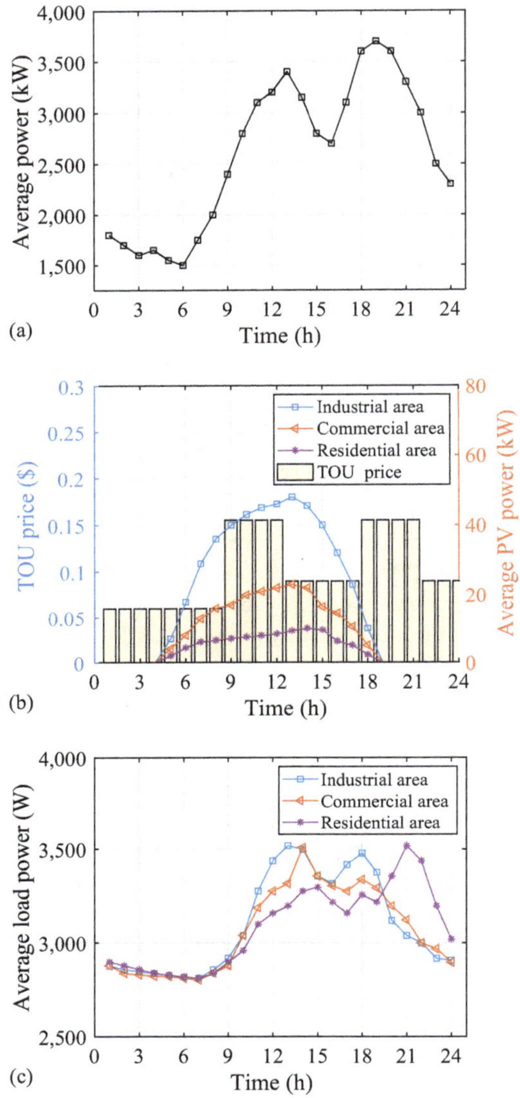

Figure 8.3 Distribution grid energy management scenario: (a) original daily load curve; (b) time-of-use (TOU) price and PV power in industrial, commercial, and residential areas; and (c) typical load curves of 5G BS in industrial, commercial, and residential areas

provoke an escalating global loss function. Meanwhile, outcomes produced via MDRL maintain constant global loss function values despite varying ζ_{max}^{AoI}. Such stability emerges because integrating any ULAoI constraint remains ignored by MDRL, which exclusively targets minimizing said global loss function.

Table 8.2 Simulation parameters

Parameter	Value	Parameter	Value
T	200	M	20
N_1, N_2	3,2	τ_g	10 ms
ξ_0	10^6 cycles	N_0	−114 dBm
$B_{m,n}$	0.2 MHz	$\alpha, \sigma^{th}, \xi^{th}$	0.15, 0.4, 0.2
ψ	0.001	ρ	0.99
V_m^{AoI}, V_m^E	3,3	V_m^K, V_m^Z	10,20
$\|\mathcal{F}_m(t)\|$	100 kbits	$\|\omega_m(t)\|$	200 kbits

Additionally, Figure 8.4(c) depicts that global loss function evaluated against $E_{m,max}$. Alongside growing $E_{m,max}$, those global loss functions generated through our proposed algorithm, MDRL, plus AoI-FLC experience reductions until hitting steady floors. This trend materializes because expanding $E_{m,max}$ grants devices a broader energy budget. Consequently, they successfully diminish their localized loss metrics by enlarging that assigned training batch size. Once $E_{m,max}$ exceeds specific limits, overarching channel quality alongside strict ULAoI constraints emerge as fresh bottlenecks, severely restricting further global loss function minimization.

Within Figure 8.5(a)–(c), we illustrate that extreme event occurrence probability denoted mathematically by $\Pr(\zeta_m(t) > \zeta_{max}^{AoI})$, alongside those CCDFs concerning both variables $Z_m(t)$ plus $K_m(t)$. These evaluated CCDFs regarding $Z_m(t)$ and $K_m(t)$ characterize how likely both metrics surpass established threshold boundaries. Consequently, such parameters directly indicate our system's ULAoI guarantee capability. Upon reaching $t = 200$, evaluated against MDRL alongside AoI-FLC, our introduced technique successfully fulfills that strict extreme event occurrence probability constraint. Furthermore, it diminishes this specific likelihood by exactly 84.54% plus 73.91%, respectively. Assuming said CCDF reaches exactly 0.01, our presented methodology significantly surpasses both AoI-FLC alongside MDRL. Specifically, regarding $K_m(t)$, enhancements hit 54.85% plus 82.11%, whereas $Z_m(t)$ improvements reach 84.52% alongside 97.34%. Provided numerical outcomes validate how effectively our suggested scheme eradicates any extreme event occurrence. Additionally, thanks to strict ULAoI guarantee implementations, it successfully mitigates that severe long-tail distribution characterizing AoI.

Figures 8.6–8.8 display those empirical energy management results concerning 5G BS energy storage across residential, commercial, plus industrial zones, respectively. Observations indicate how localized 5G BSs within every sector acquire electricity between 0:00 and 8:00. This strategic procurement reduces overall power purchase cost leveraging that specific valley load tariff.

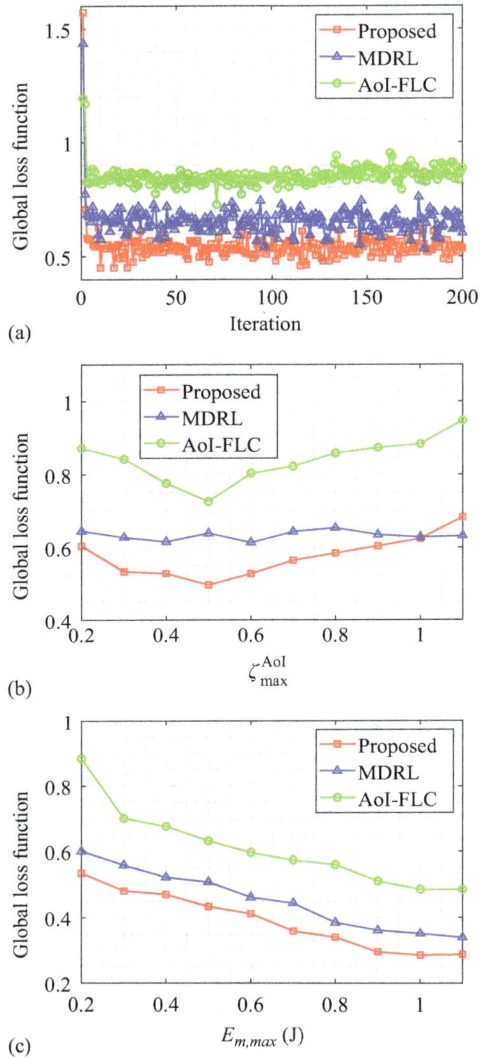

Figure 8.4 System performance: (a) global loss function versus iterations; (b) global loss function versus ζ_{max}^{AoI}; and (c) global loss function versus $E_{m,max}$

Concurrently, these automated actions deliver vital valley filling auxiliary service. Nevertheless, industrial zone 5G BSs discharge their stored power predominantly during 18:00–21:00. Conversely, equivalent infrastructure located throughout residential districts trades electricity backward between 9:00 and 11:00. Such behavioral divergence originates fundamentally from differing peak load time

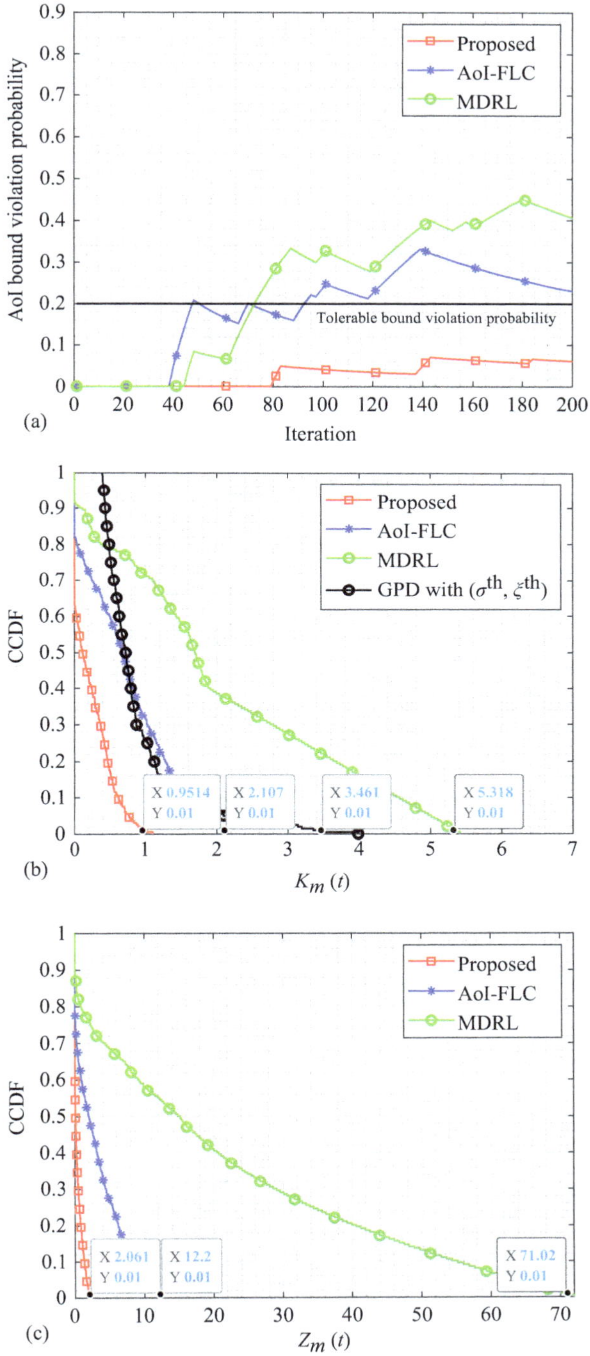

Figure 8.5 *ULAoI guarantee capability ($\sigma^{th} = 0.4$, $\xi^{th} = 0.2$): (a) AoI bound violation probability* $\Pr(\zeta_m(t) > \zeta_{max}^{AoI})$*; (b) CCDF of* $K_m(t)$*; and (c) CCDF of* $Z_m(t)$

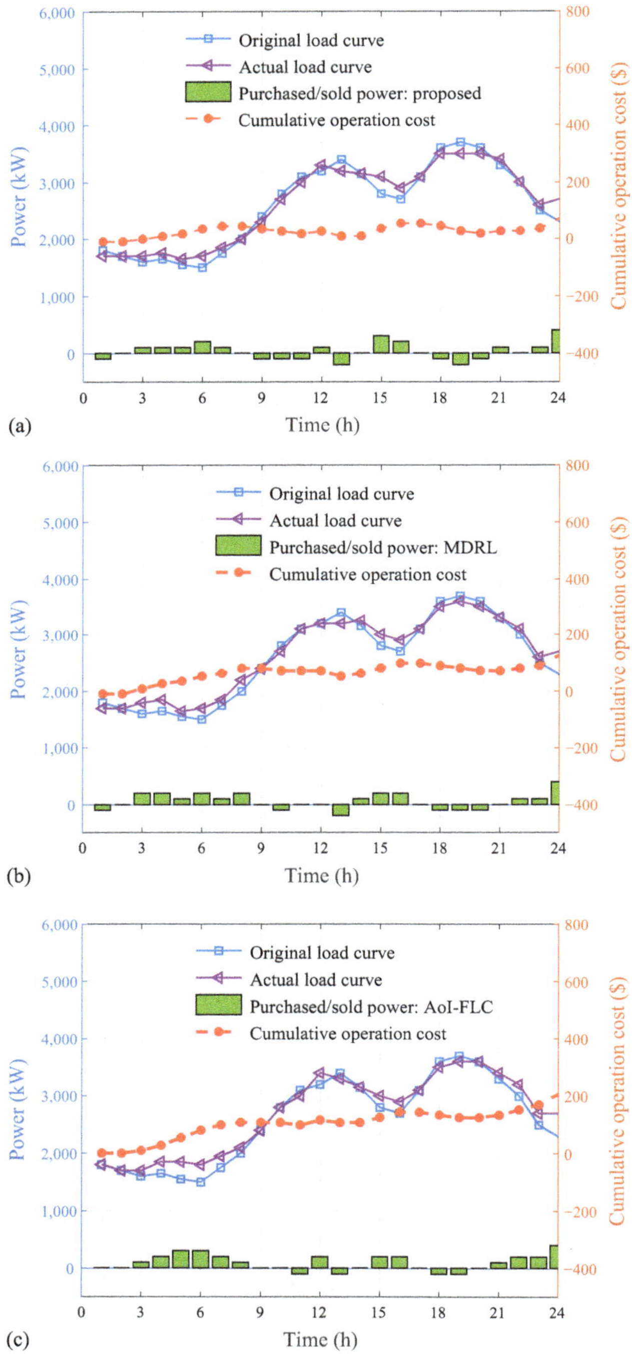

Figure 8.6 Energy management results of 5G BS energy storage in industrial area: (a) the proposed algorithm; (b) MDRL; and (c) AoI-FLC

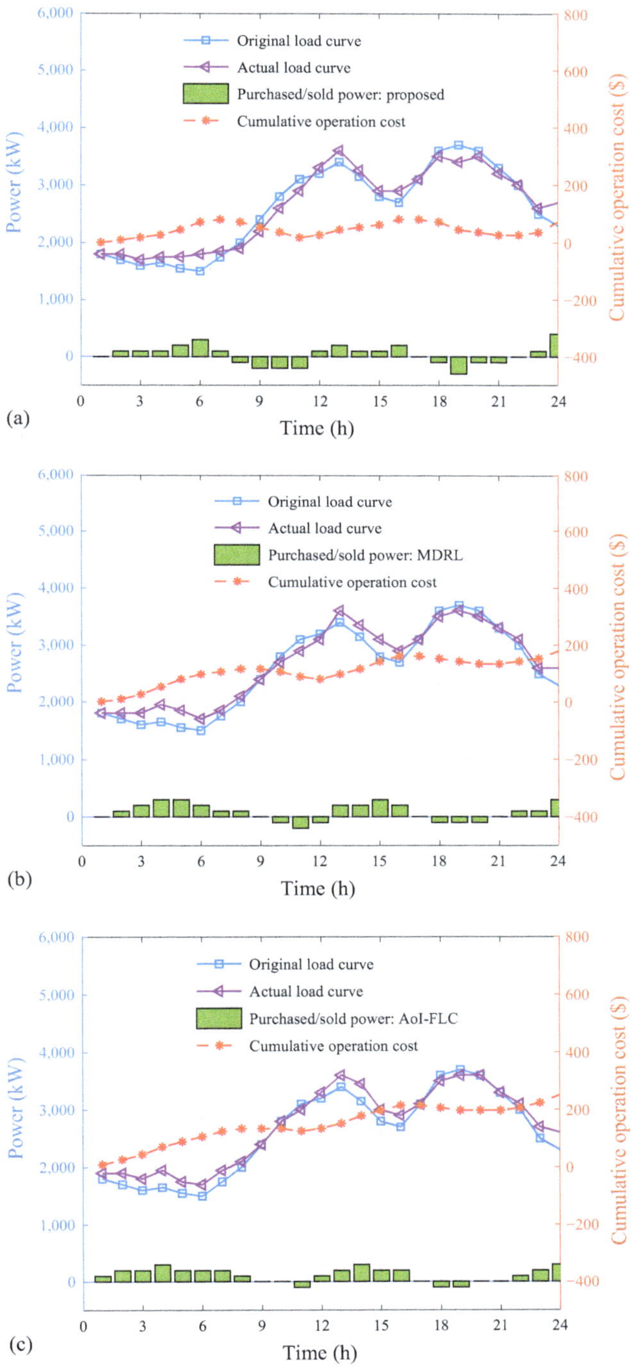

Figure 8.7 Energy management results of 5G BS energy storage in commercial area: (a) the proposed algorithm; (b) MDRL; and (c) AoI-FLC

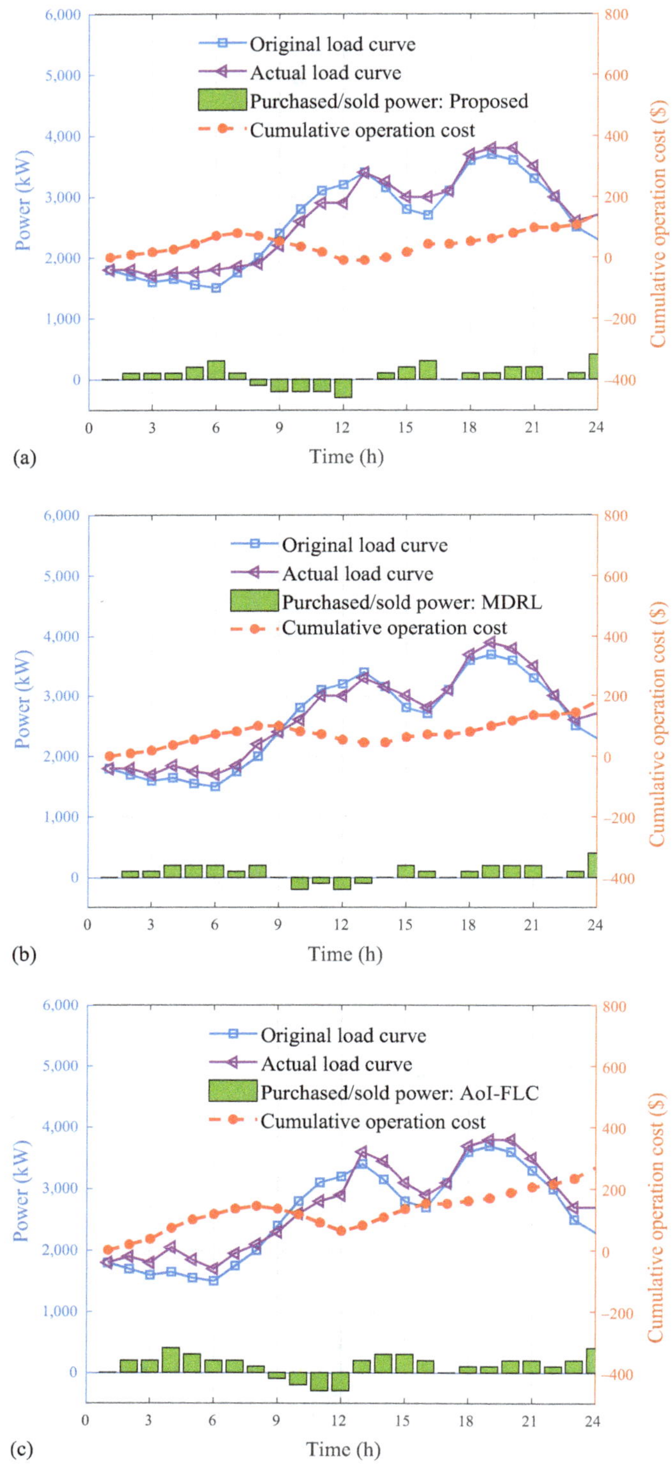

Figure 8.8 Energy management results of 5G BS energy storage in residential area: (a) the proposed algorithm; (b) MDRL; and (c) AoI-FLC

windows defining these distinct regions. Exploiting this inherent complementarity regarding peak load time helps optimize overarching distribution grid energy management. Moreover, such strategies effectively alleviate recurring daily load fluctuation while simultaneously lowering that total cumulative operation cost characterizing deployed 5G BSs.

Evaluated numerical outcomes depicted within Figures 8.6–8.8 confirm ULAoI-DT's capability delivering exceptional performances regarding valley filling alongside peak cutting operations. Furthermore, it generates substantial cumulative operation cost savings. Examining that residential area specifically, benchmarked against AoI-FLC alongside MDRL, our ULAoI-DT framework successfully suppresses load curve fluctuation by roughly 46.66% plus 20%. Similarly, total cumulative operation cost drops by nearly 5.7% alongside 1.7%, respectively. This performance advantage emerges because our presented algorithm intelligently acquires that optimal scheduling strategy concerning channels, training batch sizes, plus devices. By incorporating ULAoI awareness alongside essential DT assistance, this methodology dramatically accelerates global loss function reduction while fostering enhanced energy management precision. Summarizing these findings, such verified capabilities regarding stabilizing grid fluctuations plus reducing operational costs clearly prove something vital. Specifically, modern Web X.0 DTs transcend simple theoretical constructs, acting instead as highly practical accelerators driving our ongoing green energy transition. Through facilitating robust seamless integration concerning distributed renewables, these advanced technologies establish one concrete pathway toward successfully achieving those critical UN SDGs. Consequently, they help guarantee an upcoming future energy Internet remaining universally accessible, highly resilient, and remarkably efficient.

Within this current chapter, we formulated an innovative ULAoI-DT-assisted resource allocation framework tailored toward comprehensive distribution grid energy management. Our primary emphasis centers around utilizing emerging Web X.0 technologies for significantly advancing both UN SDG 13 alongside UN SDG 7. Minimizing that overarching global loss function during energy management model training constitutes our central objective. We accomplish this goal via jointly optimizing channel assignments, training batch size configurations, and overall scheduling of devices. All actions remain strictly bounded by extended long-term energy consumption limitations plus rigid ULAoI constraints. Consequently, formulating this mathematical problem yields extreme complexity, featuring intertwined multidimensional constraints alongside severe computational challenges. Drawing inspiration directly from virtual queue theory coupled with the standard Markov decision process, we successfully converted this initially intractable optimization problem. It became a perfectly solvable framework wherein real-time data support alongside reliable constraint guarantee are delivered directly via Web X.0's ULAoI-DT. This happens through seamlessly integrating control, communication, plus sensing operations inside one unified closed-loop system. Furthermore, introducing our novel ULAoI-prioritized DQN algorithm helped expertly optimize resource allocation. By strategically leveraging those massive data-driven advantages inherent within Web X.0, we can effectively cut carbon emissions while simultaneously boosting overall renewable energy utilization. Conducted extensive simulations rigorously validate our scheme's undeniable superiority regarding reducing costs, actively stabilizing grids, plus consistently advancing SDGs. Ultimately, adopting this innovative Web X.0-enabled approach casts exciting new light upon optimizing sustainable energy resource allocation, thereby rapidly accelerating tomorrow's green energy transition.

Suggested further readings

1. **Cyber-Physical Interdependence for Power System Operation and Control**
   IEEE Transactions on Smart Grid (2025)
   This literature explores the critical interdependence between the information and physical layers in modern power systems. The study utilizes digital twin and co-simulation technologies to evaluate and identify potential system vulnerabilities. It provides a macro-theoretical foundation for deploying ULAoI-DT architectures in distribution grid energy management.
2. **Adaptive Asynchronous Federated Learning for Digital Twin Driven Smart Grid**
   IEEE Transactions on Smart Grid (2025)
   Targeting the issue of equipment state update delays in smart grids, this research designs a framework combining asynchronous federated learning with digital twins. The methodology aligns closely with the optimization direction of the AoI-FLC and DQN models evaluated in this chapter. It offers a contemporary approach to resolving non-IID data distribution and local model obsolescence.
3. **Distributed Model Predictive Control Strategy for Multi-energy Virtual Power Plant Based on Digital Twin**
   IEEE Transactions on Smart Grid (2025)
   This paper focuses on digital twin multi-time-scale rolling optimization strategies for multi-energy virtual power plants. It directly addresses the coordination of source-load-storage, the flexible aggregation of distributed resources, and dynamic carbon emission trading optimization. The research provides a valuable extension for readers exploring comprehensive testing schemes and AI scheduling technologies for diverse virtual power plant configurations.
4. **Smart Home HVAC Digital Twin ML Meta-Model for Electric Power Distribution Systems With Solar PV and CTA-2045 Controls**
   IEEE Transactions on Industry Applications (2025)
   The authors propose an ultra-fast hybrid machine learning model as a digital twin for precise PV and load predictive control in distribution networks. The research discusses characterizing equipment as generalized energy storage to unify control protocols between virtual power plants and underlying devices. This presents a practical application reference for low-carbon situation assessment and flexible resource scheduling platforms.

Standards

(1) **NIST Framework and Roadmap for Smart Grid Interoperability Standards** serves as a fundamental policy framework. It standardizes the system architecture, data transmission mechanisms and cybersecurity specifications required for the integrated application of smart grid technologies and high-fidelity digital twins.
(2) **IEEE 2030 Series (Guide for Smart Grid Interoperability),** formulates unified technical specifications. It helps define and regulate the interoperability between power systems, end-user applications and distributed energy resources within smart grid scenarios.
(3) **EU NIS2 Directive (Directive 2022/2555)** constitutes a key European cybersecurity regulation. It underscores the importance of advanced simulation and real-time monitoring technologies represented by digital twins, which support risk assessment and safety assurance for critical infrastructure including smart grids.

References

[1] Lin Y, Gao Z, Du H, *et al.* Blockchain-Based Semantic Information Sharing and Pricing for Web 3.0. *IEEE Trans Network Sci Eng*. 2024;11(5):3918–30.
[2] Abishu HN, Seid AM, Jhaveri RH, Gadekallu TR, Erbad A, and Guizani M. Blockchain-Empowered Resource Allocation in HAPS-Assisted IoV Digital Twin Networks: A Federated DRL Approach. *IEEE Trans Intell Veh*. 2025;10(10):4710–26.
[3] Tang L, Wang A, Xia B, Tang Y, and Chen Q. Research on Integrated Sensing, Communication Resource Allocation, and Digital Twin Placement Based on Digital Twin in IoV. *IEEE Internet Things J*. 2025;12(11):17300–15.
[4] Noroozi K, Todd TD, Zhao D, and Karakostas G. Age of Information in Digital Twin Migration. *IEEE Trans Veh Technol*. 2025;74(10):16281–94.
[5] Zhuo X, Wu W, Tang L, Qu F, and Shen X. Value of Information-Based Packet Scheduling Scheme for AUV-Assisted UASNs. *IEEE Trans Wireless Commun*. 2024;23(7):7172–85.
[6] Wang L, Liang H, Tang Y, Mao G, Zhang H, and Zhao D. DRL-Based Joint Resource Allocation and Platoon Control Optimization for UAV-Hosted Platoon Digital Twin. *IEEE Internet Things J*. 2024;11(22):37114–26.
[7] Xu YH, Ding RX, Xu XR, Zhou D, and Zhou W. A DDPG Hybrid with Graph Scheme for Resource Management in Digital Twin-Assisted Biomedical Cyber-Physical Systems. *IEEE Trans Network Serv Manage*. 2025; 22(4):2956–70.
[8] Fu X, Wang T, Pace P, Aloi G, and Fortino G. Low-AoI Data Collection for UAV-Assisted IoT with Dynamic Geohazard Importance Levels. *IEEE Internet Things J*. 2025;12(11):18279–302.

[9] Tang L, Pu Z, Hou Q, Fang D, and Chen Q. Deterministic Delay of Digital-Twin-Assisted End-to-End Network Slicing in Industrial IoT via Multiagent Deep Reinforcement Learning. *IEEE Internet Things J.* 2025;12(1):1064–80.

[10] Zhou Z, Jia Z, Liao H, *et al.* Secure and Latency-Aware Digital Twin Assisted Resource Scheduling for 5G Edge Computing-Empowered Distribution Grids. *IEEE Trans Ind Informat*. 2022;18(7):4933–43.

[11] Wang L, Liang H, Mao G, *et al.* Resource Allocation for Dynamic Platoon Digital Twin Networks: A Multi-Agent Deep Reinforcement Learning Method. *IEEE Trans Veh Technol*. 2024;73(10):15609–20.

[12] Dai Y, Zhao J, Zhang J, Zhang Y, and Jiang T. Federated Deep Reinforcement Learning for Task Offloading in Digital Twin Edge Networks. *IEEE Trans Network Sci Eng*. 2024;11(3):2849–63.

[13] Lan J, Jia X, and Kou Z. Age of Information and Energy-Efficiency Optimization in RIS-Assisted Vehicular Edge Computing via Hierarchical Deep Reinforcement Learning. *IEEE Internet Things J.* 2025;12(20):43681–95.

[14] Al-Habob AA, Tabassum H, and Waqar O. Non-Orthogonal Age-Optimal Information Dissemination in Vehicular Networks: A Meta Multi-Objective Reinforcement Learning Approach. *IEEE Trans Mob Comput*. 2024;23(10):9789–803.

[15] Pan C, Wang Z, Liao H, *et al.* Asynchronous Federated Deep Reinforcement Learning-Based URLLC-Aware Computation Offloading in Space-Assisted Vehicular Networks. *IEEE Trans Intell Transp Syst*. 2023;24(7):7377–89.

[16] Kurma S, Sharma PK, Singh K, Mumtaz S, and Li C. URLLC-Based Cooperative Industrial IoT Networks with Non-Linear Energy Harvesting. *IEEE Trans Ind Informat*. 2023;19(2):2078–88.

[17] Zhou Z, Wang Z, Yu H, *et al.* Learning-Based URLLC-Aware Task Offloading for Internet of Health Things. *IEEE J Sel Areas Commun*. 2021;39(2):396–410.

[18] Wang C, Yu X, Xu L, and Wang W. Energy Efficient Task Scheduling Based on Traffic Mapping in Heterogeneous Mobile Edge Computing: A Green IoT Perspective. *IEEE Trans Green Commun Netw*. 2023;7(2):972–82.

[19] Zhang Y, Zhao X, Zhou Z, *et al.* Robust Resource Allocation for Lightweight Secure Transmission in Multicarrier NOMA-Assisted Full Duplex IoT Networks. *IEEE Internet Things J*. 2022;9(9):6443–57.

[20] Liao H, Zhou Z, Zhao X, *et al.* Learning-Based Context-Aware Resource Allocation for Edge-Computing-Empowered Industrial IoT. *IEEE Internet Things J*. 2020;7(5):4260–77.

[21] Neely MJ. *Stochastic Network Optimization with Application to Communication and Queueing Systems*. San Rafael, CA: Morgan and Claypool; 2010.

[22] Wang C, Yu X, Xu L, Wang Z, and Wang W. Multimodal Semantic Communication Accelerated Bidirectional Caching for 6G MEC. *Future Gener Comput Syst*. 2023;140:225–37.

[23] Zhu B, Chi K, Liu J, Yu K, and Mumtaz S. Efficient Offloading for Minimizing Task Computation Delay of NOMA-Based Multi-Access Edge Computing. *IEEE Trans Commun*. 2022;70(5):3186–203.

[24] Jia L, Liao H, Zhou Z, *et al.* Social-Aware Learning-Based Online Energy Scheduling for 5G Integrated Smart Distribution Power Grid. *IEEE Trans Computat Social Syst*. 2024;11(3):3157–67.

[25] Wang Y, Zheng Y, Xue H, and Mi Y. Optimal Dispatch of Mobile Energy Storage for Peak Load Shifting Based on Enhanced Firework Algorithm. *Autom Elect Power Syst*. 2021;45(5):48–56.

[26] Mahmood A, Hong Y, Ehsan MK, and Mumtaz S. Optimal Resource Allocation and Task Segmentation in IoT-Enabled Mobile Edge Cloud. *IEEE Trans Veh Technol*. 2021;70(12):13294–303.

[27] Ma X, Liu Z, Wang Y, and Feng X. Research on Photovoltaic Absorption Capacity of 5G Base Station Considering Communication Load Migration and Energy Storage Dynamic Backup. *Trans Electr Technol*. 2023;38 (21):5832–45.

[28] Lu Y, Huang X, Zhang K, Sabita M, and Zhang Y. Low-Latency Federated Learning and Blockchain for Edge Association in Digital Twin Empowered 6G Networks. *IEEE Trans Ind Informat*. 2021;17(7):5098–107.

[29] Liu X, Qin X, Chen H, Liu Y, Liu B, and Zhang P. editors. *Age-Aware Communication Strategy in Federated Learning with Energy Harvesting Devices*. Kansas City, MO: IEEE Int. Conf. Commun. (ICCC); 2021.

Chapter 9

Ethical, social, and legal challenges in Web X.0

Dasaradharami Reddy Kandati[1], S. Anusha[2], B. Koteswara Rao[2], N. Ashalatha[3] and Thippa Reddy Gadekallu[4,5]

Abstract

Web X.0 represents the next phase in the evolution of the Internet, characterized by the convergence of artificial intelligence, blockchain, decentralized infrastructures, and immersive technologies. Although these technologies enable advanced digital services, improved connectivity, and increased user autonomy, they also introduce significant ethical, social, and legal challenges that require careful consideration. This chapter examines key governance issues in Web X.0 ecosystems, including data ownership, privacy protection, algorithmic bias, decentralized governance, misinformation, and regulatory adaptation. It analyzes how the integration of intelligent and distributed technologies transforms digital interactions, economic systems, and institutional responsibilities across sectors such as education, healthcare, finance, and public governance. Furthermore, the chapter proposes a multi-layered governance framework that incorporates ethical-by-design principles, transparent artificial intelligence practices, decentralized accountability mechanisms, and adaptive regulatory strategies. By integrating technological analysis with socio-legal perspectives, the chapter identifies approaches for balancing technological innovation with user rights, digital trust, and inclusive access. The study provides a conceptual framework to support policymakers, researchers, and system designers in guiding the responsible development and governance of Web X.0, with the aim of promoting transparent, equitable, and human-centric digital ecosystems.

[1]Department of Computer Science and Engineering, Navodaya Institute of Technology, India
[2]Department of Computer Science and Engineering, N.B.K.R. Institute of Science and Technology, India
[3]Department of Computer Science and Engineering, Annamacharya Institute of Technology and Sciences, India
[4]College of Mathematics and Computer Science, Zhejiang A&F University, China
[5]Division of Research and Development, Lovely Professional University, India

9.1 Introduction

The rapid evolution of digital technologies is transforming the structure and governance of the Internet. The emerging concept of Web X.0 represents a new phase in the development of the web, characterized by increasingly intelligent, immersive, and decentralized digital environments [1]. Although these developments promise significant improvements in connectivity, automation, and digital interaction, they also introduce complex ethical, social, and legal challenges that must be carefully addressed.

As digital ecosystems become more interconnected and data-driven, issues such as privacy protection, algorithmic bias, data ownership, accountability, and digital inequality are gaining increasing attention among researchers, policymakers, and technology developers [2]. The integration of advanced technologies into everyday digital services raises critical questions about how personal data is collected, processed, and governed, as well as how automated decision-making systems influence social and economic outcomes.

Beyond technical innovation, the development of Web X.0 requires a broader governance perspective that considers the societal impact of digital transformation [3]. Ethical concerns such as fairness, transparency, and user autonomy must be balanced with technological progress, while legal systems must adapt to address emerging challenges related to decentralized platforms, digital identities, and cross-border data governance [4]. At the same time, social issues such as the digital divide, accessibility, and technological inclusion play an important role in determining whether the benefits of Web X.0 are distributed equitably.

This chapter focuses specifically on the ethical, social, and legal dimensions of Web X.0, moving beyond purely technical discussions to examine the broader implications of this evolving digital ecosystem. It analyzes key challenges related to data governance, algorithmic accountability, privacy protection, and regulatory frameworks, while also highlighting the social consequences of emerging digital infrastructures [5]. In addition, the chapter proposes governance strategies and policy recommendations aimed at supporting the responsible, inclusive, and sustainable development of Web X.0 technologies.

By examining these issues through an integrated perspective, the chapter contributes to the growing discussion on how technological innovation can be aligned with ethical principles, social responsibility, and effective legal governance, ensuring that the future web evolves in a manner that benefits society as a whole.

9.2 Ethical, social, and legal challenges: an integrated framework for Web X.0

The emergence of Web X.0, an advanced, interconnected digital ecosystem integrating artificial intelligence (AI), blockchain technologies, immersive environments, and decentralized infrastructures introduces profound ethical, social, and governance challenges [6]. Unlike earlier iterations of the web that relied heavily on centralized platforms, Web X.0 emphasizes decentralization, automation, and data-driven intelligence. While these developments promise greater transparency, user empowerment, and innovation, they also raise complex issues surrounding digital rights, accountability, trust, and regulation. This section examines five key areas: digital rights and data ownership, AI ethics, governance of decentralized networks, disinformation, and digital trust, and the evolving role of governments and regulatory frameworks.

9.2.1 Digital rights and data ownership

Digital rights refer to the fundamental rights of individuals in digital environments, including control over personal data, privacy, identity, and freedom of expression online [7]. In the context of Web X.0, these rights take on new dimensions as decentralized technologies enable users to participate more directly in data generation, storage, and exchange. Traditionally, user data in Web 2.0 environments have been largely controlled by centralized platforms such as social media companies and cloud service providers [6]. These entities collect, analyze, and monetize user data, often without transparent consent or an equitable distribution of value.

The Web X.0 technologies aim to redefine this relationship through decentralized data ownership models. Blockchain-based identity systems and decentralized storage frameworks allow individuals to retain ownership of their digital identities and personal information [8]. Concepts such as self-sovereign identity (SSI) and user-controlled data vaults enable users to determine how their data is shared and monetized. Instead of centralized platforms extracting value from user data, decentralized ecosystems propose mechanisms where individuals can grant temporary access to their data via smart contracts while maintaining ownership [9].

However, implementing true data ownership raises several practical and legal challenges. One critical issue concerns the definition of ownership itself: whether individuals can fully "own" data that may involve multiple parties or collective contributions. Furthermore, decentralized storage solutions complicate the enforcement of data protection laws, particularly when data fragments are distributed across global networks. Regulatory frameworks such as the General Data Protection Regulation (GDPR) in the European Union emphasize rights such as the "right to be forgotten," which can be difficult to enforce in immutable blockchain systems [10].

Another debate concerns the economic implications of data ownership. Emerging models propose that users may receive compensation for providing access to their data in digital marketplaces [11]. Although these models promise greater fairness, they also risk creating new inequalities if individuals feel pressured to monetize sensitive personal information. Consequently, ensuring equitable digital rights in Web X.0 requires balancing technological innovation with ethical safeguards, legal clarity, and user empowerment.

9.2.2 AI ethics

AI plays a central role in Web X.0, enabling autonomous decision-making, intelligent data analysis, and personalized digital services [12]. However, the increasing reliance on AI systems raises significant ethical concerns related to bias, transparency, accountability, and autonomy. AI algorithms often rely on large datasets that may contain embedded social biases, potentially leading to discriminatory outcomes in areas such as employment, financial services, or content moderation [13].

Algorithmic bias has become a widely discussed issue in AI ethics. Studies have demonstrated that machine learning models can unintentionally reinforce racial, gender, or socioeconomic disparities if training data reflect historical inequalities. In decentralized environments, where AI models can operate across distributed networks and interact with blockchain-based infrastructures, addressing bias becomes even more complex [14]. The responsibility for correcting algorithmic outcomes may be difficult to assign when systems operate autonomously across multiple nodes or organizations.

Transparency and explainability are also critical challenges. Many advanced AI systems operate as "black boxes," making it difficult for users and regulators to understand how decisions are made [15]. In Web X.0 ecosystems, AI agents may perform automated tasks such as financial transactions, identity verification, or content filtering without direct human oversight. Without transparent decision-making processes, users may struggle to contest unfair outcomes or errors.

Existing ethical frameworks provide guidance on how to address these issues. Organizations such as UNESCO, the European Commission, and the IEEE Global Initiative on Ethics of Autonomous and Intelligent Systems have published guidelines that emphasize principles such as fairness, accountability, transparency, and human oversight [16]. These frameworks highlight the importance of "human-in-the-loop" governance, where automated systems remain subject to human supervision and ethical evaluation.

Real-world cases further illustrate the importance of AI ethics. Instances of biased facial recognition systems and controversial algorithmic decisions in financial lending or predictive policing have demonstrated the societal impact of flawed AI models. As Web X.0 integrates AI with decentralized infrastructures, ensuring ethical oversight requires collaborative governance mechanisms, transparent algorithms, and continuous auditing processes [17].

9.2.3 Governance of decentralized networks

One of the defining features of Web X.0 is the shift from centralized control toward decentralized governance. Blockchain networks, distributed ledgers, and peer-to-peer architectures enable digital ecosystems where authority is distributed among participants rather than concentrated in a single organization [18]. While decentralization offers advantages such as transparency and resilience, it also raises fundamental questions about governance: who makes decisions, how rules are enforced, and how conflicts are resolved.

In decentralized systems, governance often occurs through consensus mechanisms and community participation. Blockchain platforms commonly use protocols such as proof-of-work, proof-of-stake, or other consensus models to validate transactions and maintain network integrity [19]. However, governance extends beyond technical validation to include decisions about protocol updates, economic incentives, and community standards.

Decentralized Autonomous Organizations (DAOs) have emerged as a prominent governance model in Web X.0 ecosystems. DAOs use smart contracts to enable collective decision-making, where stakeholders vote on proposals using tokens or other governance mechanisms. This structure aims to create transparent and democratic governance processes without relying on centralized leadership.

Despite their promise, DAOs and decentralized governance models face several challenges. Token-based voting systems may concentrate power among large stakeholders, potentially undermining the goal of decentralization. Additionally, decision-making processes can be slow and complex when large communities are involved. Legal recognition of DAOs also remains uncertain in many jurisdictions, raising questions about liability, accountability, and regulatory compliance.

Another governance challenge involves dispute resolution. Without centralized authorities, decentralized networks must develop mechanisms to address conflicts, fraudulent activity, and protocol vulnerabilities. Some platforms implement arbitration systems or decentralized courts, while others rely on community consensus. Nevertheless, ensuring effective governance in decentralized ecosystems remains an ongoing experiment that combines technological design with social coordination.

9.2.4 Disinformation and digital trust

The proliferation of digital platforms and automated content systems has significantly affected the dynamics of information dissemination. Web X.0 technologies—including AI-generated media, decentralized social networks, and immersive digital environments—have the potential to both amplify and mitigate the spread of misinformation [20]. On one hand, advanced generative AI systems can produce convincing synthetic media, such as deepfakes, that blur the boundaries between authentic and fabricated content. On the other hand, blockchain-based verification systems may provide new mechanisms for establishing the authenticity and traceability of information.

Disinformation campaigns have already demonstrated their ability to influence public opinion, elections, and social stability. The integration of AI-driven content generation into decentralized platforms may accelerate the scale and speed at which misinformation spreads [21]. Unlike traditional social media platforms that can implement centralized moderation policies, decentralized networks may lack clear mechanisms for removing harmful or misleading content.

The erosion of digital trust represents a major societal risk. When users cannot reliably distinguish between accurate and manipulated information, confidence in digital platforms and institutions may decline. Scholars have emphasized that trust is a critical component of digital ecosystems, influencing user participation, economic transactions, and civic engagement.

Several technological and policy solutions have been proposed to address these challenges. AI-based detection systems can identify patterns associated with synthetic media or coordinated misinformation campaigns [22]. Blockchain technologies may support content provenance frameworks that record the origin and modification history of digital media [23]. Additionally, collaborative fact-checking initiatives and digital literacy programs can help users critically evaluate online information.

Ultimately, addressing disinformation in Web X.0 requires a combination of technological innovation, responsible platform design, and public awareness. Maintaining digital trust will depend on establishing transparent systems that balance freedom of expression with mechanisms to reduce harmful misinformation.

9.2.5 Role of governments and regulation

As Web X.0 technologies reshape digital ecosystems, governments and regulatory institutions face the challenge of adapting existing legal frameworks to emerging technological realities. Policymakers must balance the need to encourage innovation with the responsibility to protect citizens from potential harms such as privacy violations, algorithmic discrimination, and financial instability [24].

Different regions have adopted varying regulatory approaches. The European Union has implemented comprehensive frameworks such as the GDPR and the Artificial Intelligence Act, which emphasize data protection, algorithmic transparency, and risk-based regulation of AI systems [25]. These policies aim to establish clear standards for responsible technology development while safeguarding individual rights.

In contrast, other regions have taken more flexible or market-driven approaches, focusing on innovation and industry-led standards [26]. However, the rapid evolution of decentralized technologies often challenges traditional regulatory models that rely on identifiable intermediaries or centralized entities. For example, regulating decentralized finance platforms or blockchain-based networks can be difficult when operations are distributed across multiple jurisdictions.

Another key issue concerns the global nature of Web X.0 technologies. Digital platforms and blockchain networks operate across national boundaries, requiring international cooperation to establish consistent standards and enforcement mechanisms [27]. Organizations such as the Organisation for Economic Co-operation and Development (OECD), United Nations, and World Economic Forum have initiated discussions on global digital governance frameworks to address these challenges.

At the same time, excessive regulation may hinder innovation by imposing strict compliance requirements on emerging technologies. Policymakers therefore face a delicate balance between fostering technological progress and ensuring ethical accountability [28]. Adaptive regulatory approaches—such as regulatory sandboxes, collaborative policymaking, and technology-neutral legal frameworks—may provide more effective mechanisms for governing the rapidly evolving Web X.0 landscape.

Table 9.1 presents a mapping between key ethical challenges in Web X.0 ecosystems and potential regulatory responses.

This table helps connect technological risks with concrete policy responses, supporting the governance framework discussed in the chapter.

Table 9.2 presents a mapping between key ethical challenges in Web X.0 ecosystems and potential regulatory responses.

Web X.0 governance requires collaboration among multiple actors.

This table clarifies the multi-stakeholder nature of Web X.0 governance, emphasizing shared responsibility across sectors.

Figure 9.1 illustrates the interrelationship between digital rights, AI ethics, decentralized governance, and algorithmic governance within the Web X.0

Table 9.1 Mapping ethical challenges to regulatory and governance responses

Ethical challenge	Description	Potential regulatory response	Governance mechanisms
Privacy erosion	Continuous data collection across AI, IoT, and XR platforms threatens user privacy	Data protection laws, privacy-by-design mandates	Decentralized identity systems, encrypted storage, and user-controlled data vaults
Algorithmic bias	AI systems may reinforce racial, gender, or socioeconomic inequalities	Algorithmic transparency requirements, mandatory AI audits	Explainable AI (XAI), fairness evaluation metrics
Data ownership ambiguity	Unclear ownership rights over personal or shared digital data	Legal recognition of user data ownership	Blockchain-based SSI and smart contracts
Disinformation and deepfakes	AI-generated content can manipulate public opinion	Platform accountability regulations, digital media authentication policies	Blockchain-based content provenance tracking
Governance of decentralized systems	Difficulty assigning responsibility in distributed networks	Regulatory frameworks for DAOs and decentralized platforms	Token governance models, decentralized dispute resolution
Digital divide	Unequal access to advanced digital infrastructure	Public investment in digital infrastructure and education	Digital literacy programs and inclusive technology design
Environmental impact	High energy consumption from AI models and blockchain networks	Sustainability regulations for digital infrastructure	Energy-efficient consensus mechanisms and green computing

Table 9.2 Stakeholders and responsibilities in Web X.0 governance

Stakeholder	**Primary responsibilities**	**Key challenges**
Governments and regulators	Develop legal frameworks, protect digital rights, and enforce accountability	Regulating decentralized technologies across jurisdictions
Technology companies	Design ethical AI systems and secure digital platforms	Balancing innovation with regulatory compliance
Developers and researchers	Create transparent, fair, and secure technological architectures	Addressing bias and ensuring responsible system design
Civil society organizations	Advocate for digital rights and public interest	Monitoring corporate and governmental power
Users and digital citizens	Responsible participation in digital ecosystems	Understanding data rights and digital literacy
International organizations	Coordinate global digital governance standards	Aligning diverse regulatory approaches

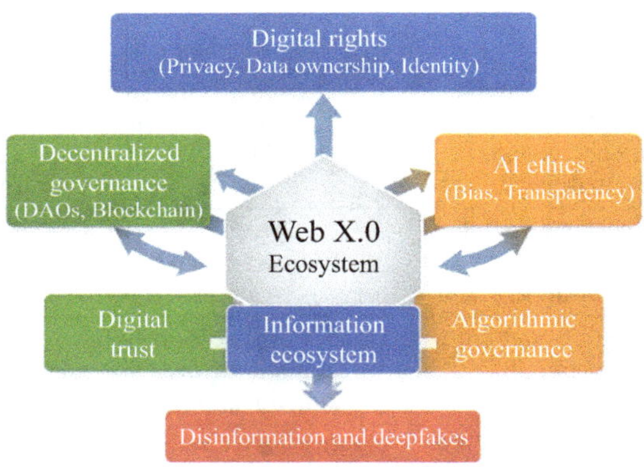

Figure 9.1 Conceptual framework linking digital rights, AI ethics, and disinformation

ecosystem. These components collectively influence digital trust and the dynamics of information integrity, including the risks posed by disinformation and deepfakes.

This framework illustrates the interconnected ethical dimensions of Web X.0:

- Digital rights form the foundation of user autonomy and privacy.
- AI ethics influences how automated decision systems operate.

- Decentralized governance structures regulate blockchain-based systems.
- Digital trust depends on transparent and accountable systems.
- Disinformation risks arise when AI-generated content spreads without verification.

9.3 Future directions, emerging trends, and open research questions

The evolution toward Web X.0 represents not only merely a technological transition but also a profound transformation of the digital ecosystem in which AI, decentralized infrastructures, extended reality, and ubiquitous connectivity converge [29]. While these technologies promise unprecedented levels of personalization, transparency, and user autonomy, they simultaneously generate complex ethical, legal, and societal challenges that require sustained interdisciplinary research and policy innovation.

Future research must therefore focus not only on technological capabilities but also on governance frameworks, ethical design principles, and social inclusion strategies that ensure Web X.0 develops in ways that benefit society as a whole [6]. The following subsections explore key emerging trends, future research directions, and unresolved questions that will shape the next generation of the Internet.

Table 9.3 presents key future research directions in Web X.0, highlighting emerging areas that are expected to shape next-generation intelligent and decentralized web systems. Ethical AI focuses on developing responsible decision-making frameworks to ensure transparency and trustworthiness in automated systems. Privacy-preserving AI emphasizes secure data sharing techniques to protect user information while enabling intelligent services. Decentralized governance explores DAO-based models to promote transparency and community-driven decision-making. Green computing addresses the need for energy-efficient

Table 9.3 Future directions in Web X.0 research

Research area	Description	Expected impact
Ethical AI	Responsible decision systems	Trustworthy AI systems
Privacy-preserving AI	Secure data sharing mechanisms	Enhanced user privacy protection
Decentralized governance	DAO-based governance systems	Transparent decision-making
Green computing	Energy-efficient blockchain infrastructure	Sustainable digital ecosystems
Digital identity	SSI management	Secure authentication and access control

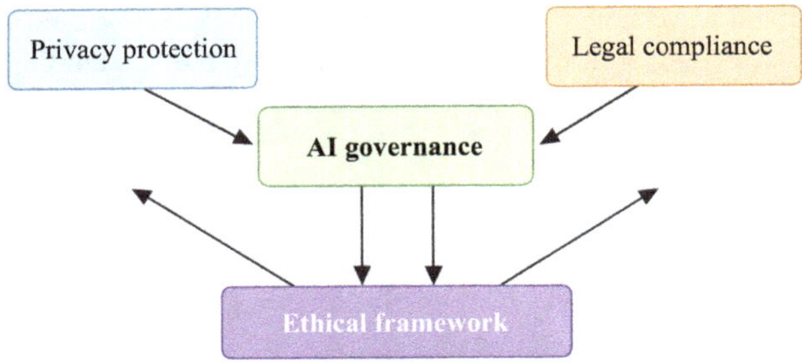

Figure 9.2 Ethical governance framework for Web X.0 systems

blockchain and computing infrastructures to support sustainable digital ecosystems. Additionally, digital identity research concentrates on SSI mechanisms that enhance secure authentication and user control over personal data. Collectively, these directions provide a roadmap for building secure, ethical, and sustainable Web X.0 environments.

Figure 9.2 illustrates the ethical governance framework for Web X.0 systems, highlighting the key components required to ensure responsible and trustworthy digital ecosystems. Privacy protection and legal compliance act as foundational pillars that guide AI governance in managing data usage, decision-making, and automated processes. AI governance integrates these regulatory and ethical considerations to develop transparent and accountable intelligent systems. The resulting ethical framework ensures that Web X.0 technologies operate within acceptable societal, legal, and moral boundaries. This framework supports the development of secure, fair, and user-centric digital environments while addressing emerging challenges related to data privacy, regulatory compliance, and responsible AI deployment.

9.3.1 Human-centric and ethical-by-design web architectures

One of the most significant future directions for Web X.0 involves the transition toward human-centric digital ecosystems, in which ethical considerations are embedded directly into system architectures rather than addressed retrospectively through regulation.

Traditional digital platforms have often prioritized efficiency, scalability, and profit optimization over ethical considerations [30]. As Web X.0 integrates autonomous AI agents, decentralized infrastructures, and immersive environments, this approach becomes increasingly problematic. Ethical-by-design frameworks propose that values such as fairness, accountability, transparency, and privacy must be integrated into technology development from the earliest design stages.

9.3.1.1 Emerging technological approaches

Several emerging approaches aim to operationalize ethical design principles:

Explainable artificial intelligence

Many AI systems used in Web X.0 environments operate as complex machine learning models whose internal decision-making processes are difficult to interpret [31]. Explainable artificial intelligence (XAI) seeks to address this problem by creating models whose decisions can be understood and audited by humans [32]. For example, financial institutions increasingly deploy XAI to justify automated loan decisions and prevent discriminatory outcomes.

Privacy-preserving machine learning

Techniques such as federated learning and differential privacy allow AI models to learn from distributed data sources without exposing sensitive information [33]. These methods may enable large-scale data analysis while protecting individual privacy, which is particularly important in sectors such as healthcare and smart city infrastructures.

Ethical auditing mechanisms

Future Web X.0 systems may incorporate automated auditing frameworks that continuously evaluate AI behavior for fairness, bias, and compliance with regulatory standards [34].

Case study: AI bias in hiring algorithms

A widely cited example illustrating the importance of ethical design is the case of automated hiring algorithms used by technology companies. In several instances, machine learning systems trained on historical hiring data developed biases that disadvantaged female candidates because historical data reflected male-dominated hiring practices. Such outcomes highlight the need for algorithmic auditing and diverse training datasets.

Multiple perspectives

Researchers and policymakers hold differing views regarding how ethical principles should be implemented:

- **Technological optimism perspective:** Advocates argue that technological solutions such as XAI and fairness metrics can effectively mitigate ethical risks.
- **Critical governance perspective:** Others argue that ethical design cannot rely solely on technical fixes; instead, strong regulatory frameworks and democratic oversight are necessary to ensure accountability.

Figure 9.3 illustrates the emerging Web X.0 technology ecosystem, highlighting the convergence of key enabling technologies that collectively shape the next-generation Internet. AI, Blockchain, extended reality, and the Internet of Things (IoT) act as foundational components that contribute to the development of Web X.0. AI enables intelligent automation and decision-making, while blockchain provides decentralized trust and secure transactions. Extended reality enhances immersive digital experiences, and IoT facilitates real-time connectivity between physical and digital environments. The integration of these technologies leads to

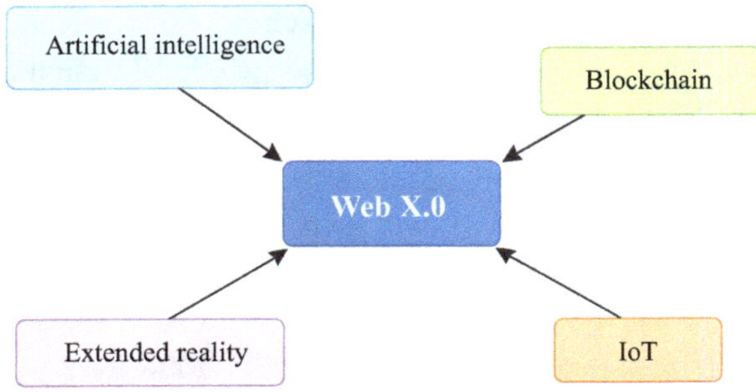

Figure 9.3 Emerging Web X.0 technology ecosystem

Table 9.4 Emerging trends and open research questions

Emerging trend	**Research challenge**	**Open question**
Metaverse integration	Identity security	How can virtual identities be securely managed?
Decentralized web	Governance models	Who governs decentralized platforms and decision-making?
AI automation	Bias mitigation	How can fairness and transparency be ensured in AI systems?
Blockchain adoption	Scalability	How can transaction speed and scalability be improved?
Web intelligence	Privacy concerns	How can personal data privacy be protected effectively?

the creation of a decentralized, intelligent, and immersive Web X.0 ecosystem capable of supporting advanced digital applications and services.

Open research questions

Several fundamental questions remain unresolved:

- How can ethical principles be systematically encoded into autonomous digital infrastructures?
- What quantitative metrics can effectively measure fairness and transparency in large-scale AI ecosystems?
- How can human oversight be maintained when decision-making is increasingly automated?

Table 9.4 outlines the major emerging trends in Web X.0 along with their corresponding research challenges and open questions. Metaverse integration raises concerns regarding secure management of virtual identities, while decentralized

Figure 9.4 Open research challenges in Web X.0

web technologies introduce governance complexities in distributed environments. AI automation continues to evolve, creating challenges related to fairness, transparency, and bias mitigation in intelligent decision-making systems. Blockchain adoption highlights scalability and transaction efficiency issues that require further innovation. Additionally, web intelligence advancements raise critical privacy concerns, emphasizing the need for effective personal data protection mechanisms. These emerging trends and associated research questions provide valuable directions for future investigation and technological advancement in Web X.0 ecosystems.

Figure 9.4 illustrates the open research challenges in Web X.0, emphasizing four critical areas that influence the development of next-generation web technologies. Security focuses on protecting decentralized systems, smart contracts, and user data from emerging cyber threats. Privacy addresses challenges related to data ownership, identity protection, and secure information sharing in distributed environments. Scalability highlights the need for efficient infrastructure capable of supporting large-scale decentralized applications and real-time interactions. Governance involves developing regulatory frameworks and decentralized decision-making mechanisms to ensure transparency and accountability. These interconnected challenges collectively define the research landscape of Web X.0 and guide future innovations toward secure, scalable, and ethically governed digital ecosystems.

9.3.2 Decentralized governance and digital policy frameworks

A defining feature of Web X.0 is the shift from centralized platform governance toward decentralized decision-making structures based on blockchain technologies and distributed networks.

Decentralized governance models promise greater transparency and resilience but also challenge traditional legal and institutional frameworks [35].

DAOs

One of the most prominent governance innovations emerging in Web X.0 is the DAO. DAOs use smart contracts to facilitate collective decision-making among stakeholders [36].

For example, blockchain-based financial platforms often rely on DAO structures in which token holders vote on protocol changes, treasury management, and governance policies.

Case study: the DAO hack

A significant early example illustrating the risks of decentralized governance occurred in 2016 when a blockchain investment fund known as "The DAO" was exploited due to a vulnerability in its smart contract code. The incident resulted in the loss of millions of dollars in digital assets and forced the underlying blockchain network to implement a controversial software fork to recover the funds.

This event sparked an ongoing debate about whether decentralized systems should prioritize immutability or allow intervention when catastrophic failures occur.

Governance challenges

Despite their innovative potential, decentralized governance models face several challenges:

- **Power concentration:** Large token holders may dominate voting processes.
- **Legal uncertainty:** Many jurisdictions lack clear regulatory frameworks for DAOs.
- **Dispute resolution:** Decentralized systems often lack effective mechanisms for resolving conflicts.

Policy perspectives

Different policy approaches are currently being explored globally:

Regulatory intervention approach

Some policymakers argue that governments must regulate decentralized platforms to protect users from financial risks and fraud.

Innovation-first approach

Others argue that excessive regulation may undermine innovation and discourage technological experimentation.

Open research questions

Future research must address questions such as:

- How can decentralized governance systems balance efficiency with democratic participation?
- What legal frameworks are necessary to recognize and regulate DAOs?
- How can global regulatory coordination address the cross-border nature of decentralized networks?

9.3.3 Privacy, data sovereignty, and digital identity

As Web X.0 systems increasingly rely on data-driven services and immersive digital interactions, issues surrounding privacy, digital identity, and data ownership will become central societal concerns [37].

Traditional Web 2.0 platforms often maintain centralized control over user data, enabling large technology companies to monetize personal information through targeted advertising and analytics [38]. Web X.0 technologies propose alternative models based on user-controlled data infrastructures.

SSI

SSI frameworks enable individuals to maintain control over their digital identities without relying on centralized authorities. Blockchain-based identity systems allow users to selectively share credentials with service providers while retaining ownership of their data [8].

Case study: digital identity systems

Several governments and organizations are experimenting with decentralized digital identity systems. For example, Estonia's digital governance infrastructure provides citizens with secure digital identities that enable access to government services, banking, and healthcare platforms.

While such systems enhance efficiency and security, they also raise concerns regarding surveillance and potential misuse of personal data.

Ethical concerns in immersive environments

Future Web X.0 platforms integrating extended reality technologies may collect highly sensitive data, including:

- Biometric information
- Eye movement patterns
- Emotional responses
- Behavioral interactions

Such data not only enable unprecedented levels of personalization but also create new forms of digital surveillance.

Multiple perspectives

The debate around data ownership includes contrasting viewpoints:

Data monetization advocates

Some researchers propose that individuals should be able to sell access to their data through decentralized data marketplaces.

Privacy protection advocates

Others argue that commodifying personal data may pressure individuals—especially those in economically vulnerable positions—to trade privacy for financial benefits.

Open research questions

- How can data ownership rights be effectively implemented in decentralized ecosystems?

- What mechanisms ensure informed consent in highly automated digital environments?
- How can privacy protections evolve alongside technologies such as IoT and extended reality?

9.3.4 Inclusive digital ecosystems and bridging the digital divide

Although Web X.0 technologies promise transformative capabilities, they also risk exacerbating existing digital inequalities.

Access to high-speed Internet, computational resources, and advanced digital technologies remains uneven across regions and socioeconomic groups.

Global digital inequality

According to international development reports, billions of people worldwide still lack reliable Internet access. Without targeted policies, the benefits of Web X.0 may remain concentrated in technologically advanced regions.

Case study: remote education during global crises

During global disruptions such as the COVID-19 pandemic, digital learning platforms enabled educational continuity for many students [39]. However, millions of learners in developing regions were unable to participate due to limited Internet access and inadequate digital infrastructure.

This example highlights how digital inequalities can amplify existing social disparities.

Strategies for digital inclusion

Future policy initiatives should prioritize:

- Expanding affordable broadband infrastructure
- Developing low-cost computing technologies
- Promoting digital literacy education
- Designing accessible interfaces for diverse populations

Open research questions

- How can Web X.0 technologies be designed to support low-resource environments?
- What policies can ensure equitable access to emerging digital infrastructures?
- How can marginalized communities participate meaningfully in decentralized digital economies?

9.3.5 Sustainable and green web infrastructure

The rapid expansion of Web X.0 technologies also raises significant environmental concerns. Large-scale AI models, blockchain networks, and immersive computing systems require substantial computational resources and energy consumption [40].

Environmental impact of emerging technologies

Certain blockchain networks have historically consumed large amounts of electricity due to energy-intensive consensus mechanisms [41]. Similarly, training advanced machine learning models may require enormous computational resources.

Emerging sustainability solutions

Researchers are exploring several strategies to reduce the environmental footprint of digital infrastructures:

- Energy-efficient blockchain consensus mechanisms
- Green data centers powered by renewable energy
- Edge computing architectures that reduce centralized processing loads
- Optimization techniques for energy-efficient AI training

Case study: green blockchain initiatives

Several blockchain platforms have transitioned from energy-intensive consensus mechanisms to more efficient alternatives, significantly reducing electricity consumption while maintaining network security [42,43].

Open research questions

- How can sustainable computing practices be integrated into large-scale digital infrastructures?
- What policy incentives can encourage environmentally responsible technology development?
- How can digital innovation be aligned with global sustainability goals?

9.3.6 Interdisciplinary collaboration for responsible innovation

The complexity of Web X.0 ecosystems requires collaboration across multiple disciplines, including computer science, law, ethics, economics, sociology, and public policy.

Technological innovation alone cannot address the societal implications of digital transformation.

Emerging collaborative approaches

Several initiatives are exploring interdisciplinary approaches to responsible technology development:

- Ethical AI research centers
- International technology governance forums
- Public–private partnerships for digital innovation

Institutional challenges

Despite increasing recognition of interdisciplinary collaboration, institutional barriers remain:

- Academic disciplines often operate in isolation
- Policy development may lag behind technological innovation
- Global governance frameworks remain fragmented

Open research questions

- What institutional structures can support interdisciplinary research on digital governance?
- How can ethical considerations be integrated into engineering education and technological design processes?
- What global governance models can effectively regulate emerging digital ecosystems?

9.3.7 Societal impact and long-term technological futures

Ultimately, the long-term success of Web X.0 will depend on whether it creates sustainable, inclusive, and trustworthy digital ecosystems.

Future research must therefore examine not only technical performance but also broader societal impacts.

Transformations in labor and economic systems

Automation and AI-driven decision-making may reshape labor markets by altering the demand for specific skills [44,45]. While automation may improve productivity, it may also displace certain categories of workers.

Human–machine interaction

Web X.0 technologies integrating extended reality and AI may transform how humans interact with digital systems. These interactions may become increasingly immersive, emotional, and autonomous.

Democratic governance in digital environments

A critical challenge for future societies will be maintaining democratic values, transparency, and accountability in digital ecosystems dominated by automated decision-making and decentralized governance structures [46,47].

Key long-term questions

- How will Web X.0 reshape economic models of digital ownership and value creation?
- What ethical dilemmas will arise as human–machine interactions become more immersive?
- How can societies maintain democratic governance in technologically mediated environments?

Addressing these questions will help ensure that Web X.0 evolves in ways that enhance human well-being, strengthen digital rights, and promote inclusive technological progress.

9.4 Conclusion

Web X.0 represents a transformative stage in the evolution of the Internet, characterized by the integration of AI, decentralized infrastructures, immersive technologies, and data-driven digital ecosystems. This chapter examined the ethical, social, and legal challenges emerging from this convergence, including concerns related to data ownership, privacy protection, algorithmic bias, governance of decentralized networks, disinformation, and regulatory adaptation. While these technologies offer significant opportunities for enhanced transparency, personalization, and user empowerment, they also introduce complex risks that require careful management. Addressing these challenges demands a balanced approach that combines ethical-by-design technological development, inclusive digital policies, and adaptive governance mechanisms. Ultimately, the responsible advancement of Web X.0 depends on aligning technological innovation with principles of trust, fairness, accountability, and societal well-being to ensure that the next generation of the web benefits individuals, institutions, and global digital communities.

Suggested further readings

1. Floridi, L. (2023). The ethics of artificial intelligence: Principles, challenges, and opportunities.
2. Zuboff, S. (2023). The age of surveillance capitalism. In Social theory re-wired (pp. 203-213). Routledge.
3. Unesco. (2022). Recommendation on the ethics of artificial intelligence. United Nations Educational, Scientific and Cultural Organization.
4. Cannarsa, M. (2021). Ethics guidelines for trustworthy AI. The Cambridge handbook of lawyering in the digital age, 30, 97-283.
5. Comert, O. (2020). Blockchain revolution: how the technology behind bitcoin and other cryptocurrencies is changing the world.

Standards

The following international standards and governance frameworks are relevant to the ethical, social, legal, and technical governance issues discussed in this chapter:

- **ISO/IEC 42001:2023** – Artificial intelligence management system (AIMS) requirements.
- **ISO/IEC 23894:2023** – Guidance on risk management for artificial intelligence.
- **ISO/IEC 27001:2022** – Information security management systems requirements.
- **ISO/IEC 27701:2019** – Privacy information management systems.
- **ISO/IEC 29100:2024** – Privacy framework.

- **IEEE 7000-2021** – Model process for addressing ethical concerns during system design.
- **IEEE 7001-2021** – Transparency of autonomous systems.
- **IEEE 7003-2024** – Algorithmic bias considerations.
- **NIST AI Risk Management Framework (AI RMF 1.0, 2023)** – Framework for trustworthy AI risk management.
- **General Data Protection Regulation (GDPR) (EU) 2016/679** – European Union data protection regulation.
- **EU Artificial Intelligence Act (2024)** – Risk-based regulation of AI systems in the European Union.

References

[1] Mattiello, H. (2024). Sailing the X. 0 wave theory: Navigating the future of civilization. *Intelligent and Sustainable Manufacturing*, 1(2), 10021.

[2] Ijaiya, H. (2024). Balancing data privacy and technology advancements: Navigating ethical challenges and shaping policy solutions. *International Journal of Research Publication and Reviews*, 4(7), 3405–3416.

[3] Mohammadian, H. D., and Wittberg, V. (2024). Edu-tech mirrors culture as an infrastructure and solution for future-oriented engineering Edu-tech challenges in the digital transformation and industry 5.0/Society 6.0 Era via X. 0 wave/age theory. *In 2024 IEEE Global Engineering Education Conference (EDUCON)* (pp. 1–10). IEEE.

[4] Mustafa, G., Rafiq, W., Jhamat, N., Arshad, Z., and Rana, F. A. (2025). Blockchain-based governance models in e-government: A comprehensive framework for legal, technical, ethical and security considerations. *International Journal of Law and Management*, 67(1), 37–55.

[5] Eke, D., and Stahl, B. (2024). Ethics in the governance of data and digital technology: An analysis of European data regulations and policies. *Digital Society*, 3(1), 11.

[6] Bernovskis, A., Sceulovs, D., and Stibe, A. (2024). Society 5.0: Shaping the future of e-commerce. *Journal of Open Innovation: Technology, Market, and Complexity*, 10(4), 100391.

[7] Siagian, R., Siahaan, L., and Hamzah, M. I. (2023). Human rights in the digital era: Online privacy, freedom of speech, and personal data protection. *Journal of Digital Learning and Distance Education*, 2(4), 548–558.

[8] Ahmed, M. R., Islam, A. M., Shatabda, S., and Islam, S. (2022). Blockchain-based identity management system and self-sovereign identity ecosystem: A comprehensive survey. *IEEE Access*, 10, 113436–113481.

[9] Balcerzak, A. P., Nica, E., Rogalska, E., Poliak, M., Klieštik, T., and Sabie, O. M. (2022). Blockchain technology and smart contracts in decentralized governance systems. *Administrative Sciences*, 12(3), 96.

[10] Angón, O. C. (2024). General data protection regulation, right to be forgotten, blockchain technology and human rights. *The Age of Human Rights Journal*, (23), e8702–e8702.

[11] Azcoitia, S. A., and Laoutaris, N. (2022). A survey of data marketplaces and their business models. *ACM SIGMOD Record*, 51(3), 18–29.

[12] Khan, I. U., Ouaissa, M., Ouaissa, M., Fayaz, M., and Ullah, R. (Eds.). (2024). *Artificial Intelligence for Intelligent Systems: Fundamentals, Challenges, and Applications.*

[13] Khan, F. (2025). Data justice and algorithmic bias: Understanding the social, ethical, and legal implications of algorithmic decision-making and its impact on marginalized communities. *Frontiers in Multidisciplinary Studies*, 2(01), 54–65.

[14] Al Jasem, M. S., De Clark, T., and Shrestha, A. K. (2025). Toward decentralized intelligence: A systematic literature review of blockchain-enabled AI systems. *Information*, 16(9), 765.

[15] Chaudhary, G. (2024). Unveiling the black box: Bringing algorithmic transparency to AI. *Masaryk University Journal of Law and Technology*, 18 (1), 93–122.

[16] Jedlickova, A. (2024). Ensuring ethical standards in the development of autonomous and intelligent systems. *IEEE Transactions on Artificial Intelligence*, 5(12), 5863–5872.

[17] Tyagi, A. K., and Tiwari, S. (2024). Blockchain-enabled smart healthcare applications in 6G networks. *Digital Twin and Blockchain for Smart Cities*, 459–494.

[18] Anthony Jnr, B. (2023). Distributed ledger and decentralised technology adoption for smart digital transition in collaborative enterprise. *Enterprise Information Systems*, 17(4), 1989494.

[19] Kaur, S., Chaturvedi, S., Sharma, A., and Kar, J. (2021). A research survey on applications of consensus protocols in blockchain. *Security and Communication Networks*, 2021(1), 6693731.

[20] Sundaravadivazhagan, B., Gnanasankaran, N., Raj, P., and Raja, A. S. (Eds.). (2025). *Virtual Reality and Augmented Reality with 6G Communication*. John Wiley & Sons.

[21] Rao, D. N., Mouneshwari, K., Kiran, P. R., Kumar, Y. J. N., Soy, A., and Srihari, T. (2025). AI-powered real-time misinformation detection a deep learning framework for combating fake news and deepfakes. *In 2025 International Conference on Metaverse and Current Trends in Computing (ICMCTC)* (pp. 1–4). IEEE.

[22] Saeidnia, H. R., Hosseini, E., Lund, B., Tehrani, M. A., Zaker, S., and Molaei, S. (2025). Artificial intelligence in the battle against disinformation and misinformation: A systematic review of challenges and approaches. *Knowledge and Information Systems*, 67(4), 3139–3158.

[23] Pawlicki, M., and Jahankhani, H. (2022). Advancing governance of news provenance posted on social media platforms with the use of blockchain technology. *In Social Media Analytics, Strategies and Governance* (pp. 1–30). CRC Press.

[24] Selvakumar, P., Sudheer, P., and Kannan, N. (2025). Balancing innovation and privacy: Understanding AI in the digital world. *In Digital Citizenship and the Future of AI Engagement, Ethics, and Privacy* (pp. 279–304). IGI Global Scientific Publishing.
[25] BeltrÃ¡n, M. (2025). AI algorithms under scrutiny: GDPR, DSA, AI Act and CRA as pillars for algorithmic security and privacy in the European Union. *Computers & Security*, 104628.
[26] Kulothungan, V., and Gupta, D. (2025). Towards adaptive AI governance: Comparative insights from the US, EU, and Asia. *In 2025 IEEE 11th Conference on Big Data Security on Cloud (BigDataSecurity)* (pp. 32–38). IEEE.
[27] Hung, A. H. C. (2024). How AI-enabled blockchain technology facilitates US sanctions on foreign businesses: An analysis based on international regulatory harmonization. *International Journal of Ethics and Technology*, 151.
[28] Kumar, D., and Suthar, N. (2025). Balancing innovation and regulation: Ethical frameworks for AI policy and governance. *In Navigating the Intersection of AI Policy, Technology, and Governance* (pp. 171–200). IGI Global Scientific Publishing.
[29] Alzahrani, S., Shakir, K., Yazeed, A., Salauddin, N., and Ahmed, S. (2025). Navigating the technological frontier: Tracing the journey from Library 2.0 to Library 5.0 and its impact on knowledge repositories. *Information Development*, 02666669251348907.
[30] Santoso, A., and Surya, Y. (2024). Maximizing decision efficiency with edge-based AI systems: Advanced strategies for real-time processing, scalability, and autonomous intelligence in distributed environments. *Quarterly Journal of Emerging Technologies and Innovations*, 9(2), 104–132.
[31] Barbierato, E., and Gatti, A. (2024). The challenges of machine learning: A critical review. *Electronics*, 13(2), 416.
[32] Mathew, D. E., Ebem, D. U., Ikegwu, A. C., Ukeoma, P. E., and Dibiaezue, N. F. (2025). Recent emerging techniques in explainable artificial intelligence to enhance the interpretable and understanding of AI models for human. *Neural Processing Letters*, 57(1), 16.
[33] Ma, C., Li, J., Wei, K., *et al.* (2023). Trusted AI in multiagent systems: An overview of privacy and security for distributed learning. *Proceedings of the IEEE*, 111(9), 1097–1132.
[34] Koshiyama, A., Kazim, E., Treleaven, P., *et al.* (2024). Towards algorithm auditing: Managing legal, ethical and technological risks of AI, ML and associated algorithms. *Royal Society Open Science*, 11(5), 1–34.
[35] Li, S., and Chen, Y. (2024). Governing decentralized autonomous organizations as digital commons. *Journal of Business Venturing Insights*, 21, e00450.
[36] Esposito, M., Tse, T., and Goh, D. (2025). Decentralizing governance: Exploring the dynamics and challenges of digital commons and DAOs. *Frontiers in Blockchain*, 8, 1538227.
[37] Mattiello, H. (2024). Exposing the hidden costs of 'free': Personal data commodification in the digital economy via X. 0 theory, fuzzy Delphi,

thematic analysis, and problem-solving frameworks. *Journal of Policy and Society*, 2(2), 1–53.

[38] Dixit, A. R. T. I. (2024). Web 2.0 technologies and its application. *Journal of Rural and Agricultural Research*, 24, 28–34.

[39] Adedoyin, O. B., and Soykan, E. (2023). COVID-19 pandemic and online learning: The challenges and opportunities. *Interactive learning environments*, 31(2), 863–875.

[40] Uddin, M., Obaidat, M., Manickam, S., *et al.* (2024). Exploring the convergence of Metaverse, Blockchain, and AI: A comprehensive survey of enabling technologies, applications, challenges, and future directions. *Wiley Interdisciplinary Reviews: Data Mining and Knowledge Discovery*, 14(6), e1556.

[41] Hussein, Z., Salama, M. A., and El-Rahman, S. A. (2023). Evolution of blockchain consensus algorithms: a review on the latest milestones of blockchain consensus algorithms. *Cybersecurity*, 6(1), 30.

[42] Lv, Y. (2023). Transitioning to sustainable energy: Opportunities, challenges, and the potential of blockchain technology. *Frontiers in Energy Research*, 11, 1258044.

[43] Fernandez-Carames, T. M., and Fraga-Lamas, P. (2024). A comprehensive survey on green blockchain: Developing the next generation of energy efficient and sustainable blockchain systems. *arXiv preprint arXiv*:2410.20581.

[44] Zubair, S. (2024). AI-driven automation: Transforming workplaces and labor markets. *Frontiers in Artificial Intelligence Research*, 1(3), 373–411.

[45] Bera, S., Pillai, S., Pathak, P., and Yadav, V. (2024). Navigating the AI Impact: Job markets and evolving skillsets. *In International Conference on Artificial Intelligence and Networking* (pp. 139–158). Springer Nature Singapore.

[46] Chaffer, T. J., Goins II, C. V., Okusanya, B., Cotlage, D., and Goldston, J. (2024). Decentralized governance of autonomous AI agents. *arXiv preprint arXiv*:2412.17114.

[47] Kassen, M. (2025). Blockchain and digital governance: Decentralization of decision making policy. *Review of Policy Research*, 42(1), 95–121.

Chapter 10

The future of work, business, and innovation in Web X.0

Ahmed Naeem[1], Muhammad Tariq[2] and Houbing Herbert Song[3]

Abstract

With Web X.0, a completely new paradigm of human–technology interaction that transcends the incremental improvements of its predecessors has evolved, signifying a turning point in the evolution of the digital economy. This chapter provides a comprehensive, interdisciplinary examination of the convergent organizational, social, and technological dynamics that characterize the Web X.0 era. It charts the development from Web 1.0's read-only infrastructure to Web 3.0's ownership architecture, Web 2.0's participatory platforms, and Web X.0's intelligent, immersive, and ambient computing environment. The chapter's core argument is that Web X.0 is a combination of edge computing, brain–computer interfaces, extended reality, blockchain-enabled decentralization, and artificial intelligence (AI), rather than a single technology. As a result of this convergence, decentralized autonomous organizations, tokenized contributor economies, and AI-augmented knowledge work are emerging, replacing centralized organizational hierarchies and altering employment contracts. The chapter examines how business models are being drastically rethought, from platform-based value extraction to protocol-based value distribution, and provides a methodical strategic roadmap for businesses navigating this transition. While the metaverse economy introduces entirely new degrees of digital ownership, immersive commerce, and creator-driven value creation, innovation is shown to be accelerating via self-reinforcing cycles of AI-driven discovery and open collaboration. The significance of leadership and talent development is comprehensively covered, with a particular emphasis on the life-long learning pathways, skills, and competencies required to remain competitive in

[1]Department of Electrical and Computer Engineering, National University of Sciences and Technology (NUST), Pakistan
[2]Department of Computer Engineering, School of Engineering, Smart Technologies and Applied Intelligence Research (STAIR) Lab, National University of Computer and Emerging Sciences (NUCES), Pakistan
[3]Department of Information Systems, University of Maryland, Baltimore

a Web X.0 employment market. The chapter concludes by confronting the transformation's ethical and distributional stakes, investigating the digital divide, proposing an inclusive innovation framework, and mapping four plausible future scenarios, ultimately arguing that a human-centered Web X.0 outcome is achievable, but only through deliberate governance, equitable policy, and collective institutional will.

10.1 Introduction: from Web 1.0 to Web X.0

The Internet has always evolved and never stood still. Since its inception as a network of static pages restricted to government researchers and academics, it has experienced numerous fundamental alterations that have transformed how people interact, communicate, produce, and consume. Each of these innovations was given a version number, such as Web 1.0, Web 2.0, and Web 3.0 [1]. This is not because the Internet was technically updated like a software patch, but because human interaction with digital technology changed so radically that a new classification was required.

Web 1.0, a read-only environment, ruled the Internet from the early 1990s to the early 2000s. The typical person was a passive consumer of content produced by companies, organizations, and a select group of highly skilled individuals; websites were static, and information only flowed in one direction. The idea that regular people could contribute to the web was largely theoretical, and there was little customization or interaction.

With Web 2.0, everything changed. The read-write web, a dynamic, interactive online environment where users engage as producers, emerged around the mid-2000s [2]. Social networking sites, blogs, wikis, video sharing services, and collaborative tools have given billions of people a voice and a presence on the Internet. By gathering user attention and data and creating platform economies that produced enormous profits, companies like Google, Facebook, Amazon, and Twitter rose to previously unheard-of levels of dominance, raising grave concerns about privacy, monopoly power, and the commodification of human behavior.

Additionally, Web 3.0 brought ownership and decentralization. Based on blockchain technology, it suggested a read-write-own model in which people could own digital assets, manage their own data, and take part in governance processes via smart contracts and tokens. Although Web 3.0 is still in its early stages of development, its fundamental concepts including trustless systems, digital ownership, and decentralized finance, have fundamentally changed the debate over who owns and uses the Internet [3,4].

Now the next frontier is represented by Web X.0. An Internet that is ambient, intelligent, and deeply ingrained in all facets of human life is the result of the convergence of AI, spatial computing, decentralized infrastructure, ubiquitous connectivity, and biological–digital interfaces rather than a single technology or established standard. The line between the digital and physical worlds starts to blur in Web X.0. You now live on the Internet rather than just visiting it.

This chapter investigates the implications for the workplace, business models, and organizational structures, as well as the nature of innovation itself. It contends that Web X.0 is a civilizational revolution, not just a technological one, and that comprehending its contours is critical for anyone who wants to prosper personally, professionally, or institutionally in the next decades. As illustrated in Figure 10.1, the web has evolved through four distinct generations, from passive consumption in Web 1.0 to the intelligent, immersive, and ambient paradigm of Web X.0.

10.2 Understanding the Web X.0 ecosystem

One must first comprehend the technological ecology that enables Web X.0 to comprehend the future of work and business. The convergence and mutual reinforcement of multiple transformational technologies, each of which is potent on its own but exponentially more significant when combined with the others, are what propel Web X.0 rather than a single game-changing invention [5].

- **Artificial intelligence (AI) and machine learning** are at the heart of Web X.0. AI has progressed from a limited set of rule-based tools to systems capable of reasoning, producing, and behaving autonomously, which was unthinkable just a decade ago. Large language models, generative AI, autonomous agents, and multimodal systems are changing the way knowledge is formed, decisions are made, and organizations operate [6]. AI in Web X.0 is not a department or a tool; rather, it is the operating system of the new digital economy.
- **Blockchain and decentralized infrastructure** form the trust layer for Web X.0. Blockchain technology enables new kinds of digital ownership, economic organization, and governance by allowing peer-to-peer transactions and agreements to be conducted without the use of central middlemen. Smart contracts, which are code-based agreements that execute themselves, automate complex procedures that were previously handled by lawyers, accountants, or institutional middlemen. Decentralized finance (DeFi), non-fungible tokens (NFTs), and decentralized autonomous organizations (DAOs) are some early examples of what this technology may do [7].
- **Extended reality (XR)**, which includes augmented reality, virtual reality, and mixed reality, produces immersive digital worlds that revolutionize education, commerce, work, socializing, and creativity [8]. In Web X.0, XR is the principal interface for human interaction with digital devices, rather than a specialized entertainment technology. The metaverse, a persistent, shared virtual reality, represents the most ambitious manifestation of XR's potential, creating totally new avenues for trade, collaboration, and community.
- **The Internet of Things (IoT)** connects the physical and digital worlds. Billions of sensors, devices, machines, and things continuously provide data

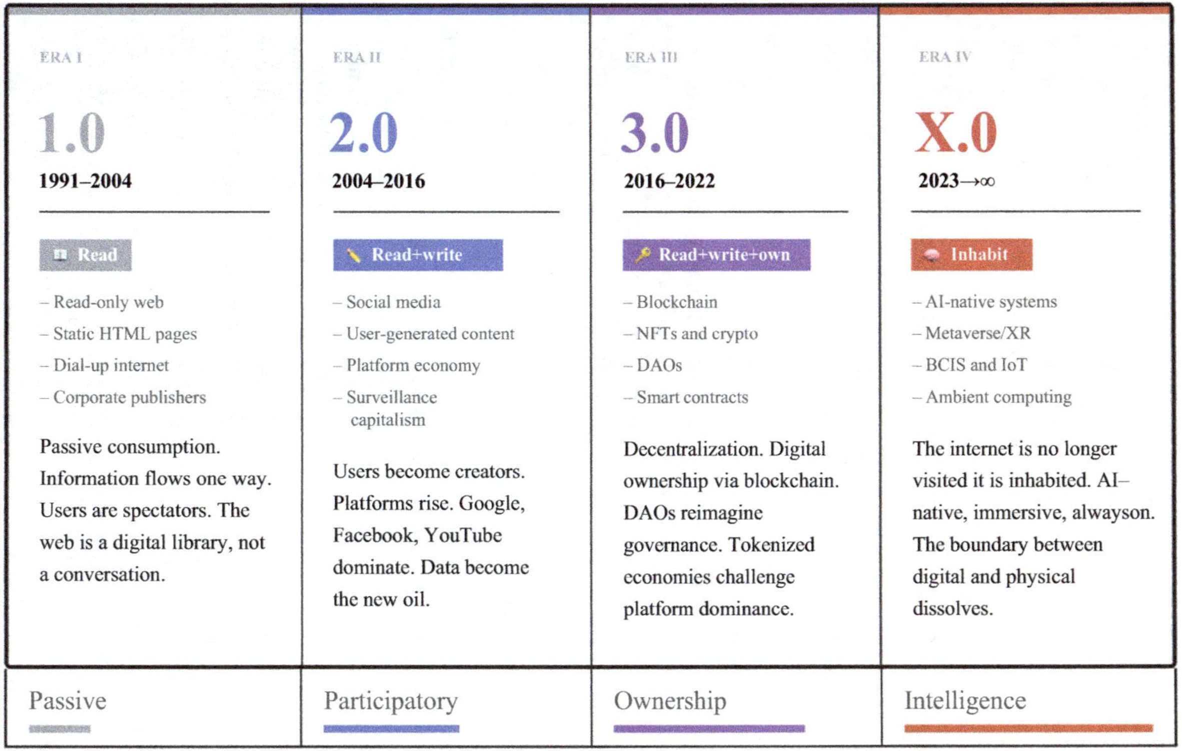

Figure 10.1 Web evolution timeline

about the real world, allowing for unprecedented levels of monitoring, optimization, and automation. In Web X.0, the IoT includes smart cities, intelligent supply chains, connected healthcare systems, and agricultural technologies that feed data into AI systems capable of making real-time, large-scale decisions.

- **Edge computing** addresses one of the main obstacles of prior Internet generations: latency. Edge computing allows for real-time responsiveness in applications such as driverless vehicles, remote surgery, and immersive XR environments by processing data closer to where it is created rather than routing it all through centralized cloud servers. It also improves privacy by lowering the quantity of sensitive data that needs to be transferred across networks.
- **5G and beyond** serve as the networking backbone for all of these technologies. With far faster speeds, lower latency, and the ability to support far more connected devices per square kilometer, 5G and its successors make the ambient, always-on Internet of Web X.0 technically conceivable on a worldwide scale.
- **Brain–computer interfaces** are the most speculative yet potentially transformational frontier of Web X.0. Companies such as Neuralink are developing technology that enables direct contact between the human brain and digital systems, suggesting fundamental possibilities and ethical concerns about the future of human cognition, identity, and autonomy.

These technologies work together to recreate the existing Internet, rather than merely upgrading it. Web X.0 is an ecosystem in which intelligence is pervasive, ownership is dispersed, experience is immersive, and the distinction between human and machine becomes progressively blurred. Figure 10.2 maps the seven core technologies that together constitute the Web X.0 ecosystem, each transformative independently, but collectively forming a new civilizational paradigm.

10.3 The transformation of work

The implementation of Web X.0 has had a more direct and obvious impact on work than any other domain. The types of vocations, organizational structures, meanings of employment, and skills required for individuals to thrive economically are all rapidly evolving. Understanding these patterns is more than a theoretical exercise; it is a practical requirement for employees, educators, policymakers, and managers. Table 10.1 compares job characteristics between the Web 2.0 and Web X.0 periods, demonstrating a significant shift not only in technologies and tools, but also in the fundamental structures of employment, income, and organization.

10.3.1 The displacement and augmentation of labor

Work automation is the aspect of Web X.0's effects on work that is most frequently discussed. A growing number of jobs that were previously performed

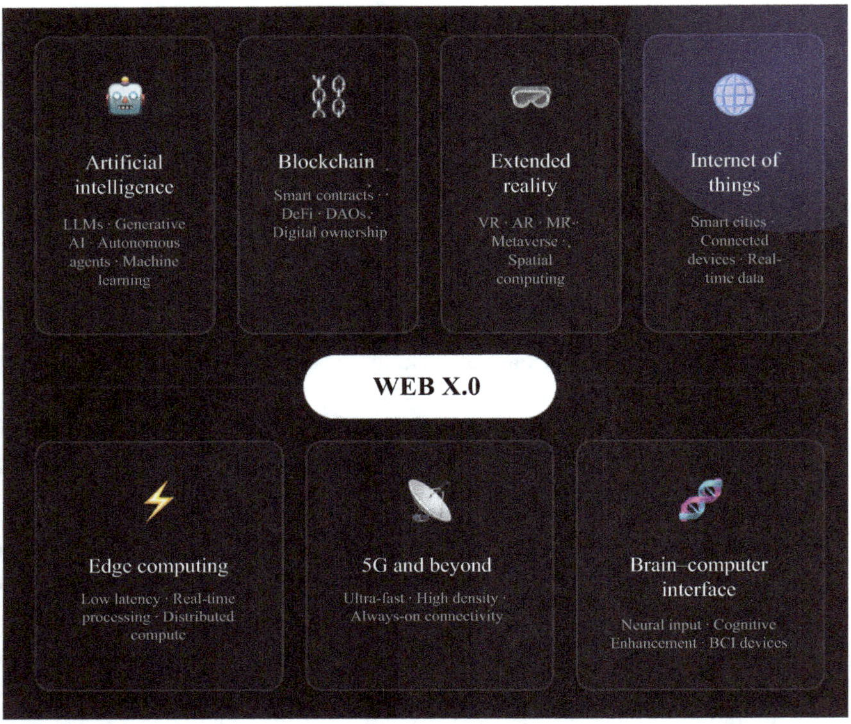

Figure 10.2 Technology ecosystem

Table 10.1 Comparison of work characteristics across the Web 2.0 and Web X.0 eras across eight key organizational dimensions

Dimension	**Web 2.0 era**	**Web X.0 era**
Workplace	Office-first, hybrid emerging, video calls standard	Immersive virtual offices, location-irrelevant, XR collaboration hubs
Employment	Full-time dominant, gig economy emerging	Contributor model, DAOs, token-based participation, creator economy
Skills	Technical skills + soft skills, degree-centric hiring	AI fluency + meta-skills, micro-credentials, adaptability paramount
Organization	Hierarchical, matrix structures, centralized authority	Network-based, flat, decentralized, DAO governance models
Compensation	Salary, equity, bonuses in fiat currency	Tokens, crypto, revenue sharing, community ownership stakes
Management	Performance management, key performance indicator (KPIs), top-down direction	Purpose-led, trust-based, AI-assisted, servant leadership

(Continues)

Table 10.1 (Continued)

Dimension	Web 2.0 era	Web X.0 era
Innovation	R&D departments, patents, internal teams	Open-source, decentralized science, AI co-creation, community-driven
Talent access	Resume screening, interviews, geographic constraints	Skills-based hiring, global talent pools, on-chain reputation systems
	Platform era—centralized and siloed	Protocol era—decentralized and open

only by human workers can now be completed by AI and robotics, including cognitive as well as physical and repetitive labor [9]. AI is exhibiting capabilities that match or surpass human performance in specific circumstances across a number of fields, including data analysis, legal research, financial modeling, content creation, customer service, and medical diagnosis. However, the history of technological revolutions indicates that while automation eliminates certain types of employment, it also creates others. The question is not whether employment would be lost, but which jobs, at what rate, and whether displaced workers will have access to other options. The change will be uneven, with considerable human costs if not managed proactively [10].

The idea of augmentation, AI, and digital tools that improve human capabilities rather than replace them, is more complex than simple replacement. The most valued employees in Web X.0 will be those who successfully cooperate with machines rather than those who compete with them. This calls for new literacies: the capacity to collaborate with AI systems, analyze and evaluate their results, recognize the issues they are unable to resolve, and contribute the moral insight, inventiveness, and judgment that computers are unable to supply.

10.3.2 The distributed workplace

The COVID-19 pandemic hastened the shift to remote and hybrid work, which Web X.0 technologies are making more advanced and permanent. Digital project management systems, cloud-based processes, and virtual collaboration tools have already helped a sizable section of the global knowledge workforce divorce work from physical location. To go one step further, Web X.0 introduces immersive virtual workplaces, which are persistent digital spaces where groups can interact, work together, and meet in ways that more closely mimic the richness of in-person interactions.

The implications are significant. Geographic limits on talent acquisition are eliminated, allowing businesses to hire internationally and employees to live anywhere. Urban centers lose part of their economic dominance. Work–life integration becomes increasingly flexible and difficult to manage. In remote companies, questions of belonging, culture, and connection take on strategic importance rather than being peripheral considerations.

10.3.3 The rise of decentralized work

Fundamentally, new types of economic organization are made possible by Web X.0. Smart contracts and token-based governance are used by DAOs to organize group activities without the need for conventional management hierarchies. Contributors to a DAO challenge the conventional employer–employee relationship by earning tokens for their work, taking part in governance choices, and sharing in the organization's success. In Web X.0, the gig economy, which was already substantial in Web 2.0, grows significantly. Through platforms, people can make money from a greater variety of abilities, resources, and artistic creations. With the help of Web X.0 tools that allow direct monetization without middlemen, the creator economy, in which people establish audiences and enterprises around their knowledge, personality, and creative work, becomes a significant area of economic activity.

10.3.4 Skills and the future of human capital

The effects of Web X.0 on skills and human capital are arguably the most important aspect of its effects on the workplace. Certain technical talents have a much shorter half-life; what is innovative now could be automated tomorrow. Meta-skills, the capacity to pick things up quickly, adjust to new situations and tools, think critically and creatively, work well with others, and confidently handle ambiguity, are highly valued. Cross-cultural communication, systems thinking, emotional intelligence, and ethical judgment are some of the uniquely human skills that will always be valued since they are hard to automate. Companies, businesses, and educational institutions will be better positioned for the Web X.0 economy than those that continue to rely on technical qualifications if they recognize this and make the required investments.

10.4 The new business landscape

The development of Web X.0 is radically changing what a company or business is, how it creates value, and how it engages with its staff, clients, and other stakeholders. The businesses that dominated the Web 2.0 era might not be the same as those that will rule the Web X.0 economy [11].

10.4.1 From platform to protocol

In Web 2.0, platform firms such as Google, Uber, Amazon, and Airbnb became well-known. Through centralized platforms that they owned and controlled, these businesses connected buyers and sellers, manufacturers and consumers, creating value. These platforms profited immensely from portraying themselves as crucial intermediaries and utilizing network effects to cement their dominance. In contrast, Web X.0 drastically alters this paradigm. Decentralized blockchain-based protocols enable peer-to-peer trade by doing away with the requirement for a central platform operator. The network's participants, who include users, donors, and token holders, profit more than the centralized corporate owner. The shift from platform to protocol has far-reaching ramifications for competitive dynamics, economic value distribution, and regulatory frameworks tailored to a world of corporate intermediaries. Digital markets offer enormous rewards to scale and winner-take-all dynamics, fundamentally altering competitive strategy and forcing firms to reevaluate previous assumptions about market entry and sustainability [12].

Figure 10.3 shows the value flow in Web X.0 protocol economies, where value is distributed back to all contributing parties, as opposed to Web 2.0 platform economies, where value is extracted by a central platform.

10.4.2 Decentralized autonomous organizations: the new organizational frontier

As Web X.0 eliminates barriers between owners, workers, and users, one of the most radical organizational innovations to emerge is the decentralized autonomous organization, or DAO. Unlike traditional firms, which are governed by boards of directors and hierarchical management structures, DAOs are jointly owned and democratically managed entities, with rules inscribed directly into blockchain-based smart contracts [7]. Governance is decentralized, with token holders voting on everything from treasury allocation to strategic direction. This reflects a fundamental reimagining of what an organization is, who it belongs to, and how collective decisions are legally made in the digital economy.

10.4.2.1 How DAOs function

DAOs rely on three interdependent mechanisms: smart contracts, governance tokens, and community voting. Smart contracts serve as the DAO's constitution, enforcing organizational standards automatically and transparently, eliminating the need for human mediators [7]. When a member makes a governance proposal, such as sponsoring a new project, changing a protocol parameter, or allocating treasury resources, token holders vote on it. If the proposal reaches a predefined quorum and approval level, the smart contract will execute the decision without requiring central authority approval.

Through token sales, contribution-based prizes, or community airdrops, creators, contributors, and investors receive governance tokens that confer voting rights proportionate to holdings. For DAOs, the token distribution technique is essential, as it determines power distribution and whether the organization is indeed centralized or decentralized. A shared treasury, typically held in cryptocurrency and managed collaboratively by member votes, is another feature of many DAOs. This creates a form of participatory budgeting that has no obvious counterpart in conventional corporate governance. DAO treasuries were significant participants in the broader digital economy, with assets of billions of dollars by 2023 [4]. From proposal submission to on-chain execution, the DAO governance cycle functions through five automated stages, as shown in Figure 10.4, without the need for a central authority or human middleman at any point.

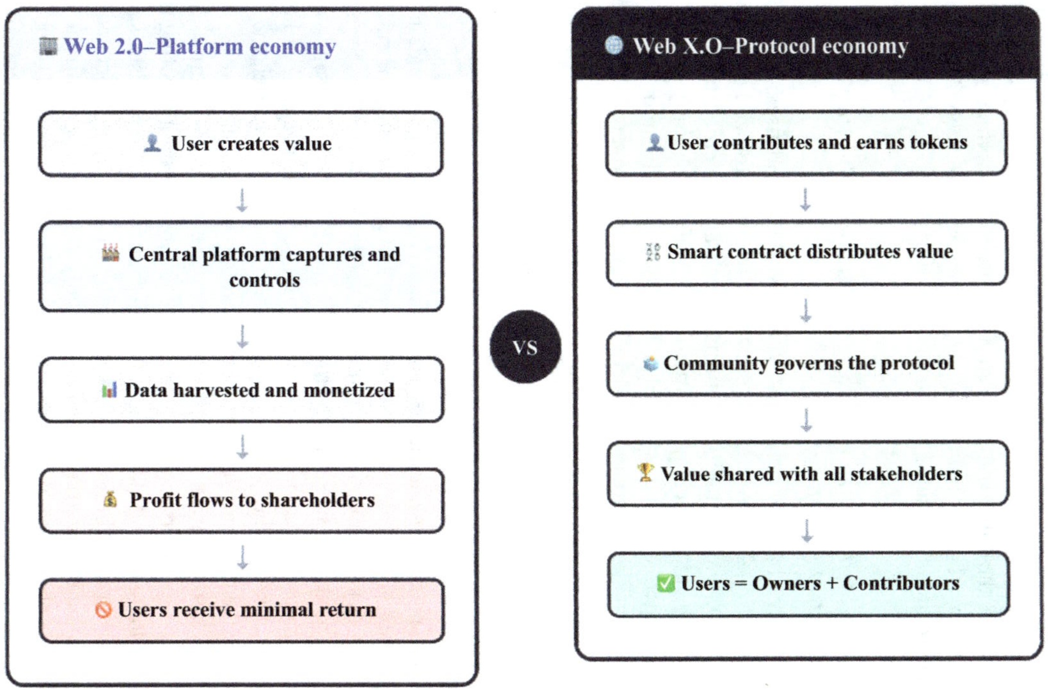

Figure 10.3 *Comparing Web X.0 protocol economies with Web 2.0 platform economies in terms of value flow models*

Figure 10.4 The five-stage DAO governance cycle: from proposal submission to automatic on-chain execution via smart contracts, without human intermediaries

10.4.2.2 Real-world examples

The variety of DAOs currently in use demonstrates the model's wide applicability as well as the range of ways it has been implemented. The DAI stablecoin is governed by MakerDAO, which essentially acts as a decentralized central bank overseeing billions of dollars' worth of assets. Token holders vote on interest rates, collateral kinds, and risk factors. One of the most researched models of large-scale decentralized governance in practice is provided by Uniswap, which assigns governance of its multibillion-dollar decentralized exchange protocol to UNI token holders, who discuss and vote on fee structures, grant allocations, and protocol improvements.

Through a community-governed awards program, the Gitcoin DAO has given tens of millions of dollars to open-source software development projects, proving that DAOs are capable of allocating funds to public goods. With intellectual property held collectively by the DAO community rather than by academic institutions or pharmaceutical companies, VitaDAO pioneers decentralized funding for longevity research in the scientific field. This concept has important implications for the ownership and dissemination of scientific knowledge. Constitution DAO brilliantly proved the mobilization power of DAOs, raising about $47 million from 17,000 donors in less than a week, while ultimately failing to purchase an actual copy of the US Constitution at auction [4].

10.4.2.3 Challenges and criticisms

DAOs face significant, well-documented challenges despite their transformative promise. Voter apathy is the most persistent; most token holders never or rarely vote, and participation rates in most DAOs are quite low. An ironic reversal of the decentralization ideal, this results in a de facto oligarchy in which a small number of highly active or heavily tokenized people have disproportionate power. This issue is frequently exacerbated by token concentration among early investors and founding teams, which essentially grants whale wallets veto power over community decisions.

Vulnerabilities in smart contracts are a big technological concern. A contentious hard fork of the Ethereum blockchain was required to address the 2016 DAO attack, which resulted in the theft of nearly $60 million in Ether [7]. Code-based governance failure remains a systemic risk, despite major improvements in smart contract security since then. Another difficulty is legal ambiguity; the majority of countries do not recognize DAOs as legal corporations, thus exposing members to personal liability and limiting their ability to participate in regular contracts or employment agreements.

10.4.2.4 Implications for work and business

A DAO-based economy eliminates the traditional distinction between employees, investors, and customers. Contributors earn tokens that grant governance rights as well as a percentage of organizational upside, making it a realistic alternative to employment and gig work [3]. Companies and lawmakers must now take DAOs seriously, whether through hybrid governance experiments, contributions to new legislative frameworks, or strategic collaborations with DAO-native groups. It is a necessity for effectively competing and collaborating in the Web X.0 economy.

10.4.3 AI-first business models

AI is the foundation of competitive advantage in Web X.0, not merely a feature or department. AI-first enterprises rely only on intelligent system capabilities to power their operations, services, and goods. They use AI to automate complex operations, enhance supply chains in real time, adapt customer experiences on a large scale, and derive insights from data that humans would be unable to comprehend on their own.

There are important ramifications for competition. Businesses with superior data and AI skills can run at significantly reduced costs, respond to market changes more quickly, and drastically provide different customer experiences when compared to conventional firms [13]. This creates winner-take-all dynamics in many industries and opens new opportunities for specialized AI-powered firms. Generative AI has the potential to increase global gross domestic product (GDP) by \$2.6–\$4.4 trillion annually, with the largest impacts in marketing, customer operations, software engineering, and R&D [14].

10.4.4 Tokenized business models

A key component of Web X.0 business models is tokenization, which uses digital tokens on a blockchain to represent ownership, value, and governance rights. Organizations can eliminate conventional boundaries between clients, staff, and investors through tokenization [15]. Tokens that grant users economic stakes and governance rights may be awarded to users who contribute to a platform. This creates stakeholder groups that play a significant role in the company's success by aligning incentives in ways that standard stock structures cannot.

Innovative methods for value distribution, liquidity, and finance are made possible by tokenized models. As alternatives to traditional venture capital and public markets, initial coin offerings, security token offerings, and decentralized funding mechanisms increase investment opportunities while posing new regulatory challenges.

10.4.5 Hyper-personalization and the experience economy

Businesses can now offer experiences tailored to each individual customer with previously unheard-of accuracy and depth thanks to Web X.0 technology. Real-time product, service, and information selection is possible for AI systems that comprehend people's preferences, behaviors, and environments. Consumers can connect with businesses in immersive settings, try products before they buy them, and co-create unique experiences that increase engagement and loyalty by using augmented and virtual reality technologies.

Web X.0 represents the pinnacle of the experience economy, in which people pay for unique, meaningful experiences rather than items or services. Companies that understand the art and science of experience design will command high prices and strong loyalty in marketplaces where functional differences are becoming increasingly difficult to maintain.

10.4.6 Sustainability and stakeholder capitalism

Web X.0 is also associated with a broad shift in attitudes around the purpose of business. Stakeholder capitalism, the idea that firms should deliver value to all stakeholders, not just shareholders, is gaining traction as the public becomes more conscious of the social and environmental costs of profit-driven enterprise. Web X.0 technologies empower and compel enterprises to take these greater obligations seriously. Blockchain-based supply chain transparency makes it more difficult to hide unsustainable or immoral behavior. AI-powered environmental monitoring enables businesses to measure and manage their ecological footprints with unparalleled accuracy. Furthermore, the distributed ownership models offered by tokenization provide communities a true role in the governance of the businesses that touch their lives.

10.5 Innovation in the Web X.0 era

Innovation has long been the driving force behind economic growth, but Web X.0 is changing the nature, pace, and geography of innovation in ways that affect enterprises, governments, and societies [16]. The innovation ecosystem of Web X.0 is more dispersed, collaborative, AI-accelerated, and unpredictable than it has ever been.

10.5.1 AI-accelerated discovery

AI is becoming more than just a tool to carry out human commands; it is becoming a co-inventor, a collaborator in the process of discovery and production. AI systems are discovering patterns, developing hypotheses, and investigating solution spaces at rates and scales much beyond human cognitive capacity in a variety of fields, including software engineering, drug discovery, and materials research. An early but potent illustration of what AI-accelerated discovery may achieve is AlphaFold's solution to the protein folding problem, which had evaded biologists for 50 years [17]. The Web X.0 innovation acceleration cycle, shown in Figure 10.5, is a self-reinforcing cycle that significantly reduces the time from discovery to worldwide deployment by combining AI analysis, open collaboration, and rapid prototyping.

Figure 10.5 The Web X.0 innovation acceleration cycle

There are important implications for innovation timescales. AI-assisted methods can solve problems in years or even months that would take decades to resolve using traditional research methods [18]. The compression of invention cycles will expedite technological progress, resulting in both tremendous disruption and unprecedented opportunity.

10.5.2 Agentic AI: autonomous agents as innovation engines

One of the most significant advancements in the Web X.0 technology environment is the rise of agentic AI systems that can pursue complex, multi-step goals autonomously, eliminating the need for continual human guidance at each level. Unlike classical AI tools, which respond to single orders, agentic systems analyze their environment, plan, select, and utilize tools, maintain memory across interactions, and carry out activities to achieve a specific purpose [6]. This shift from AI as a reactive assistant to AI as a proactive agent is a qualitative leap in machine intelligence, with far-reaching implications for how innovation unfolds in the Web X.0 era.

- **How agentic AI systems function:** Agentic AI differs from classical AI in four essential ways: goal-directed planning, tool use, memory, and self-reflection. As illustrated in Figure 10.6, these capabilities operate in a continuous autonomous loop in which the agent receives inputs from its surroundings, organizes a sequence of subtasks, acts by invoking external tools, and evaluates its results before looping back to improve its approach. Goal-directed planning enables agents to break down high-level objectives into executable subtasks without requiring human intervention at any stage. Agents can communicate with other systems via tools such as browsers, code interpreters, APIs, and databases, allowing them to act outside of the language model [6]. Memory allows agents to retain context and improve their approach over time. It distinguishes between short-term working memory while doing a task, long-term memory between sessions, and episodic memory of earlier actions and outcomes. Self-reflection enables agents to evaluate their own performance, identify flaws, and adjust their strategy accordingly [17]. Multi-agent architectures involve networks of specialized agents interacting, one researching, another writing, and another executing, all coordinated by an orchestrating agent, like the organization of human teams but functioning at machine speed and scale. This division of cognitive work represents a new paradigm in automated problem-solving, in which the complexity of tasks that an AI system can meaningfully manage is not limited by the capability of a single model.
- **Applications and examples:** Agentic AI applications have already emerged in a range of fields. In software development, technologies such as GitHub Copilot Workspace can take a natural-language task and automatically write, test, and debug code, reducing development time from days to minutes [17].

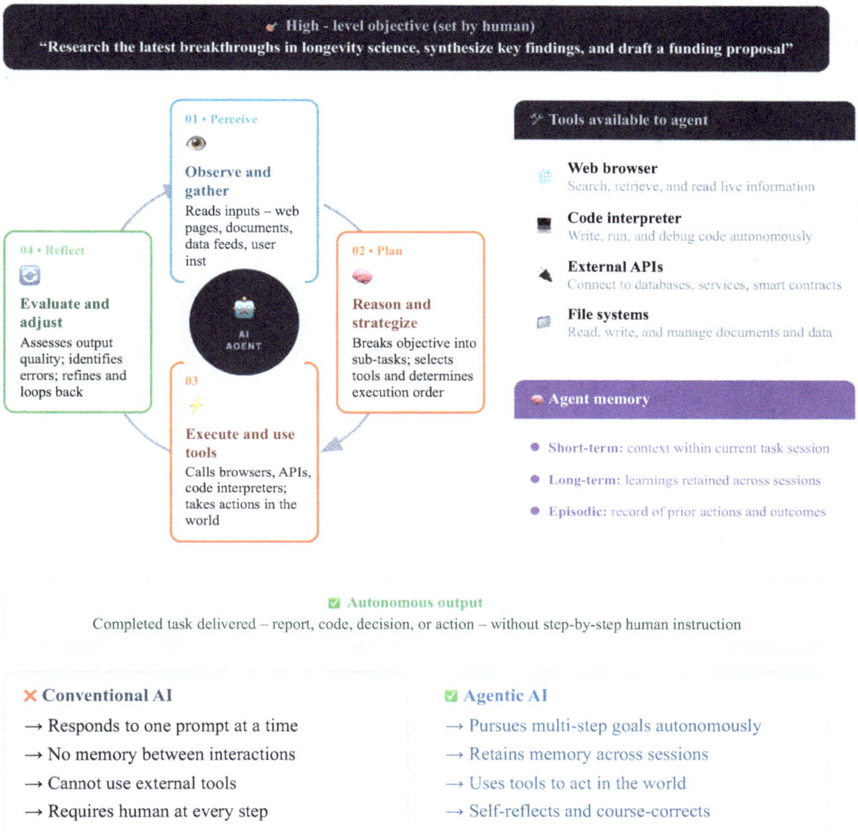

Figure 10.6 The four main phases of the agentic AI autonomous loop: perceive, plan, act, and reflect

Agentic systems review literature independently, formulate hypotheses, and interpret experimental data in scientific research, speeding up medication development and materials science discovery. Agentic AI automates complex workflows in corporate operations, such as market research and supply chain optimization, which previously required human judgment at each stage [14]. Personal AI agents that manage calendars, handle transactions, and monitor data are becoming commercially available, signaling a shift in human–digital relations. The combination of agentic AI and decentralized infrastructure opens new possibilities: DAOs can use AI agents as autonomous contributors to perform governance tasks, manage treasury operations, and conduct due diligence, allowing decentralized organizations to operate at scales that human governance cannot match [7].

- **Risks and governance:** The autonomy that makes agentic AI so powerful also creates novel vulnerabilities. When agents work through long action sequences without human supervision at each step, the alignment problem becomes much more complex; slight misalignments in the objective specification can spread and accumulate, resulting in unforeseen effects. Accountability is also challenging when an autonomous agent causes harm; existing liability frameworks make it difficult to identify blame along a large causal chain from designer to outcome. Agents with web access and code-execution capabilities are vulnerable to prompt-injection attacks, which can hijack their objectives during a task. The risk is particularly apparent in agentic systems utilized in financial or critical infrastructure settings, where a single compromised action sequence might have major real-world consequences. Robust human oversight, capability constraints, and sandboxing are critical protections as agentic AI enters meaningful real-world implementation. Emerging governance frameworks, such as the EU AI Act and the OECD AI principles, are beginning to handle agentic systems specifically; however, regulatory development is still lagging technological capacity. For both individuals and businesses, agentic AI necessitates a rethinking of skills and governance systems. Those who gain the ability to successfully command and supervise autonomous agents, known as agentic literacy, will have a significant edge in the Web X.0 innovation economy [10].

10.5.3 Open and collaborative innovation

The open innovation model, the notion that useful knowledge resides outside organizational borders and that the most successful innovators are those who can access, integrate, and build upon the ideas of others is amplified and expanded by Web X.0. Decentralized research networks, open data efforts, and collaborative innovation platforms that cut across organizational and national boundaries are the Web X.0 manifestations of open-source software development, which in the Web 2.0 period revealed the power of dispersed cooperation [19].

To make research financing, data sharing, peer review, and knowledge distribution more open, transparent, and equitable, a new movement known as decentralized science (DeSci) uses blockchain technology and tokenization to organize scientific research [20]. If DeSci succeeds in its goals, it has the potential to significantly democratize knowledge production, lessen the power of big research institutions, and allow gifted people from all over the world to advance science.

10.5.4 The startup ecosystem in Web X.0

Startups have historically been disproportionately important sources of disruptive innovation, and Web X.0 exacerbates this trend in multiple ways. The cost of developing and implementing digital products continues to decline rapidly, eliminating entry barriers to entrepreneurship. AI tools lessen the requirement for huge engineering teams. Decentralized financing systems offer an alternative to traditional venture funding. Furthermore, global connections allow entrepreneurs to have access to talent and markets that were previously unavailable due to geographic limitations.

The stakes for incumbents are also increased by Web X.0 [21]. Businesses that do not innovate run the danger of losing market share as well as being structurally irrelevant as AI-native competitors and new decentralized protocols circumvent the platforms and business models that underpin their supremacy. Incumbents frequently misjudge the speed and thoroughness of such shifts, according to the history of digital disruption.

10.5.5 Innovation at the intersection

Some of the most important Web X.0 developments are occurring at the nexus of previously distinct fields, such as biology and AI to create personalized medicine, blockchain and energy to create peer-to-peer electricity markets, and education and spatial computing to create immersive learning environments. Because they do not cleanly fit into current organizational structures or competitive frameworks, these intersectional innovations are frequently the hardest for established actors to predict or react to. Thus, one of the most important innovative skills in the Web X.0 age is the capacity to think and work across disciplinary boundaries. The innovators who influence the next decade will be disproportionately represented by organizations that foster interdisciplinary teams, promote experimentation that crosses boundaries, and establish cultures that reward curiosity and creative risk-taking.

10.6 The metaverse economy

One of the most notable and important examples of Web X.0 is the term "metaverse," which has attracted a lot of interest, major investment, and skepticism in recent years. Stripped of its exaggeration, the phrase "metaverse" refers to three-dimensional, shared, persistent digital places where people can work, play, communicate, create, and do commerce. In its most ambitious form, it is not a single platform or commodity that creates a parallel economy with the physical one, but rather an ecosystem of connected virtual locations.

10.6.1 The architecture of the metaverse

The metaverse is built on convergent technologies, including high-bandwidth, low-latency connectivity that permits large-scale real-time interaction, blockchain infrastructure that permits digital ownership and interoperability, AI systems that give virtual worlds intelligent agents and customized experiences, and extended reality hardware that permits immersive access, which are the foundation of the metaverse [22,23]. Through the creation of technical standards and governance agreements, the goal of an open, interoperable metaverse where people can move between virtual locations with ease while bringing their identities, assets, and social interactions with them is currently being fulfilled.

10.6.2 Virtual commerce and digital assets

The metaverse is already a significant economic sector. Real-world values for virtual commodities, such as digital apparel, accessories, artwork, real estate, and experiences, are determined by their scarcity, desirability, and social signaling value. The idea that digital items can have actual economic worth has been proven by the market for digital assets, such as NFTs and virtual real estate, which in peak years reached tens of billions of dollars despite extreme volatility.

In a developed metaverse economy, companies will continue to operate virtual stores where consumers can browse and buy goods in immersive settings [24]. Digital clothes for avatars will be sold by fashion brands. Architects will create virtual places. There will be virtual places where musicians will perform. This potential will also give rise to a whole ecosystem of metaverse-native companies, including virtual event planners, digital interior designers, avatar stylists, and virtual real estate developers.

10.6.3 Work and collaboration in the metaverse

The metaverse presents enticing potential for the future of work. Virtual offices and collaboration spaces can replicate the social and geographical richness of physical workplaces while removing geographic constraints. Teams from around the world can interact in shared virtual worlds that allow spatial audio, gesture, and presence in ways that flat video conferences cannot. Training simulations, design collaboration, and virtual prototyping can reduce expenses and expedite schedules. To improve internal communication, several sizable businesses, including significant IT firms and financial institutions, have already made investments in metaverse infrastructure. The basic value proposition of improved remote collaboration is attractive enough to support further investment and development, despite early reception being mixed [25].

10.6.4 The creator economy in virtual worlds

By providing more venues for artistic expression and financial gain, the metaverse broadens the creator economy. In metaverse environments, producers of virtual worlds, experience designers, game developers, and digital artists can produce and sell their work directly to customers, earning cryptocurrencies or other digital currencies that can be exchanged for fiat money. Among the most significant infrastructure providers in the metaverse ecosystem will be platforms that provide easy-to-use creation tools [26].

10.7 Leadership and management reimagined

In addition to new technology and business models, the shift to Web X.0 necessitates new management and leadership techniques. The leadership paradigms of the industrial period, and even the Web 2.0 era, are unsuitable for organizations that are distributed, AI-augmented, tokenized, and move at the speed of digital marketplaces. Web X.0 necessitates a thorough rethinking of what leadership is and what it entails. Figure 10.7 identifies the seven core leadership competencies for the Web X.0 era, extending traditional emotional intelligence and systems thinking with the critical new additions of AI literacy, ethical judgment, and decentralized thinking.

10.7.1 From hierarchy to network

Traditional organizational structures were established for an era of limited knowledge and centralized decision-making. In Web X.0, information is available, decisions must be made at the edges of companies where knowledge and context are most prevalent, and the most valued contributors are frequently members of distributed communities and ecosystems rather than workers [27]. Effective Web X.0 leaders recognize that their purpose is not to direct and manage, but to foster circumstances of trust, alignment, and capacity that allow scattered networks of contributors to achieve amazing outcomes [28].

This transition to a network-centric organization demands leaders who can set direction without micromanaging implementation, are at ease with ambiguity, and thrive at fostering trust across boundaries and differences. It necessitates communication cultures that promote transparency and psychological safety, governance systems that delegate true authority, and recognition schemes that emphasize contribution over tenure.

10.7.2 Human-centered leadership in an AI world

As AI systems take on more of the analytical, administrative, and even strategic tasks of management, the distinctive value of human leaders is increasingly found in the areas that machines cannot replicate, such as empathy, ethical judgment, creative vision, cultural stewardship, and the ability to inspire and motivate. Web X.0 leaders must be highly human-centered, genuinely interested in their followers, committed to their development and welfare, and capable of creating a feeling of shared purpose that transcends the transactional [29].

In Web X.0, emotional intelligence, the capacity to identify, comprehend, and control one's own emotions as well as those of others becomes a fundamental leadership skill rather than a nice-to-have. Emotionally intelligent leaders create teams that are more resilient, creative, and dedicated, according to a wealth of research. The caliber of leadership is a key factor in determining whether an organization can draw in and keep the contributors it needs in a world where there is tough competition for talent and a growing number of alternatives to traditional employment.

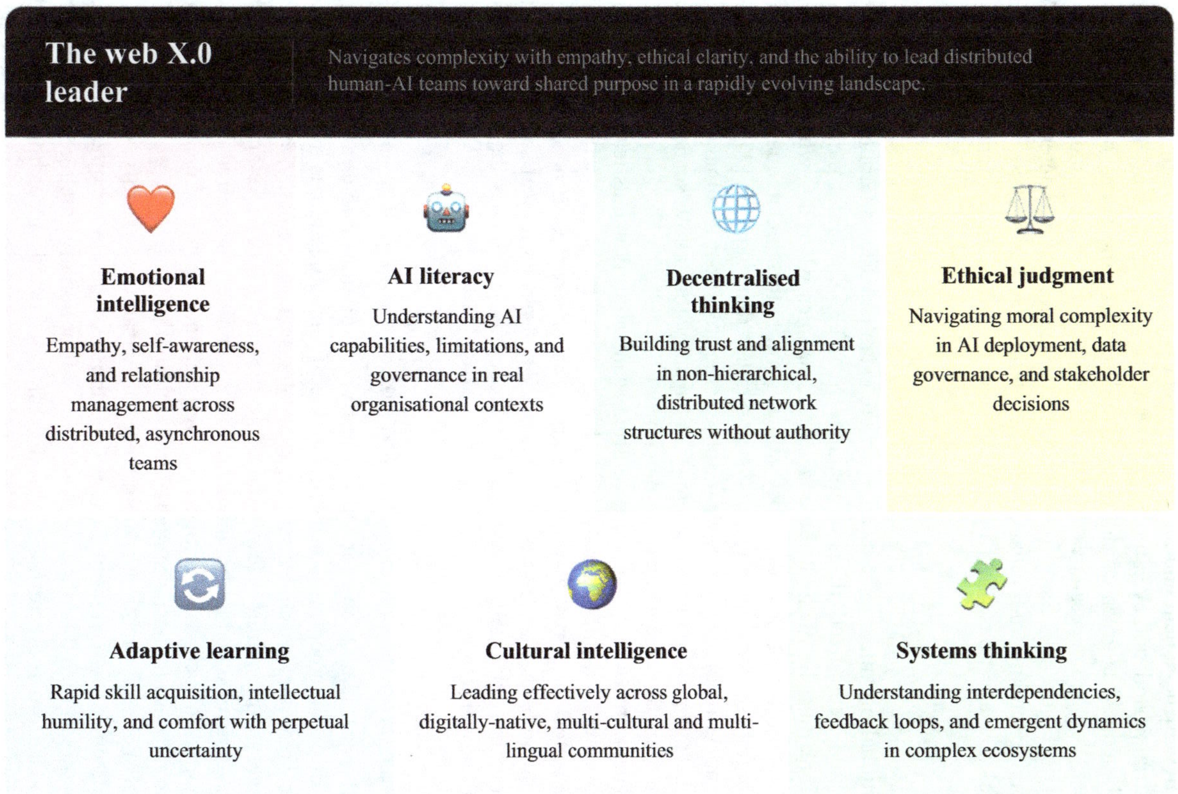

Figure 10.7 The seven Web X.0 leadership competencies

10.7.3 Leading through continuous change

Web X.0 companies work in a constantly disruptive market and technology context. Therefore, a distinguishing leadership talent is the capacity to guide organizational learning and adaptation, assisting teams in navigating uncertainty, developing new capabilities, and sustaining performance through change. This calls for not only personal resilience but also the capacity to model and foster resilience in others: to celebrate learning, to normalize experimentation and failure, and to keep a clear sense of direction and purpose even in the face of uncertainty.

10.8 Education, skills, and talent in the Web X.0 world

The education and talent systems that educate individuals for the future of work in Web X.0 must be completely rethought if it is marked by dispersed cooperation, AI augmentation, and constant change. The front-loaded education model of the industrial period, where people receive degrees in their twenties that are intended to support jobs spanning decades, is structurally insufficient to meet the demands of the Web X.0 economy.

10.8.1 The lifelong learning imperative

In Web X.0, education is not a stage of life but a permanent requirement for economic engagement. The ability to continuously learn new abilities is more valuable than any technical qualification because of the speed at which technology is developing, making talents obsolete more quickly than in the past. Establishing a structure and culture of lifelong learning is the responsibility of individuals, governments, and organizations.

Strong metacognitive abilities, such as the capacity to learn how to learn, must be developed, along with a growth mindset that welcomes challenge and views failure as information rather than a judgment. Instead of viewing learning as a separate activity, organizations must engage in programs for ongoing development, cultivate cultures that promote experimentation and inquiry, and include learning in the regular flow of work. Governments must reconsider social safety nets, credential recognition programs, and school funding methods to assist employees in adjusting to increasingly frequent and quick changes.

10.8.2 Micro-credentials and alternative pathways

Traditional four-year university degrees are already being supplemented, and in some cases, replaced by shorter, more targeted certifications that recognize certain skills and abilities. Micro-credentials, digital badges, bootcamps, and online courses offered by platforms such as Coursera, edX, and LinkedIn Learning are increasing in popularity among employers who prioritize demonstrated capacity over institutional affiliation. Blockchain-based credential verification systems in Web X.0 will enable people to keep portable, tamper-proof records of their abilities and accomplishments across industries and regions.

10.8.3 AI as an educational partner

AI is revolutionizing education by delivering personalized learning experiences based on each student's needs, speed, and learning style. AI tutors can offer patient, on-demand guidance with a wide range of courses. AI evaluations can provide more detailed, nuanced feedback than standardized exams [30,31]. Furthermore, AI curriculum design technology can assist teachers in identifying knowledge gaps and developing more effective learning experiences to address them. The democratization of high-quality, individualized education using AI has the potential to significantly reduce educational inequality; however, realizing this potential necessitates careful consideration of accessibility and equity.

10.8.4 Talent acquisition in Web X.0

Traditional recruitment tactics are becoming increasingly unproductive as businesses compete for talent in the Web X.0 economy. The best contributors can be found anywhere in the world, prefer decentralized work arrangements, and have unique credentials that do not easily fit into application tracking systems designed for a different era. Forward-thinking organizations are developing novel approaches to talent identification, such as skills-based hiring that focuses on demonstrated capability, project-based assessments that simulate real-world work, and community-based recruitment, which seeks contributors within ecosystems and open-source projects where top talent already exists.

10.9 Ethics, privacy, and governance

Web X.0 technologies not only have exceptional potential, but they also carry enormous risks and obligations. As the digital and physical worlds collide, AI systems play more roles in significant decisions, and massive amounts of personal data become the raw material of the new economy, Web X.0's ethical, privacy, and governance concerns require immediate and serious consideration.

10.9.1 The ethics of AI

AI systems are increasingly making or informing judgments that have far-reaching consequences for people's lives, including credit decisions, job decisions, medical diagnoses, criminal justice evaluations, and more. These systems are only as good as the data on which they are trained and the values built into their design, both of which are usually wrong. Algorithmic bias, or the tendency of AI systems to duplicate and amplify biases found in their training data, is a well-documented and deeply disturbing issue. AI systems trained on past data are more likely to maintain discriminatory behaviors unless explicitly and regularly corrected [32,33].

Another significant ethical difficulty is explaining AI decisions. When an AI system refuses someone a loan, flags them as a fraud risk, or advises against their parole, the impacted individual has a legal right to know why. Many of the most powerful AI systems, particularly deep learning models, are essentially black boxes with internal logic that is difficult or impossible to explain in human words. The development of explainable AI is a technological and moral imperative.

10.9.2 Data privacy and digital sovereignty

Web X.0 generates data of unprecedented size and granularity. Smart cities, wearable devices, always-on AI assistants, and immersive virtual worlds gather real-time information about people's locations, habits, health, emotions, and social interactions. The collection of this data results in surveillance capabilities that, if not properly handled, constitute a serious danger to individual privacy and autonomy [34].

The concept of digital sovereignty, or the right of individuals, communities, and nations to control their own digital data and infrastructure, is gaining appeal as a counterweight to the data colonialism perpetrated by huge technical platforms. Regulatory frameworks such as the European Union's General Data Protection Regulation are early attempts to establish genuine privacy rights in the digital age, but they were designed for a Web 2.0 environment and will require major evolution to meet Web X.0 challenges.

10.9.3 Governance of decentralized systems

Decentralized systems have a variety of governance challenges. Traditional regulatory systems presume the existence of identifiable legal entities, firms, and persons that can be held accountable for the consequences of their products and services. This concept excludes decentralized protocols, distributed autonomous organizations, and anonymous networks. Regulators worldwide are debating how to apply consumer protection, financial regulation, and law enforcement in situations where there is no central authority to supervise or hold accountable. There is a lot of experimentation going on in DAO governance. Early DAO governance models revealed significant challenges, such as low participation rates, plutocratic dynamics where token concentration gives large holders disproportionate influence, and vulnerability to governance attacks. Developing more dependable, equitable, and effective governance mechanisms for dispersed organizations is both a technical and political challenge.

10.10 The digital divide and inclusive innovation

One of the most crucial and underrated aspects of the Web X.0 transition is its potential to aggravate current inconsistencies if not actively and properly managed. Web X.0 innovations are predominantly created in wealthy countries by privileged populations, with the benefits going to those who already have access to finance, knowledge, and connectivity. Without conscious action, Web X.0 risks generating a more technologically proficient but less equitable world, with a growing inequality between those who own and control the new digital infrastructure and those who rely on it. The Web X.0 readiness gap across nine demographic and geographic characteristics is quantified in Figure 10.8, which shows that the advantages of Web X.0 will mostly favor those who are already digitally advanced in the absence of targeted intervention.

10.10.1 The infrastructure gap

Roughly one-third of the world's population still lacks reliable Internet access, and many more have access to inadequate, expensive, or restricted connectivity, making it impossible for them to engage meaningfully in the digital economy. By 2023, there will be about 2.6 billion individuals without Internet access, most of whom live in rural and low-income nations [40]. Compared to earlier Internet generations, Web X.0 requires far more advanced computer systems, high-bandwidth networks, extended reality devices, and infrastructure. The Web X.0 economy runs the risk of being exclusive to those who live in affluent urban areas if substantial investments in digital infrastructure are not made in poor nations.

This gap is being filled by efforts to increase global connectivity, such as community mesh networks, public investment in broadband infrastructure, and satellite Internet constellations like SpaceX's Starlink. However, the deployment rate must be significantly accelerated to keep up with the rate of technological advancement.

10.10.2 The skills gap

Even when infrastructure is available, effective participation in Web X.0 necessitates skills such as digital literacy, data fluency, and AI literacy, which are unevenly distributed among populations. Many areas of the world's education institutions are still unprepared to acquire these abilities on a large scale, and the informal learning paths that are becoming increasingly crucial in the Web X.0 economy necessitate Internet access, time, and cultural capital that not everyone possesses [41,42].

Inclusive innovation in Web X.0 necessitates investment in education and skill development not only at elite institutions and technology hubs, but also in

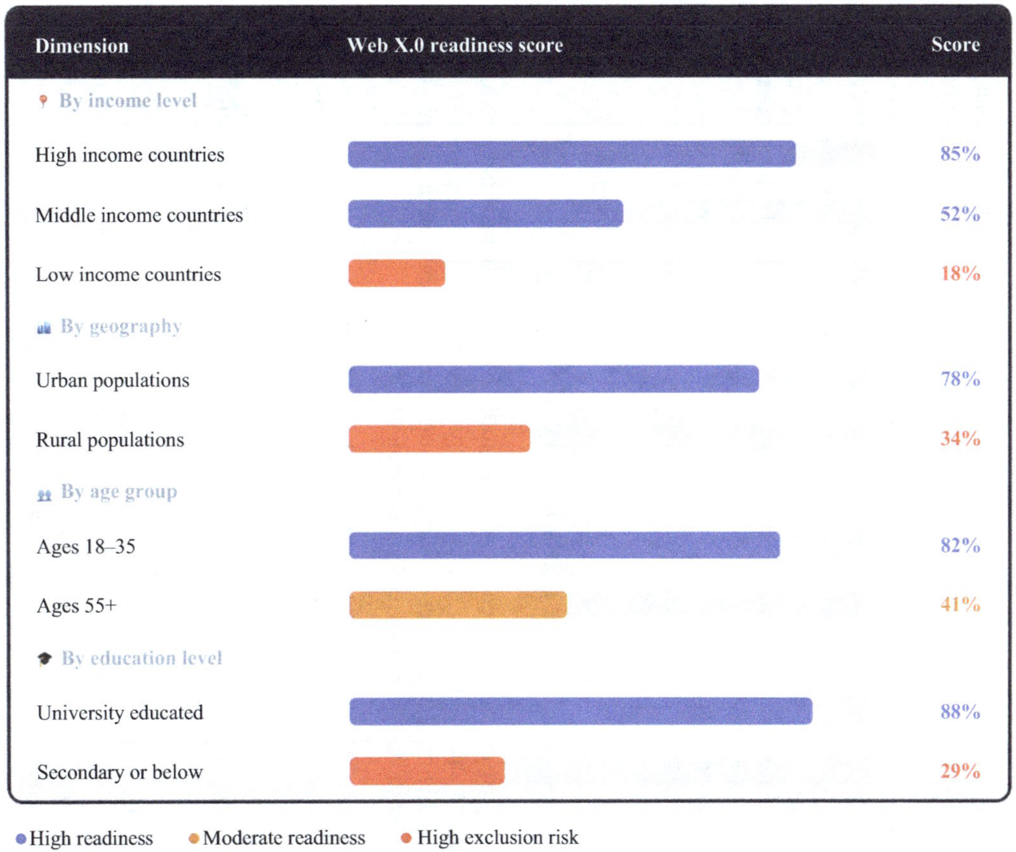

Figure 10.8 *Web X.0 readiness gap by regional and demographic factors [35–39]. The populations most at danger of being left out of the Web X.0 economy in the absence of focused policy intervention are shown by red bars.*

community colleges, vocational programs, rural schools, and informal learning contexts. It demands building learning aids that are accessible in low-bandwidth situations, available in numerous languages, and culturally meaningful for varied groups.

10.10.3 The governance gap

Many of the communities most affected by Web X.0 technologies, whether by algorithmic decisions that affect their creditworthiness or employment prospects, or by surveillance technologies deployed in their neighborhoods, or by platform moderation decisions that shape their access to information, have little voice in how those technologies are designed, deployed, or regulated. Inclusive governance of Web X.0 necessitates tools for various communities to participate meaningfully in decisions that affect them: not simply public comment periods on regulatory proposals, but actual co-design of the technologies and governance frameworks that will shape their future. The UN Human Development Report highlights digital exclusion as one of the key drivers of rising global inequality, warning that without purposeful intervention, the Web X.0 transition may exacerbate rather than close development inequalities [43,44].

10.11 Case studies: pioneers of Web X.0

Theory is most appealing when it is based on the lived experiences of real-world organizations and individuals negotiating the transition to Web X.0. The case studies below highlight the variety of approaches, problems, and actual possibilities that early Web X.0 pioneers are demonstrating.

Case study 1: Ethereum and the smart contract revolution
Ethereum, announced in 2015 by Vitalik Buterin and a small group of partners, is arguably the most significant infrastructure project of the Web 3.0/Web X.0 era. Ethereum paved the way for a thriving ecosystem of decentralized apps, DeFi protocols, and tokenized organizations by enabling programmable smart contracts, which are self-executing agreements with terms stated directly in code. The Ethereum ecosystem demonstrates that it is technically possible to conduct complex financial transactions, creative trade, and governance operations without the use of centralized middlemen. For years to come, Web X.0 infrastructure will be defined by the lessons learnt from its successes and failures in terms of decentralized governance, scalability, and user experience.

Case study 2: MakerDAO and decentralized governance
MakerDAO is one of the most advanced and broad experiments in decentralized autonomous organization governance. It manages the DAI stablecoin via a complex smart contract and community governance framework. MKR token holders vote on risk parameters, protocol changes, and strategic decisions. MakerDAO's

experience demonstrates both the possibilities and the problems of decentralized governance. While it has demonstrated remarkable resilience in the face of multiple market crises, it has also met challenges with voter apathy, plutocratic tendencies, and the difficulty of employing democratic processes to make sophisticated technological decisions.

Case study 3: NVIDIA and the AI infrastructure economy
NVIDIA's transformation from a graphics chip manufacturer to the primary provider of AI computing infrastructure is one of the most incredible business tales of the Web X.0 era. By anticipating the processing demands of deep learning and investing heavily in graphic processing unit (GPU) architectures and software ecosystems, particularly the compute unified device architecture (CUDA) platform, NVIDIA established itself as the critical infrastructure provider for the AI revolution. Its market capitalization has risen from tens of billions to over a trillion dollars, implying that whoever controls AI compute infrastructure controls a critical chokepoint in the Web X.0 economy.

Case study 4: Coursera and the future of learning
Coursera's evolution from a Stanford spinoff offering free online courses to a publicly traded company collaborating with hundreds of universities and corporations to provide credentials and career guidance exemplifies both the opportunities and the challenges of rethinking education for the Web X.0 economy. Coursera has demonstrated that high-quality educational knowledge can be delivered on a large scale at a considerably lower cost than traditional higher education. It has also proven the difficulty of translating information access into meaningful learning outcomes and professional advancement, particularly for students who lack the social capital and support structures that traditional university contexts offer.

Case study 5: Shopify and the democratization of commerce
Shopify's objective to improve commerce for everyone, including independent entrepreneurs with fewer resources than huge businesses, exemplifies Web X.0's democratizing potential. Shopify has helped millions of small businesses compete in the global digital economy by offering sophisticated e-commerce infrastructure, payment processing, logistical support, and increasingly AI-powered marketing and operations solutions. Its transition to a more decentralized, ecosystem-based model, in which partners and developers enhance its capabilities via an open app marketplace, exemplifies how platform businesses may add value to their ecosystems rather than extract it.

10.12 Strategies for individuals, businesses, and governments

Understanding Web X.0 transforms is only useful if it helps you make better judgments and take more effective actions. This section transforms the previous sections' analysis into practical strategic counsel for the three main types of actors who will shape and be shaped by the Web X.0 transition: individuals, businesses, and governments.

10.12.1 Strategies for individuals

Individuals navigating the Web X.0 economy should prioritize investing in adaptation. This entails laying a solid foundation in meta-skills such as critical thinking, communication, collaboration, and creativity, as well as acquiring the technical fluency required to work effectively with AI tools, understand the fundamentals of blockchain and decentralized systems, and navigate immersive digital environments.

Building a strong personal brand and professional network in digital contexts is becoming increasingly vital as geographic labor market boundaries fall away and reputation takes precedence over institutional membership as a measure of worth. Contributing to open-source projects, building a portfolio of publicly available work, and actively participating in professional groups are all strategies to increase credibility and visibility in the Web X.0 economy. Financial literacy in the context of Web X.0 refers to understanding cryptocurrencies, digital assets, tokenized investments, and decentralized finance, all of which are becoming increasingly important components of personal financial management, despite the fact that it necessitates being aware of the very real risks of speculation and fraud in developing markets.

10.12.2 Strategies for businesses

For businesses, the most important strategic goal is to establish genuine AI capability, which entails not only procuring AI technologies but also developing the organizational capacity to successfully deploy AI, find the highest-value applications, manage risks, and learn and evolve. This includes investments in data infrastructure, AI talent, and the change-management skills needed to incorporate AI into workflows and cultures based on human decision-making [45].

Even well-established companies should experiment with novel business models such as tokenization, decentralized governance, and community ownership, not to fully embrace them, but to understand their consequences and develop the organizational capacity required to respond when they disrupt established markets. Organizations that begin learning about decentralized systems now, rather than waiting until disruption forces them to do so, will be best positioned for Web X.0.

In an era when consumers, employees, and regulators are increasingly demanding accountability from the organizations with which they interact, building trust through radical transparency, strong data privacy practices, ethical AI governance, and genuine stakeholder engagement is both a moral obligation and a strategic advantage [46]. To provide practical recommendations for each of the four primary stakeholder groups, governments, large corporations,

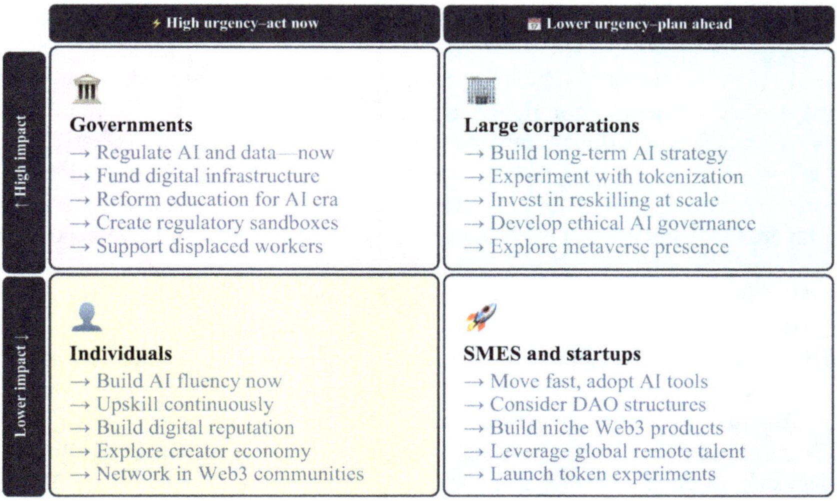

Figure 10.9 Web X.0 stakeholder strategy matrix. Depending on the urgency and impact scale of the Web X.0 transition, each quadrant corresponds to a specific stakeholder category and their optimal strategic approach.

individuals, and small and medium-sized enterprise (SMEs), Figure 10.9 maps suggested strategic priorities by urgency and impact scale.

10.12.3 Strategies for governments

The Web X.0 transition provides governments with an opportunity to increase economic growth while also requiring them to manage the risks involved with the transition. Strategic public investment in digital infrastructure, such as open data platforms, public AI compute resources, and Internet connectivity, can help spread the benefits of the Web X.0 economy and remove barriers to participation.

While avoiding the dual traps of regulatory capture by incumbents and regulatory overreach, which stifles innovation, regulatory frameworks must evolve swiftly to address concerns such as AI governance, data privacy, cryptocurrencies, and decentralized systems. Because digital systems are inherently cross-border, the most effective regulatory methods will be evidence-based, adaptable, and internationally coordinated. As G20 countries adhere to shared standards for trustworthy AI that strike a balance between innovation and risk mitigation, international coordination on AI governance is becoming increasingly important [47].

Investing in education and workforce development is economically and ethically vital, particularly for people who are most vulnerable to automation. The Web X.0 transition will generate massive amounts of money, but unless active redistribution measures are in place, this wealth will be distributed unfairly.

10.13 Conclusion—navigating the next frontier

One of the most pivotal moments in human history is upon us. AI, decentralized infrastructure, immersive computing, and ubiquitous connectivity are combining to create Web X.0, a new digital universe that will alter work, business, creativity, and society in ways we do not yet fully understand. Whether this technological revolution promotes or exacerbates human inequality, distributes or concentrates power, and favors the many or the few will be determined by the decisions we make at this critical juncture.

The analysis presented in this chapter draws several general conclusions. First, the velocity and scope of change in Web X.0 will exceed most enterprises' and individuals' expectations. Technology is changing faster than governance frameworks, education systems, and business models can keep pace, creating a dangerous gap between capability and knowledge. Closing this gap will necessitate immediate investment in institutional capacity, regulatory agility, and human development. Second, the most important predictors of Web X.0 results are human, not technical. Web X.0 technologies are tools, though extremely powerful ones. The judgments made by people responsible for their development, deployment, and regulation decide whether technologies serve or harm human goals. The most pressing issue of our time is developing ethical frameworks, governance systems, and cultural standards to direct these technologies towards human flourishing.

Third, the benefits of Web X.0 will not be distributed in an automatic or equitable manner. To realize these technologies' democratizing promise, particularly their power to extend access to economic opportunity, education, healthcare, and artistic expression, requires conscious, consistent, and politically challenging involvement. Markets alone will not guarantee that the benefits of the Web X.0 economy are widely distributed.

Finally, the future of Web X.0 has not been resolved. It is actively shaped by the actions of entrepreneurs, investors, regulators, educators, and citizens worldwide. The myth of technological inevitability, the notion that technology development comes to us rather than something we shape, is both factually incorrect and dangerously disempowering. We have more agency in creating the nature of Web X.0 than we realize, and using that authority wisely and ethically is both our greatest challenge and opportunity. Figure 10.10 depicts four conceivable Web X.0 futures plotted against two axes: AI autonomy and degree of decentralization, demonstrating that the aspirational Human-Centered Web X.0 outcome in the top-left quadrant is not predetermined but necessitates purposeful governance decisions. The next frontier is ours to explore. The question is whether we will approach the situation with the necessary knowledge, guts, and solidarity.

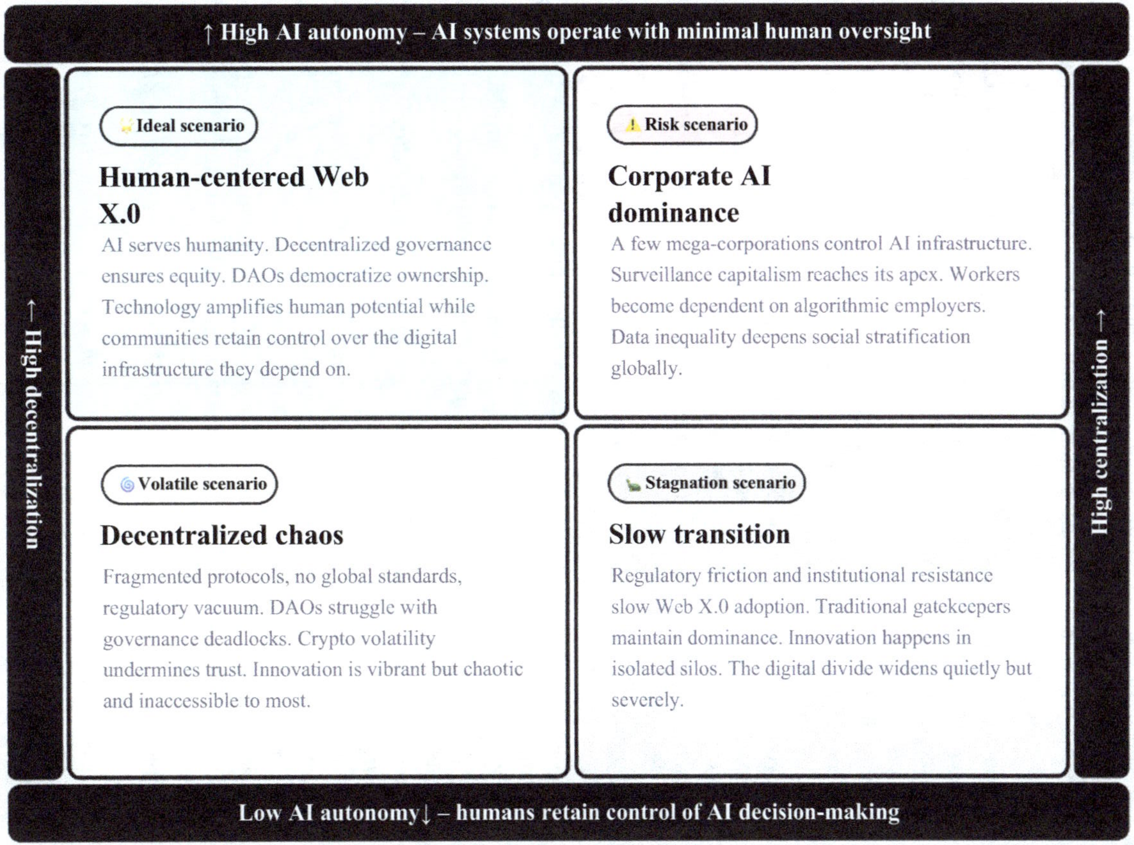

Figure 10.10 Web X.0 future scenarios matrix. The top-left quadrant represents the intended outcome, which requires deliberate governance and an inclusive innovation strategy.

Suggested further readings

The following works are recommended for readers wishing to deepen their understanding of the themes explored in this chapter. They are organized by thematic area to facilitate targeted exploration. Annotations are provided to guide selection based on the reader's background and interests. These readings are distinct from the chapter's bibliography and represent a curated pathway for further scholarship, professional development, and strategic reflection on the Web X.0 transition.

[1] Berners-Lee, T., and Fischetti, M. (2000). *Weaving the Web: The Original Design and Ultimate Destiny of the World Wide Web.* HarperBusiness.

[2] Tapscott, D., and Williams, A. D. (2006). *Wikinomics: How Mass Collaboration Changes Everything.* Portfolio.

[3] Jeremy, R. (2014). "The zero marginal cost society: The Internet of Things, the collaborative commons, and the eclipse of capitalism." Palgrave Macmillan, 18: 422–425.

[4] Schwab, K. (2024). "The fourth industrial revolution: What it means, how to respond." *Handbook of Research on Strategic Leadership in the Fourth Industrial Revolution*. Edward Elgar Publishing, 29–34.

[5] Russell, S. (2022). "Human-compatible artificial intelligence." *Human-Like Machine Intelligence* 1: 3–22.

[6] Beltramini, E. (2019). "Life 3.0. Being human in the age of artificial intelligence, by max tegmark." *Religion and Theology* 26 (1–2): 169–171.

[7] Tan, J. M. (2025). "Co-intelligence: Living and working with AI." *Anesthesiology* 142 (6): 1195–1196.

[8] Narayanan, A., and Kapoor, S. (2025). "AI snake oil: What artificial intelligence can do, what it can't, and how to tell the difference." Princeton University Press, 1–384.

[9] Marcus, G., and Davis, E. (2019). *Rebooting AI: Building Artificial Intelligence We Can Trust.* Vintage.

[10] Tapscott, D., and Tapscott, A. (2016). *Blockchain Revolution: How the Technology Behind Bitcoin Is Changing Money, Business, and the World.* New York: Penguin Random House, 348 pages.

[11] Hansen, K. (2020). "Book Review: 'The Bitcoin Standard: The Decentralized Alternative to Central Banking'." The Quarterly Journal of Austrian Economics, 22: 634–641.

[12] Werbach, K. (2018). *The Blockchain AND The New Architecture of Trust.* MIT Press.

[13] Burniske, C., and Tatar, J. (2017). *Cryptoassets: The Innovative Investor's Guide to Bitcoin and Beyond.* McGraw Hill Professional.

[14] Brynjolfsson, E., and McAfee, A. (2014). *The Second Machine Age: Work Progress and Prosperity in a Time of Brilliant Technologies.* WW Norton & Company.

[15] Dweck, C. S. (2006). *Mindset: The New Psychology of Success.* Random House.

[16] Hamel, G., and Zanini, M. (2020). *Humanocracy: Creating Organizations as Amazing as the People Inside Them.* Harvard Business Review Press.
[17] Brown, B. (2018). *Dare to Lead: Brave Work, Tough Conversations, Whole Hearts.* Random House.

Relevant industry standards and policies

The following standards and policies are directly relevant to the technologies, organizational models, and governance challenges examined in this chapter. They are organized by domain to reflect the eight principal technology and governance areas covered. Where a standard is explicitly cited in the chapter text, the relevant section reference is provided. Standards bodies referenced include ISO (International Organization for Standardization), IEC (International Electrotechnical Commission), IEEE (Institute of Electrical and Electronics Engineers), NIST (National Institute of Standards and Technology), ETSI (European Telecommunications Standards Institute), W3C (World Wide Web Consortium), and key regulatory and intergovernmental bodies.

1. Artificial intelligence

Standard/policy	Full title and description
ISO/IEC 42001:2023	Artificial Intelligence Management System (AIMS). Specifies requirements for establishing, implementing, maintaining, and continually improving an AI management system within organizations.
ISO/IEC 23053:2022	Framework for AI Systems Using Machine Learning. Defines terminology, concepts, and a general framework for ML-based AI systems.
ISO/IEC TR 24028:2020	Overview of trustworthiness in AI. Addresses bias, robustness, transparency, explainability, and security in AI systems.
ISO/IEC TR 24368:2022	AI Ethical and Societal Concerns. Overview of ethical and societal concerns related to AI applications.
NIST AI RMF 1.0 (2023)	AI Risk Management Framework. Voluntary US framework for identifying, assessing, and managing AI risks across the full AI lifecycle, organized around four functions: Govern, Map, Measure, and Manage.
IEEE 7000-2021	Model Process for Addressing Ethical Concerns During System Design. Establishes a process model for embedding ethical values into systems and software engineering.
IEEE 7010-2020	Recommended Practice for Assessing the Impact of Autonomous and Intelligent Systems on Human Well-Being. Defines metrics for well-being impact assessment.

(Continues)

(*Continued*)

Standard/policy	Full title and description
EU AI Act (2024)	The European Union's comprehensive legal framework for AI—the world's first. Classifies AI systems by risk level (unacceptable, high, limited, minimal) and sets binding compliance obligations for providers and deployers.
OECD AI Principles (2023)	Internationally adopted principles for trustworthy AI covering transparency, accountability, robustness, security, and human oversight. Adopted by 46+ countries.
G20 AI Principles	AI governance principles adopted by G20 nations, based on OECD AI Principles, committing member states to shared standards for trustworthy AI development.

2. Data privacy and digital sovereignty

Standard/policy	Full title and description
ISO/IEC 27001:2022	Information Security Management Systems (ISMS). The internationally recognized standard specifying requirements for establishing, implementing, maintaining, and continually improving an ISMS.
ISO/IEC 27701:2019	Privacy Information Management System (PIMS). Extension to ISO 27001 specifically for managing personal data and demonstrating GDPR compliance.
ISO/IEC 29100:2011	Privacy Framework. Defines terminology, actors, roles, and privacy safeguarding requirements for protecting personally identifiable information (PII) in ICT systems.
NIST Privacy Framework (2020)	Voluntary tool for improving privacy risk management through five functions: Identify-P, Govern-P, Control-P, Communicate-P, and Protect-P.
EU GDPR (2018)	General Data Protection Regulation. The EU's landmark data privacy law establishes rights for individuals over their personal data and obligations for organizations processing it. Sets the global benchmark for data protection legislation.
OECD Privacy Guidelines (2013)	OECD Guidelines on the Protection of Privacy and Transborder Flows of Personal Data. The foundational international policy instrument for cross-border data governance establishes eight core privacy principles.

3. Blockchain and decentralized systems

Standard/policy	Full title and description
ISO 22739:2020	Blockchain and Distributed Ledger Technologies—Vocabulary. The foundational international standard defines terminology and concepts for blockchain and DLT.

(*Continues*)

(*Continued*)

Standard/policy	Full title and description
ISO/TR 23576:2020	Blockchain and DLT—Security Management of Digital Asset Custodians. Technical report on security practices for entities managing digital assets.
ISO/TR 23244:2020	Blockchain and DLT—Privacy and PII Protection. Technical report on privacy considerations in blockchain system design.
ISO/TC 307	ISO Technical Committee 307—Blockchain and Distributed Ledger Technologies. The body responsible for developing international standards across all aspects of blockchain, including interoperability, security, identity, and governance.
IEEE P2418.2	Standard for Data Format for Blockchain Systems. Specifies data formats ensuring interoperability between different blockchain platforms.
FATF Recommendations on Virtual Assets	Financial Action Task Force guidance on anti-money laundering (AML) and counter-terrorism financing (CTF) for cryptocurrency exchanges, DeFi platforms, and virtual asset service providers.

4. Extended reality and the metaverse

Standard/policy	Full title and description
IEEE 2048.1	Standard for Virtual Reality Floor Plan. Defines the foundational architecture and floor plan for VR environments and experiences.
IEEE 2048.101	Standard for Augmented Reality—Device Taxonomy and Definitions. Establishes a classification system for AR devices and their capabilities.
ISO/IEC JTC1 SC24	ISO/IEC Subcommittee 24—Computer Graphics, Image Processing and Environmental Data Representation. Develops standards for 3D graphics, VR/AR interchange formats, and spatial data.
OpenXR (Khronos Group)	Industry-led open standard for cross-platform XR device access and rendering. Enables applications to run across different VR/AR hardware without platform-specific code.
Metaverse Standards Forum	Industry consortium including IEEE, ISO, W3C, and major technology firms, coordinating on interoperability standards for metaverse infrastructure, identity, payments, and content.
W3C WebXR Device API	World Wide Web Consortium standard enabling web browsers to access VR and AR hardware, making immersive experiences accessible without proprietary apps.

5. Internet of Things (IoT)

Standard/policy	Full title and description
ISO/IEC 30141:2018	Internet of Things—Reference Architecture. Provides a standardized IoT reference architecture defining the entities, communication patterns, and characteristics of IoT systems.
IEEE P2413	Standard for an Architectural Framework for the Internet of Things. Defines the cross-domain framework for IoT systems, including design abstractions and interoperability.
NIST SP 800-213	IoT Device Cybersecurity Guidance for the Federal Government. Provides cybersecurity requirements for IoT devices, widely adopted as an industry best practice beyond federal use.
ETSI EN 303 645	Cybersecurity for Consumer Internet of Things. The European baseline standard for IoT device security covers requirements such as unique passwords, vulnerability disclosure, and secure updates.

6. Edge computing and connectivity (5G)

Standard/policy	Full title and description
ETSI MEC (Multi-access Edge Computing)	ETSI's industry specification group defines the architecture, APIs, and use cases for multi-access edge computing—processing data at the network edge rather than in centralized cloud infrastructure.
3GPP Release 15–18 (5G Standards)	3rd Generation Partnership Project technical specifications defining the 5G New Radio (NR) standard, including enhanced mobile broadband, ultra-reliable low-latency communications, and massive machine-type communications.
IEEE 802.11 (Wi-Fi Standards)	Family of wireless local area network standards defining the technical specifications for Wi-Fi, including the latest Wi-Fi 6E and Wi-Fi 7 generations, providing high-throughput, low-latency local wireless connectivity.
ITU-T Y.3170 Series	ITU Telecommunication Standardization Sector recommendations for IMT-2020 (5G) network requirements and architectures, providing the international framework within which 3GPP standards operate.

7. Cybersecurity and agentic AI

Standard/policy	Full title and description
NIST CSF 2.0 (2024)	NIST Cybersecurity Framework version 2.0. The widely adopted voluntary framework organizing cybersecurity activities around six functions: Govern, Identify, Protect, Detect, Respond, and Recover.
ISO/IEC 27032:2023	Cybersecurity—Guidelines for Internet Security. Provides guidance on improving the state of cybersecurity, including coordination between Internet stakeholders and addressing Internet-specific threats.
OWASP Top 10 for LLM Applications (2023)	Open Web Application Security Project's list of the most critical security risks in large language model applications, including prompt injection, insecure output handling, and training data poisoning.
ISO/IEC 27035:2023	Information Security Incident Management. Provides guidelines for planning and preparing for incident response, including in AI and automated system contexts.

8. Education, skills, and digital credentials

Standard/policy	Full title and description
W3C Verifiable Credentials (VC) Data Model	World Wide Web Consortium standard defining a data model for cryptographically verifiable digital credentials—enabling tamper-proof, portable, and privacy-preserving credential verification.
IMS Global Open Badges 3.0	The 1EdTech (IMS Global) technical standard for digital badges—verifiable, portable records of skills, achievements, and competencies issued by educational institutions and employers.
IEEE P2881	Recommended Practice for Learning Technology Standards Architecture. Defines the architectural framework for interoperable learning technology systems.
ISO/IEC 40180:2017	Information Technology for Learning, Education, and Training—Quality Framework. Establishes a quality framework for digital learning resources and systems.

References

[1] Berners-Lee T., Hendler J., and Lassila O. 'The semantic web'. *Scientific American*. 2001;284(5):34–43.

[2] O'Reilly T. 'What is Web 2.0: Design patterns and business models for the next generation of software' [online]. 2005. Available from http://www.oreillynet.com/pub/a/oreilly/tim/news/2005/09/30/what-is-web-20.html

[3] Tapscott D., and Tapscott A. *Blockchain Revolution: How the Technology Behind Bitcoin Is Changing Money, Business, and the World*. New York: Penguin Random House; 2016.

[4] Hassan M.A., Jamshidi M.B., Manh B.D., *et al.* 'Enabling technologies for Web 3.0: A comprehensive survey'. *Computer Networks*. 2025;264:111242

[5] Xu M., David J.M., and Kim S.H. 'The fourth industrial revolution: Opportunities and challenges'. *International Journal of Financial Research*. 2018;9(2):90–95.

[6] LeCun Y., Bengio Y., and Hinton G. 'Deep learning'. *Nature*. 2015;521 (7553):436–444.

[7] Buterin V. 'A next-generation smart contract and decentralized application platform' [online]. 2014. Available from https://ethereum.org/en/whitepaper/.

[8] Cheng R., Wu N., Chen S., and Han B. 'Will metaverse be NextG internet? Vision, hype, and reality'. *IEEE Network*. 2022;36(5):197–204.

[9] Brynjolfsson E., and McAfee A. *The Second Machine Age: Work, Progress and Prosperity in a Time of Brilliant Technologies*. New York: W.W. Norton & Company; 2014.

[10] Acemoglu D., and Restrepo P. 'Automation and new tasks: How technology displaces and reinstates labor'. *Journal of Economic Perspectives*. 2019;33(2):3–30.

[11] Rogers D.L. *The Digital Transformation Playbook: Rethink Your Business for the Digital Age*. New York: Columbia University Press; 2016.

[12] Sturgeon T.J. 'Upgrading strategies for the digital economy'. *Global Strategy Journal*. 2021;11(1):34–57.

[13] Davenport T.H., and Mittal N. *All in on AI: How Smart Companies Win Big with Artificial Intelligence*. Boston, MA: Harvard Business Review Press; 2023.

[14] Chui M., Hazan E., Roberts R., Singla A., and Smaje K. *The Economic Potential of Generative AI: The Next Productivity Frontier [online]*. McKinsey Global Institute; 2023. Available from https://www.mckinsey.com/capabilities/mckinsey-digital/our-insights/the-economic-potential-of-generative-ai

[15] Heines R., Dick C., Pohle C., and Jung R. 'The tokenization of everything: Towards a framework for understanding the potentials of tokenized assets'. *Presented at Hawaii International Conference on System Sciences (HICSS)*; Maui, Hawaii, 2021.

[16] Chesbrough H.W. *Open Innovation: The New Imperative for Creating and Profiting from Technology*. Boston, MA: Harvard Business Press; 2003.

[17] Jumper J., Evans R., Pritzel A., *et al.* 'Highly accurate protein structure prediction with AlphaFold'. *Nature*. 2021;596(7873):583–589.

[18] Correia M.J., and Matos F. 'The impact of artificial intelligence on innovation management'. In: *Proceedings of the 16th European Conference on Innovation and Entrepreneurship (ECIE)*; 2021. pp. 1–9.

[19] Murray F., Aghion P., Dewatripont M., Kolev J., and Stern S. 'Of mice and academics: Examining the effect of openness on innovation'. *American Economic Journal: Economic Policy*. 2016;8(1):212–252.

[20] Shilina S. *Decentralized science (DeSci): Web3-mediated future of science* [online]. Paradigm Research, Medium; 2022. Available from https://medium.com/paradigm-research/decentralized-science-desci-web3-mediated-future-of-science-2547f9a88c40.

[21] Isaacson W. *The Innovators: How a Group of Hackers, Geniuses, and Geeks Created the Digital Revolution*. New York: Simon & Schuster; 2014.

[22] Park S.M., and Kim Y.G. 'A metaverse: Taxonomy, components, applications, and open challenges'. *IEEE Access*. 2022;10:4209–4251.

[23] Ball M. *The Metaverse: And How It Will Revolutionize Everything*. New York: Liveright Publishing; 2022.

[24] Hollensen S., Kotler P., and Opresnik M.O. 'Metaverse – The new marketing universe'. *Journal of Business Strategy*. 2023;44(3):119–125.

[25] Dincelli E., and Yayla A. 'Immersive virtual reality in the age of the metaverse: A hybrid-narrative review based on the technology affordance perspective'. *Journal of Strategic Information Systems*. 2022;31(2):101717.

[26] Dionisio J.D.N., Burns W.G., and Gilbert R. '3D virtual worlds and the metaverse: Current status and future possibilities'. *ACM Computing Surveys*. 2013;45(3):1–38.

[27] Hamel G., and Zanini M. *Humanocracy: Creating Organizations as Amazing as the People Inside Them*. Boston, MA: Harvard Business Review Press; 2020.

[28] Ismail S., Diamandis P.H., and Malone M.S. *Exponential Organizations ExO 2.0: The New Playbook for 10x Growth and Impact*. Ethos Collective; 2023.

[29] Gurdjian P., Halbeisen T., and Lane K. 'Why leadership-development programs fail'. *McKinsey Quarterly*. 2014;1(1):121–126.

[30] Mollick E. *Co-intelligence: Living and Working with AI*. New York: Portfolio/Penguin; 2024.

[31] Selingo J.J. *College (Un)bound: The Future of Higher Education and What It Means for Students*. New York: Houghton Mifflin Harcourt; 2013.

[32] Wachter S., Mittelstadt B., and Russell C. 'Why fairness cannot be automated: Bridging the gap between EU non-discrimination law and AI'. *Computer Law and Security Review*. 2021;41:105567.

[33] Narayanan A., and Kapoor S. *AI Snake Oil: What Artificial Intelligence Can Do, What It Can't, and How to Tell the Difference. Princeton, NJ*: Princeton University Press; 2024.

[34] Zuboff S. 'Surveillance capitalism or democracy? The death match of institutional orders and the politics of knowledge in our information civilization'. *Organization Theory*. 2022;3(3):26317877221129290.
[35] ITU. *Measuring Digital Development: Facts and Figures 2023*. Geneva: International Telecommunication Union; 2023. Available from https://www.itu.int/en/ITU-D/Statistics
[36] World Bank. *World Development Report 2023: Migrants, Refugees, and Societies*. Washington, DC: World Bank Group; 2023. Available from https://doi.org/10.1596/978-1-4648-1941-4
[37] OECD. *OECD Digital Economy Outlook 2023: Shaping an Enabling Environment for the Digital Transition*. Paris: OECD Publishing; 2023. Available from https://doi.org/10.1787/9e446ede-en
[38] UNDP. *Human Development Report 2021/2022: Uncertain Times, Unsettled Lives*. New York: United Nations Development Programme; 2022. Available from https://hdr.undp.org
[39] Broadband Commission for Sustainable Development. *The State of Broadband* 2023. Geneva: ITU & UNESCO; 2023. Available from https://broadbandcommission.org
[40] Oloyede A.A., Faruk N., Noma N., Tebepah E., and Nwaulune A.K. 'Measuring the impact of the digital economy in developing countries: A systematic review and meta-analysis'. *Heliyon*. 2023;9(7):e17654.
[41] Chetty R., Jackson M.O., Kuchler T., *et al.* 'Social capital I: Measurement and associations with economic mobility'. *Nature*. 2022;608(7921):108–121.
[42] Ragnedda M., and Ruiu M.L. *Digital Capital: A Bourdieusian Perspective on the Digital Divide*. Bingley: Emerald Publishing; 2022.
[43] Conceição P. *Human Development Report 2023/24: Breaking the Gridlock: Reimagining Cooperation in a Polarized World*. New York: United Nations Development Programme; 2024.
[44] Eubanks V. *Automating Inequality: How High-Tech Tools Profile, Police, and Punish the Poor*. New York: St. Martin's Press; 2018.
[45] Daugherty P.R., and Wilson H.J. *Radically Human: How New Technology Is Transforming Business and Shaping Our Future*. Boston, MA: Harvard Business Review Press; 2022.
[46] Astaiza Dorado L.I., and Kleven O. 'Should we call it AI? Investigating brand building in AI-native startups'. *Master's Thesis*. 2025.
[47] G20. 'G20 ministerial statement on trade and digital economy' [online]. G20 Presidency, Osaka, Japan; 2019. Available from https://www.mofa.go.jp/policy/economy/g20_summit/osaka19/pdf/documents/en/annex_08.pdf

Appendix A

The evolution of the web: from Web 1.0 to Web X.0

Muhammad Tariq[1], *Irum Saba*[2] *and Sana Saleh*[1]

A.1 Timeline of major web milestones (1969–2024)

Year	Milestone	Web generation
1969	ARPANET established	Pre-Web
1983	TCP/IP adoption as a standard protocol	Pre-Web
1989	Tim Berners-Lee proposed the World Wide Web at CERN	Pre-Web
1991	First public web browser (World Wide Web) released	Web 1.0 begins
1993	NCSA Mosaic browser released	Web 1.0
1994	Netscape Navigator launched; W3C founded	Web 1.0
1995	Amazon and eBay founded; Internet Explorer released	Web 1.0
1998	Google founded	Web 1.0
2001	Wikipedia launched	Transition to Web 2.0
2004	Facebook launched	Web 2.0
2005	YouTube launched; AJAX popularized	Web 2.0
2006	Twitter (now X) launched; AWS launched	Web 2.0
2008	Bitcoin white paper published	Web 3.0 beginnings
2009	Bitcoin network launched	Web 3.0
2014	Ethereum white paper published	Web 3.0
2015	Ethereum mainnet launched	Web 3.0

(Continues)

[1]Department of Computer Engineering, School of Engineering, Smart Technologies and Applied Intelligence Research (STAIR) Lab, National University of Computer and Emerging Sciences (NUCES), Pakistan
[2]Department of Electrical Engineering, School of Engineering, Smart Technologies and Applied Intelligence Research (STAIR) Lab, National University of Computer and Emerging Sciences (NUCES), Pakistan

(*Continued*)

Year	Milestone	Web generation
2017	CryptoKitties popularizes NFTs	Web 3.0
2020	DeFi "Summer" – explosion of decentralized finance	Web 3.0
2021	NFT boom; Metaverse announcements	Web 3.0/Web X.0
2022	Ethereum Merge (transition to Proof-of-Stake)	Web 3.0
2023	EU AI Act and MiCA finalized	Web X.0 policy
2024	Major LLM integration across platforms	Web X.0 emerging

A.2 Key terminology definitions

Term	Definition
Ambient intelligence	Electronic environments that are sensitive and responsive to the presence of people, embedding computing capabilities seamlessly into the environment
Blockchain	A distributed, immutable ledger that records transactions across a network of computers without a central authority
Cryptographic trust	Trust established through mathematical verification rather than institutional authority or interpersonal relationships
Decentralization	Distribution of authority, control, and data across a network rather than concentration in a single entity
Digital sovereignty	The ability of individuals or entities to maintain control over their digital identities, data, and assets
Disintermediation	The removal of intermediaries (such as banks or platforms) from transactions or interactions
Network effect	The phenomenon where a service becomes more valuable as more people use it
Platform economy	An economic model centered on digital platforms that facilitate interactions between user groups
Proof-of-Stake (PoS)	A consensus mechanism where validators are selected based on the amount of cryptocurrency they "stake" as collateral
Proof-of-Work (PoW)	A consensus mechanism requiring computational work to validate transactions and create new blocks
Self-Sovereign Identity (SSI)	An identity model where individuals have sole control over their digital identity and associated data
Semantic Web	An extension of the web where data is structured to be machine-readable, enabling intelligent agents to process information automatically

(Continues)

(*Continued*)

Term	Definition
Smart contract	Self-executing code on a blockchain that automatically enforces agreements when conditions are met
Surveillance capitalism	An economic system centered on the commodification of personal data through its extraction, analysis, and monetization
Tokenization	The process of representing real-world or digital assets as tradable tokens on a blockchain
Trustless system	A system where participants can transact securely without needing to trust any specific counterparty

A.3 Comparison of web generation characteristics (extended)

Characteristic	Web 1.0	Web 2.0	Web 3.0	Web X.0
Primary interface	Desktop browser	Desktop + mobile browser	Mobile + browser extension	AR/VR/MR + AI agents
Content format	Static HTML pages	Dynamic, user-generated	Tokenized assets	Immersive 3D + AI-generated
Identity model	Anonymous (per-site)	Platform-specific profiles	SSI	Biometric + AI-managed
Data storage	Local servers	Centralized cloud	Distributed/block-chain	Hybrid (Edge/Fog/ Cloud)
Key risk	Server attacks	Data breaches	Smart contract exploits	AI misalignment + systemic
User skill required	Technical (HTML)	Basic digital literacy	Crypto literacy	AI interaction literacy
Innovation cycle	Slow (years)	Medium (months)	Fast (weeks)	Real-time
Governance model	Centralized (owners)	Corporate-controlled	Community DAOs	Multi-stakeholder

A.4 Glossary of acronyms (cross-reference for readers)

This appendix provides a quick-reference glossary of all acronyms used in this chapter.

Acronym	Definition	First use (section)
AI	Artificial Intelligence	1.1
AJAX	Asynchronous JavaScript and XML	1.4
API	Application Programming Interface	1.4
AR	Augmented Reality	1.1
ARPANET	Advanced Research Projects Agency Network	1.1
DAO	Decentralized Autonomous Organization	1.5
DApp	Decentralized Application	1.5
DeFi	Decentralized Finance	1.2
DID	Decentralized Identifier	1.8
DoS	Denial of Service	1.3
HTML	HyperText Markup Language	1.1
HTTP	Hypertext Transfer Protocol	1.1
IoT	Internet of Things	1.1
IPFS	InterPlanetary File System	1.8
LLM	Large Language Model	1.6
ML	Machine Learning	1.2
NFT	Non-Fungible Token	1.2
NPC	Non-Player Character	1.2
PoS	Proof-of-Stake	1.5
PoW	Proof-of-Work	1.2
RDF	Resource Description Framework	1.5
SDG	Sustainable Development Goal	1.9
SSL	Secure Sockets Layer	1.3
SSI	Self-Sovereign Identity	1.5
TCP/IP	Transmission Control Protocol/Internet Protocol	1.1
URI	Uniform Resource Identifier	1.1
URLLC	Ultra-Reliable Low Latency Communication	1.6
UX	User Experience	1.5
VR	Virtual Reality	1.6
W3C	World Wide Web Consortium	1.8
XR	Extended Reality	1.1

Appendix B

Metaverse, Virtual Reality (VR), and Augmented Reality (AR) in Web X.0

Irum Saba[1], Sana Saleh[2] and Memoona Sadaf[3]

B.1 Timeline of major milestones in Metaverse, VR, and AR (1968–2026)

Year	Milestone	Significance
1968	Ivan Sutherland's "The Sword of Damocles"	First head-mounted display (HMD) system
1989	Jaron Lanier coins "Virtual Reality"	Popularization of the VR concept
1992	"Snow Crash" novel by Neal Stephenson	Introduction of the "Metaverse" term
1999	The Matrix film	Mainstream awareness of VR concepts
2010	Oculus Rift prototype announced	Modern VR revival
2012	Google Glass announced	AR smart glasses for consumers
2014	Facebook acquires Oculus for $2B	Major corporate investment in VR
2016	Pokémon Go launched	First mass-market AR game
2017	Microsoft HoloLens 2 announced	Enterprise MR leadership
2018	Decentraland launches	First blockchain-based virtual world
2019	Fortnite Travis Scott concert (12M+ viewers)	Metaverse live events proof-of-concept
2020	COVID-19 accelerates VR adoption	Remote work and virtual events boom
2021	Facebook rebrands to Meta	Major corporate commitment to Metaverse

(Continues)

[1]Smart Technologies and Applied Intelligence Research (STAIR) Lab, Department of Electrical Engineering, School of Engineering, National University of Computer & Emerging Sciences (NUCES), Islamabad, 44000, Pakistan
[2]Smart Technologies and Applied Intelligence Research (STAIR) Lab, Department of Computer Engineering, School of Engineering, National University of Computer & Emerging Sciences (NUCES), Islamabad, 44000, Pakistan
[3]School of Information Technology, Murdoch University, Australia

(*Continued*)

Year	Milestone	Significance
2022	Apple Vision Pro announced	High-end MR headset from a major tech
2023	Major AI integration in XR	Generative AI for world-building
2024	6G research accelerates	Sub-1 ms latency for holographic comms
2025	Widespread BCI prototypes	Neural interfaces for accessibility
2026	Convergence toward Web X.0	Integrated immersive ecosystems

B.2 Comparative framework of enabling technologies

Technology	Primary function	Latency requirement	Key challenge	Maturity level
VR HMDs	Full immersion	<20 ms	Motion sickness, cost	High
AR glasses	Digital overlays	<10 ms	Field of view, battery	Medium
Edge computing	Local processing	<5 ms	Resource allocation	Medium–high
Fog computing	Regional aggregation	<20 ms	Standardization	Medium
Cloud computing	Global storage, AI	>50 ms	Latency, bandwidth	High
Blockchain	Trust, ownership	Variable (seconds)	Scalability, energy	Medium
AI/ML	Intelligence, personalization	Real-time	Bias, ethics	Medium–high
5G networks	Connectivity	1–10 ms	Coverage, deployment	High
6G networks	Holographic comms	<1 ms	Research phase	Low (research)
BCI	Direct neural control	<50 ms	Signal accuracy, invasiveness	Low
Spatial audio	3D sound localization	<10 ms	Realism, tracking	High

B.3 Applications of immersive technologies by sector

Sector	Key applications	Primary technologies	Section reference
Gaming	VR games, AR games, virtual concerts	VR HMDs, AR, Spatial audio	5.3.1
Education	Virtual classrooms, skill training, personalized learning	VR, AI, Haptics	5.3.2
Healthcare	AR surgery, VR therapy, and medical training	AR, VR, Haptics, IoT	5.3.4
Remote work	Virtual offices, 3D collaboration	VR, AR, AI	5.3.3
Digital commerce	NFT marketplaces, virtual retail, immersive shopping	Blockchain, AR, NFTs	5.3.5
Governance	Virtual town halls, smart city planning, DAOs	VR, AR, Blockchain, DAOs	5.3.6
Social interaction	Virtual worlds, cultural preservation	VR, AR, Spatial audio	5.3.7

B.4 Summary of challenges and mitigation strategies

Challenge category	Key risks	Mitigation strategies	Responsible actors
Privacy and data protection	Biometric data theft, surveillance	Data minimization, encryption, and user consent	Developers, regulators
Cybercrime	Identity theft, asset theft	MFA, smart contract audits, ZTA	Platform operators, security firms
Ethical governance	Harassment, manipulation, wealth-based voting	AI moderation, equitable DAO design, guidelines	Community, regulators
Digital divide	Economic barriers, connectivity gaps	Affordable devices, 5G/6G investment, universal design	Industry, governments
Psychological impacts	Addiction, identity confusion	Usage limits, digital wellness tools, and education	Platform operators, families
Interoperability	Platform lock-in, fragmentation	Open standards (glTF, OpenXR), cross-platform APIs	Standards bodies, industry

(Continues)

(*Continued*)

Challenge category	Key risks	Mitigation strategies	Responsible actors
Environmental	High energy use, e-waste	Green computing, renewable energy, PoS	Data centers, developers
Legal and regulatory	Jurisdictional uncertainty	International frameworks, updated IP laws	Governments, international bodies

B.5 Glossary of key terms

Term	Definition
Ambient intelligence	Electronic environments that are sensitive and responsive to human presence
Avatar	A digital representation of a user in a virtual environment
Cybersickness	Discomfort, nausea, or disorientation experienced during VR use
Digital twin	A virtual representation of a physical object, system, or environment
Foveated rendering	A rendering technique that prioritizes resolution where the user is gazing
Haptic feedback	Tactile sensations are simulated through devices to mimic touch
Holographic communication	Real-time 3D projection of users for remote presence
Interoperability	The ability of different systems to exchange and use information seamlessly
Latency	Delay between user action and system response
Metaverse	Persistent, shared, interoperable virtual world connecting real and virtual realities
Non-Fungible Token (NFT)	Unique digital asset with verified ownership on a blockchain
Presence	Psychological feeling of "being there" in a virtual environment
Self-Sovereign Identity (SSI)	An identity model where individuals control their own digital identity
Smart contract	Self-executing code on blockchain that automatically enforces agreements
Spatial audio	3D sound reproduction that simulates direction and distance
Telepresence	Technology that gives users a feeling of presence at a remote location
Zero Trust Architecture (ZTA)	Security model requiring continuous verification of all users and devices

Appendix C

Real-world use cases and case studies in Web X.0

Adeel Anjum[1], Muazzam Ali Khan Khattak[2] and Jawad Ali[1]

C.1 Web X.0 technology stack overview

Web X.0 integrates multiple layers of advanced technologies:

- Infrastructure layer: Cloud, edge computing, and quantum systems
- Protocol layer: Blockchain, smart contracts, and decentralized identity
- Intelligence layer: Artificial intelligence and machine learning
- Interaction layer: XR and natural interfaces
- Application layer: Healthcare, finance, and governance

C.2 Comparative features of web generations

Feature	Web 2.0	Web 3.0	Web X.0
Data control	Centralized	Decentralized	Self-sovereign
Intelligence	Limited	Semantic	AI-driven
Interaction	Social	Context-aware	Immersive and emotional
Security	Platform-based	Blockchain	Zero-trust + AI

C.3 Key challenges in Web X.0 adoption

- Data privacy concerns
- Interoperability limitations
- High infrastructure cost
- Ethical AI challenges
- Regulatory uncertainty

[1]Institute of Information Technology, Quaid-i-Azam University Islamabad, Pakistan
[2]Department of Computer Sciences, Quaid-i-Azam University Islamabad, Pakistan

Index

www.ingramcontent.com/pod-product-compliance
Lightning Source LLC
LaVergne TN
LVHW020313061026
849616LV00003B/27
* 9 7 8 1 8 3 7 2 4 5 3 4 5 *